The Succession of Imperial Power under the Julio-Claudian Dynasty (30 BC–AD 68)

Paweł Sawiński

The Succession of Imperial Power under the Julio-Claudian Dynasty (30 BC–AD 68)

PETER LANG

Bibliographic Information published by the Deutsche Nationalbibliothek
The Deutsche Nationalbibliothek lists this publication in the Deutsche Nationalbibliografie; detailed bibliographic data is available online at http://dnb.d-nb.de.

Library of Congress Cataloging-in-Publication Data
A CIP catalog record for this book has been applied for at the Library of Congress.

This Publication was financially supported by Faculty of Pedagogy and Fine Arts of Adam Mickiewicz University in Poznań.

Cover Design: © Olaf Gloeckler, Atelier Platen, Friedberg
Cover illustration: Courtesy of the Trustees of the British Museum

Printed by CPI books GmbH, Leck

ISBN 978-3-631-75773-4 (Print)
E-ISBN 978-3-631-75774-1 (E-PDF)
E-ISBN 978-3-631-75775-8 (EPUB)
E-ISBN 978-3-631-75776-5 (MOBI)
DOI 10.3726/b14206

Peter Lang – Berlin · Bern · Bruxelles · New York · Oxford · Warszawa · Wien

This publication has been peer reviewed.

www.peterlang.com

Acknowledgements

When writing this book, I had the help of many people and institutions that I would now like to thank. First of all, let me thank Adam Ziółkowski, with whom I have had the opportunity to again and again discuss the claims made in this book. His critical and discerning reading of the chapters has also influenced the final shape of this publication. I am also grateful to Danuta Okoń, who gave me valuable advice in her review, and to Leszek Mrozewicz and Jakub Pogoń for their many important and inspiring suggestions. To Andrzej Wypustek, Krzysztof Królczyk, Lechosław Olszewski and Adam Jarych, all of whom read through chapters of this work, I am grateful for their remarks and suggestions, thanks to which I was able to avoid many errors. I would also like to thank Robert Suski, Michał Faszcza, Michał Baranowski and Karol Kłodziński, with whom I was able to discuss some of the claims I make here. Then I must thank Andrzej Wypustek, Katarzyna Balbuza, Agata Kluczek, Anna Tatarkiewicz and Monika Kubiaczyk for making titles available to me which could not be obtained in Polish libraries. I am grateful to the De Brzezie Lanckoronski Foundation for granting me a scholarship in Rome in 2008, which made it possible for me to peruse the impressive collections of the libraries there.

I owe particular thanks to my wife Dace and my children, Emilia, Paula and Edgar for their understanding and the most pleasant work environment they created for me. It is to the four of them that I dedicate this book.

Contents

Introduction

The succession of imperial power makes for one of the most riveting aspects of the history of the Roman Empire. This is largely due to the specificity of the principate, a *de facto* monarchy officially perceived as a continuation and "restoration" of the Republic[1]. The position of the princeps was never inheritable nor were there any legal documents in existence regulating succession. These features fundamentally distinguish the principate from most mediaeval or modern monarchies known to us. Even so, a distinct majority of Roman emperors pursued dynastic policies, undertaking various measures intended to prepare and ensure the succession of their chosen heir. Furthermore, from the times of Augustus onward, a clear tendency of attempting to pass on the purple within one's family can be observed, thus confirming a dynastic rule.

This dissertation focuses on the succession of imperial power under the Julio-Claudian dynasty, thus encompassing the period from 30 BC to AD 68. There are two reasons why I limit my analysis to the first imperial dynasty. First, the enormous size of the subject matter dissuaded me from my original intention of discussing the problem as it unfolded throughout the principate. Second, after Nero's death certain new trends appeared with regard to the procedure for appointing the new princeps: to counteract the dynastic principle there was a rising demand for the best to be chosen, with the candidate's qualifications and merits being decisive rather than his family connections, whereas the Year of the Four Emperors demonstrated it was possible to be made princeps away from Rome and by the legions as well as by the Praetorian Guard and the Senate. Both these tendencies would make themselves known in the future, as successive emperors came into power, and until the end of the principate.

The book has been divided into two parts, with the discussion organized chronologically and thematically. In the five chapters of Part One, I mostly investigate the mechanisms of the succession policies of the Julio-Claudian emperors, where by *succession policy* I mean primarily those deliberate actions of the princeps

---

1 Many books have been written on the essence of the principate as a system of government, as well as on the position of the princeps within the new political regime. The most significant works on the subject include Hammond 1933; Von Premerstein 1937; Béranger 1953; id. 1959, 151–170; Kunkel 1961, 353–370; Alföldi 1970; Castritius 1982; Badian 1982, 18–41; Wallace-Hadrill 1982, 32–48; Eder 1990, 71–122; Linderski 1990, 42–53; Lacey 1996; Welwei 2004, 217–229; Gruen 2005, 33–51; and Veyne 2008, 9–73.

aimed at determining political succession and ensuring that his chosen successor would assume power smoothly. Under that term I also include any actions of the incumbent emperor taken with a view to increasing the popularity of his anticipated successors, intended to secure them the support of various circles of Roman society, particularly the army and the plebs, as well as dynastic murders used by any current princeps to eliminate potential rivals in the struggle for the throne or to pave the road to succession for his envisioned successor. In Part One, I concentrate on determining the roles played by certain members of the imperial family in the succession plans of the rulers from the first dynasty. I also look into the *cursus honorum*, the public presentation and honours of the intended successors, which made it possible to establish the hierarchy within the ruling family, and into dynastic adoption and marriages, both of which were important parts of the succession policies of Augustus and his successors.

In Part Two of the book, comprising four chapters, I analyse the various stages of the accessions of Tiberius, Caligula, Claudius and Nero. I also try to determine who decided the appointment of the new ruler in situations where the previous emperor had not, and what the Julio-Claudian model of the investiture of a new princeps was. My discussion is completed by the Appendix, where I attempt to discern how the various rulers in the first imperial dynasty dated the beginning of their reign (or the *dies principatus*).

The rule of the Julio-Claudian dynasty and the succession policies of its emperors both enjoy fairly solid documentation in the source material. Of course that does not mean we are able to find the answers to all the questions asked in this book in the sources; in many respects we are still forced to settle for mere guesses—some likely, others less so.

The first group of sources is made up from the accounts of ancient historians. Here, I only mention those which were the most vital for my work. To follow the chronological order, I shall begin with the *Historia Romana* by Velleius Paterculus, an author active under Augustus and Tiberius. In book two of his work, Paterculus recounts, among other things, the events of Augustus' principate and the most salient aspects of Tiberius' reign. While he witnessed many of the things he wrote about, we need to approach his text with great caution, as many of his passages are a kind of a panegyric in Tiberius' honour. Moreover, before Tiberius' adoption, Paterculus' narrative frequently exaggerates his actual standing within the *domus Augusta*.

The next sources to be listed must be *Bellum Iudaicum* and *Antiquitates Iudaicae* by Flavius Josephus, active under the Flavii. Those two works, books 2 and 19, respectively, contain the most extensive account of the stormy events surrounding Caligula's assassination and Claudius' rise to power.

Another ancient source to take into account is Tacitus' *Annales*, dated to the end of Trajan's or the beginning of Hadrian's reign. In there, we find a brief summary of Augustus' principate, a comprehensive account of Tiberius' rule (in books 1–6) and a description of the closing part of Claudius' principate as well as all of Nero's, excluding the last two years (in books 11–16). Unfortunately, books 7–10, which dealt with the reign of Caligula and the first part of Claudius', are not extant, and book 5 is only preserved in part, meaning that some years are missing from the account of Tiberius' principate as well. And while the author states *sine ira et studio* to be his guiding principle, he fails to remain objective: in his descriptions of Tiberius, Agrippina the Younger and Nero there are echoes of the literary tradition hostile to them, which clearly influenced him. However, such reservations aside, Tacitus' work is undoubtedly one of the most significant and valuable sources on the first imperial dynasty.

Another key text is *De vita Caesarum* by Suetonius, who was active during the reign of Hadrian. The book contains biographies of all the *principes* in the Julio-Claudian dynasty, and while it is often anecdotal and gossipy, it does provide much valuable information on the succession policies of Augustus and his successors.

Finally, I must not omit *Historia Romana* by Cassius Dio, a historian active at the turn of the 2nd and 3rd centuries. This book is a monumental history of Rome—from its origins until Severus Alexander, or to be precise, until AD 229. For my purposes, books 51–63 are crucial, as they detail the rule of the Julio-Claudian dynasty. Unfortunately, some passages of those books (especially those on Claudius and Nero) have only come down to us in epitomes made by the Byzantine authors Xiphilinos and Zonaras, and in mediaeval excerpts. Despite this reservation, and the considerable time gap separating Cassius Dio from the events he wrote about, his work is no doubt next to that of Tacitus, the most extensive and important historical text for researching the first imperial dynasty.

The other type of sources, and of particular importance to the problem discussed in this book, are the epigraphic ones. Of those, the first that ought to be listed are the two inscriptions from Pisa containing the texts of the honorific decrees passed by the authorities of that Italian town for Gaius and Lucius Caesar, Augustus' grandsons and adoptive sons[2], which make it possible to see the Pisans' reaction to the death of the princeps' intended successors and provide detailed information on their posthumous honours.

2 For the most important editions of the Pisan inscriptions, see especially Rowe 2002, 119–123; and Lott 2012, 57–77.

Then there are three monumental inscriptions worthy of particular notice: the *Tabula Hebana*, the *Tabula Siarensis* and the *Senatus Consultum de Cn. Pisone patre*. The first two contain the Senate decrees passed after Germanicus' death and are an invaluable source of information on his posthumous honours, but there is the problem of the *Tabula Siarensis* being incomplete in places, forcing us to resort to reconstruction; the third inscription contains the text of the *senatus consultum* passed in connection with the trial of Gnaeus Calpurnius Piso, who was charged with contributing to Germanicus' death, and supplies important information on the relations between the ruling dynasty, the Senate, the equestrian order, the plebs and the army[3].

It is also worth mentioning the inscriptions from Aritium (in *Hispania Lusitania*) and Assos (in Asia province), which contain the text of the oath the people of those two towns swore to Caligula after he was made princeps, and make for an important source of information on the mood among the inhabitants of the provinces regarding Germanicus' son's rise to imperial power.

Finally, the *Acta Fratrum Arvalium* (abbreviated hereafter to *AFA*) prove invaluable, as they make it possible to reconstruct the various stages of Caligula's and Nero's imperial accessions[4].

The third category of sources I have used in writing this book comprises coins, the so-called official series being the most important[5]. Those include the coins struck in the imperial mint located in Lugdunum until Caligula's time and later in Rome, as well as those produced in the mint administered by the Senate, also in Rome. Scholars hotly dispute the degree to which their legends and iconography reflected the intentions of the incumbent princeps, and whether coins were a medium of official propaganda[6]. Personally, I fully agree with Carlos Noreña, who asserted that "Each coin minted at Rome was an official document and as such represented an official expression of the emperor and his regime."[7] Thus the official coin series is fundamental to examining the succession policies

3 These three inscriptions have had many editions, of which the most important ones include: Crawford 1996; Eck, Caballos, Fernandéz 1996; Sànchez-Gutiérrez 1999; and Lott 2012.

4 For the standard edition, see Scheid 1998.

5 I primarily make use of the classical corpus of official coins that is *The Roman Imperial Coinage*, I^2: *From 31 BC to AD 69*, ed. C. H. V. Sutherland, London 1984.

6 See, among others, Grant 1952, 79–85; Jones 1956, 13–33; Sutherland 1959, 46–55; Göbl 1978; Crawford 1983, 47–64.

7 Noreña 2001, 147.

of the various *principes*. Provincial coins also hold considerable significance[8]. Their message usually correlates with that of imperial coins, which demonstrates that the inhabitants of the provinces were familiar with the current hierarchies within the imperial family and the current succession order, as they knew quite well whom and how to honour.

Lastly, iconographic sources need to be mentioned. My analysis includes, without being limited to, the famous relief sculptures of the Ara Pacis, the Boscoreale skyphoi, the *gemma Augustea* and a number of *phalerae* depicting members of the imperial family. Still, it ought to be emphasized that any discussion based on this category of sources may only be hypothetical. There are two major reasons for this. First, it is impossible to be certain which members of the reigning dynasty are depicted on those relics; and second, they cannot be dated accurately.

Imperial succession under the Julio-Claudian dynasty has not received treatment to date in the form of a comprehensive monograph[9]. Not that the questions I raise in this book have not been investigated in scholarship before. Since the literature which to varying degrees deals with the topics I discuss here is immense, I shall limit myself to listing the most crucial titles. First of all, there is Alexander Mlasowsky's extensive paper[10] analysing certain selected aspects of the succession-related propaganda of all the Julio-Claudian emperors. However, his perspective is largely that of numismatic and iconographic sources, with less attention paid to literature and inscriptions. Nor is it possible to accept all his findings. Then one must remember the publications about selected aspects of the succession policies of the rulers from the first imperial dynasty, most of them focusing on Augustus. They include especially the work of Barbara Levick, Peter

---

8 The standard edition of provincial coins minted under the Julio-Claudian dynasty is *Roman Provincial Coinage*, I: *From the Death of Caesar to the Death of Vitellius* (*44 BC–AD 69*), eds. A. Burnett, M. Amandry, P. P. Ripollès, London 1992.

9 Although there is Blanche Parsi's book (1963); still, this mostly deals with the legal aspects of designating and investing the new princeps in the first two centuries of the Empire, and the author devotes only very little attention to succession policies during the principate. Then we have *The Julio-Claudian Succession. Reality and Perception of 'Augustan Model'* (ed. A. G. G. Gibson), Leiden–Boston 2013, a collection of articles published by the prestigious Brill, but it is not exhaustive; the articles collected there touch on only some of the issues I discuss here. This is also the right place to mention M. Hammond's paper (1956); still, this only looks into the succession of imperial power in the period from Nero's death until Severus Alexander, and devotes only a few introductory pages to Julio-Claudian times.

10 Mlasowsky 1996, 249–388.

Sattler, John H. Corbett, Glen Bowersock, Mark D. Fullerton, Hartwin Brandt, Frédéric Hurlet, Andrew Pettinger, Tom Stevenson and Robin Seager[11]. Other works worthy of mention are the monographs by Maria H. Dettenhofer and Beth Severy, both insightful accounts of the building of a dynasty by the first princeps and of the *domus Augusta* forming as the new ruling elite[12]. Tiberius' succession policy, however, has attracted scholarly attention to a lesser degree, featuring mostly in the works of Fernand de Visscher, Eckhard Meise and Paul Schrömbges[13]. Then there is a similar trend for Caligula and Claudius; of the works dealing with their dynastic policies, one needs to mention those by Edoardo Bianchi and Josiah Osgood[14].

Other than those, publications important to the problems investigated in this book include any that deal with the issues of appointing successors, transferring the imperial power and investing the new emperor under the principate, especially those by Jean Béranger, Léon Lesuisse, Dieter Timpe, Blanche Parsi and John Scheid[15].

The aspects of the Julio-Claudian reign of interest to me are also extensively discussed in the biographies of the several *principes* and other members of the dynasty, most of them centring on Augustus, of course. Those by Dietmar Kienast, Jochen Bleicken, Werner Eck and Barbara Levick are particularly noteworthy[16], and Levick has biographies of Tiberius and Claudius as well[17]. Of Caligula's biographies, those by Anthony Barrett and Alois Winterling deserve mention[18], and when it comes to Nero, there is Miriam Griffin's book[19]. Biographies of individual members of the imperial family worth listing include the work of Meyer Reinhold and Jean M. Roddaz on Agrippa, Bruno Gallotta's on Germanicus and Anthony Barrett's on Agrippina the Younger[20].

---

11 Levick 1966, 227–244; Sattler 1969, 486–530; Corbett 1974, 87–97; Bowersock 1984, 169–188; Fullerton 1985, 473–483; Brandt 1995, 1–17; Hurlet 1997 (passim); Pettinger 2012 (passim); Stevenson 2013, 118–139; Seager 2013, 41–57.

12 Dettenhoffer 2000; Severy 2003.

13 De Visscher 1964, 54–65; Meise 1966, 7–21; Schrömbges 1986 (passim).

14 Bianchi 2006, 597–630; Osgood 2011.

15 Béranger 1939 (1973), 137–152; Lesuisse 1961a, 415–428; id. 1962, 32–50; Timpe 1962; Parsi 1963; Scheid 1992, 221–237.

16 Kienast 1982; Bleicken 1998; Eck 2007; Levick 2010.

17 Levick 1990; 1999.

18 Barrett 1989; Winterling 2011.

19 Griffin 1984.

20 Reinhold 1933; Roddaz 1984; Gallotta 1987; Barrett 1996.

Terminological and Editorial Notes

In this book, I make use of terms such as *monarchy*, *dynasty*, *co-regent* or *the throne*, which some might consider anachronistic when applied to the Julio-Claudian period. That is because I believe the principate to have been a *de facto* monarchy, and in my view these terms aptly reflect the historical realities described. Furthermore, the terminology is in widespread use in scholarly literature on the subject.

All the abbreviations of the names of ancient authors and the titles of their works are those used in the *Oxford Classical Dictionary*.

The abbreviated titles of journals, publication series, catalogues of coins and inscriptions follow the convention used by *L'Année Philologique*.

Part One The Succession Policies of the Julio-Claudian Emperors

1 Augustus

1.1 Marcus Claudius Marcellus: the First Prospective Successor?

The early years of Augustus' independent rule are a peculiar stage in the process of the princeps building up his position in the new political context and the forming of the new reigning family centred on the emperor (the *domus Augusta*)[1]. Initially, an important place in that family fell to Marcus Claudius Marcellus, the son of C. Claudius Marcellus, a consul in 50 BC, and of the emperor's sister Octavia the Younger[2]. Not having any male issue of his own, the future princeps began to use his nephew for his own political purposes from very early on. In 39 BC, Marcellus, then three years old, was betrothed to the daughter of Sextus Pompeius[3]. In accordance with the practice applied by the Roman aristocracy of strengthening alliances through marriages, that betrothal was to confirm the political truce made in the same year in Misenum between Sextus Pompeius on the one hand, and Octavian[4] and Mark Antony on the other[5]. In the end, though, the marriage was cancelled, as eventually the alliance fell apart and Pompeius died in 35 BC.

The marriage to Livia, which took place in 38 BC, did not give Octavian the son he so desired. This caused him to fairly quickly start showing Marcellus off publicly, assigning to him the role which would certainly have otherwise fallen to his own son. In 29 BC, the lad, then thirteen, took part alongside Tiberius, Octavian's stepson, in Octavian's triumph over Dalmatia and Egypt[6]. The participation of

1 It bears noting here that the expression *domus Augusta* only appears expressly in the sources towards the end of Augustus' reign. First in Ovid, *Ponto* 2, 2, 74; 3, 1, 135; and 4, 15, 16. See also Millar 1993, 1–17; Flory 1996, 287–306; Wardle 2000, 479–493; Severy 2003, 214–219. In spite of that reservation I see no reasons not to use that term to refer to the imperial family already at the beginning of Augustus' principate.

2 Kienast 1996, 70.

3 App. *B. Civ.* 5, 73; Cass. Dio 48, 38, 3.

4 When recounting Augustus' doings before 27 BC, I apply the convention of referring to him as *Octavian*. Still, it should be emphasized that after his adoption by Julius Caesar the would-be princeps no longer used his old name of *Octavius*, calling himself *Caesar* instead. See Kienast 1996, 61. Referring to the young Caesar as Octavian is also widespread in literature. See e.g. Levick 2010, 5.

5 Importantly, Marcellus was at the time a stepson of Antony.

6 Suet. *Tib.* 6, 4.

the two boys in the ceremony was in keeping with the Republican practice, as under the Republic sons would take part in their father's triumphs[7]. In that context, it is clear that both youths made their first public appearance as "replacement sons" of the future Augustus[8]. From Suetonius' account, we know they rode on horseback next to the triumphator's chariot; Suetonius probably points out that Marcellus rode on the right of the quadriga for a reason[9]. It is also telling that on the occasion of that triumph Octavian had sums of money doled out to plebeian children in Marcellus' name only[10]. It was certainly no accident that Tiberius was excluded from this act, the obvious purpose of which was to win Octavian's nephew popularity with the poorer inhabitants of Rome. This clearly proves, as is borne out by Augustus' later actions towards both boys, that the emperor distinctly favoured his nephew from the start.

Augustus' stay in Spain from 26 to 25 BC in connection with the campaign against the Cantabri was a good opportunity to present Marcellus and Tiberius to the legions there[11]. From Cassius Dio's account we know that after the hostilities were over, the princeps entrusted them with hosting a show for the soldiers held in the legionary camp, which they presided over[12].

The year 25 BC proved a pivotal year for Marcellus: it was then that Augustus brought about his marriage to his only daughter, Julia. Since the emperor was absent, the marriage ceremony was presided over personally by Agrippa[13]. Marcellus' standing within the *domus Augusta* was undoubtedly considerably reinforced due to that marriage. As Augustus' son-in-law, he formally won the status of the second most important person in the imperial family, right after the princeps[14]. The union was also an important step in the process of Augustus constructing a reigning family centred on him. It ought to be emphasized here

---

7 Lucius Aemilius Paullus' triumph of 167 BC can serve as an example. Cf. Liv. 45, 40, 8.

8 Dettenhofer 2000, 96; Severy 2003, 68.

9 Suet. *Tib.* 6, 4.

10 Cass. Dio 51, 21, 3; cf. also Dettenhofer 2000, 96.

11 Marcellus and Tiberius were military tribunes then. Cf. Suet. *Tib.* 9, 1; Hurlet 1997, 33.

12 Cass. Dio 53, 26, 1.

13 Plut. *Marc.* 30, 6; Suet. *Aug.* 63, 1; Cass. Dio 53, 27, 5; see also Treggiari 1991, 169; Brandt 1995, 7–9; Corbier 1995, 179, 182; Hurlet 1997, 33; Severy 2003, 68. Levick (2010, 80) dates the marriage to 24 BC.

14 Cf. Dettenhofer 2000, 96. Now of course that does not change the fact that Augustus' second-in-command and the actual second power in the state was still Agrippa, even though in the hierarchy of the *domus Augusta* he stood behind Marcellus (since at the time Agrippa was merely the husband of the emperor's niece Claudia Marcella).

that in the Roman world, marriages between first cousins were quite common and had already been made under the Republic[15]. Some scholars are of the opinion that Marcellus' marriage to Julia is commemorated on the dupondii minted in 25 BC at the instigation of proconsul M. Acilius Glabrio, perhaps in Africa province[16]. The obverse of that series shows Augustus' head with the legend IMP CAESAR DIVI F AUGUST COS IX, which is what makes it possible to date it; the reverse has two heads facing each other, of a young woman and a man, which some historians identify as being depictions of Marcellus and Julia, and the legend M ACILIUS GLABRIO PRO COS[17].

In 24 BC, Augustus began to successively introduce Marcellus to politics by persuading the Senate to grant the youth certain special privileges meant to speed up his career. From Cassius Dio's account we learn he was co-opted into the Senate and gained the right to vote with the ex-praetors. He was also accorded the right to run for consulship ten years before the minimum age prescribed at the time and designated aedile for the following year[18]. Tacitus adds to this that Marcellus was also made a *pontifex*[19]. At the same time, Tiberius was granted certain less spectacular honours: the special right to run for every magistracy five years before the age determined by custom, and a quaestorship[20]. Comparing the scale of the privileges granted to the two young men further demonstrates that Tiberius was clearly eclipsed by Marcellus. The most prestigious of the honours accorded Julia's husband in 24 BC was beyond any doubt the right to run for consul at a younger age than normal. According to that exemption, Marcellus

---

15 Cf. Liv. 42, 34, 2–4; Tac. *Ann.* 12, 6, 3. Drusus the Younger's marriage to Livilla can serve as a later example within the imperial family. Cf. Kienast 1996, 82; Severy 2003, 64. For general information on marriages between cousins in the Roman society, see esp. Treggiari 1991, 110–119; Corbier 1991a, 140–141.

16 It is possible he was the governor of that province at that time. Cf. *RPC* I 5415 (the commentary on that coin issue).

17 Cf. Sutherland 1951, 55; Grant 1954, 27; Kienast 1982, 91 note 97; Dettenhofer 2000, 101 note 75. According to another interpretation, they are images of Octavia and Augustus. Cf. the commentary on that coin in the *RPC* I 5415; see also Brandt 1995, 9. Identifying the characters on the coin as Marcellus and Julia is supported by the fact it was minted exactly in the year they were married. Still, one must remember the claim is only hypothetical, since the coin bears no legend referring to the depictions on the reverse.

18 Cass. Dio 53, 28, 3; cf. also Brandt 1995, 10–11; Dettenhofer 2000, 96; Severy 2003, 68.

19 Tac. *Ann.* 1, 3, 1; cf. also Hurlet 1997, 34.

20 Cass. Dio 53, 28, 3.

could have become a candidate when he was twenty-three[21]. Granting Marcellus those privileges, which were intended to accelerate his *cursus honorum*, initiated the practice of distinguishing members of the imperial family in the same way later on in Augustus' reign[22].

According to the majority of ancient authors, the way Augustus favoured Marcellus and gradually introduced him to public life caused a conflict between Marcellus and Marcus Agrippa, which eventually brought about the latter's departure from Rome in 23 BC[23]. However, this story is highly questionable; I do not think it likely that Augustus' actions regarding Marcellus could have hurt the ambition of Agrippa, the princeps' actual second-in-command and closest associate, who had loyally stood by Octavian since the very outset of his political career and whose position in the emperor's retinue was incontestable. Accordingly, it seems unlikely Agrippa could have seen Augustus' son-in-law as serious competition[24]. In my opinion, seeing Agrippa's departure through the prism of any rivalry between him and Marcellus, as most ancient historians do, obfuscates the real reasons for his stay in the East. The only author who never even mentions Marcellus in the context of Agrippa's eastern mission is Flavius Josephus, who clearly states Agrippa was dispatched to overseas provinces in order to govern them in the emperor's name[25]. On the basis of his account we can accept that the objective of Agrippa's eastern journey was to put a number of affairs in that region in order, including the Parthian question, the relations between Rome and the rulers of the vassal kingdoms, and inspecting the administration in the provinces[26]. As the emperor's special emissary, he was to prepare

---

21 In the light of the regulations in force under Augustus, one could run for consul only after reaching the age of thirty-three. Cf. Brandt 1995, 11; Pettinger 2012, 65.

22 In 19 BC, Drusus the Elder was allowed to run for magistracies five years before the regulations then provided (Cass. Dio 54, 10, 4). In 5 and 2 BC, respectively, Gaius and Lucius Caesar were designated consuls by the Senate and the People, and they were to hold consulship before they were twenty (*Mon. Anc.* 14, 1). In AD 9, the right to run for consul early was granted Germanicus (Cass. Dio 56, 17, 2); four years later, Drusus the Younger (Cass. Dio 56, 28, 1).

23 Vell. Pat. 2, 93, 2; Plin. *HN*. 7, 149; Suet. *Aug*. 66, 3; *Tib*. 10, 1; Cass. Dio 53, 32, 1. So also Corbett (1974, 88), who sees the event as Agrippa yielding to Marcellus. Cf also Boruch 2010, 9.

24 So Reinhold 1933, 81.

25 Joseph. *AJ*. 15, 350.

26 Velleius Paterculus, too, wrote between the lines on the political nature of that mission (2, 93, 2).

the ground for Augustus' visit to the East, planned for the near future[27]. It is possible that in suggesting there was open strife between Agrippa and Marcellus, most of these authors drew inspiration from the later rivalry between Tiberius and the young Caesars, which would eventually convince Augustus' stepson to withdraw from political life to Rhodes in 6 BC, and so they applied the same perspective to Agrippa's earlier departure to the East[28].

Marcellus' unexpected death in 23 BC—the year he became aedile—not merely thwarted Augustus' plans regarding the young man, but was also a heavy personal blow for him[29]. Cassius Dio mentions the rumours that Livia was responsible; supposedly she got rid of Marcellus, seeing him as a serious threat to Tiberius' standing. Dio is right to doubt that version of the events; instead he concludes that Marcellus was probably among the many victims of the epidemic which swept through Rome in 23 BC[30]. From Dio's account we learn that the princeps commemorated the youth with a public funeral, during which he gave the speech (the *laudatio funebris*) himself. The ceremony took place in the Forum Romanum, and then the body was moved to the Campus Martius. There it was cremated and laid to rest in the Mausoleum of Augustus[31]. Interestingly, Marcellus was the first member of the imperial family to be buried in the family tomb erected by the princeps. Further, because of his death public mourning was called[32]. Among the posthumous honours accorded to Marcellus at Augustus' instigation, Cassius Dio lists an image made of gold, a golden wreath and a curule chair, all to be displayed publicly during the *ludi Romani*. The crowned curule chair on which the aforementioned *imago* presumably sat was to be placed among the chairs of the officials responsible for those games[33]. Exhibiting the *sella curulis* during those festivities was meant to commemorate Marcellus' aedileship, which reached its climax in the preparation of *ludi Romani*[34]. Dio also tells us of another form of posthumously honouring the deceased man, that is naming a theatre on the Campus Martius after him. That theatre was probably

---

27 For Agrippa's eastern mission in 23/22 BC, cf. among others Magie 1908, 145–152; Reinhold 1933, 83–85; Roddaz 1984, 319–328; Dąbrowa 1998, 201; Sawiński 2004, 242–244.

28 Cf. Syme 2002, 342 note 7.

29 Vell. Pat. 2, 93, 1; Plut. *Marc.* 30, 6.

30 Cass. Dio 53, 33, 4; cf. also Kienast 1982, 92.

31 Cass. Dio 53, 30, 5; *Cons. ad Liv.* 67–68.

32 Wesch-Klein 1993, 15 note 85, 92.

33 Cass. Dio 53, 30, 6. See Heinemann 2007, 62.

34 Vell. Pat. 2, 93, 1; cf. also Rich 1990, 166–167.

dedicated to him in 13 or 11 BC[35]. Moreover, at Octavia's instigation a Graeco-Latin library was founded[36].

I would now like to take a stand on two important issues which have led to some controversy. The first regards Marcellus' alleged adoption by Augustus; the second, the question asked in this chapter's title: should we see Marcellus as Augustus' first intended successor? The first problem seems simpler. Information on Marcellus' adoption can only be found in Plutarch and Servius—in his commentary on the *Aeneid*[37]. Scholars tend to consider this information spurious[38], as the credibility of these two authors is challenged by other sources, most importantly epigraphical ones. Both the *Res gestae* and an inscription from the Mausoleum of Augustus refer to Marcellus only as *gener*[39].

The question remains open as to whether the princeps ever *planned* to adopt his nephew, but speculation is all we have on this issue. In Ronald Syme's opinion, Augustus meant to adopt Marcellus in 23 BC, but was ultimately dissuaded from the idea by his closest associates, primarily Agrippa. The historian goes so far as to imply a veiled coup d'état which stopped the princeps from carrying out his plan[40]. In my view, Syme's notion is purely speculative, since we have no source material to even slightly confirm it. Furthermore, adopting Marcellus would first have necessitated his divorce from Julia[41]. It seems unlikely the princeps would have brought that marriage about if he had been going to adopt his nephew; it would have been utterly irrational.

The second issue would appear more complex, even though the ancient authors are nearly unanimous in seeing Marcellus as Augustus' intended

35 Cass. Dio 53, 30, 5–6. Dio (54, 26, 1) dates the building of the theatre to 13 BC, and his chronology is accepted by, among others, Heinemann 2007, 45, while other scholars accept Pliny's dedication date of May 11 BC (*HN*. 8, 65). Cf. e.g. Rich 1990, 204; Kienast 1996, 70.

36 Plut. *Marc*. 30, 6. The library was inside the Porticus Octaviae. For information on that structure, see esp. *LTUR*, 4, 1999, 141–145 (A. Wiscogliosi, s.v. *Porticus Octaviae*).

37 Plut. *Ant*. 87, 2; Serv. *in Aen*. 6, 861.

38 See e.g. Instinsky 1966, 336.

39 *Mon. Anc*. 21, 1; cf. Hesberg, Panciera 1994, 91–94; Brandt 1995, 2 note 9; Cooley 2009, 200.

40 Syme 2002, 342–343; 368.

41 Cf. Dettenhofer 2000, 101 note 72. A little differently Treggiari (1991, 38), in whose opinion adopting one's son-in law automatically annulled the marriage.

successor. Seneca the Younger[42] and Tacitus unambiguously say Augustus saw his son-in-law so:

> Divus Augustus amisit Octaviam sororem carissimam et ne ei quidem rerum natura lugendi necessitatem abstulit, cui caelum destinaverat, immo vero idem omni genere orbitatis vexatus sororis filium successioni praeparatum suae perdidit[43].
>
> The deified Augustus lost his darling sister Octavia, and not even was he, whom Nature had destined for heaven, made exempt from the necessity of mourning - nay, he was harassed by every sort of bereavement, and, when he had planned to make his sister's son his own successor, he lost him[44].
>
> Exemplo divi Augusti qui sororis filium Marcellum, dein generum Agrippam, mox nepotes sus, postremo Tiberium Neronem privignum in proximo sibi fastigio conlocavit. sed Augustus in domo successorem quaesivit, ego in re publica[45].
>
> Herein I follow the example of the deified Augustus, who placed in high station next his own, first his sister's son Marcellus, then his son-in-law Agrippa, afterwards his grandsons, and finally Tiberius Nero, his step-son. But Augustus looked for a successor within his own house, I in the whole state[46].

Velleius Paterculus and Dio add to those accounts that in the eyes of the public opinion of the time, Marcellus was the primary candidate for accession in the event of the princeps' death:

> Ante triennium fere, quam Egnatianum scelus erumperet, circa Murenae Caepionisque coniurationis tempus, abhinc annos quinquaginta, M. Marcellus, sororis Augusti Octaviae filius, quem homines ita, si quid accidisset Caesari, successorem potentiae eius arbitrabantur futurum, ut tamen id per M. Agrippam securo ei posse contingere non existimarent, magnificentissimo munere aedilitatis edito decessit admodum iuvenis, sane, ut aiunt, ingenuarum virtutum laetusque animi et ingenii fortunaeque, in quam alebatur, capa[47].

---

42 It is worth emphasizing here that Seneca (*Cons. ad Marc.* 3, 1) also counts as an intended successor (*futurus princeps*) Drusus the Elder who was actually a plan B candidate to succession. Thus he obviously exaggerates the role Livia's younger son played in the *domus Augusta*, and so he probably does the same in Marcellus' case. I suppose Seneca, who was in exile, did that to ingratiate himself with the emperor Claudius, who was Drusus' son and Marcellus' nephew. Depicting his closest relatives as special and as Augustus' successors was important in the context of legitimizing his own succession. I discuss that more fully in Chapter Eight, section 8.3.

43 Sen. *Cons. ad Polyb.* 15, 3.

44 Translated by J. W. Basore (Loeb Classical Library, 254).

45 Tac. *Hist.* 1, 15.

46 Translated by C. H. Moore (Loeb Classical Library, 111).

47 Vell. Pat. 2, 93, 1.

Some three years before the plot of Egnatius was exposed, about the time of the conspiracy of Murena and Caepio, fifty years from the present date, Marcus Marcellus died, the son of Octavia, sister of Augustus, after giving a magnificent spectacle to commemorate his aedileship and while still quite a youth. People thought that, if anything should happen to Caesar, Marcellus would be his successor in power, at the same time believing, however, that this would not fall to his lot without opposition from Marcus Agrippa. He was, we are told, a young man of noble qualities, cheerful in mind and disposition, and equal to the station for which he was being reared[48].

Ὁ δ᾽ Αὔγουστος ἑνδέκατον μετὰ Καλπουρνίου Πίσωνος ἄρξας ἠρρώστησεν αὖθις, ὥστε μηδεμίαν ἐλπίδα σωτηρίας σχεῖν· πάντα γοῦν ὡς καὶ τελευτήσων διέθετο, καὶ τάς τε ἀρχὰς τούς τε ἄλλους τοὺς πρώτους καὶ τῶν βουλευτῶν καὶ τῶν ἱππέων ἀθροίσας διάδοχον μὲν οὐδένα ἀπέδειξε, καίτοι τὸν Μάρκελλον πάντων προκριθήσεσθαι ἐς τοῦτο προσδοκώντων [...][49].

When Augustus was consul for the eleventh time, with Calpurnius Piso, he fell so ill once more as to have no hope of recovery; at any rate, he arranged everything as if he were about to die, and gathered about him the magistrates and the foremost senators and knights. He did not, to be sure, appoint a successor, though all were expecting that Marcellus would be preferred for this position [...][50].

A similar opinion is held by some modern scholars, who see evidence for Augustus intending that Marcellus would be his political successor in particular in the fact that he married the young man to his only daughter, Julia[51]. However, that opinion does not seem justified to me. Since Augustus did not have a son, Marcellus' status as his son-in-law beyond doubt made him a strong candidate for the succession. Still, I do not think his marriage to Julia proves the emperor unequivocally indicated him as his successor[52]; that would require adoption, which would have made Marcellus not merely the future heir to Augustus' name, property and clients, but would also have in the eyes of the Roman society predestined him to take the princeps' place on the public scene after his death[53]. But as we know, that never happened, and as I discuss above there are no reasons

48 Translated by F. W. Shipley (Loeb Classical Library, 152).

49 Cass. Dio 53, 30, 1–2.

50 Translated by E. Cary (Loeb Classical Library, 83).

51 Cf. e.g. Kienast 1982, 177, 376 note 38; Kleiner 2005, 200; Syme 2002, 341, 346; Boruch 2010, 8, 92, 149–150; *contra* Brandt 1995, 1–16; Simpson 2005, 180–181; id. 2008, 361.

52 One finds similar scepticism in Instinsky 1966, 335–336; Severy 2003, 68–69; Wells 2005, 78–79.

53 The notion that a man's son is not only his heir privately, but also especially predisposed to becoming the successor to his political position, including to specific

to believe it was ever going to. It seems more likely that, with the chances of his having a son of his own being minute[54], Augustus hoped Julia and Marcellus' marriage would produce a son whom he would later be able to adopt and make his political successor[55]. In other words, Marcellus' role was to sire the emperor's potential successor and so help him actualize his dynastic plans[56]. I suspect that if Julia had given birth to a son, Marcellus would have risen to imperial power in the event of the princeps' premature death, and held it until Augustus' grandson cum-son was ready to reign in his own right[57]. That hypothesis is borne out by Augustus' later actions as regards dynastic policy, which indicate that he regarded his natural descendants as his potential successors first[58]. Of course, in Marcellus' case we need to remember that all this is pure speculation; in the light of his early death we do not know the role he would have ultimately played in the imperial family.

Some historians suppose the image of Marcellus as intended successor, which emerges from the ancient sources quoted above, may result from their authors writing about the beginnings of the principate *ex post*[59]; consequently, they elevated Marcellus to the rank held by Agrippa, later by Gaius and Lucius Caesar, and finally by Tiberius, overestimating his significance in the imperial family

---

offices or public posts, was characteristic of the Republican *nobilitas*. It is well illustrated by the case of P. Cornelius Scipio, who in 211 BC in Spain received a special *imperium* after the deaths of his father and uncle, even though he had only been aedile before. See Liv. 26, 18. Doubtless the most spectacular illustration of the power of family ties in Rome's public life is the case of Octavian himself; as Caesar's adoptive son, Octavian built on his political capital from the beginning of his career. More on that below.

54 Considering his marriage to Livia remained childless for thirteen years, it would seem unlikely the princeps could still hope for her to bear him a male child. Suetonius (*Aug.* 63, 1) does report Livia was pregnant with Augustus' child, but the baby was born premature. Still, we do not know when that happened and can only guess it was during the early years of their marriage.

55 See the later case of Gaius and Lucius Caesar. Cf. Instinsky 1966, 336.

56 In that spirit esp. Brandt 1995, 10 note 51. Cf. also Corbier 1995, 182.

57 With that assumption in mind the German term *Platzhalter* used for Marcellus would appear very apt; so for instance Bleicken (1998, 339). The princeps would later assign a similar role in his succession plans to Agrippa. On that, see below.

58 Instinsky 1966, 342; Bleicken 1998, 339.

59 Still, it is important to note that according to Velleius Paterculus and Cassius Dio's reports, it was only the Roman public and not Augustus himself that saw his future successor in Marcellus. See above.

and in the new order in general[60]. Brandt also correctly observed that the image of Marcellus preserved in literary sources does not agree with the message of the numismatic sources; the almost utter lack of coins depicting him is striking[61]. This sharply contrasts with Augustus' practice of presenting his intended successors on coinage; we have numerous coin series with Gaius and Lucius Caesar, and after his adoption, with Tiberius, issued by the senatorial mint in Rome, the imperial mint in Lugdunum and by provincial mints as well. On the one hand, such coins informed the public of Augustus' dynastic plans; on the other, they were a way of endorsing and celebrating the intended successors[62]. In this context, it seems no accident that we only have one coin series related to Marcellus, and that is provincial and uncertain.

To sum up, we have too little evidence to assume the princeps wanted Marcellus to be his political successor. It is here worth considering whether at that stage the emperor had even thought about choosing one at all; it would seem the problem did not occupy him too much in the early years of his rule. I think during that time the princeps concentrated more on consolidating his power and providing it with a definite legal framework rather than on choosing a specific successor; it is telling he did not even pick one when he expected to die during the grave illness from which he suffered in 23 BC[63]. Contrary to the opinion of certain other scholars, I do not believe that by handing over his personal ring

---

60 Cf. e.g. Brandt 1995, 4; Severy 2003, 68–69.

61 As mentioned above, the only coins featuring the supposed representations of Marcellus and Julia were probably minted in Africa, and we cannot be absolutely certain that is whom they depict.

62 Brandt 1995, 4, 8–9, 13–14; see also Kuhoff 1993a, 58. For coin series with the images of the young Caesars, see, among other places, *RIC* I² *Aug.* 205–209; 404–405; *RPC* I 96–97, 319, 2361, 2363, 2428; of Tiberius, *RIC* I² *Aug.* 221–222; 469–470; *RPC* I 215, 1140, 1565. On the other hand, those members of the emperor's family who were his plan B candidates for the succession are very rarely seen on Augustan era coins. Drusus the Elder is a good example. The only series minted in Augustan times and related to Drusus is one of the aurei and denarii issued in the mint in Lugdunum, generally dated to 15–12 BC: some scholars think the coins show Drusus and Tiberius in military attire giving Augustus olive branches, which in that context stand for victory. The princeps sits in a *sella curulis* placed on a special platform. See Kuhoff 1993a, 65; Zanker 1999, 227; Severy 2003, 89–90. However, not all scholars identify those characters as Augustus' stepsons. See the description of that series in *RIC* I² *Aug.* 164ab–165ab, and *HCC* I *Aug.* 191–193. Cf. also Rose 1997, 15.

63 As clearly noted by Cassius Dio (53, 30, 1–2).

to Agrippa during that illness he appointed Agrippa his successor[64]. And so, in Marcellus' lifetime the question of Augustus' succession remained unresolved[65].

1.2 Marcus Agrippa: Augustus' *collega imperii* or Successor?

It is no doubt a commonplace that Marcus Agrippa was Octavian's closest associate and second-in-command from the beginning of the latter's political career. Nor can it be doubted it is to Agrippa's superior military skill that the would-be princeps owed his sparkling career in the period from 44 to 30 BC, culminating in the victory over Antony and Cleopatra, which opened the door to his ruling the whole Empire. Octavian appreciated Agrippa's crucial contribution to the victory at Actium by according his friend many honours after they returned to Rome in 29 BC. Cassius Dio says those were numerous, but only lists one of them: the so-called dark-blue flag (*vexillum caeruleum*). The special character of that award is indicated primarily by the fact it had never been granted before[66]. Present-day historians suppose Agrippa was also made patrician and included in the college of *quindecemviri sacris faciundis*, and handing over to him Antony's old residence on the Palatine and his estate in Egypt was a reward of sorts as well[67]. The years right after Octavian came into independent power prove he had no intention of giving up Agrippa's services as his partner in administering the state. In 28 and 27 BC, the two of them held consulship together[68]. The moment was hardly incidental. It was the time of the preparation for—and eventually realization of—the so-called restoration of the Republic, which actually heralded the onset of a monarchic regime in Rome: the principate. Among the more important undertakings carried out by Octavian and Agrippa during their consulship of 28 BC were a census of citizens and the first senator list (*lectio senatus*), the aim of which was to exclude any unwanted person from the Senate and introduce their political allies in their place. As a result, a new senator list (*album*) was made, opened naturally by Octavian himself as the *princeps senatus*[69]. Agrippa's

64 I discuss this more extensively in the next section (1.2).

65 See Gruen 2005, 38.

66 Cass. Dio 51, 21, 3. Cf. also Roddaz 1984, 185; Kienast 1996, 72. In Suetonius (*Aug.* 25, 3) that honour was awarded Agrippa for his victory over Sextus Pompeius at Naulochus in 36 BC, but it is likely the author confused the two events. For information about that award, see Maxfield 1981, 82.

67 Roddaz 1984, 186–187; Reinhold 1988, 155.

68 Degrassi 1952, 3; Kienast 1996, 72.

69 *Mon. Anc.* 8, 2; Suet. *Aug.* 35, 1. Cassius Dio (52, 42, 1–2) dates that review of the membership of the Senate to 29 BC. It remains an open question what prerogatives

involvement in those early crucial projects closely connected to rolling in the new regime definitely demonstrates that Augustus assigned him a special role within the political system he was creating.

In this section, I mean to establish the place of Agrippa in the monarchy Augustus was building. The discussion will largely revolve around two questions. One of those is the problem, widely disputed in scholarship, of Agrippa's so-called co-regency; the other relates to the question of whether we can see Agrippa as Augustus' intended successor, or was he merely his helper (*collega imperii, adiutor*) in ruling the state? I believe, in order to determine the answers one needs to examine Agrippa's political career after 23 BC and the coin series related to him. That will make it possible to determine the position he held within the new order of power.

I shall begin with an analysis of an interesting passage in book fifty-three of Cassius Dio's *Roman History*, where he mentions the grave illness which befell Augustus during his eleventh consulship in 23 BC[70]. Expecting the illness to perhaps prove fatal this time, the emperor called for a meeting of his most important officials, representatives of the Senate and influential equites, to issue them with his last orders. This is how Dio recounts the course of that meeting:

> Ὁ δ᾽ Αὔγουστος ἑνδέκατον μετὰ Καλπουρνίου Πίσωνος ἄρξας ἠρρώστησεν αὖθις, ὥστε μηδεμίαν ἐλπίδα σωτηρίας σχεῖν· πάντα γοῦν ὡς καὶ τελευτήσων διέθετο, καὶ τάς τε ἀρχὰς τούς τε ἄλλους τοὺς πρώτους καὶ τῶν βουλευτῶν καὶ τῶν ἱππέων ἀθροίσας διάδοχον μὲν οὐδένα ἀπέδειξε, καίτοι τὸν Μάρκελλον πάντων προκριθήσεσθαι ἐς τοῦτο προσδοκώντων, διαλεχθεὶς δέ τινα αὐτοῖς περὶ τῶν δημοσίων πραγμάτων τῷ μὲν Πίσωνι τάς τε δυνάμεις καὶ τὰς προσόδους τὰς κοινὰς ἐς βιβλίον ἐσγράψας ἔδωκε, τῷ δ᾽ Ἀγρίππᾳ τὸν δακτύλιον ἐνεχείρισε[71].

> When Augustus was consul for the eleventh time, with Calpurnius Piso, he fell so ill once more as to have no hope of recovery; at any rate, he arranged everything as if he were about to die, and gathered about him the magistrates and the foremost senators and knights. He did not, to be sure, appoint a successor, although all were expecting that

---

allowed Octavian and Agrippa to carry out the census and the *lectio senatus*. The sources are ambiguous. The princeps himself says in the *Res gestae* (8, 2) they did that in their capacity as consuls. In the *Fasti Venusini* (Degrassi 1963, 60–61) and in Cassius Dio (52, 42, 1) we find the information they based their action on their authority as censors (*censoria potestas*). See Reinhold 1933, 68–69 note 35; Roddaz 1984, 201–203; Ziółkowski 2004, 362; Cooley 2009, 139–142.

70 It should be noted here that Augustus had already been unwell before, including gravely ill a few times, including during the military campaign against Caesar's killers in 42 BC, and then in 25 BC during Julia's marriage to Marcellus: Suet. *Aug.* 81, 1.

71 Cass. Dio 53, 30, 1–2.

> Marcellus would be preferred for this position, but after talking with them awhile about the public affairs, he gave Piso the list of the forces and of the public revenues written in a book, and handed his ring to Agrippa[72].

This passage gives rise to several questions. First of all, one must inquire whether the events described actually took place. I agree with the majority of modern scholars who believe the passage is historical[73]. This possibility is borne out by Cassius Dio's account being largely confirmed in Suetonius, who also mentions a meeting between Augustus, senators and magistrates during the princeps' aforementioned illness:

> De reddenda re p. bis cogitavit: primum post oppressum statim Antonium, memor obiectum sibi ab eo saepius, quasi per ipsum staret ne redderetur; ac rursus taedio diuturnae valitudinis, cum etiam magistratibus ac senatu domum accitis rationarium imperii tradidit. Sed reputans et se privatum non sine periculo fore et illam plurium arbitrio temere committi, in retinenda perseveravit [...][74].

> He twice thought of restoring the republic; first immediately after the overthrow of Antony, remembering that his rival had often made the charge that it was his fault that it was not restored; and again in the weariness of a lingering illness, when he went so far as to summon the magistrates and the senate to his house, and submit an account of the general condition of the empire. Reflecting, however, that as he himself would not be free from danger if he should retire, so too it would be hazardous to trust the State to the control of more than one, he continued to keep it in his hands [...][75].

Now Suetonius' account would indicate that in view of his poor health the princeps was going to transfer power over to the Senate, as is evidenced by his giving its representatives a report on the current affairs of the state, among other things, but ultimately he changed his mind. However, there is no mention in Suetonius of the princeps giving Agrippa his personal ring, and if we accept the story told in both Cassius Dio and Suetonius as true, the question arises of the meaning and message of Augustus' actions in the face of imminent death.

There are many different interpretations of the emperor's behaviour among scholars. Some believe that by handing over his signet ring to Agrippa, the princeps informally indicated him as his political successor, supposedly inspired by the earlier actions of Alexander the Great, who reputedly gave his ring to

72 Translated by E. Cary (Loeb Classical Library, 83).

73 Rich 1990, 165–166; Brandt 1995, 12–13; Dettenhofer 2000, 100. *Contra* Simpson 2005, 187–188.

74 Suet. *Aug*. 28, 1.

75 Translated by J. C. Rolfe (Loeb Classical Library, 31).

Perdiccas as he lay dying[76]. In my opinion, that interpretation is questionable. First, Cassius Dio himself clearly notes that during the meeting Augustus did not indicate anybody as his political successor; thus he does not see a connection between giving Agrippa the ring and making him the successor, whether formally or informally[77], although sadly he does not explain the meaning of the gesture in this passage. Second, if the handing over of Augustus' personal ring was meant to indicate who would be the successor, then we would have to assume it was at the time regarded as a symbol of the emperor's power or possibly a symbol of an office held (in this case, the consulship), and it would have had to be seen as such by the senators and other officials who took part in the meeting. However, we know that both under the Republic and Augustus' reign the major visual trappings of power were the curule seat (*sella curulis*) and the *fasces* carried by the lictors accompanying the official[78], and nothing indicates a ring could have had that function. Moreover, Christopher J. Simpson pointed out that in the Roman context receiving somebody's ring did not give one the right to inherit anything, let alone succeed to their political position; he rather thinks that the ring acquired the status of an official symbol of a princeps' power, one that could then be passed to one's chosen successor, only under the Flavian dynasty[79].

A slightly different interpretation of the passage in question is to be found in Brandt, who assumes handing over the ring mostly meant indicating Agrippa as Augustus' private successor and the executor of his will. The historian emphasizes that this in turn predisposed Agrippa to political succession[80], but that interpretation seems incorrect too; there are no grounds for believing that Agrippa receiving the ring was tantamount to him becoming Augustus' private heir. According to Roman law, the only person entitled to inheriting the emperor's property was still his daughter, Julia[81], which could have changed if the princeps had adopted Agrippa or included him specifically in his last will.

---

76 See. eg. Reinhold 1933, 78–79; Sattler 1960, 67; Rich 1990, 165–166; Bleicken 1998, 347.

77 Cass. Dio 53, 30, 1. Suetonius (*Aug.* 28, 1) does not mention Augustus then indicating a successor either.

78 For information on external attributes of power in Rome cf. especially Schäfer 1989, *passim.*

79 Simpson 2005, 182, 184, 186. Now Suetonius' account of the last moments of Tiberius' life could suggest a ring was already a sign of a princeps' power during that emperor's lifetime. Cf. Suet. *Tib.* 73, 2; *Calig.* 12, 2. However, we cannot be certain that is not an anachronism.

80 Brandt 1995, 12–13. Sattler 1960, 67 takes a similar tone.

81 Cf. Dettenhofer 2000, 100.

Furthermore, only adoption would have allowed Agrippa, then the heir to Augustus' name, to aspire to taking over from him in the public arena[82]. That had been demonstrated by the case of Octavian himself, who owed all of his dazzling career after coming to Rome in 44 BC to the magic of Caesar's name, who had adopted him in his will[83]: thanks to that adoption he became not simply the murdered dictator's main heir, but as the bearer of his name the head of the Julian family, he inherited Caesar's political alliances and his clientele. Thus, for his contemporaries Octavian became the new Caesar and so the natural successor to the remarkable position held on the Roman public scene by his adoptive father[84]. With this borne in mind, I fail to see how simply having Augustus' ring could have been enough of an asset for Agrippa to take his place, should Augustus have died[85]. It is also difficult to imagine the senatorial elite accepting as the future princeps a man with such a lowly name and origin as Agrippa[86]. Still, one can agree with Brandt that the transfer of Augustus' personal ring confirmed Agrippa's special role in the new system of power as the ruler's closest aide and second-in-command[87].

The most convincing explanation of the issue in question has in my opinion been put forward by Dettenhofer, who rightly points out that the problems solved by Augustus during his meeting with officials and senators when seriously ill were both public and private in nature. From Cassius Dio we know the man to receive Augustus' report on the situation in the state was incumbent consul Gnaeus Calpurnius Piso, so it is possible that any directions given Agrippa were all about Augustus' private affairs. In Dettenhofer's view, passing the ring to Agrippa did not make him Augustus' successor or heir; instead, it only meant

82 But of course we have no grounds for supposing the princeps was going to adopt Agrippa. T. Stevenson (2013, 125) believes on the other hand that Augustus handing the ring over to Agrippa might mean the princeps had recently chosen him as his heir in his will.

83 As emphatically indicated by two passages in Cicero's *Philippicae*; see Cic. *Phil.* 11, 8, 20; 13, 11, 24.

84 See Syme 2002, 112–122; Bleicken 1998, 339; Ziółkowski 2004, 355, 400; Stevenson 2013, 119–120. Confirming the adoption and accepting the name *Caesar* also made it Octavian's duty to avenge the murdered dictator's death. See Sawiński 2008, 141–150; Flaig 2013, 148.

85 *Contra* Reinhold 1933, 78.

86 Velleius Paterculus (2, 96, 1) writes of Agrippa's *novitas* and Tacitus (*Ann.* 1, 3, 1) terms him *ignobilis*. See also Dettenhofer 2000, 102; Stevenson 2013, 124.

87 Brandt 1995, 12–13.

entrusting him with carrying out his last will[88]. To continue this line of thought, we can surmise Agrippa was expected to use Augustus' signet ring to settle all his private and family matters if he were to die[89]. It is also possible that by giving his personal ring to his closest and most reliable friend, the emperor entrusted him with both his property and family (the *domus Augusta*). It bears mentioning here that Agrippa had replaced Augustus as *pater familias* before, such as at Julia's and Marcellus' wedding in 25 BC, when in the princeps' absence (incidentally, also due to an illness), he personally presided over the wedding ceremony[90]. His choice of this trusted friend for that role is thus quite understandable[91]. To sum up, I see no reasons to conclude that the transfer of the ring to Agrippa had anything to do with making him a public successor or private heir[92].

Cassius Dio's text also informs us that after his recovery Augustus suggested that his last will be read in the Senate to prove he had not appointed a political successor (*τῆς ἀρχῆς διάδοχον*), which is presumably to mean he had not adopted anybody in that document. However, the Senators predictably prevented the contents of the will from becoming public knowledge:

> Ταῦτα μὲν ὕστερον ἔπραξε, τότε δὲ σωθεὶς τὰς διαθήκας ἐσήνεγκε μὲν ἐς τὸ συνέδριον καὶ ἀναλέξασθαι ἠθέλησεν, ἐνδεικνύμενος τοῖς ἀνθρώποις ὅτι οὐδένα τῆς ἀρχῆς διάδοχον καταλελοιπὼς ἦν, οὐ μέντοι καὶ ἀνέγνω· οὐδεὶς γὰρ ἐπέτρεψεν[93].
>
> This he did later; at the time, after being restored to health, he brought his will into the senate and desired to read it, by way of showing people that he had left no successor to his realm; but he did not read it, for none would permit it[94].

I think that passage is actually anachronistic[95]; it probably reflects later practices, when adoption would precede granting a candidate imperial prerogatives and

88 Dettenhofer 2000, 100. Cf. also Severy 2003, 69.

89 Cf. Wells 2005, 79. One must not forget the Romans used that ring to seal private letters and a variety of documents.

90 Cass. Dio 53, 27, 5.

91 Still, Richard Bauman (2003, 101) supposes Augustus gave the ring to Agrippa, because Marcellus was already ill at the time. However, Cassius Dio's account (53, 30, 4) indicates the young man only fell ill after the princeps got better.

92 That conclusion is also confirmed, I believe, by the passage in Cassius Dio (51, 3, 5–6) on the events of 31 BC. Namely Dio reports Octavian handed over his ring to Agrippa and Maecenas so they could send letters in his name to the Senate and magistrates. Clearly that had no connection to appointing a successor.

93 Cass. Dio 53, 31, 1.

94 Translated by E. Cary (Loeb Classical Library, 83).

95 *Contra* Rich 1990, 167.

so would have a close connection to designating one's successor. We must also remember that formally Augustus could only use his will to choose a private heir. Therefore, it seems unlikely the princeps intended to explain to the Senate directions which were all to do with his private affairs. Regardless of the historicity of the passage, though, it exemplifies, as does the passage on the emperor's actions during his grave illness analysed above, Dio's conviction that in 23 BC the question of the political succession to Augustus' legacy remained unresolved. Under the circumstances it is impossible to unequivocally determine who would have taken Augustus' place, had the illness proven fatal. While Marcellus was his nearest male relative, he was not part of the *Iulii Caesares* family, and more importantly, he was not a son of the emperor. In other words, he lacked the asset which had made it possible for Octavian to take Caesar's place in Roman politics[96]. Agrippa, on the other hand, was disqualified by his lowly birth[97].

As mentioned above, not naming a specific successor could have been caused by the fact that in the early years of his independent reign the princeps focused more on consolidating his power and on looking for a legal foundation for the rising monarchy. What is more, it is difficult to imagine what such an appointment could have looked like formally, as rules for it had not yet been established[98]. Not that this means Augustus had no dynastic aspirations; those were to be realized in the future by handing the imperial power over to a close family member. And since he had no son, his only daughter, Julia, was to help him carry out those plans. However, her marriage to Marcellus failed to give Augustus the male descendants he so desired. It is for that reason that two years after his nephew's death (in 21 BC) he married Julia to Agrippa, who had first had to divorce Octavia's daughter, Claudia Marcella[99]. Plutarch highlights Octavia's special role as the driving force behind that marriage. Supposedly it was Octavia who suggested the notion to the princeps when he was considering the choice of a husband for his daughter[100]. Still, Plutarch seems to overestimate Augustus' sister's role in this regard, although of course it is possible he might have consulted her on a matter which did involve her daughter's divorce and her current son-in-law's remarriage. According to Frank B. Marsh, by marrying Agrippa to Julia, Augustus intended to tie his closest aide and friend to himself even more closely. The marriage was also supposedly to guarantee Agrippa's loyalty towards the princeps. Also, in that

96 Of course it is possible to guess there was a clause adopting Marcellus in Augustus' will, but that is mere speculation.

97 See above.

98 Adoption was not in itself enough to publically designate a successor.

99 Vell. Pat. 2, 93, 2; Suet. *Aug.* 63, 1; Cass. Dio 54, 6, 5.

100 Plut. *Ant.* 87, 2–3. Cf. also Bauman 2003, 101.

scholar's opinion the fact the emperor gave Agrippa his daughter in marriage clearly meant designating him as the successor[101]. Only the first part of this view seems to be correct; it would be hard to agree that the princeps wanted to obtain Agrippa's loyalty in that way, since he had proven himself loyal many times before by standing by Octavian from the beginning of his political career. Rather, the marriage to Julia was a reward, after a manner, for all of Agrippa's earlier services, rather than the price of his continued loyalty. While the relation between that marriage and Augustus' dynastic policy is obvious, in my opinion it hardly proves the princeps intended Agrippa to be his final successor. As I have mentioned above, I believe Augustus hoped Julia would bear sons, from among whom he would be able to pick his future successor. Thus Agrippa's role lay in siring that successor. There can be no question that the marriage to Julia was a significant point in Agrippa's career: due to it he was brought even closer to Augustus, and as his son-in-law became the second most eminent person in the imperial family, right after the princeps.

Agrippa's political career certainly reached its crowning point in 18 BC, when, at Augustus' instigation, he was granted tribunician powers for five years[102]. It bears pointing out here that he was the first member of the *domus Augusta* (excluding the princeps himself) to receive those prerogatives. At the same time, his *imperium proconsulare*, probably conferred for the first time in 23 BC, was also prolonged for another five years[103]. Just like Augustus' *imperium*, his too was presumably *maius* in relation to those of all the provincial governors[104]. Thus from 18 BC on, Agrippa held the two highest powers in the state, which

101 Marsh 1931, 33. Similarly Corbett 1974, 88.

102 Tac. *Ann.* 3, 56, 2; Cass. Dio 54, 12, 4. Dio also mentions that at the time Agrippa was granted a number of other privileges on top of the tribunician power, ones Augustus had already enjoyed; sadly, he does not list them. Cf. also Roddaz 1984, 357; Kienast 1996, 72.

103 See Eck 2007, 66.

104 Scholars have been engaged in a heated discussion on the nature of Agrippa's *imperium* for years now. The starting point is interpreting the fragment of the Greek version of the funeral speech (*laudatio funebris*) Augustus gave over his friend's grave, preserved in papyrus form. Generally, two opinions can be encountered. Some believe the text mentions granting Agrippa *imperium aequum*, that is, power equal to that of other governors. Others see Agrippa's *imperium* as superior to theirs (that is, as *maius*). On that subject, see Koenen 1970, 217–283; Gray 1970, 227–238; Bringmann 1977, 219–234; Badian 1980, 97–107; Haslam 1980, 193–199; Roddaz 1984, 343–347; Rich 1990, 168; Fraschetti 1990b, 83–98; Ameling 1994, 1–28; Hurlet 1997, 38–52; Galinsky 2012, 115–118. Personally, I stand with the scholars who maintain Agrippa had *imperium maius* in relation to other governors' powers, and I have expressed my point of view before in other publications. See Sawiński 2004, 246–249 and id. 2005, 27–29.

since 23 BC had been the legal foundation of Augustus' power as princeps. Some historians assume that this meant elevating Agrippa to the rank of Augustus' co-regent[105], and formally speaking, they may be right. Having *tribunicia potestas* and *imperium maius*, the two crucial components of imperial power, combined, nominally made Agrippa Augustus' partner on an equal footing[106]. Still, it does not follow that a double monarchy was thereby introduced[107]. The state was still ruled by a single princeps, the commander-in-chief of the Empire's armies, sworn in to his name and his alone. Moreover, it was under his auspices that all the military campaigns proceeded[108]. However, what particularly distinguished Augustus from Agrippa was *auctoritas*. Now that term had a broad semantic field, but Romans mostly used it to mean somebody's dignity, distinction and authority. No doubt in this respect, as the son of the godlike Caesar (*divi filius*), Augustus surpassed Agrippa by a wide margin, as Agrippa was low-born and had no such lofty ancestry to his name[109]. Thus, while the 18 BC regulations made Agrippa Augustus' equal legally, his actual standing as that of the second most influential man in the state and the emperor's first aide did not change.

Agrippa's political career after 18 BC demonstrates he retained his status of *collega Augusti* until his death in 12 BC. In 17 BC, he and the princeps presided together over the Secular Games (*ludi saeculares*), celebrated as the beginning of a new era in the history of Rome[110]. In the same year, he was sent as the emperor's special envoy to the East, where he was to conduct an inspection of the provinces and vassal kingdoms[111]. Agrippa's sojourn in the region from 17 to 13 BC was a good opportunity for the inhabitants of those provinces to confirm their loyalty to the *domus Augusta* by appropriately celebrating its second most important member. The type and number of honours granted Agrippa at the time confirm his special standing in the imperial family and within the new order of power. Among

105 Cf. among others Reinhold 1933, 98–101; Parsi 1963, 47; Roddaz 1984, 351–381; Rich 1990, 189; Ziółkowski 2004, 364.

106 A conclusion unchanged, in my opinion, by Agrippa receiving tribunician powers through a *senatus consultum* rather than a *lex* passed by the Comitia (as had been the case with Augustus) or by those powers being limited in time. See Lacey 1979, 29.

107 *Contra* Kornemann 1930, 12–20.

108 Cf. Jacques, Scheid 1992, 33.

109 In that context, the famous passage in *Res gestae* (34, 3) is quite telling. Cf. also Reinhold 1933, 100–101; Roddaz 1984, 366, 377.

110 *CIL* VI 32323; Roddaz 1984, 370–374; Severy 2003, 70.

111 For information on Agrippa's second visit to the East, cf. among others Reinhold 1933, 106–123; Roddaz 1984, 419–475; Halfmann 1986, 164–166; Dąbrowa 1998, 202–203; Sawiński 2005, 79–81.

the more prestigious ones there were statues erected in his honour by many cities there. Alas, in most cases only honorific inscriptions remain of these, demonstrating Agrippa was celebrated with epithets such as *εὐεργέτης*, *σωτήρ*, *κτίστης*, or *συγγενής*[112]. One of the Greek cities to honour Agrippa in that way was Athens. The monument was placed on the Acropolis opposite the Propylaea. It is supposed that it was a statue standing in a triumphal quadriga. The only preserved part is the huge pedestal with an inscription stating the whole thing was erected by a decision of the Athenian assembly[113]. As another example, there is the statue dedicated to Agrippa on Delos, likely placed in the naos of the temple of Apollo there, since that is where it was discovered, and the decision was again taken by the Athenian assembly and the Areopagus. It is estimated that it was founded between 16 and 13 BC[114]. An interesting statuary group was also erected by the people of Thespiae in Boeotia, likewise dated to 16–13 BC. Besides Agrippa, the group included statues of Julia, Gaius and Lucius Caesar, Agrippina the Elder and Livia, and the whole cycle was most likely located in or near the local sanctuary of the Muses[115]. The high rank of those honours is indicated primarily by the fact the statues were all placed in the highest and most prestigious locations of any given city, such as the acropolis or a temple.

After Agrippa's return from the East in 13 BC, the Senate prolonged his *tribunicia potestas* and *imperium* for another five years[116]. At the same time, the senatorial mint in Rome issued a series of coins with his image. Of special interest are the series minted by two *monetales*, C. Marius and C. Sulpicius Platorinus, in principle dated to 13 BC[117]. The obverse of C. Marius' denarii has an image of Augustus with a *lituus* in the background, with the legend AUGUSTUS; the reverse shows Augustus and Agrippa in togas, each holding a scroll in his left hand, with the triumvir's signature, C MARIUS C F TRO III VIR[118]. (fig. 1) The coins most likely refer to the third *lectio senatus*, carried out by Augustus and Agrippa together in 13 BC[119]. Then there is the series of aurei and denarii signed by Sulpicius Platorinus.

---

112 Among other places, we have such inscriptions from Athens (*IG* III 575), Corcyra (*CIG* II 1878), Thermis on Lesbos (*IGRR* IV 21), Gythium (*IG* V.1 1666) and Troy (*IGRR* IV 204). Cf. also Reinhold 1933, 106–108; 116; Roddaz 1984, 441–444.

113 Cf. Reinhold 1933, 108; Roddaz 1984, 439.

114 Rose 1997, 151 (no. 83).

115 Rose 1997, 149–151 (no. 82); Boschung 2002, 144–145.

116 Cass. Dio 54, 28, 1; Kienast 1996, 72.

117 Cf. Fullerton 1985, 474–475.

118 *RIC* I² *Aug*. 397; Reinhold 1933, 100 note 7; Fullerton 1985, 475.

119 There is a reminder of the selection of the membership of the Senate in 13 BC in Cassius Dio (54, 26, 3–4), among other sources. Cf. also Fullerton 1985, 477.

Fig. 1. Denarius of Gaius Marius, Rome, 13 BC. Obverse: an image of Augustus with a *lituus* in the background; legend: AUGUSTUS. Reverse: images of Augustus and Agrippa wearing togas, each holding a scroll in his left hand; triumvir's signature: C MARIUS C F TRO III VIR (*RIC* I² *Aug*. 397).

The obverse of the aurei contains Augustus' head wearing an oak-leaf crown and the legend, CAESAR AUGUSTUS; the reverse has Agrippa wearing a combination of *corona rostrata* and *corona muralis*, completed by the legend M AGRIPPA and the triumvir's name, PLATORINUS III VIR[120]. (fig. 2) The denarii have Augustus' head on the obverse, again with the legend CAESAR AUGUSTUS, while on the reverse the emperor sits side by side with Agrippa in a *bisellium*, the traditional seat of the tribunes of the plebs, placed on a platform decorated with *rostra*; here, the triumvir's signature is C SULPIC PLATORIN[121]. (fig. 3) The series probably commemorated the renewing of Agrippa's tribunician powers in 13 BC[122]. His role as that of Augustus' co-wielder of the *tribunicia potestas* was also highlighted by a provincial coin series minted at the behest of the proconsul of Crete and Cyrenaica and dated to sometime between 18 and 12 BC. The obverse depicted the heads of Augustus and Agrippa facing each other, and the legend was CAESAR TR POT AGRIPPA[123]. All these coin series very clearly exhibited Agrippa's position as

120 *RIC* I² *Aug*. 409; Fullerton 1985, 474; Grant 1990, 12–13.
121 *RIC* I² *Aug*. 406; *HCC* I *Aug*. 49; Reinhold 1933, 100 note 7; Fullerton 1985, 474, 477; Grant 1990, 13–14.
122 Fullerton 1985, 477; Severy 2003, 75.
123 *RPC* I 942; Reinhold 1933, 99 note 4a.

Fig. 2. Aureus of Gaius Sulpicius Platorinus, Rome, 13 BC. Obverse: an image of Augustus wearing an oak wreath; legend: CAESAR AUGUSTUS. Reverse: a portrait of Agrippa in a combined *corona rostrata* and *corona muralis*; legend: M AGRIPPA; triumvir's signature: PLATORINUS III VIR (*RIC* I[2] *Aug*. 409).

Fig. 3. Denarius of Gaius Sulpicius Platorinus, Rome, 13 BC. Obverse: Augustus' head; legend: CAESAR AUGUSTUS. Reverse: an image of Augustus and Agrippa seated on a *bisellium* placed on a platform; triumvir's signature: C SULPIC PLATORIN (*RIC* I[2] *Aug*. 406).

Augustus' closest collaborator, sharing the toil of managing the Empire with the princeps[124].

There is one more interesting denarius series related to Agrippa, signed by a Cossus Cornelius Lentulus. The obverse prominently featured Augustus' head in the oak-leaf crown and the legend AUGUSTUS COS XI; the reverse depicts Agrippa's head, again with the combined *corona muralis* and *rostrata*, the legend being M AGRIPPA COS TER and the signature, COSSUS LENTULUS[125]. The coins were probably minted after Agrippa's death (in March of 12 BC) and were a posthumous commemoration of his military successes[126].

The course of his political career outlined above, and the analysis of the coin series relating to him, both irrefutably prove that from 18 BC on, Agrippa formally had the status of *collega Augusti* and in actual fact was the second most powerful man in the state and the emperor's second-in-command. One can agree with Roddaz's opinion that the princeps introduced co-regency out of a concern to provide the new monarchy with some permanence and stability[127]. It was also an important stage in the forming of a reigning dynasty centred on the emperor. At this point, we ought to return to the question asked above regarding Agrippa's place in Augustus' dynastic plans, and whether his formally becoming the co-regent in 18 BC entailed his appointment as successor as well.

Tacitus has no doubts; in his opinion, granting Agrippa the *tribunicia potestas* meant Augustus was indicating that he would be his political successor[128]. A number of modern historians consider the matter less obvious. Namely, they observe that conferring those "imperial" powers on Agrippa merely elevated him to the status of co-regent[129]. Their perspective is largely justified, since Augustus adopting Gaius and Lucius in 17 BC demonstrates he actually intended one of them to eventually succeed him. For now, however, the prospect was remote, as the two brothers were still young children[130], so the sickly princeps had to take

---

124 Fullerton 1985, 480; Wallace-Hadrill 1986, 71–72, 79; Severy 2003, 76.

125 *RIC* I² *Aug.* 414; *HCC* I *Aug.* 53; Fullerton 1985, 475.

126 Fullerton 1985, 478; Ziółkowski 2007, 467.

127 Roddaz 1984, 379.

128 Tac. *Ann.* 3, 56, 1–2. Some modern scholars agree and believe Agrippa's assumption of tribunician powers meant not only that he rose to the position of co-regent, but also was designated the princeps' successor. Cf. e.g. Bauman 2003, 101–102; Ziółkowski 2004, 364.

129 So among others Reinhold 1933, 101–102; Severy 2003, 70, 75–76.

130 At the moment of the adoption, Gaius was two years old, and Lucius had only just been born. Cf. Kienast 1996, 73, 75.

into consideration he might die before his adoptive sons reached the age when they were fit to rule. I believe introducing and then reinforcing the co-regency, which remained in force until Agrippa's death, was actually closely connected to ensuring the young Caesars' succession. Having the tribunician power and *imperium proconsulare*, the two most vital legal foundations of the emperor's authority, was in fact supposed to make it possible for Agrippa to smoothly take over the reins of power in the case of Augustus' unexpected death, which in turn was to guarantee in future that one of the young Caesars would become princeps. After all, it seems certain Agrippa would have done all he could for his natural sons to take Augustus' place. Therefore, I think Augustus saw Agrippa not so much as a successor, but rather as a potential regent or temporary successor, who could wield imperial power in the event of his sudden death, until Gaius or Lucius were of age[131]. It does not seem likely the princeps supposed one of his adopted sons would assume power only after Agrippa died[132], since in the eyes of the Roman society it was Gaius and Lucius, as heirs to Augustus' name, that would also naturally succeed to his political position. What is more, Agrippa's low birth disqualified him from the senatorial aristocracy, which Augustus must have known very well[133]. Of course, we must not forget that any such speculation is purely hypothetical, since we cannot be certain how events would have unfolded had the princeps died before his friend did.

With Agrippa's illness and unexpected death in Campania after his return from the Pannonian campaign in 12 BC, the problem of his possible succession or regency solved itself. News of his aide's illness made the emperor leave for Campania immediately, but he found Agrippa already dead. From Cassius Dio we know Augustus personally accompanied the funeral procession of his friend's body from Campania to Rome[134], and his account of Agrippa's burial

131 So also Brunt, Moore 1967, 55; Sattler 1969, 492–493; Roddaz 1984, 378; Rich 1990, 195; Dettenhofer 2000, 147; Severy 2003, 71. In this case the German term *Platzhalter* would describe Agrippa well.

132 A claim found, in, among others, Marsh 1931, 33; Corbett 1974, 88; Bauman 2003, 102, all of whom assume Augustus intended for Agrippa to rise to actual imperial power after him, only then to be followed by one of the young Caesars.

133 See above. The dislike in which the *nobilitas* held Agrippa may be indicated by a passage in Cassius Dio (54, 29, 6), where he says the senators were sceptical about the mourning declared after his death, attempting to boycott the funeral games in his honour. On that subject, see also Rich 1980, 217–221; id. 1990, 208; Fraschetti 1990a, 285–286; Dettenhofer 2000, 102; Syme 2002, 344.

134 Cass. Dio 54, 28, 3.

is somewhat more extensive than that of Marcellus. We know the princeps paid his last respects to the deceased by holding a *funus publicum* for him, and after reaching Rome the corpse was displayed in the Forum Romanum. Then Augustus gave a *laudatio funebris* from the rostra in front of the temple to divus Julius[135]. There is one extremely interesting detail to the account of the funeral; namely Dio mentions that while Augustus was giving the eulogy, the corpse was concealed behind a special curtain, quoting various authors' opinions as to why that was done. Some of them claimed the princeps could not look at a dead body, because he was the *pontifex maximus*[136]; others implied the prohibition resulted from the emperor holding censorial powers. However, Dio considers both those explanations erroneous, while admitting he cannot satisfactorily explain Augustus' behaviour[137]. A solution may be found in some other sources. According to Seneca, at the funeral of Drusus the Younger, his body, too, was hidden behind a special curtain while Tiberius gave the *laudatio funebris*. For Seneca it is obvious that as the *pontifex maximus*, the princeps could not come into direct contact with a corpse[138]. In that context, a passage in Tacitus is of importance as well; there, the historian mentions the harsh criticism Tiberius directed at Germanicus for taking part in the burial of the remnants of Varus' legionaries killed in AD 9 in the Teutoburg Forest. In Tacitus' opinion, among the reasons for the emperor reacting in this way was the fact that Germanicus was an augur at the time and so should not have participated in burying the dead[139]. Another relevant confirmation can be found in Servius' commentary on the *Aeneid*, which clearly states *pontifices* were strictly forbidden to look at dead bodies[140]. Those sources clearly prove that any contact with a corpse, including merely looking at it, was taboo for people who held priesthoods. Thus, contrary to Cassius Dio's opinion, among the authors he quotes those are right who claim Augustus' behaviour followed from his being the *pontifex maximus*, and it was for that reason that he had to give Agrippa's funeral eulogy as described.

---

135 Cass. Dio 54, 28, 3. See Fraschetti 1990a, 284.

136 Augustus took over as *pontifex maximus* on 6th March 12 BC, after Marcus Lepidus died. See the *Fasti Praenestini* (Degrassi 1963, 120–121). Agrippa's funeral was probably held in late March or early April of that year. See Kienast 1996, 64.

137 Cass. Dio 54, 28, 3–4.

138 Sen. *Cons. ad Marc.* 15, 3. See also Roddaz 1984, 486–487.

139 Tac. *Ann.* 1, 62, 2.

140 Serv. *In. Aen.* 3, 64; 6, 176. See Rich 1990, 207.

Moreover, from the same historian's account we know the situation would be repeated during Octavia's funeral[141].

After the *laudatio*, Agrippa's body was carried from the Forum to the Campus Martius in a solemn procession and there cremated. Even though he had his own tomb within the Campus Martius, the bones were laid in the Mausoleum of Augustus[142]. Choosing the Mausoleum over the tomb as the place of burial was hardly an accident; rather, it followed from Agrippa's standing. As the emperor's son-in-law, he could be buried in no other place than Augustus' family tomb[143].

Since Agrippa had been quite active in the provinces and client states, thereby winning considerable popularity, news of his death spread among the inhabitants. His memory was especially cultivated by Herod[144], who had a town in Judea renamed from Anthedon to *Ἀγρίππειον*, and a grandson of his, born in 10 BC, was named M. Julius Agrippa[145]. On Kos, games were regularly held in Agrippa's honour, and his memory endured in Ephesus, where the southern gate leading to the agora, dated to 4 or 3 BC, was dedicated to Augustus, Agrippa and their wives Livia and Julia. Finally, a number of cities in Asia Minor would mint coins with Agrippa's image long after his death[146].

Cassius Dio further informs us that successive anniversaries of Agrippa's death were likewise celebrated with solemnity. On the fifth (in 7 BC), games were held in his honour in the Campus Martius, focusing on gladiatorial combat, with all the spectators wearing mourning garb. The only exception was the princeps; as explained above, he needed to abstain from contact with anything related in any way to death[147].

Agrippa's death doubtless complicated the political succession after Augustus, since in 12 BC Gaius and Lucius Caesar were still too young to take over, should the princeps have died within the next few years. Consequently, Augustus had to include one of his stepsons in his plans as a potential temporary successor or regent, who might carry the burden of governance until one of his sons could rule in his own right.

141 Cass. Dio 54, 35, 4–5.

142 Cass. Dio 54, 28, 5; Reinhold 1933, 127.

143 Cf. Wesch-Klein 1993, 110.

144 M. Reinhold (1933, 133) supposes Herod personally took part in Agrippa's funeral.

145 Joseph. *AJ*. 13, 357; *BJ*. 1, 87; 416; Reinhold 1933, 133–134; Roddaz 1984, 453.

146 Reinhold 1933, 134–135.

147 Cass. Dio 55, 8, 5. See Rich 1990, 226.

1.3 Tiberius, Drusus the Elder and the Problem of Succession from 12 to 6 BC

In this section, I mostly intend to establish what standing Tiberius and Drusus had in the *domus Augusta* between 12 and 6 BC, and what roles they played in Augustus' succession plans at the time. Both stepsons were certainly taken into consideration as potential successors, but only as distant ones; as I have mentioned above, as of 17 BC the primary candidates to succession were Gaius and Lucius Caesar. Still, at the moment of Agrippa's death the brothers were too young to take over as rulers in the event of Augustus' death in the near future; too young, too, for the princeps to entrust them with any administrative or military tasks. Thus he had to rely on his stepsons to help him govern the Empire; in that role, they were meant to replace the dead Agrippa.

Tiberius had received his first serious mission as early as 20 BC. He was then sent to the East, presumably as a *legatus Augusti*, and contained the political situation in Armenia by setting a pro-Roman ruler on its throne[148]. Then in 15 BC, Augustus' stepsons were entrusted with their first major military campaign, this being the war against the Alpine tribes of Raeti and Vindelici[149]. In 12 BC, the princeps dispatched Tiberius to Pannonia, where he was to finish the campaign started by M. Agrippa. At the same time, Drusus received a command in Germania. In 11 BC, the brothers were granted an independent *imperium* (*proconsulare*), so that they could hold an ovation for their successes in the German and Pannonian campaigns[150]. Besides, Tiberius and Drusus both held consulships, in 13 and 9 BC, respectively[151]. Thus, the course of their civilian and military careers in that period was roughly similar, implying that Cassius Dio was wrong to suggest Tiberius took Agrippa's place at the time, complete with his duties as the emperor's first assistant[152]; the tasks assigned Drusus had equal responsibility and prestige[153]. However, if the *cursus honorum* of the stepsons was close, their standing within the imperial family differed fundamentally.

---

148 Vell. Pat. 2, 94, 4; Tac. *Ann.* 2, 3, 2; *Mon. Anc.* 27, 2. See Kienast 1996, 76; Levick 1999, 26; Cooley 2009, 231.

149 Vell. Pat. 2, 95, 2; Cass. Dio 54, 22, 1–5; Flor. 2, 22.

150 Vell. Pat. 2, 96, 3; Cass. Dio 54, 33, 5; 34, 3; 55, 2, 4; Suet. *Tib.* 9, 2; *Claud.* 1, 3; see also Syme 1979, 312–314; Kienast 1996, 69, 76, 78; Sawiński 2005, 30–31, 88, 91–92.

151 Degrassi 1952, 4–5; Kienast 1996, 69, 78.

152 Cass. Dio 54, 31, 1.

153 John Rich (1990, 209) is also critical towards this suggestion of Dio. Cf. also Dettenhofer 2000, 161–162.

Tiberius undoubtedly stood higher in the hierarchy of the *domus Augusta*, primarily due to his marriage to Julia. Already in 12 BC, Augustus had convinced his stepson to divorce Vipsania Agrippina, Agrippa's daughter from his first marriage, and had him engaged to Julia[154]. Since after Agrippa's death Julia was expected to observe one year of mourning (an *annus luctus*), it is likely that they only actually got married in 11 BC[155]. According to Suetonius, Augustus spent a long time pondering the possible candidate and even considered marrying her off to a member of the equestrian order, but eventually he chose Tiberius[156]. I view this piece of information as highly suspect. Considering that until then the princeps had always chosen his sons-in-law from among the people closest to him, it seems very unlikely he would have settled on a man from outside the narrow circle of the *domus Augusta*. Tiberius and Drusus simply had to be the only candidates of note at the time[157], and Suetonius' account probably reflects the literary tradition hostile to Tiberius, which consistently belittled his place in the imperial family.

I think this marriage of Julia's, just like her previous two, failed to make the emperor's son-in-law his successor, especially since at the time Augustus already had sons, who were widely perceived as his intended successors[158]. On the other hand, Wood's claim that Tiberius might have taken over the throne, had Augustus died within the next few years, seems sound, as the two Caesars would still have been too young to rule on their own. In that case, he would have acted as a regent of sorts until one of Augustus' sons reached the age when he could become princeps[159]. In other words, by arranging that marriage, the emperor assigned his new son-in-law a role similar to the one Agrippa had played[160].

---

154 Cass. Dio 54, 31, 2. Suetonius (*Tib.* 7, 2) says Tiberius was reluctant to leave his wife, to whom he was supposedly very attached.

155 Vell. Pat. 2, 96, 1; Cass Dio 54, 35, 4; Suet. *Aug.* 63, 2; *Tib.* 7, 2; Treggiari 1991, 155; Kienast 1996, 76; Bauman 2003, 103, while Rich (1990, 209, 216) supposes the marriage ceremony may have taken place late in 11 or early in 10 BC in Gaul or some place in northern Italy, or only after Tiberius' return to Rome in 10 BC.

156 Suet. *Aug.* 63, 2.

157 Although it is difficult to determine why it was the elder of his two stepsons that Augustus chose to be Julia's husband.

158 Similarly Meise 1966, 11; Rose 1997, 20; Severy 2003, 67, 161. *Contra* Ehrhardt 1978, 54.

159 Wood 2001, 66.

160 See Syme 2002, 416.

Velleius Paterculus is no doubt correct when he claims that the marriage to Julia brought Tiberius even closer to Augustus[161].

Sattler believes Tiberius may have also hoped for a son with Julia, who would then have become a serious alternative candidate to succession, able to compete with Gaius and Lucius. Now from Suetonius we know Julia did give birth to a son, but he died in infancy[162]. Sattler supposes that, had he lived longer, the boy would have been adopted by the princeps, and as a descendant of both Augustus and Livia he would have been better predisposed to coming into the emperor's inheritance than either of the young Caesars[163]. In my opinion, his claim is unfounded. Firstly, any speculation on the emperor's possible plans regarding the son of Julia and Tiberius, who died in infancy, remains purely hypothetical. And secondly, if Augustus had wanted the future successor to be not merely descended from himself, but also to be related to Livia, he would have given Julia to Tiberius in the first place, and would not have arranged her marriages to Marcellus and, later, Agrippa. As I have emphasized more than once before, this points to Julia's key role in his dynastic plans: since he had no sons of his own, his daughter became, to quote Mireille Corbier, responsible for conceiving the future successor[164]. Thus, I suppose Augustus mostly wanted the successor to continue his bloodline, and any relation he might have had to Livia would have been of secondary importance. And thirdly and finally, the case of Agrippa Postumus, born in 12 BC, demonstrates that the princeps did not intend to adopt Julia's younger sons: it was only the death of the young Caesars that made him adopt Postumus and Tiberius in AD 4. So, it seems unlikely that Augustus would have made the succession unnecessarily complicated by adopting further candidates to imperial power.

After Drusus died in 9 BC, Tiberius in fact became Augustus' second-in-command, partly because the emperor's adoptive sons were still too young to be entrusted with responsible political or military missions. In 8 BC, Tiberius set out for Germania, to finish the work of his prematurely dead brother. Since Velleius Paterculus panegyrizes Tiberius, and all his accounts of his military achievements are exaggerated, we can certainly expect the same when he claims the campaign ended in the near-instant conquest of Germania, which was subsequently turned

161 Vell. Pat. 2, 96, 1. See also Sattler 1969, 497; Dettenhofer 2000, 165.

162 Suet. *Tib.* 7, 3. The child was most likely born in 10 BC; see Kienast 1996, 79.

163 Sattler 1969, 497–498; 502.

164 See Corbier 1995, 182.

into a Roman province[165]. For these accomplishments, Tiberius was acclaimed *imperator* for the second time, and awarded a triumph, which would be held a year later[166]. Interestingly, he was the first person to hold a triumph since 19 BC, when Augustus all but reserved that honour for the princeps[167].

In 7 BC, Tiberius also held his second consulship[168]. The following year, he was granted the unquestionable honour of five years of *tribunicia potestas*, at Augustus' instigation[169]. Most historians assume that at the same time his *imperium proconsulare*, first granted in 11 BC, was prolonged by five years, and suggest that since he was entrusted with a mission in Armenia, that *imperium* was valid in all the eastern provinces (*transmarinae provinciae*) and *maius* relative to those of the governors there[170]. Considering the nature of his mission, which involved the possibility of encroaching on the senatorial proconsuls' prerogatives, this assumption seems logical; giving Tiberius that level of power could prevent conflict with the governors. However, we must remember no sources explicitly confirm that he was granted such extensive powers. From Cassius Dio, we only learn that Tiberius was to go to Armenia, where after Tigranes' death events had taken a turn unfavourable for Rome, but the specific powers based on which Tiberius was supposed to act there are not provided[171]. Now some scholars believe granting Tiberius those powers meant elevating him to the position of Augustus'

165 Vell. Pat. 2, 97, 4. On how Tiberius is made to look in Paterculus' narrative, see especially Küntze 1985, passim; Schmitzer 2000, passim.

166 Vell. Pat. 2, 97, 4; Suet. *Tib.* 9, 2; Cass. Dio 55, 6, 4–5; 8, 2; Sawiński 2005, 88, 90.

167 Prior to him, a triumph was twice granted Agrippa, first in 19 BC for suppressing the insurrection of the Cantabri in Spain, and then in 14 BC for controlling the situation in the Bosporan Kingdom, a client state of Rome. However, in both cases he refused. Cass. Dio 54, 11, 6; 24, 7.

168 Degrassi 1952, 5; Kienast 1996, 78.

169 Vell. Pat. 2, 99, 1; Cass. Dio. 55, 9, 4; Suet. *Tib.* 9, 3. For reasons I do not understand (since she does not explain the grounds for the chronology she accepts), Severy (2003, 163) dates Tiberius first receiving tribunician powers to 7 BC. Generally it is assumed it only happened in 6 BC. Cf. e.g. Kienast 1982, 108; Rich 1990, 228; Dettenhofer 2000, 169.

170 Levick 1972a, 781–782; Bringmann 1977, 228; Kienast 1982, 108; Rich 1990, 228; Hurlet 1997, 104–105; Levick 1999, 35–36; Swan 2004, 85; Syme 2002, 416; Stevenson 2013, 132.

171 Cass. Dio 55, 9, 4. Suetonius (*Tib.* 11, 3), whose passage is used by, among others, Barbara Levick (1999, 238 note 24), only says that Tiberius made use of his tribunician prerogatives while on Rhodes, but does not mention any *imperium maius* being granted him.

co-regent, which had previously been occupied by Agrippa[172], and basically one could agree, except we cannot be certain that Tiberius' *imperium* at the time was *maius* the way Agrippa's had been[173]. The fact remains, of course, that he was then the second most influential man in the state (or, as Velleius Paterculus aptly put it, *civium post unum … eminentissimus*[174]).

At this point, it would make sense to ask whether granting Tiberius tribunician powers was, as Tacitus would have it, a sign of Augustus designating him as his successor[175]. In my opinion, the question is arguable[176]. In 6 BC, Gaius Caesar virtually stood on the threshold of adulthood—he would don the *toga virilis* in the following year—and was already venturing into the political arena. Moreover, two years earlier (in 8 BC) he had been officially presented as the intended successor to the legions on the Rhine[177]. His brother Lucius was going to follow in his footsteps soon, and in that context I do not think Augustus decided to designate Tiberius as his successor right when his sons, whom he had meant for the role from the beginning, were gradually entering public life. This would have been particularly strange considering Augustus did not take such a step regarding Tiberius directly after Agrippa's death, when the boys were still very young. Finally, it does not stand to reason that Tiberius would sulk and ostentatiously leave Rome for Rhodes if the grant of tribunician powers had meant his appointment to successor[178]; that would have been an extremely irrational thing to do. Thus, paradoxically, it is precisely Tiberius' rise in status in 6 BC that I believe to be his main reason for leaving[179]. Namely, I believe Tiberius was well

---

172 See Lacey 1979, 31; Kienast 1982, 108; Swan 2004, 85; Levick 2010, 181.

173 Perhaps in 6 BC he was only granted a prolongation of the *imperium* he had received five years prior for his Pannonian campaign. As we know that was an *imperium proconsulare*, which was however not *maius*. See Sawiński 2005, 30–31.

174 Vell. Pat. 2, 99, 1. One can agree with Levick (1972a, 782) that had Augustus died just then, with the *tribunicia potestas* and the *imperium proconsulare* (possibly *maius*?), Tiberius would have taken his place. Stevenson's (2013, 132) suggestion that in the case of Augustus' sudden death, he would have been supposed to ensure Gaius' or Lucius' succession, is convincing as well.

175 Tac. *Ann.* 3, 56, 2.

176 Similarly, among others, Syme 2002, 416; Ziółkowski 2004, 401. *Contra* Bowersock 1984, 170; Levick 1999, 36.

177 Cass. Dio 55, 6, 4. I discuss the episode in more detail in the next section (1.4.2).

178 As one of the reasons for that trip, Cassius Dio (55, 9, 7) lists Tiberius' bitterness resulting from the fact he was not made "Caesar".

179 Not, of course, that we can with any certainty rule out the other reasons for the departure given by ancient authors. Among those, they list especially the wish to give way to Augustus' sons as they entered politics, marital strife with Julia and weariness with

aware that his position as the second most important person in the state was temporary, and soon he would have to yield ground to the young Caesars. His departure to Rhodes would then have been a demonstration of his displeasure with the growing importance of Gaius and Lucius, whom Augustus had begun to publicly present as his successors. Why, then, did the emperor decide to confer *tribunicia potestas* on Tiberius? Personally, I do not see a satisfactory answer to this question. Perhaps it was a reward, after a manner, for his service to the princeps thus far[180], and it is possible Augustus wanted Tiberius to partly relieve him of the burden of ruling the state until he could rely on the young Caesars in that respect. Whatever the exact truth, Tiberius no doubt realized the honour was temporary and left for Rhodes, because he was tired of his role as the spare successor.

1.4 Gaius and Lucius Caesar as Intended Successors

1.4.1 Adoption

Julia and Agrippa's marriage finally gave Augustus his long desired male descendants. In 20 BC, she gave birth to Gaius, and three years later, Lucius[181]. The great importance this had for the princeps can be indicated by the fact that public sacrifices were made on every anniversary of Gaius' birth[182]. In 17 BC, right after the younger boy was born, Augustus adopted them both[183]. From Suetonius we find out that the adoption was private and took place in Agrippa's house: the old *mancipatio* procedure was used, according to which Augustus bought Gaius and Lucius from under their natural father's authority with a token coin and a set of scales (*per assem et libram*). As a result, the boys came under the emperor's *patria*

---

public duties. See Vell. Pat. 2, 99, 2; Tac. *Ann.* 1, 53, 1; Suet. *Tib.* 10, 2; 11, 5; Cass. Dio 55, 9, 5–8. For information on the subject of Tiberius' withdrawal to Rhodes, see esp. Sattler 1969, 509–514; Levick 1972a, 779–813; Sidari 1978–1979, 51–69; Huttner 2004, 133–134.

180 So Gruen 2005, 45–46.

181 Gaius was presumably born at some point between 14th August and 13th September; and Lucius between 14th June and 15th July. See Kienast 1996, 73, 75. Wolfgang Kuhoff (1993a, 61) incorrectly dates Gaius' birth to 12th July, as the mention in the *Fasti Amiternini* (Degrassi 1963, 188–189) he draws on probably refers to Julius Caesar's birth.

182 Cass. Dio 54, 8, 5.

183 Vell. Pat. 2, 96, 1; Tac. *Ann.* 1, 3, 2; Suet. *Aug.* 64, 1; Cass. Dio 54, 18, 1.

potestas[184]. For Cassius Dio, the adoption was equivalent to officially appointing the young Caesars Augustus' successors (διαδόχους τῆς ἀρχῆς)[185], but that is of course anachronistic. In this case, he had in mind the later practice, whereby adoption did precede conferring "imperial" prerogatives on the chosen candidate by the Senate and the people. However, in that case there are two reasons why actually designating successors is out of the question. First, the brothers were still young children, and second, the princeps adopted them both, thus not deciding which of the two should succeed him in the future[186]. Formally, the adoption mostly meant choosing one's private heirs. From that moment on, the brothers were both heirs to Augustus' name and property in the light of Roman law[187]. Still, Roman tradition dictated that, as Augustus' sons, after his death they would also inherit his friends, clients and political connections[188], and for their contemporaries it had to be self-evident that one of them would in time succeed to Augustus' position as well.

Naming his heirs, one of whom would also in the future become his political successor, was certainly not the only point of the *mancipatio*. Hans U. Instinsky correctly observed that by adopting Agrippa's sons the princeps also wanted to stop *gens Iulia* from dying out. As new *gens* members, Gaius and Lucius were supposed to cultivate the family tradition after Augustus' death and take over ancestor worship from him. Here, the princeps very clearly drew on Republican tradition, since back then *nobiles* who had no sons of their own very often resorted to *mancipatio* in order to prolong the family[189].

Severy supposes there was a reason why Gaius and Lucius were adopted in 17 BC; she thinks Augustus' decision was related to the marital legislation he had introduced a year previously, which condemned celibacy and childlessness and provided special privileges for those with three or more children (the *ius trium liberorum*). If those laws were to have the intended results, their originator had to give the people a shining example himself, and after adopting the boys the princeps did fulfil the criteria[190]. Her observation is certainly interesting: the public

184 Suet. *Aug.* 64, 1. For information on the legal consequences of Gaius' and Lucius' *mancipatio, see* Prevost 1949, 37–39.
185 Cass. Dio 54, 18, 1.
186 See Kienast 1982, 97.
187 Rich 1990, 195; Severy 2003, 71.
188 Cf. Dettenhofer 2000, 163; Veyne 2008, 15.
189 Instinsky 1966, 342. For an example of the practice, see Polyb. 31, 28, 2.
190 Severy 2003, 71. The fact Gaius and Lucius were not the emperor's natural sons was irrelevant, as the *ius trium liberorum* refered to any father of three children regardless of whether they were his own or adopted. See Zabłocka 1986, 258. For Augustus'

image of Germanicus, depicted as a model father surrounded by his many offspring, is evidence Augustus paid special attention to his family being an *exemplum* of sorts to the Roman society[191]. However, that was certainly not the main reason why Julia and Agrippa's sons were adopted.

Then there is the observation of Brian Rose, who noted the adoption coincided with the *ludi saeculares*; in his view there was a reason they were held in the exact same year. Augustus' "propaganda" gave a special rank to both those events: the Secular Games were to be the symbolic beginning of a new, golden age in the history of Rome, while the adoption of Gaius and Lucius meant the birth of a dynasty and securing the succession of imperial power within that dynasty for another generation[192].

1.4.2 *Cursus honorum*, Public Presentation and Honorifics

It was very early on that Augustus began to publicly style his adoptive sons as planned successors. In 13 BC, Gaius was among the boys from well-off Roman families who took part in a horsemanship contest (the *lusus Troiae*) held on the occasion of dedicating the Theatre of Marcellus. Such games had already been held under the Republic. Augustus drew on that tradition by organizing them regularly in order to encourage young Romans to practice sports which were to ensure they would be fit[193].

In the same year, the senatorial mint in Rome issued a series of extremely interesting coins. The obverse of those denarii, signed by a Gaius Marius, shows Augustus' head in the oak-leaf crown and the legend AUGUSTUS DIVI F. The reverse depicts three persons, identified by most numismatists and historians as Julia, Gaius and Lucius. The image is completed with the signature of the triumvir monetalis, C MARIUS TRO III VIR. Above Julia's head, there is a *corona civica*, which from 27 BC was a hallmark of the Julian dynasty[194]. (fig. 4) The use

---

marital laws, see e.g. Raditsa 1980, 278–339; Galinsky 1981, 126–144; Cohen 1991, 109–126.

191 See Suet. *Aug.* 34, 2.

192 Rose 1997, 13. See also Haselberger 2007, 152–153; Hekster 2015, 6.

193 Cass. Dio 54, 26, 1; Suet. *Aug.* 43, 2. We owe a detailed description of the *lusus Troiae* to Vergil (*Aen.* 5, 545–602). Cf. also Rich 1990, 204; Zanker 1999, 218–219.

194 *RIC* I^2 *Aug.* 405; *HCC* I *Aug.* 47; Fullerton 1985, 475–476; Wallace-Hadrill 1986, 79 note 75; Trillmich 1988a, 490, 526 (no. 372); Kuhoff 1993a, 60; Hurlet 1997, 115; Zanker 1999, 218–219; Severy 2003, 76–77; Galinsky 2012, 124; Stevenson 2013, 129 note 51. Still, not all scholars accept this identification; some believe the coins in question depict Julia with Augustus and Agrippa, or Livia with Tiberius and Drusus. Their reasoning rests

Fig. 4. Denarius of Gaius Marius, Rome, 13 BC. Obverse: Augustus' head in an oak wreath; legend: AUGUSTUS DIVI F. Reverse: an image of Julia with Gaius and Lucius Caesar (?); triumvir's signature: C MARIUS TRO III VIR (*RIC* I² *Aug*. 405).

of this motif clearly indicates the triumvir's intention was to emphasize the close kinship between the three persons on the reverse and Augustus, stressing the notion that Gaius and Lucius were part of *gens Iulia* and presenting them as the emperor's future successors[195].

primarily on the claim the characters shown next to the woman's figure are the same size as her. That is supposed to indicate the two male figures cannot be the emperor's sons, since at the time they were still children. See Rose 1997, 15; Kleiner, Buxton 2008, 76–77. I find those arguments unconvincing; in Roman iconography, children were often depicted out of proportion to their actual age. Cf. Zanker 1999, 219, 348. Moreover, it should be remembered that images on coins are not realistic representations. On the other hand, there is some substantial evidence for identifying the two characters as Gaius and Lucius. First, such a subject would fit other series signed by Gaius Marius minted in the same year, which show Augustus and Agrippa, the boys' adoptive and natural father, as partners in managing the Empire (see above for a description of those coin series). In this context, it appears quite likely the same triumvir would have minted another series in the honour of Julia and the young Caesars. Second, we know the brothers were quite often depicted in their mother's company during that period, as illustrated by the statuary groups decicated in Delphi, Thespiae and on Paros, where the boys' statues stood next to those of Julia, Agrippa and their sister Agrippina the Elder. See Rose 1997, 139–140 (no. 70); 149–151 (no. 82); 156–157 (no. 92).

195 Fullerton 1985, 476; Kuhoff 1993a, 60; Zanker 1999, 218; Severy 2003, 76–77.

On the reverse of another coin series of G. Marius, there is an image of a woman, identified as Julia based on her hairstyle. The emperor's daughter is shown here as Diana, as indicated by the quiver next to her, a traditional attribute of this goddess[196]. According to Paul Zanker, the quiver unambiguously alludes to the idea that Diana herself watched over the birth of the boys[197]. The appearance of Julia on the coins in question reflected her exceptional role at the time as that of the mother of the future successors and thus, as Diana Kleiner aptly put it, "the first mother of Rome."[198] It is worth highlighting that Augustus' daughter was the first woman from the imperial family to have her face put on official coinage[199]. In addition, the coins promoted the image of a perfect family, a concept which would soon find its fullest expression in the relief sculptures of the *Ara Pacis*. Scholars are quite right to emphasize the fact it was on those coins that Augustus' succession plans were first displayed; they confirm his dynastic policy centred on the aspiration to pass the imperial power on to his closest relative[200]. Not that this means the idea was only born in 13 BC; I am convinced it had been with the princeps since the time when he came to rule independently, possibly even longer. Still, it was only then that it was so emphatically articulated through coins; after the adoption of Gaius and Lucius, Augustus' plans regarding his future successor were specific enough as to the persons involved that they could be shared with the public.

Some historians see further evidence for the leading role Augustus' adopted sons were to play in his dynastic plans in the way they were portrayed on the relief sculptures of the Altar of Peace (the *Ara Pacis*). The Senate voted to erect this monument on the occasion of the emperor's successful return from Spain and Gaul in 13 BC, and it was consecrated on 4th July 9 BC[201]. These historians claim that members of the imperial family were depicted on the altar in the order of established succession. Gaius was supposedly sculpted on the outside of the

196 *RIC* I^2 *Aug.* 403; *HCC* I *Aug.* 46; Fullerton 1985, 475–476; Zanker 1999, 218–219.

197 Zanker 1999, 218.

198 Kleiner 2005, 201.

199 Earlier only Octavia had been honoured in such a way, but coins with her depictions were minted during the second triumvirate. See Trillmich 1988a, 479, 499 (no. 300); 481, 503 (no. 312); Wallace-Hadrill 1986, 79.

200 Fullerton 1985, 480.

201 *Fasti Amiternini* (Degrassi 1963, 188–189); *Mon. Anc.* 12, 2. The literature on the *Ara Pacis* is extensive. See e.g. Simon 1967, *passim*; Torelli 1982, 27–61; Settis 1988, 400–426; Zanker 1999, 164–165; 177–184; 206–208; 218–220; Kleiner, Buxton 2008, 57–89.

Fig. 5. A detail from the *Ara Pacis Augustae*, featuring an image of Gaius Caesar (?).

southern wall, right behind the princeps and Agrippa, (fig. 5) whereas Lucius was on the northern wall, but otherwise in the exact same position as his elder brother. He was shown next to Julia, leading the imperial family as they joined the priests opening the procession. (fig. 6) The main argument for identifying those two figures as the young Caesars is the fact that compared to the other members of the *domus Augusta*, they hold central places in the procession, as well as being portrayed in Trojan dress complete with the characteristic *torques*. That would allude not merely to the elder brother taking part in the aforementioned *lusus Troiae*, during which the youths probably wore the costume, but also clearly to the Trojan origins of the Julian family, who derived their genealogy from the mythical Julus, son of Aeneas[202]. In principle, that interpretation seems acceptable, although we need to remember the identification of several figures in the reliefs is purely speculative. Thus, any attempt to reconstruct the

202 See, among others, Fullerton 1985, 481; Zanker 1999, 218–220. According to another interpretation, the boys sculpted on the northern and southern walls of the altar are

Fig. 6. A detail from the *Ara Pacis Augustae*, featuring an image of Lucius Caesar (?).

hierarchy within the *domus Augusta* based on the order in which its members feature on the altar is fraught with risk.

One of the key elements which guaranteed the stability of the new monarchy was beyond doubt the support of the army. From the very start, Augustus paid a lot of attention to having all the major military campaigns led, if possible of course, by members of the *domus Augusta*. Victories by commanders from the imperial family won great popularity for themselves and especially for the

barbarian princes who were then hostages in Augustus' home. That version is put forward by Rose (1990, 453–467), among others, but his idea is highly questionable: it would be difficult to explain why the barbarians should be there right in the middle of the procession, among members of the *domus Augusta*. What is more, it would be most odd if the images on the altar did include all the other important members of the imperial family, but lacked those of the princeps' sons and prospective successors. For the various attempts at identifying the figures on the *Ara Pacis*, see also Holloway 1984, 625–628; Syme 1984, 583–589; Pollini 1986, 453–460; Settis 1988, 414–416; Severy 2003, 108–112. For children's images on the *Ara Pacis*, see especially Uzzi 2005, 142–155.

princeps, under whose auspices they fought. Their successes were also of considerable significance for shaping the soldiers' loyalty towards the reigning family. No wonder Augustus regarded presenting his intended successors properly to the army as so important. In 8 BC, Gaius was introduced for the first time to the legions stationed on the Rhine. From Cassius Dio we know that he took part in the exercises of the units there, which were paid special *donativa* on the occasion[203]. Most likely, it was this episode that was reflected in the series of aurei and denarii produced by the imperial mint in Lugdunum soon after the event. The obverse had Augustus' head wearing the laurel crown, with the legend AUGUSTUS DIVI F; the reverse showed Gaius on a horse in gallop, sword and shield in hand, with legion standards and C CAES AUGUS F in the background[204]. (fig. 7) The coins

203 Cass. Dio 55, 6, 4. For information on Gaius Caesar's sojourn in Germania, see Janssen 1920, 205–206.

204 *RIC* I² *Aug.* 198–199; *HCC* I *Aug.* 213–215; Sutherland 1951, 68–69; Hurlet 1997, 115; Rose 1997, 17; Heinemann 2007, 46; Kleiner, Buxton 2008, 75. *Contra* Romer 1978, 187–202; Bowersock 1984, 173. They reject the traditional interpretation of this series and instead claim the coins were only minted in 2 BC in connection with the consecration of the temple to Mars Ultor in the Forum of Augustus, where the standards recovered earlier from the Parthians were deposited. Placing Gaius' image against the background of those standards was to predict his victories in the eastern campaign he was entrusted with and to depict him as the future conqueror of the Parthians and a worthy successor to Augustus in that regard, an interpretation I do not find convincing; in my opinion we have no grounds to be certain, as Frank E. Romer and Glen Bowersock are, that the *signa* on the coins refer precisely to the legion standards recovered from Parthians and moved to the new temple of Mars Ultor in 2 BC. I think if the intention had been to recall that event, then the coins would have had an image of that temple complete with a legend to identify it and the standards inside, so that the message was clear. After all, we do know there were such depictions on coins minted earlier (in 19 BC) on the occasion of recovering the standards. They included the round temple, erected by Augustus to Mars Ultor on the Capitoline, where the *signa* returned by the Parthians were originally exhibited. On one of the series, inside the temple there, was Mars holding a legion's eagle; on another, the temple held the *signa* themselves. See *RIC* I² *Aug.* 68–72; 507; Zanker 1999, 190. I am convinced the *signa* on the coins discussed here simply stand in for the legions, and depicting Gaius Caesar with them in the background was meant to stress the special relationship between Augustus' son and the army. For that reason I lean towards the opinion held by most scholars, that the series in question not so much predicted Gaius' future victories in the East as commemorated his participation in the exercises of the legions. Rose (1997, 221 note 92) further observes Gaius was shown wearing a *bulla* around his neck. Since young Roman men no longer wore the *bulla* after they donned

Fig. 7. Aureus, Lugdunum, c. 8 BC. Obverse: Augustus' head in a laurel wreath; legend: AUGUSTUS DIVI F. Reverse: an image of Gaius riding a horse in gallop, sword and shield in his left hand, with legion standards in the background; legend: C CAES AUGUS F (*RIC* I² *Aug*. 198).

were probably part of the gratuities the legionaries received, and the image on the reverse was intended to remind the soldiers to whom they owed the unexpected gift[205]. It is hard to imagine better endorsement of Gaius to the army stationed on the Rhine. As with the series from 13 BC mentioned previously, this one clearly stressed the family relationship between Augustus and Gaius, this time accentuated by the legend on the reverse.

Some interesting information on how the princeps introduced his sons to the army can also be found in archaeological sources. One of those is a bronze sword scabbard dated to Augustus' day, found in what is today Bonn. It was decorated with an engraving portraying a woman flanked by two young men wearing armour and military cloaks (*paludamenta*). (fig. 8) Some scholars believe those to be images of Julia and her sons[206], while other reject this possibility and identify the persons depicted as Livia, Tiberius and Drusus instead[207]. According to

the *toga virilis*, one can see this as another argument in favour of the coins having been minted before 5 BC.

205 Rich 1990, 224; Kuhoff 1993a, 60; Zanker 1999, 220–221.

206 Boschung 1987, 227; id. 1996, 401–402; Zanker 1999, 220–221.

207 Rose 1997, 15; Severy 2003, 86–87.

Fig. 8. Ornaments on a sword scabbard, Bonn, Augustus' times. A putative image of Julia with the young Caesars, depicted wearing armour and military cloaks (*paludamenta*).

Rose, who is one of the major supporters of that interpretation, the ornamentation on the scabbard was probably made shortly after 15 BC[208], and occasioned by the victorious campaign the two brothers led in 15 BC against Alpine tribes. Rose supposes it was a gift given to one of the soldiers who had then fought under the command of Augustus' stepsons, and we cannot identify the figures on the object as Gaius and Lucius, because at the time they had not as yet taken part in any warfare[209].

However, I do not find his arguments convincing. First, there is no evidence that would allow us to date the scabbard with precision. Second, Rose assumes the ornamentation is supposed to be reminiscent of past historical events, namely Tiberius and Drusus' command during the Alpine campaign of 15 BC, a precarious conclusion if we consider that Roman art was not fundamentally

208 Another dates was suggested by Ernst Künzl (1996, 402), who would have it made between 10 and 2 BC.

209 Rose 1997, 15.

documentary. As a result, I see nothing in particular that would preclude Gaius and Lucius from being depicted in a military style even if they had not led any campaigns yet[210]. Rather, we can agree with the scholars who see the armoured figures as the young Caesars and hypothesize the person who commissioned the scabbard meant to see the emperor's sons as commanders ready to act, who would soon begin to shoulder the burden of waging the greatest wars[211]. That type of graphic representation was particularly addressed to the army and in this case intended to win the soldiers' affection for the young Caesars [212]. It would have certainly worked well with Augustus' style, since the princeps was well aware that the support and loyalty of the legions might be of fundamental importance in the future for one of his sons to take over smoothly.

The princeps also took care to suitably endorse the young Caesars among the inhabitants of Rome, especially the senators and the urban plebs. In 7 BC, Gaius co-presided with Gnaeus Calpurnius Piso over the *ludi votivi* held on the occasion of Augustus' safe return from Gaul, standing in for Tiberius, who was the other consul that year, but was absent from Rome due to the war in Germania[213]. Entrusting Gaius with that task was an extraordinary honour, as he was only thirteen[214]. More were to come in the following year: Cassius Dio reports he was elected to the college of *pontifices* and allowed to participate in Senate meetings. He could also sit with the senators during various shows and

---

210 There is actually another depiction of a member of the imperial family in armour even though he held no military functions: the statue of Nero Julius Caesar, son of Germanicus, erected in Caere in Etruria, probably in the local theatre. Cf. Rose 1997, 83–86 (no. 5).

211 Similarly, also Zanker 1999, 220.

212 Possibly scabbards with this kind of ornamentation were a reward for the particularly deserving legionaries, as were *phalerae* depicting members of the imperial family. Cf. Boschung 1987, 227.

213 *CIL* VI 36789; Cass. Dio 55, 8, 3. Cf. also Halfmann 1986, 159; Rich 1990, 226, Kienast 1996, 74.

214 Later, Augustus would hold various games in Gaius and Lucius' names several more times (*Mon. Anc.* 22, 1). That may be illustrated by the grandiose gladiatorial competition which added some festive spirit to the consecration of Mars Ultor's temple in the Forum of Augustus in 2 BC. Cassius Dio (55, 10, 6–8) reports that in addition to gladiators' combat, the spectators could see *venationes* and *naumachia*. Such moves were no doubt intended to win Augustus' future successors the affection of the *plebs urbana*. See also Cooley 2009, 202.

games and take part in feasts held by them[215]. Rich supposes that unlike other sons of senatorial families, who after donning the toga of manhood could listen in on Senate sessions[216], Gaius also had the right to speak and vote[217], but his suggestion is not confirmed by any sources. The option of participating in senatorial banquets was no doubt an interesting privilege, as it made the conditions perfect for Gaius to strengthen his connections with senators and to socialize with them.

No doubt 5 BC was a year of special importance to Gaius Caesar; it was then that he donned his *toga virilis* and was listed as a citizen. As mandated by tradition, the ceremony took place in the Forum Romanum. It was accorded special splendour by the fact that Augustus, who led his son into the Forum as the *pater familias*, was also consul. The princeps had especially taken a consulship for the first time in seventeen years in order to impart the event with extra significance, making it not merely a private, but a public occasion. In the same year, the Senate designated Gaius consul, an office he was supposed to hold five years later. Moreover, the equestrian order gifted the boy with a silver shield and spear, and the title of *princeps iuventutis*. Three years later, Lucius put on his toga of manhood under the same circumstances[218], receiving all the same honours[219]. The princeps wanted the moments his sons entered manhood to endure in the memory of the inhabitants of Rome, so the Roman plebs received gifts of money on the occasion. The gesture was doubtless aimed at winning the boys popularity among the *plebs urbana*[220].

Other than that, Augustus made sure his sons would have the support of influential Roman families by arranging the right marriages for them. Thus, soon after donning the *toga virilis*, and before the end of 2 BC, Lucius Caesar was

---

215 Cass. Dio 55, 9, 4. Still, he could only take advantage of that privilege and take part in the sessions after he donned the toga of manhood in the following year. See *Mon. Anc.* 14, 1; Cass. Dio 55, 9, 9. See also Rich 1990, 228.

216 Suet. *Aug.* 38, 2.

217 Rich 1990, 228.

218 Stevenson (2013, 133–134) supposes the ceremony took place in the newly built Forum of Augustus.

219 Except Lucius became an augur rather than a *pontifex*. *CIL* II 3828; *CIL* VI 36908; *Mon. Anc.* 14, 1–2; Tac. *Ann.* 1, 3, 2; Cass. Dio 55, 9, 9–10; Suet. *Aug.* 26, 2–3. See also Kienast 1982, 109–110; Vassileiou 1984, 827–840; Rich 1990, 229–230; Kienast 1996, 74–75; Dettenhofer 2000, 171; Wolters 2002, 297–323; Swan 2004, 89–91.

220 *Mon. Anc.* 15, 2, 4; Cass. Dio 55, 10, 1; Kienast 1982, 110; Dettenhofer 2000, 171; Severy 2003, 164; Cooley 2009, 172.

betrothed to Aemilia Lepida, a great-granddaughter of Pompey the Great and of Sulla, and in the following year, Gaius was married off to Claudia Livia, known as Livilla, the daughter of Drusus the Elder and Antonia the Younger, so a member of the *Claudii Nerones*, who was moreover a granddaughter of Mark Antony and Octavia on the distaff side[221].

Officially designating both sons of the princeps for consulship, which they were to hold before they were twenty, was an honour awarded to no other member of the imperial family during Augustus' reign[222]; suffice it to say that Marcellus could only run when he was twenty-three[223], Tiberius was first consul at twenty-eight, and Germanicus, before he was twenty-six[224]. The analogy with the swift career of Augustus, who had also held his first consulship at nineteen, had to be evident. The event was commemorated on two monumental inscriptions discovered in the Forum Romanum, which emphasized the two brothers were only fourteen when designated[225]. The inscription dedicated to Gaius, whose marble pedestal was unearthed near the *Basilica Iulia*, is especially interesting; it meticulously noted Gaius was the first Roman to have ever been designated consul at such a tender age[226]. It is worth mentioning here that when Gaius started his consulship in AD 1, he had not held any previous offices, a dispensation the princeps granted to no other member of the *domus Augusta*.

Granting the young Caesars the title of *princeps iuventutis* automatically brought to mind the term *princeps* as it referred to Augustus' special position as the first citizen[227], which implies the brothers were treated as future successors by their contemporaries[228]. That is clearly confirmed by Ovid's *nunc iuvenum princeps, deinde future senum*, referring in his *Ars Amatoria* to Gaius (the

221 Tac. *Ann.* 3, 22, 1; 3, 23, 1; 4, 40, 4. Cf. also Kienast 1996, 74–75; Dettenhofer 2000, 180.

222 Gaius assumed his consulship on January 1 of AD 1, during his eastern mission. He was nineteen. In Lucius' case, premature death prevented him from ever becoming consul.

223 See above.

224 Kienast 1996, 78, 80.

225 A piece of information found also in the *Res Gestae* (14, 1), which says the boys were in their fifteenth year (*annum quintum et decimum*).

226 *CIL VI* 3748 = 31271 = 36893; *CIL* VI 36908. See also Cooley 2009, 164.

227 See e.g. *Mon. Anc.* 30, 1; 32, 3; Hor. *Carm.* 4, 14, 6; Vell. Pat. 2, 90; Tac. *Ann.* 1, 1, 2; cf. also Syme 2002, 311.

228 From then on, the title of *princeps iuventutis* was only ever accorded the intended successors of the current princeps; see Kienast 1982, 110; Rich 1990, 230; Zanker 1999, 220; Cooley 2009, 166. The rule remained in force until the end of the principate.

poet mentioned his mission to the East in 1 BC)[229]. Epigraphic sources are also suggestive in this context. In the Pisan inscription containing the text of the honorific decree passed by the local authorities in AD 4 after Gaius' death, he explicitly features as *designatus princeps*[230]. It is certainly a rhetorical formula rather than any official title[231]; the colony in Pisa had special ties to the imperial family, and its inhabitants based high hopes on the future succession of one of the Caesars[232]. While the terminology used to refer to Gaius was not official, it very aptly reflects his actual standing within the *domus Augusta*, held since 2 BC when his younger brother died and he became the only successor. We can see the inhabitants of Pisa were quite up to date with the current situation in the imperial family. Still, that does not allow the conclusion that he had that position *de iure*. It would also be good to note the term is not used of Lucius, either in the honorific decree passed by the authorities of Pisa after his death two years previously, or in the decree honouring his elder brother[233]. I think the explanation is quite simple: calling the younger brother *designatus princeps* would have been most infelicitous, since before his death the princeps had not yet decided which of the brothers would succeed him. The death of his younger son changed the situation fundamentally: Gaius became the leading—and in fact only—candidate to the throne and his succession seemed a foregone conclusion. No wonder the Pisans saw him as the future princeps and stressed this so scrupulously in the decree.

The entry of Augustus' sons onto the Roman political scene was soon after commemorated with a series of interesting aurei and denarii produced by the imperial mint in Lugdunum. The obverse of those coins had Augustus' portrait and the legend CAESAR AUGUSTUS DIVI F PATER PATRIAE; the reverse showed Gaius and Lucius wearing togas and, between them, the silver shields and

229 Ov. *Ars am.* 1, 194. See also Lebek 1991a, 65; Swan 2004, 90.

230 *CIL* XI 1421 = *ILS* 140, ll. 12–13. I am relying on the edition found in Rowe (2002, 121–123).

231 See Lott 2012, 200, who however fails to convince, as he claims the expression *designatus princeps* was used in the decree to stand for the title *princeps iuventutis*, for which I see no evidence, especially as in Lucius' case the same text uses the term explicitly. See Rowe 2002, 121, ll. 15–16. Moreover, the context of the expression on the inscription in question clearly suggests a different meaning.

232 Lucius was the town's patron (*CIL* XI 1420 = *ILS* 139, l. 8), while Gaius was referred to in the honorific decree passed after his death as *unicum praesidium coloniae* (*CIL* XI 1421 = *ILS* 140, ll. 13–14). Cf. also Rowe 2002, 116; Lott 2012, 200.

233 See Instinsky 1966, 324 note 3.

Fig. 9. Aureus, Lugdunum, 2 BC–AD 4. Obverse: a portrait of Augustus; legend CAESAR AUGUSTUS DIVI F PATER PATRIAE. Reverse: Gaius and Lucius Caesar wearing togas, with silver shields and spears between them, and a *simpulum* and a *lituus* above their heads; legend: C L CAESARES AUGUSTI F COS DESIG PRINC IUVENT (*RIC* I² *Aug*. 206).

spears granted them by the *ordo equester*. Above them, there are a *simpulum* and a *lituus*, denoting their membership in the colleges of *pontifices* and augurs. The whole thing was complemented by the telling legend C L CAESARES AUGUSTI F COS DESIG PRINC IUVENT[234]. (fig. 9) The series must have been minted after 2 BC, which was when Augustus received the honorary title of *pater patriae*. The coins on the one hand stressed—again—the close family ties between Augustus and the young Caesars, and on the other highlighted the public role of the brothers as priests and future consuls. The title *princeps iuventutis* seen on the coins clearly identified Gaius and Lucius as Augustus' future successors[235].

There were also many coin series dedicated to Gaius and Lucius minted in the provinces[236]. In this context, one such series deserves particular attention: that of the dupondii, minted in Caesaraugusta in Spain by the local duumviri Cn. Domitius Ampianus and C. Veturius Lancianus. The obverse shows three statues,

234 *RIC* I² *Aug*. 205–207; *HCC* I *Aug*. 216–218; Kuhoff 1993a, 60; Zanker 1999, 221.

235 Rose 1997, 17; Mellado Rivera 2003, passim; Severy 2003, 164.

236 See among others *RPC* I 96 (Gades, Spain); 210 (Tarraco, Spain); 319 (Caesaraugusta, Spain); 779 (Hadrumetum, Africa); 1564 (Thessalonica, Macedonia); 2121–2122 (Sinope, Bithynia and Pontus). The coin series are dated to between 6 BC and AD 4.

which according to the legend represent Augustus and the young Caesars. The princeps is in the centre, holding a *simpulum*, which he passes to Gaius, standing in front of him. The image is complemented by the legend IMP AUG L CAESAR C CAES COS DES. On the reverse, there is a *vexillum* in between two legion standards, with the legend CAESARAUGUSTA II VIR CN DOM AMPIAN C VET LANCIA[237]. The obverse is a reference to one of the more important moments in the elder Caesar's career, namely his appointment to the college of *pontifices* in 6 BC[238].

The sons of Augustus donning their togas of manhood and commencing their political careers gave Romans a good occasion to celebrate the Empire. In an extensive inscription erected by the authorities of Sardis, we read the citizens of Sardis decided to make the day Gaius put on the *toga virilis* a public holiday. On every anniversary of that day, as well as of the day the news of that fact reached the city, the inhabitants would wear wreaths and ceremonial dress, while the *strategi* who ruled in Sardis made sumptuous sacrifices and prayed for the princeps' son. Gaius was also celebrated with a statue, which was placed next to that of Augustus in the local temple to the princeps. For that gesture of loyalty and affection, the emperor thanked the inhabitants in an official letter[239].

The designation of Gaius Caesar as consul was celebrated by the people of Messene. Interesting information on the subject comes from a honorific inscription dated to 2–3 BC, bearing the text of the decree passed by the local authorities to celebrate P. Cornelius Scipio, a *quaestor pro praetore provinciae Achaiae.* He was thus commemorated for holding festivities dedicated to Augustus' prosperity (the *Kaisareia*), thereby proving his piety towards the *domus Augusta.* The inscription also informs the reader how the Messenians honoured Gaius Caesar: among other things, Scipio organized a two-day festival to celebrate Gaius' designation as consul and decreed public sacrifices to be made on each anniversary of this event, with the inhabitants wearing wreaths. Interestingly enough, this initiative came from above; the inscription states the festivities were instituted at Scipio's command[240].

237 *RPC* I 319. See also Mlasowsky (1996, 289–290), who dates the series to between 6 and 3 BC.

238 See Rose 1997, 17.

239 *IGRR* IV 1756, ll. 6–28; see also Kuhoff 1993a, 61; Rose 1997, 179 (no. 121) Cooley 2009, 165; Levick 2010, 183–184.

240 *SEG* XXIII 206, ll. 17–21; *AEph.*1965, 110–115; Kuhoff 1993a, 62. For a detailed analysis of that inscription, see esp. Zetzel 1970, 259–266; Herz 1993, 272–288; Kantiréa 2007, 162–163, 208.

Another town to commemorate the emperor's sons was Pagus Stellatinus in Italy, whose inhabitants erected in their honour a statuary group comprised of the statues of Gaius, Lucius and Augustus. From the dedicatory inscriptions, we know they were financed by a P. Sergius Rufus and a T. Braetius Rufus, the *magistri* administering that Italian colony. The statues were in all likelihood an integral part of a place of worship built by these officials. Based on the ordinal number of Augustus' *tribunicia potestas* used in the inscriptions, we can date the group to 4–3 BC[241]. It is worth stressing that honouring Gaius also became a good occasion to honour his younger brother in the same way.

Another statuary group, this one inspired by Lucius donning the toga of manhood and receiving the same honours as his elder brother before him, was erected in the honour of Augustus' sons in Rome. This one is dated to the period from 2 BC to AD 1. Rose assumes the statues of the two brothers stood in front of the temple of Portunus in the Forum Boarium, since that is where the pedestals were discovered in the 16th century with dedicatory inscriptions celebrating the young Caesars[242]. The location seems probable, but then considering the phenomenon of "wandering inscriptions", absolute certainty is impossible. In the light of the titulature used to refer to Augustus' sons, we may assume the statues were dedicated shortly after 2 BC; we do not, however, possess any information as to who founded them.

Soon after putting on the *toga virilis*, Gaius officially entered upon his political career. As early as 5 BC, he assumed the honorary function of *sevir equitum*, the commander of one of six cavalry units. Among the duties of the *seviri* was preparing the unit in their care, and then commanding it during the ceremonial equestrian parade (*transvectio*) held yearly on 15th July[243]. Then in 2 or 1 BC, Gaius became the commander of the legions stationed on the Danube. In Cassius Dio we read he did not, however, conduct any military action, a task in which he was replaced by his legates, learning instead how to lead an army[244]. Gaius' stay on the Danube was also a good opportunity to introduce one of the emperor's intended successors to the legions there, which constituted the most important military force in the Empire, next to those on the Rhine.

241 Rose 1997, 99 (no. 27).

242 Rose 1997, 17, 106–107 (no. 34).

243 Cass. Dio 55, 9, 9. Cf. also Rich 1990, 230; Swan 2004, 90.

244 Cass. Dio 55, 10, 17. For information on Gaius' actions there, see esp. Romer 1974, 101–107.

Gaius Caesar's military career no doubt found its climax in his *imperium proconsulare* of 1 BC and the mission to the East he was given[245]. His task was primarily to control the situation in Armenia and restore regular relations with the Parthian kingdom. Bearing in mind the young man's inexperience, Augustus appointed a group of advisors to accompany his son on his eastern mission, which also created excellent opportunities to endorse Gaius to the inhabitants of the eastern provinces and the soldiers stationed there. For Gaius himself, it was a chance to gain important experience to do with administering the state and running military campaigns. Furthermore, by carrying out the task effectively he would have been able to prove himself a worthy candidate to Augustus' legacy, which was certainly of considerable importance to a future successor's public image.

A visit from the emperor's son and planned successor became a good occasion for the inhabitants of the eastern provinces to express their loyalty and affection towards the *domus Augusta*, as reflected particularly in the many honours

---

245 Vell. Pat. 2, 101–102; Plin. *HN*. 2, 168; Cass. Dio 55, 10, 18; Suet. *Tib*. 12, 2; Oros. 7, 3, 4. Klaus Bringmann (1977, 228) believes Gaius' *imperium* was *maius* relative to those of other governors, but that is pure speculation without any confirmation in sources. It is also an open question whether granting Gaius proconsular prerogatives may be taken to explicitly mean his appointment as Augustus' successor, a claim put forward by Adam Ziółkowski (2004, 401); in my opinion, such a conclusion is too far-reaching. Instead, I believe Gaius' *imperium proconsulare* was mostly to do with this mission to the East. If so, what we have here is not the grant to the intended successor of proconsular powers as one of the two crucial to the emperor's position, as was the case with Tiberius in AD 13, and then Nero in 51 (more on which below); rather, it is a grant of powers which were to enable a specific task to be carried out within a certain strictly limited area. In other words, the same situation as with Germanicus, whose *imperium* in 14 and then in 17 was connected purely to his work in Germania and the East. Thus, I do not see with regard to Gaius the powers in question as part of the process of choosing the successor. In any case, we know Augustus never officially designated a son of his future successor. For information on the nature and geographical range of Gaius' *imperium*, see e.g. Zetzel 1970, 261; Bringmann 1977, 228; Jacques, Scheid 1992, 21; Hurlet 1994, 271–272; Sawiński 2005, 31–32. Most scholars date Gaius' departure to the East to 29th January 1 BC. See e.g. Herz 1980, 287–288; Halfmann 1986, 166; Kienast 1996, 74. This is based on the reconstruction of a missing fragment of the *Fasti Praenestini* carried out by Peter Herz (1980, 288). *Contra* Romer (1978, 187-202), who believes the campaign started as early as 2 BC. For more on the subject of Gaius' eastern mission, see Zetzel 1970, 259–266; Romer 1974, 161–185; id. 1978, 187–202; id. 1979, 199–214; Dąbrowa 1998, 203–205; Sawiński 2005, 81–83.

accorded Gaius. Among the more prestigious ones were the honorific statues erected in Athens, Sparta and Lindos on Rhodes, among other places[246].

Athenians honoured Augustus' son in a most spectacular way. In the agora, a temple dedicated to Ares was raised, with Gaius' statue inside. Interestingly, the temple was built with materials obtained from a dismantled fifth-century temple to the same god, which had stood in one of the Attic demes[247]. From an inscription from the Theatre of Dionysus, we also know the Athenians gave Gaius the epithet *New Ares*[248]. Based on Ovid's text, we may see a connection between this unusual way the inhabitants of Athens chose to honour him, and the consecration of the temple to Mars Ultor in 2 BC, that is shortly before Gaius Caesar left for the East; the poet clearly connects the consecration to Gaius' Parthian campaign. His description shows the young man was endorsed as the new conqueror of the Parthians and avenger of all the insults Romans had suffered from that people: his campaign was to continue Augustus' earlier successes[249]. In addition, in the Messenian honorific inscription to Cornelius Scipio mentioned above, Gaius' eastern campaign was styled a war waged "against barbarians for the sake of saving all the people" (sc. in the Empire: "ὑπὲρ τᾶς ἀνθρώπων πάντων σωτηρίας τοῖς βαρβάροις μαχόμενον")[250]. In the context of Gaius' predicted succession, creating that kind of image was quite significant. It is also worth noting here that after the news reached Messene that during the campaign against the Parthians Gaius had managed to avoid various dangers, Scipio ordered a bull sacrificed in the intention of his safe return to Rome, again commanding the people to make offerings and wear wreaths[251].

Another Greek city to honour Gaius was Sparta. His statue was put up in the local theatre. Next to it stood a statue of Lucius, probably only dedicated after his death. In each case, the decision to erect them was taken by the local authorities[252]. Then, in Lindos the statues of the young Caesars were placed in front of Athena's temple there[253]. Unfortunately, not one of the statues in question, related to Gaius' mission to the East, survives.

---

246 The statuary groups are essentially dated to the period from 2 BC to AD 2. See Rose 1997, 149, 154.

247 See Romer 1974, 97; Bowersock 1984, 173; Rose 1997, 18; Zanker 1999, 224, 261.

248 *IG* II^2 3250; Ehrenberg–Jones 1976, 68 (no. 64); Schmalz 2009, 100–101 (no. 129).

249 See Ov. *Ars am.* 1, 177–228. On that subject see esp. Romer 1974, 95–98; Syme 1978, 8–11; Bowersock 1984, 173; Rose 1997, 17–18.

250 *SEG* XXIII 206, ll. 10–12.

251 *SEG* XXIII 206, ll. 11–16.

252 Rose 1997, 149 (no. 81).

253 Rose 1997, 154 (no. 88).

The inhabitants of the eastern provinces also honoured Augustus' son by minting coins. As an example, let us look at coins produced in Pargamum and Apamea. On the obverse of the Pergamum coins, there is Gaius' head with the legend Γ ΚΑΙΣΑΡ ΠΕΡΓΑΜΗΝΩΝ, while the reverse shows an Armenian holding a spear and an arrow, and the legend is Α ΦΟΥΡΙΟΣ ΓΥΜΝΑΣΙΑΡΧΩΝ. The Apamean series has an image of Augustus on the obverse, the legend ΣΕΒΑΣΤΟΣ; the reverse has Gaius on a quadriga and reads ΓΑΙΟΣ ΚΑΙΣΑΡ ΓΑΙΟΣ ΜΑΣΩΝΙΟΣ ΡΟΥΦΟΣ ΑΠΑΜΕΩΝ. It is most likely that the two emissions honoured Augustus' son as a conqueror of Parthians and Armenians[254]. It is worth noting here that while on the Apamean series Gaius was depicted as a triumphator, there was no relation to any actual triumph, since we know he was never granted that particular reward[255].

In 2 BC, Lucius followed in his elder brother's footsteps by being sent to Spain to be introduced to the legions there. In the Spanish provinces, he was also supposed to gain proper experience administering the state[256]. However, that prospect never came true, as Lucius died in the same year during the journey, in Massalia (modern Marseille). Then two years later in Limyra in Lycia, Gaius died of a wound suffered during his campaign in Armenia[257].

1.4.3 Posthumous Honours

The deaths of the young Caesars were no doubt heavy blows to Augustus, which he expressed most emphatically in his *Res Gestae*[258]. The first response to the news was the Senate instituting public mourning (*iustitium*), which was to remain in effect in Rome until the bones were laid in the Mausoleum[259]. Alas, our sources provide little information on the form of the funeral ceremonies held in the honour of Augustus' deceased sons. All we know is that exactly as had been the case with Drusus the Elder, after being brought to Italy the bodies of the young Caesars were carried to Rome in a solemn procession by military tribunes

254 *RPC* I 2361; 3129.

255 During Augustus and Tiberius' reigns, the emperor and his likely successors were very often depicted as *triumphatores* (on a quadriga or wearing the triumphal dress) even if they had never held a triumph. The practice was one of the ways of exalting them. See Sawiński 2014, 134–135.

256 Vell. Pat. 2, 102, 3; Tac. *Ann.* 1, 3, 3; Suet. *Aug.* 64, 1; Cass. Dio 55, 10a, 9.

257 Vell. Pat. 2, 102, 3; Tac. *Ann.* 1, 3, 3; Suet. *Aug.* 65, 1; Cass. Dio 55, 10a, 9. Lucius died on 20th August; Gaius, on 21st or 22nd February. See Kienast 1996, 74–75.

258 "Filios meos, quos iuvenes mihi eripuit Fortuna" (*Mon. Anc.* 14, 1).

259 Wesch-Klein 1993, 92; Eck 1995, 1.

in mourning garb and by the most eminent inhabitants of the towns the conduct passed through[260]. In Gaius' case, it was not so much a body as an urn containing his remains, as the body had been burnt, probably before it left Limyra; the long distance between that city and Rome made it impossible to transport the corpse before it decomposed. The situation would be similar later with Germanicus, whose body was cremated in Antioch, where he died[261]. We may assume Lucius' *funus* took place in accordance with the pattern established before and used at the funerals of members of the imperial family[262]. Thus his body would have been put on public display in the Forum Romanum, where the princeps gave the traditional *laudatio funebris*, from there, it was moved to the Campus Martius, where it was cremated, and finally the urn was deposited in the Mausoleum of Augustus. Gaius' funeral ceremony, on the other hand, presumably resembled that held later after the urn holding Germanicus' bones was brought to Rome, as reported by Tacitus[263]. Based on that, we may assume it took place in the Campus Martius, where in the presence of the imperial family, magistrates, soldiers and the urban plebs the urn with the remains of Gaius Caesar was placed in the Mausoleum.

We know much more of the posthumous honours granted to the two Caesars, with important data supplied primarily by two extensive epigraphic texts, the *Tabula Siarensis* and the *Tabula Hebana*:

***Tabula Siarensis*, fr. 2, col. a, ll. 1–5 (ed. Sánchez-Gutiérrez 1999, 60).**

1 [--- Utique a(nte) d(iem) VI id(us) Oct(obres) quotannis apud eam ara]m, quae es-
2 [set ante tumulum, quo ossa illata essent Germanici Caesaris publice i]nferiae Manibus
3 [eius mitterentur per magistros sodalium] Augustalium p[ullis] amictos togis, quibus eo-
4 [rum ius fasque esset habere e]o die sui coloris togam, eodem ritu sacricfici quo
5 [publice inferiae mitterentur] Manibus G(ai) et L(uci) Caesarum

Annually on October 10 at that altar which is in front of the burial mound where the bones of Germanicus Caesar have been interred the officers of the Augustal Brotherhood, with those of them veiled in black togas that can legally and rightly wear an uncolored toga on that day, should publicly offer sacrifices to his shades in the same manner of sacrifice in which sacrifices are made publicly to the shades of Gaius and Lucius Caesar[264].

260 Cass. Dio 55, 12, 1. Swan 2004, 136.
261 Tac. *Ann.* 2, 83, 2; *TS* fr. I, 2, ll. 35–36.
262 See Sawiński 2012, 35–41.
263 Tac. *Ann.* 3, 4, 1.
264 Translated by J. B. Lott 2012, 93.

***Tabula Hebana*, ll. 4–7 (ed. Crawford 1996, 519–521)**

4 utiq(ue) Sali carminibus suis nomen Germanici Caesa[ris pro ho-]
5 norifica memoria int<e>rponant, qui honos C(aio) quoq(ue) et L(ucio) Cae-
sarib(us) fratr(ibus) Ti(beri) Caesaris Aug(usti) habitus est; [vacat]
6 utiq(ue) AD (decem) centur(ias) Caesarum quae de co(n)s(ulibus) pr(aetoribus) destinandis
suffragium ferre solent adiciantur (quinque): centuri[ae
que quae] –
7 primae (decem) citabuntur C(ai) et L(uci) Caesar(um) appellentur, inse-
quen<t>es (quinque) Germanici Caesaris

and that the Salian priests should include the name of Germanicus in their hymns for the sake of his honored memory, an honor which has also been observed for Gaius and Lucius Caesar, the brothers of Tiberius Caesar Augustus; and that to the ten centuries of the Caesars which regularly cast a vote about destining consuls and praetors, five more should be added; and the first ten centuries which are called forward to vote should be called the centuries of Gaius and Lucius Caesar and the following five called those of Germanicus Caesar[265].

The two inscriptions mostly refer to the ways Germanicus was commemorated after his unexpected death in AD 19, but also contain mentions of posthumous honours granted to Augustus' sons earlier. It should be noted here the text of the *Tabula Siarensis* is badly damaged in exactly those places, meaning we need to resort to a hypothetical reconstruction of some passages which have been lost. Luckily, the corresponding passages of the *Tabula Hebana* are preserved much better, which makes it possible for scholars to restore the missing pieces with some probability. In the inscriptions, we read that on the anniversaries of Gaius and Lucius' deaths, priests wearing dark togas were to make offering (*inferiae*) to their Manes at the special altar in front of the Mausoleum of Augustus[266]. The two brothers' names were included in the song of the Salii, a religious brotherhood related to the worship of Mars. Additionally, ten voting centuriae were

265 Translated by J. B. Lott 2012, 107.

266 It should be noted here that Augustus' sons were probably the first members of the reigning dynasty to be posthumously honoured in this way. For Marcellus, Agrippa, Octavia and Drusus the Elder, we lack the source material to suggest *inferiae* were to be offered on the anniversaries of their deaths in front of the Mausoleum of Augustus. In Drusus' case, there is only the information in the *TS* (fr. 1, 29–32) and the mention in Suetonius (*Claud.* 1, 3) of sacrifices made every year by representatives of the Gaulish provinces near his cenotaph in Mogontiacum (modern Mainz). However, it is not known if they were instituted on the anniversary of Drusus' death or birth.

named after them (the *centuriae Caesarum*); their duty was to choose candidates for praetorships and consulships[267].

More information on their posthumous honours can be found in literary sources. From Cassius Dio we learn that the Senate decreed that the silver shields and spears Gaius and Lucius had been granted by the equestrian order when receiving the title of princeps *iuventutis* be exhibited in its house (in the *Curia Iulia*)[268]. To this, Suetonius adds that Tiberius composed a lyric poem (*carmen lyricum*) in Lucius' honour to express his grief for the young man's death[269].

Moreover, many prestigious posthumous honours were accorded to the dead Caesars by the inhabitants of Pisa, who had special ties to Augustus' sons[270]. We owe the detailed information on the subject to two extensive inscriptions containing the texts of the honorific decrees passed by the authorities of that Italian town[271].

***CIL* XI 1421 = *ILS* 140, ll. 7–33 (ed. Rowe 2002, 121–122)**

7 cum a(nte) [d(iem) II] II nonas Apriles allatus esset nuntius C(aium) Caesarem, Augusti, patris patri-
8 ae, [po]ntif(icis) maxsumi, custodis imperi Romani totiusque orbis terrarum prae-
9 si[dis, f]ilium, Divi nepotem, post consulatum, quem ultra finis extremas popu-
10 li [Ro]mani bellum gerens feliciter peregerat, bene gesta re publica, devicteis aut
11 in [fid]em receptis bellicosissimis ac maxsimis gentibus, ipsum volneribus pro re
12 pu[bli]ca exceptis ex eo casu crudelibus fatis eruptum populo Romano, iam designa-
13 tu[m i]ustissumum ac simillumum parentis sui virtutibus principem coloniaeque
14 no[st]rae unicum praesidium, eaque res nondum quieto luctu, quem ex deces –
15 su [L(ucii) C]aesaris, fratris eius, consulis designati, auguris, patroni

267 Ehrenberg–Jones 1976, 47, 51; Sánchez–Gutiérrez 1999, 196–202; 280–287; Heinemann 2007, 72–73; Lott 2012, 225–226; 241–243.

268 Cass. Dio 55, 12, 1. See Lebek 1993, 104–105; Swan 2004, 136; Heinemann 2007, 53–55.

269 Suet. *Tib.* 70, 2.

270 Lucius was that town's patron. See *CIL* XI 1420, l. 8; *CIL* XI 1421, ll. 13–14; Galsterer 2000, 178.

271 For latest editions of the Pisan inscriptions, with commentary, see Rowe 2002, 102–123; Segenni 2011; Lott 2012, 54–77; 174–209.

nostri, princ[i]-
16 pis [iu]ventutis, colonia universa susceperat, renovasset multiplicassetque
17 ma[er]orem omnium singulorum universorumque, ob eas res universi decu-
18 rio[ne]s colonique, quando eo casu in colonia neque (duo)vir(i) neque praefecti
19 er[ant] neque quisquam iure dicundo praerat, inter sese consenserunt, pro
20 ma[g]nitudine tantae ac tam improvisae calamitas oportere ex ea die
21 qu[a ei]us deces<s>us nuntiatus esset usqu[e] ad eam diem qua ossa relata atque
22 co[nd]ita iustaque eius Manibus perfecta essent, cunctos veste mutata templis –
23 qu[e d]eorum immortalium balneisque publicis et tabernis omnibus clausis
24 co[nv]ictibus sese apstinere, matronas quae in colonia nostra sunt sublugere
25 di[em]que eum, quo die C(aius) Caesar obit, qui dies est a(nte) d(iem) VIIII k(alendas) Martias, pro Alliensi
26 lu[gub]rem memoriae prodi notarique in praesentia omnium iussu ac
27 vo[lun]tate caverique, ne quod sacrificium publicum neve quae suppli –
28 ca[tio]nes nive sponsalia nive convivia publica postea in eum diem
29 eo[ve d]ie, qui dies erit a(nte) d(iem) VIIII k(alendas)Mart(ias), fiant concipiantur indican-
30 tu[rve], nive qui ludi scaenici circiensesve eo die fiant spectenturve,
31 ut[ique] eo die quodannis publice Manibus eius per magistratus eosve,
32 qu[i Pi]sis iure dicendo praerunt, eodem loco eodemque modo, quo
33 L(ucio) C[aes]ari parentari institutum est, parentetur

Since on 2 April the news was announced that Gaius Caesar—son of Augustus, father of the fatherland, chief pontiff, guardian of Roman power and protector of the whole world, and grandson of a god—after his consulship which he passed successfully waging war beyond the furthest borders of the Roman people, having governed well and defeated or received into alliance the fiercest and most powerful nations, himself wounded on behalf of the republic, had been, as a result of this disaster, snatched from the Roman people by the cruel fates, a man already designated a *princeps* most just and similar to his father in virtues and an unparalleled defender of our colony; and since this matter has renewed and multiplied the grief of everyone singly and collectively, when the mourning that the whole colony had taken up the death of Lucius Caesar his brother, consul designate, augur, our patron, and prince of the youth had not yet subsided, all the councilors and the colonists, thus, decided among themselves (since at the time of this disaster there were neither joint executives nor prefects nor anyone with jurisdiction in our colony) that, on account of the magnitude of so great and so unforeseen a calamity, it was fitting: that everyone, with their clothing changed, refrain from social engagements and that the temples of the immortal gods, the public baths and the shops all be closed from the day on which his death was announced until the day on which his remains were returned and buried and the funeral rites for his Shades completed; and that the married women of our colony help mourn; and that the day on which Gaius Caesar died, 21 February, be handed down in memory as a day of mourning like the day of Allia and be so observed at present by the command and desire of all; and that care be taken lest any public sacrifice or supplications or weddings or public banquets ever be held, planned, or announced for that day or on that day, which day will be February 21, nor should any theatrical shows or chariot races be held or watched in that day; and that on that day annually the magistrates or whoever has jurisdiction at Pisa should offer funeral rites at that same place and in the same way as was established for sacrificing for Lucius Caesar[272].

***CIL* XI 1420 = *ILS* 139, ll.17–21 (ed. Rowe 2002, 120)**

17 apud eam aram quod annis a(nte) d (iem) X [III k (alendas)
Sept(embres) p]ublice Manibus eius per magis –
18 tratus eosve, qui ibi iure dicendo pr[ae]runt, togis pullis amictos,
19 quibus eorum ius fasque erit eo die [eiu]s vestis habendae, inferiae mit-
20 tantur, bosque et ovis atri infulis caerulis infulati Diis Manibus eiu[s]
21 mactentur

and (the council directed) that at this altar annually on 20 August the magistrates or those men who will have executive power there should, veiled in black togas, if they are legally and religiously able to wear such clothing on that day, offer sacrifices at public expense to his shades; namely, that a black bull and a black ram, adorned with dark ribbons, should be slaughtered for his divine shades[273].

CIL XI 1421 = ILS 140, ll. 34–37 (ed. Rowe 2002, 122)

34 utique [ian]us celeberrimo coloniae nostrae loco constituatur orna-
35 tu[s sp]oleis devictarum aut in fidem receptarum ab eo gentium, super
36 eu[m st]atua pedestris ipsius triumphali ornatu circaque eam duae
37 eq[uest]res inauratae Cai et Luci Caesarum statuae ponantur

and that an arch should be placed in the most frequented place in our colony, decorated with the spoils of nations conquered or received in alliance by him, and on the arch should be placed a statue of him on foot in triumphal dress and two gilded equestrian statues of Gaius and Lucius Caesar should be placed on either side[274].

272 Translated by J. B. Lott 2012, 73, 75.

273 Translated by J. B. Lott 2012, 65.

274 Translated by J. B. Lott 2012, 75.

From the fragments quoted above, we learn the first thing the authorities of the colony did on receiving the news of the death of Augustus' sons was to introduce public mourning. In Gaius' case, we know the mourning was to remain in effect from the moment the news of his death reached Pisa to the day of his funeral, and while it lasted, all the temples, baths and taverns were to be closed. The citizens of Pisa were obliged to wear mourning dress during that time, and the local matrons were supposed to lament his passing[275]. It is quite likely the *iustitium* instituted earlier, after Lucius' death, was similar in nature.

The honorific decree in question also contained a number of interesting decisions regarding commemorating every anniversary of their deaths, which fell on 21st February and 20th August, respectively. We do know the day Gaius died was declared unlucky and was to be accompanied by many prohibitions: no public ceremonies, theatre performances or circus games were to be held on the anniversary. Public sacrifices were likewise forbidden, except for the special funeral sacrifices mentioned below, as were supplication, feasts and weddings[276]. Sacrifices (*inferiae*) were to be made on the two anniversary days at a specially raised altar at public expense, overseen by the local officials wearing mourning togas. In the decree honouring Lucius, even the type of sacrificial animals was specified: they were to be black bull and black ram, additionally decorated with dark ribbons to emphasize the chthonic nature of the sacrifice[277].

The text of Gaius' inscription moreover reveals an honorific arch was erected in his name. The monument was most likely placed in the local forum (*celeberrimo coloniae nostrae loco*), that is, in the most frequented and prestigious part of Pisa. The arch was decorated with the arms (*spolia*) of peoples who were conquered or accepted Rome's supremacy as a result of Gaius' eastern campaign; it was crowned with a statue of the deceased wearing the robes of triumph (the *toga picta*), flanked by gilded equestrian statues of himself and his brother Lucius, who had died two years before. The *spolia* of the defeated barbarians, which included mostly weapons and armour, were probably depicted on an ornamental relief[278].

---

275 *CIL* XI 1421 = *ILS* 140, ll. 14–16; ll. 20–24; Galsterer 2000, 181; Lott 2012, 201–202.

276 *CIL* XI 1421= *ILS* 140, ll. 25–30; Weinstock 1966, 895; Galsterer 2000, 182; Lott 2012, 202–203.

277 *CIL* XI 1420 = *ILS* 139, ll. 17–21; *CIL* XI 1421 = *ILS*, 140, ll. 31–33; Galsterer, 2000, 181; Lott 2012, 185–187; 203–204.

278 *CIL* XI 1421 = *ILS* 140, ll. 34–37. For more information on Gaius' arch, see Kleiner 1985a, 156–164; Kleiner 1985b, 35; De Maria 1988, 250–251 (no. 32); Lebek 1991a, 63–65; Rose 1997, 99–100 (no. 28); Roehmer 1997, 109–110; Sawiński 2014, 119–120.

It is worth pointing out here that it was very unusual to place two statues of the same person on an arch; this was the first documented example of the practice[279]. Rose supposes Gaius' top statue was placed in a quadriga to make it proportional to the equestrian statues on its sides[280], but he must be mistaken, since the Pisan inscription clearly mentions a *statua pedestris*[281]. Wolfgang D. Lebek, on the other hand, aptly observed the statues decorating the arch sent a double message. In his opinion, the gilt statues on horseback placed on top of the monument were a clear reference to the honorary title of *princeps iuventutis* granted the brothers by the equites, which from Augustus' day on indicated the main candidates to succession. In that context, it would appear the founders of the arch meant primarily to posthumously honour the two Caesars as the successors they would have been.

To the Pisans that was of considerable importance, as the two young men had special ties to the colony, and high hopes were placed in the town on one of them succeeding Augustus as emperor. Then there was the decision to depict Gaius as a *triumphator* and to decorate the arch with images of trophies won in the East, intended to commemorate his military achievements during the Parthian campaign[282]. The projected image chosen is interesting, because, as I have mentioned above, Gaius was never accorded the right to hold a triumph. All we know (again, from Cassius Dio) is that in AD 3 he was acclaimed *imperator*[283]. Based on that, we may surmise he would have received that honour had he returned safely to Rome. It should be noted here that Gaius Caesar was the second member of the imperial family after Drusus the Elder to be posthumously commemorated with an honorific arch[284]. The tradition of honouring members of the reigning dynasty in this way would be continued under Tiberius[285].

By granting Augustus' sons a number of posthumous honours, the Pisans not only demonstrated their loyalty to the princeps and his family, but also emphasized the special relationship between their town and the ruling dynasty. In Lucius' case, we know that as regards his posthumous honours, the Pisan authorities' point of reference was a decree of the Roman Senate, probably similar to those

279 Kleiner 1985b, 35.

280 Rose 1997, 100.

281 *CIL* XI 1421, l. 36.

282 Lebek 1991a, 64–65.

283 Cass. Dio 55, 10a, 7; see Syme 1979, 315.

284 For information on Drusus' arch, see Sawiński 2014, 116–118 (with a list of ancient sources and the more significant modern literature on the subject).

285 See below.

passed later in Germanicus' and Drusus the Younger's honour. Unfortunately, no inscription bearing its text has been uncovered so far[286].

Gaius and Lucius received many prestigious posthumous honours in the provinces as well. The famous temple commonly known as Maison Carrée was constructed in their honour in Nîmes in Narbonne[287]. In Limyra, where Gaius had died, the inhabitants put up a cenotaph in his memory[288]. In many towns of the Empire, the young Caesars were worshipped as heroes, as indicated by the statues dedicated to them. The statues erected in their honour in Corinth may serve as a good example: the sculptures were placed in the exedra of the local Basilica Julia and fortunately they both survive, Gaius' complete, Lucius' as the head and torso only. Therefore, we know the two brothers were depicted as the Dioscuri, naked, wearing only cloaks draped on their left shoulders and twisted around their left forearms[289]. Showing Gaius and Lucius in the style typical of images of heroes indicates the statues were only dedicated after their deaths; Rose has noted that, until Claudius' reign, in Roman colonies (such as Corinth) heroic nudity was exclusively reserved for images of the dead[290].

It is supposed the armoured statue based on the sculpture of Augustus from Prima Porta, found in Jol-Caesarea in Mauretania, also has a connection to Gaius. It was probably founded shortly after his death by king Juba II of Mauretania, who had accompanied Gaius on his eastern campaign[291]. The iconography of the armour indicates it commemorated Gaius' successes during the Armenian-Parthian campaign. Central to the image is a half-naked character, identified with Gaius, handing Victory with a tropaeum to Venus, the patron goddess of gens Iulia, who is here an armoured *Venus Victrix*, holding a sword and shield. Behind Augustus' son, there is Victory, holding an oak-leaf crown (*corona civica*) above his head. Below that central scene, there are two centaurs, one holding a horn of plenty, and the other, a rudder, clear references to Augustus' victory at

286 A mention of the Senate decreeing a number of posthumous honours for Lucius Caesar can be found in the Pisan inscription dedicated to him. See *CIL* XI 1420 = *ILS* 139, ll. 9–12; Lott 2012, 182. It seems virtually certain a similar *senatus consultum* was passed when Gaius died. See *TS* fr. II, col.a, ll. 5–7.

287 Zanker 1999, 223, 306.

288 For a detailed analysis of that structure, see Borchhardt 1974, 217–241; Ganzert 1984, passim.

289 See Rose 1997, 138–139 (no. 69); Boschung 2002, 64–66.

290 Rose 1997, 139.

291 Juba's connection to Augustus' son gets a mention in Pliny (*HN* 6, 141), who writes that the king wrote a lost treatise on Gaius' *expeditio Arabica*.

Fig. 10. A posthumous statue of Gaius Caesar (?), Jol-Caesarea, probably funded by Juba II, king of Mauretania.

Actium and its consequences, which were propitious for the state. In that context, as Zanker rightly notes, Gaius' success seems to have been portrayed as a continuation of the era of good fortune begun by that victory. In the top part of the image, one can see Mars in a helmet and armour, while on the tasses there are the heads of bearded barbarians, standing for the defeated Parthians and Armenians[292]. (fig. 10)

The unexpected deaths of Augustus' sons destroyed the previous concepts of succession and forced the emperor to look for new solutions in that regard. Naturally, faced with such a turn of events, we cannot definitively determine which of the young Caesars would have eventually succeeded the princeps, but I think that if Gaius and Lucius had not died young, Augustus would have considered the criterion of seniority and ended up appointing the elder brother as his successor.

1.5 The Adoptions of AD 4: the Origins of the New Order of Succession

1.5.1 Tiberius' *adrogatio* and Grant of Imperial Prerogatives

The loss of both sons forced Augustus—whether he liked it or not—to rely on the experienced Tiberius as his future successor. Tiberius returned from Rhodes to Rome already in AD 2, possibly even before Lucius' death[293]. According to Suetonius, he owed his being recalled mostly to Gaius, who agreed to it provided Tiberius would not interfere with matters of state[294]. However, we should retain some caution regarding Suetonius assertions, as he may be overestimating Gaius' influence on his father's decisions. Sattler, on the other hand, supposes the favourable circumstances which made it possible for Tiberius to come back consisted in his greatest opponents being at the time in the East with Gaius Caesar, which allowed Tiberius' friends to convince the princeps to let his stepson return to Rome[295]. Either way, we know from the moment of the younger Caesar's death he kept a low profile and held no public office. Suetonius also says after his return from Rhodes Tiberius lived away from the imperial family, in Maecenas' old estate on the Esquiline[296].

292 Zanker 1999, 225–226.

293 Vell. Pat. 2, 103, 1; Suet. *Tib.*14, 1; Cass. Dio 55, 11, 3.

294 Suet. *Tib.* 13, 2.

295 Sattler 1969, 529.

296 Suet. *Tib.* 15, 1. On the subject of Maecenas' residence, see *LTUR*, 3, 1996, 70–74 (Ch. Häuber, s.v. *Horti Maecenatis*).

All that changed completely after Augustus' sons had both died. A few months after Gaius' death, the princeps finally adopted his stepson[297]. Before I discuss the legal aspects of that adoption and the consequences it had for Tiberius' standing, I would first like to quickly deal with a passage in Velleius Paterculus, who writes:

> Sed fortuna, quae subduxerat spem magni nominis, iam tum rei publicae sua praesidia reddiderat: quippe ante utriusque horum obitum patre tuo P. Vinicio consule Ti. Nero reversus Rhodo incredibili laetitia patriam repleverat. Non est diu cunctatus Caesar Augustus; neque enim quaerendus erat quem legeret, sed legendus qui eminebat. Itaque quod post Lucii mortem adhuc Gaio vivo facere voluerat atque vehementer repugnante Nerone erat inhibitus, post utriusque adulescentium obitum facere perseveravit, ut et tribuniciae potestatis consortionem Neroni constitueret, multum quidem eo cum domi tum in senatu recusante, et eum Aelio Cato C. Sentio consulibus V. Kal. Iulias, post urbem conditam annis septingentis quinquaginta quattuor, abhinc annos septem et viginti adoptaret[298].

> But fortune, which had removed the hope of the great name of Caesar, had already restored to the state her real protector; for the return of Tiberius Nero from Rhodes in the consulship of Publius Vinicius, your father, and before the death of either of these youths, had filled his country with joy. Caesar Augustus did not long hesitate, for he had no need to search for one to choose as his successor but merely to choose the one who towered above the others. Accordingly, what he had wished to do after the death of Lucius but while Gaius was still living, and had been prevented from doing by the strong opposition of Nero himself, he now insisted upon carrying out after the death of both young men, namely, to make Nero his associate in the tribunician power, in spite of his continued objection both in private and in the senate; and in the consulship of Aelius Catus and Gaius Sentius, on the twenty-seventh of June, he adopted him, seven hundred and fifty-four years after the founding of the city, and twenty-seven years ago[299].

Velleius implies that Augustus meant to adopt Tiberius even before Gaius' death, right after Lucius Caesar died, but gave up on the idea because his stepson opposed it vehemently. I believe the account may be understood in two different ways. On the one hand, we can of course question its reliability and decide Paterculus made it all up in order to again showcase Tiberius' special role in

297 Vell. Pat. 2, 103, 3; Suet. *Tib.* 21, 2–3; Tac. *Ann.* 1, 3, 3; Cass. Dio 55, 13, 1–2; *Fasti Amiternini* (Degrassi 1963, 187) list the date of Tiberius' adoption as 26th June AD 4.

298 Vell. Pat. 2, 103, 1–3.

299 Translated by F. W. Shipley (Loeb Classical Library, 152).

the *domus Augusta* and his *moderatio*[300]; on the other, both Velleius and Cassius Dio mention that after Gaius was wounded during the Armenian campaign, he suffered a breakdown and decided to withdraw from political life. Dio says it was a big disappointment to the princeps, who also supposedly officially informed the Senate of his son's decision[301]. Now if the version of events preserved in those two authors is true, then Augustus' plans for Gaius' future succession had been thwarted even before he died, and under the circumstances I do not think we can single-handedly reject Paterculus' suggestion of the emperor's intention to adopt Tiberius and make him his successor already in Gaius' lifetime[302].

To move on to the legalities of Tiberius' adoption, one must begin by emphasizing it was fundamentally different from the earlier adoptions of Gaius and Lucius, which as we know followed the procedure of *mancipatio*, since the boys had a living father. In the case of Tiberius, who had no *pater familias* above him, the procedure applied was that of *adrogatio*, which involved a legally independent (*sui iuris*) person freely coming under the *patria potestas* of another, surrendering their property and family to their care[303]. As a result, Augustus' paternal authority extended also to Tiberius' natural son Drusus the Younger, and to Germanicus, whom Tiberius had adopted at the emperor's command before being in turn adopted by him[304]. Losing the *pater familias* status also led to certain specific financial consequences for Tiberius; in Suetonius we read from then on he could not free slaves, make donations or accept inheritance without Augustus' consent, and could only temporarily use a part of his property

300 There is a repeated tendency in Paterculus to exaggerate Tiberius' actual significance in the imperial family before his adoption. See e.g. Vell. Pat. 2, 96, 1; 2, 101, 1. A model illustration of *moderatio Tiberii* in that historian's perspective is the passage 2, 122. See also Pigoń 1996, 74–75.

301 Vell. Pat. 2, 102, 2–3; Cass. Dio 55, 10a, 8–9. Romer 1979, 212.

302 Similarly, Dettenhofer 2000, 180–181, while Syme (2002, 430) admits the possibility that that version of events was invented for Tiberius' sake after he came into power. Still, Syme's claim does not seem convincing to me; it would be difficult to suppose Tiberius wanted the rumour spread that Augustus was only going to adopt him and designate him successor, because Gaius had decided to withdraw from political life. Velleius' version is also decisively rejected by Seager 2013, 41 note 1.

303 For information on that form of adoption, see esp. Prevost 1949, 39–43; Swan 2004, 141–142; Kunst 2005, 85–92; Lindsay 2009, 146–159.

304 I shall return to Germanicus' adoption and its meaning for the new family order within the *domus Augusta* in the next section.

assigned him, the *peculium*[305]. Since the adoption was an *adrogatio*, it took place in the Forum Romanum and was officially sanctioned by a *lex curiata*[306]. The college of *pontifices* had probably been consulted as well, because adopting a *sui iuris* person involved closing down the family cult, which they had presided over until this time.

The sources unambiguously highlight the public nature of Tiberius' adoption. Velleius Paterculus and Suetonius' accounts are both extremely telling:

> Adoptatus eadem die etiam M. Agrippa, quem post mortem Agrippae Iulia enixa erat, sed in Neronis adoptione illud adiectum his ipsis Caesaris verbis: "hoc", inquit, "rei publicae causa facio"[307].

> On the same day Marcus Agrippa, to whom Julia had given birth after the death of Agrippa, was also adopted by Augustus; but, in the case of Nero, an addition was made to the formula of adoption in Caesar's own words: "This I do for reasons of state"[308].

> [...] sed expugnatum precibus uxoris adoptionem non abnuisse, uel etiam ambitione tractum, ut tali successore desiderabilior ipse quandoque fieret. Adduci tamen nequeo quin existimem, circumspectissimum et prudentissimum principem in tanto praesertim negotio nihil temere fecisse; sed vitiis Tiberi[i] virtutibusque perpensis potiores duxisse virtutes, praesertim cum et rei p. causa adoptare se eum pro contione iuraverit et epistulis aliquot ut peritissimum rei militaris utque unicum p. R. praesidium prosequatur[309].

> [...] but that overcome by his wife's entreaties he did not reject his adoption, or perhaps was even led by selfish considerations, that with such a successor he himself might one day be more regretted. But after all I cannot be led to believe that an emperor of the utmost prudence and foresight acted without consideration, especially in a matter of so great moment. It is my opinion that after weighing the faults and the merits of Tiberius, he decided that the latter preponderated, especially since he took oath before the people that he was adopting Tiberius for the good of the country, and alludes to him in several letters as a most able general and the sole defence of the Roman people[310].

Both those authors make it clear that when adopting the stepson, the princeps stated he was doing it for the sake of the state (*rei publicae causa*)[311]. By

305 Suet. *Tib.* 15, 2. Of course we cannot say, as Jerzy Linderski (1995, 380 note 15) rightly observes. to what extent the property limitations listed by Suetonius with reference to Tiberius were factual.

306 Suet. *Aug.* 65, 1.

307 Vell. Pat. 2, 104, 1–2.

308 Translated by F. W. Shipley (Loeb Classical Library, 152).

309 Suet. *Tib.* 21, 2–3.

310 Translated by J. C. Rolfe (Loeb Classical Library, 31).

311 See also Levick 1966, 228–229; Woodman 1977, 135–136; Lindsay 2009, 199.

using this expression, and there is no reason to doubt those very words were uttered during the adoption procedure, Augustus left no possible doubt as to who would succeed him, while also clearly indicating he adopted his stepson reluctantly and under the pressure of the circumstances[312]. Velleius Paterculus most picturesquely described the supposed reaction of the inhabitants of Rome to Tiberius' adoption:

> Laetitiam illius diei concursumque civitatis et vota paene inserentium caelo manus spemque conceptam perpetuae securitatis aeternitatisque Romani imperii vix in illo iusto opere abunde persequi poterimus, nedum hic implere temptemus, contenti id unum dixisse quam ille omnibus faustus fuerit. Tum refulsit certa spes liberorum parentibus, viris matrimoniorum, dominis patrimonii, omnibus hominibus salutis, quietis, pacis, tranquillitatis, adeo ut nec plus sperari potuerit nec spei responderi felicius[313].

> The rejoicing of that day, the concourse of the citizens, their vows as they stretched their hands almost to the very heavens, and the hopes which they entertained for the perpetual security and the eternal existence of the Roman empire, I shall hardly be able to describe to the full even in my comprehensive work, much less try to do it justice here. I shall simply content myself with stating what a day of good omen it was for all. On that day, there sprang up once more in parents the assurance of safety for their children, in husbands for the sanctity of marriage, in owners for the safety of their property, and in all men the assurance of safety, order, peace, and tranquillity; indeed, it would have been hard to entertain larger hopes, or to have them more happily fulfilled[314].

The account is no doubt exaggerated, as are most accounts of Tiberius by Paterculus, but I do think we can take the passage as evidence of a widespread belief at the time of a close connection between the adoption and Augustus designating Tiberius his future heir.

It is supposed the day of Tiberius' adoption (26th June) was made a public holiday by decree of the Senate; this information was most likely included under the date in the *Fasti Amiternini*. However, the text of the inscription is badly damaged in that place, so all we have is a hypothetical reconstruction of the lost passage. The emendated text of the inscription runs as follows:

> Fer(iae) ex s(enatus) [c(onsulto), q]uod e[o] die [Imp(erator) Caes(ar)] Augus[tus ado]p[tav]it [sibi] filiu[m Ti. Caesarum] Aelio [et Sentio co(n)s(ulibus)][315]

312 See Béranger 1973, 139.

313 Vell. Pat. 2, 103, 3–5.

314 Translated by F. W. Shipley (Loeb Classical Library, 152).

315 Degrassi 1963, 187. Arguments adduced in favour of such a reconstruction of the inscription by Instinsky (1966, 334) seem convincing.

From other epigraphical sources, we know that the people of the provinces reacted promptly to Tiberius' adoption too. Athens may serve as an example, where the day, especially important to the imperial family, was celebrated by erecting a monument to Tiberius as Augustus' new successor. It included statues of Germanicus and Drusus the Younger as well, who in that context were honoured as successors further down the line[316].

Shortly after the adoption, possibly on the same day, Tiberius was granted *tribunicia potestas*[317]. Sources disagree on the length of its validity. According to Suetonius, Tiberius received these powers for five years; according to Dio, for ten[318]. It is commonly accepted Tiberius was at the same time accorded an *imperium proconsulare* too[319], and while no source mentions this explicitly, the assumption seems completely correct, because it is established that soon after the adoption the princeps dispatched Tiberius with a new mission to Germania. Since he was going to command the legions stationed there, he had to have military authority[320]. Considering the direct relationship between the adoption and Tiberius receiving the two crucial component prerogatives of imperial power, we can say in AD 4, he was officially designated as Augustus' successor[321].

1.5.2 The Adoption of Germanicus

Before Tiberius was adopted by Augustus, he had had to adopt his nephew Germanicus, even though he had a son of his own[322]. The order of adoptions was dictated by the fact that after his *adrogatio* by the princeps Tiberius would lose his status of *sui iuris* and thus the ability to carry out any legal actions in his own right[323]. It is quite likely that this was a necessary condition for the princeps

316 See Bowersock 1984, 181.

317 Vell. Pat. 2, 103, 3; Suet. *Tib.* 16, 1; Tac. *Ann.* 1, 3, 3; Cass. Dio 55, 13, 2.

318 Suet. *Tib.* 16, 1; Cass. Dio 55, 13, 2. Modern scholars generally accept Cassius Dio's version. See Instinsky 1966, 325; Kienast 1996, 77; Levick 1999, 49; Severy 2003, 189.

319 Timpe 1962, 27; Syme 1979, 315; Shotter 1991, 88; Jacques, Scheid 1992, 21; Kienast 1996, 77; Hurlet 1997, 141–146; Severy 2003, 190; Ziółkowski 2004, 364, 401.

320 But I reject Peter M. Swan's (2004, 142) notion that Tiberius' *imperium* was *maius* relative to those of other proconsuls, but *minus* relative to Augustus'. Considering Tiberius' actions were to be contained in Germania, I do not see any need for such broad powers to be granted him at the time. However, I find it difficult to determine what that scholar rests his claim on.

321 See Lacey 1979, 34.

322 Suet. *Tib.* 15, 2; Tac. *Ann.* 1, 3, 5; Cass. Dio 55, 13, 2.

323 See Levick 1975b, 30; Dettenhofer 2000, 182 note 98; Rivière 2016, 69.

to adopt him[324]. This immediately begs the question of why Augustus made Tiberius adopt his nephew, and to answer it we must first of all determine the place the princeps appointed Germanicus in his succession plans.

In both Tacitus and Suetonius, we find the information that Augustus seriously considered passing Tiberius over and designating Germanicus his successor, but in the end he chose his stepson, mostly due to pressure from Livia, something that both authors are careful to stress[325]. Of course, we are not able to definitively determine whether Augustus did wrestle with this dilemma, but it does not seem very likely. Even if he had no special affection for Tiberius, when designating him as successor in AD 4, he mostly had the best interests of the state in mind[326]. Therefore, it would be hard to suppose Augustus, who had always acted pragmatically, seriously considered passing over Tiberius, who was fully familiar with the difficulties of administering the Empire, only to choose the thoroughly inexperienced Germanicus to be his direct successor. In AD 4, Augustus was already sixty-six, so he needed somebody suitably prepared, who could take over from him immediately if he died[327]. Nor would I exaggerate Livia's influence on that decision of his. I do not think her interference was even necessary in that case; the princeps was well aware Tiberius was the best candidate at the moment. Moreover, Sajkowski rightly observes the intention to make Germanicus direct successor, attributed to Augustus by ancient historians, may reflect their ill will towards Tiberius, "born in senatorial circles" at the time he was already princeps[328]; reading through the first few book of Tacitus' *Annals* leaves no room to doubt that his account is filled with spite directed at Tiberius, whereas his references to Germanicus, whose personality was allegedly the exact opposite of his uncle's sullen, duplicitous character, exude sympathy[329].

---

324 So e.g. Corbier 1991b, 66. *Contra* Levick 1975b, 30.

325 Tac. *Ann.* 4, 57, 3; Suet. *Tib.* 21, 2; *Calig.* 4, 1. See also Levick 1975b, 29; Kienast 1982, 116; Corbier 1995, 186; Bauman 2003, 104–105.

326 As indicated by the formula *rei publicae causa*, supposedly spoken by Augustus during the adoption, if by nothing else. The same point is argued by Suetonius (*Tib.* 21, 2–7) who writes that while Augustus personally disliked his stepson, he really valued his military and political talents, which ended up shifting the scales in Tiberius' favour and convincing the emperor to make him his successor.

327 Germanicus was hardly ready for that at that stage, as he only began to hold offices in AD 7. Cf. Kienast 1996, 80.

328 Sajkowski 2006, 369.

329 See e.g. Tac. *Ann.* 1, 33, 1–3; 2, 5, 1–2; 2, 26, 2–5; 2, 40, 1–3; 2, 43, 4–5; 6, 51, 3. For information on Tacitus' approach to Tiberius and Germanicus in his narrative, see Shotter 1968, 194–214; Borzsák 1969, 588–600; Baar 1990, passim.

Some scholars claim the decisive factor which ultimately weighed in favour of adopting Tiberius and designating him, rather than Germanicus, was the bad situation in Germania, which required an experienced commander to intervene. Tiberius was at the time the only member of the *familia Caesaris* Augustus could entrust with that. The promise of succession in the future was to be his reward for taking command in that difficult campaign[330]. I find that view too extreme. First, in AD 4, the situation in Germania was not yet grave enough to absolutely require Tiberius' presence, unlike five years later, after Varus' defeat. Second, I think Augustus would have adopted his stepson and designated him successor even had there been no need to intervene in Germania; as I have noted above, he needed someone suitably prepared to take over as princeps.

David Shotter believes that choosing Tiberius, one of the Claudii Nerones, to succeed him, was Augustus' nod to the old Republican families. He thinks this particular branch of the patrician *gens Claudia* played a greater role under the Republic than the *Iulii Caesares* did, so designating a member of that gens was meant to win the emperor the support of the "old aristocracy."[331] I find his opinion very questionable. First, I do not know Shotter's grounds for claiming the *Claudii Nerones* had more influence under the Republic than the *Iulii Caesares*. During the final sixty years of its existence, the latter family held the consulship several times, whereas the last Claudius Nero assumed that office in 202 BC. Second, after his adoption Tiberius moved from his old gens into *gens Iulia*, as did all his descendants. Thus imperial power was to remain in the hands of the *Iulii*.

To sum up, I do not see sufficient evidence to conclude that Augustus planned to make Germanicus his direct successor. Rather, all the evidence points to the princeps intending that he would only take over from Tiberius. That, then, would have been the primary purpose of that adoption, since it gave Germanicus the same rights to succession as those enjoyed by Drusus the Younger, Tiberius' natural son[332].

In my view, two facts indicate Augustus' intention was for imperial power to fall in the long term to Germanicus and then to whatever descendants he might have. Firstly, an analysis of Germanicus' political career clearly shows the princeps favoured him over Drusus and saw to it that, from the start, he would gain experience governing the state[333]. Between AD 7 and 9 Germanicus took

330 Cf. Instinsky 1966, 331–332; Birch 1981, 445; Dettenhofer 2000, 182–183.

331 Shotter 1992, 12–13.

332 Levick 1966, 232.

333 That aspect was also recently pointed out by Bellemore 2013, 79–84.

part, under Tiberius' command, in suppressing the uprising in Pannonia and Dalmatia, for which he was awarded the *ornamenta triumphalia*[334]. In AD 9, he was counted among the members of the Senate as a praetor and granted the right to run for consul early and to speak in the Senate directly after the ex-consuls[335]. Two years later, he was sent to Germania in proconsular rank to help Tiberius normalize the situation there after Varus' defeat[336]. In AD 12, he assumed his first consulship, even though he had not previously held a praetorship[337]. In the following year, he was given the general command over the legions stationed on the Rhine[338].

Drusus the Younger's career was a far cry from that of Germanicus. He was granted his first privilege in AD 9, when he was given the right to take part in sessions of the Senate in praetorial rank. The only magistracy he held under Augustus was a quaestorship, to which he ascended in AD 11[339]. In 13, he was granted the right to run for consul in two years' time and without having to hold a praetorship first[340]. Thus Drusus' "civilian" *cursus honorum* did not diverge from that of Germanicus very much[341]. However, unlike his adoptive brother, Drusus held no military functions under Augustus, and those were an important part of endorsing future successors. Levick disagrees, trying to demonstrate Drusus' political career at the time was in fact similar to Germanicus' *cursus honorum*. In her opinion, Germanicus rose to certain honours earlier simply for having been the elder of the two and the fact does not in any way indicate that Augustus favoured him[342]. That opinion is questionable; it would be difficult

334 Vell. Pat. 2, 116, 1; Cass. Dio 55, 32, 1–4; 56, 11, 1; 12, 2; 15, 1; 17, 1–2.

335 Cass. Dio 56, 17, 2. See Hurlet 1997, 167; Dettenhofer 2000, 197. Bellemore (2013, 81) on the other hand, when referring to that passage in Dio, erroneously says Germanicus was allowed to express his opinion in the Senate right after the consuls then in office. Meanwhile, Cassius Dio clearly refers to consulars.

336 Cass. Dio 56, 25, 2. The problem of the exact nature of Germanicus' *imperium* during his actions in Germania in ad 11 is controversial. See e.g. Hurlet 1997, 168–169; Sawiński 2005, 32–33.

337 Cass. Dio 56, 26, 1.

338 Vell. Pat. 2, 123, 1; 125, 1; Tac. *Ann.* 1, 31, 1–2; see Kienast 1996, 80.

339 Cass. Dio 56, 17, 3; 25, 4. See also Sumner 1967, 428; Hurlet 1997, 212; Bellemore 2013, 81.

340 Cass. Dio 56, 28, 1; Sumner 1967, 428.

341 The difference was that Germanicus rose to the same privileges and offices younger. Consulship may serve as an example; it fell to Germanicus at twenty-five, but to Drusus only at twenty-seven or twenty-six. See Sumner 1967, 432–433.

342 Levick 1966, 233–244.

to explain the differences in the careers of Tiberius' sons by pointing to the age difference, as it was relatively small. While we do not know the exact date of Drusus' birth, it is generally accepted he was one or at most two years younger than Germanicus[343], so he could easily have held certain military functions during Augustus' principate.

And secondly, shortly after Tiberius adopted Germanicus, Augustus brought about his marriage to his granddaughter Agrippina the Elder. That union no doubt additionally strengthened Germanicus' position in the *domus Augusta* and tied him more closely to the princeps[344]. I believe that by arranging that marriage, Augustus primarily counted on the couple having sons, one of whom would eventually become the emperor. Thus his plans included Germanicus as princeps after Tiberius, for the imperial power to pass to a son of his next, ultimately remaining in the hands of a natural descendant of Augustus[345].

The family arrangements made by the princeps and Germanicus' *cursus honorum* clearly point to only a minor role for Drusus the Younger and any potential issue of his in the new order of succession created after AD 4[346]. Still, whether that order of succession within the imperial family were kept no longer depended directly on Augustus. Tiberius' stance in that respect would no doubt have been crucial, since he would appoint his own successor, and we have no way to be certain he would have followed Augustus' wishes by designating

---

343 *Feriale Cumanum* (*CIL* X 8375) lists Drusus' birthday (7th October), but does not specify the year. Therefore I find Mlasowski's claim (1996, 339) based on that inscription that Drusus *must* have been born in 15 BC, unjustified. Bellemore's conjecture (2013, 81 note 10) that Drusus may have been a year older than Germanicus is not very likely either. For various proposals regarding the date of Drusus the Younger's birth, see Rogers 1943, 91–92; Sumner 1967, 427–430; Shaw 1990, 3–5; Kienast 1996, 82.

344 Tac. *Ann.* 1, 33, 1; Suet. *Aug.* 64, 1. The marriage was probably made in AD 5. See Schrömbges 1986, 160; Kienast 1996, 80; Rivière 2016, 71. Agrippina was an extremely prestigious bride to win, as indicated by passages in Tacitus (*Ann.* 3, 4, 2; 4, 52, 2), who writes the people of Rome called her *decus patriae, solum Augusti sanguinem* and *unicum antiquitatis specimen*. See also Corbier 1995, 183–184; Seager 2013, 47.

345 See Marsh 1931, 41; Griffin 1984, 191; Dettenhofer 2000, 182; Ziółkowski 2004, 400; Boruch 2010, 12. One should also remember Germanicus himself was related to Augustus on his mother's side. See Tac. *Ann.* 2, 43, 5. Antonia the Younger was the emperor's favourite niece. I think that was one of the reasons Augustus put Germanicus above Drusus.

346 There may be more evidence for that in Augustus' last will, where Germanicus and Drusus were both included as second-line heirs, but Drusus' share in the emperor's property was to be smaller. Suet. *Aug.* 101, 2. See also Sumner 1967, 433.

Germanicus and passing over his natural son. Since both his sons died early, all we can do is speculate.

1.5.3 The Adoption and *abdicatio* of Agrippa Postumus

Another integral element of the adoptions of AD 4 was Augustus' adopting Agrippa Postumus, the third son of Julia and Agrippa, and, as his *cognomen* indicates, he was born after his father's death. He was adopted on the same day as Tiberius and from then on, his name was officially *Agrippa Iulius Caesar*[347]. In other words, formally speaking, the young Agrippa gained the same standing in the *domus Augusta* that Tiberius had. Two questions must be asked here: why did Augustus decide to adopt Agrippa Postumus? And, did he see a place for him in the succession order created after AD 4? Unfortunately, ancient authors have nothing to say on his motivations in that regard, merely making a note of the adoption. As a result, modern historical literature abounds with diverse hypotheses meant to explain the reasons behind it. In this section, I shall only present the more important views on the matter found in scholarship.

Shelagh Jameson and Barbara Levick believe the parallel adoptions of Agrippa and Tiberius are important evidence in favour of Augustus intending to introduce double principate. Supposedly, such plans had been indicated earlier by the adoption of Gaius and Lucius, who were to rule together after Augustus' death as co-regents. Under the new circumstances caused by their unexpected death, Tiberius and Agrippa Postumus were to be that pair. Thus these historians accept the notion of "Doppelprinzipat", created by Ernst Kornemann[348]. The claim is very much questionable, since we have no reasons to suppose the princeps aimed to have Rome ruled by two *principes* after his death. While in the case of Gaius and Lucius their very similar careers could have led those scholars to the belief that Augustus intended for the two Ceasars to co-rule in the future, with Tiberius and Agrippa any such conjecture is quite baseless; after all, we do know Postumus never held any public functions, and Augustus never took any steps to endorse the young man as a successor.

Another solution to the problem in question was put forward by Severy, who proposed that by adopting Agrippa, Augustus protected himself from making Tiberius his rival, who might have threatened his position within the *domus Augusta*. In this context, as Augustus' other son, whose rights to the succession were equivalent to those of Tiberius, Postumus would have been a trump card

347 Vell. Pat. 2, 104, 1; Suet. *Aug*. 65, 1; *Tib*.15, 2; Kienast 1996, 75.
348 Levick 1966, 229; Jameson 1975, 287. Cf. also Kornemann 1930, 24–26.

that could have been played against Tiberius, had he proven disloyal. The scholar also supposes that the young man's difficult character was another factor which convinced the princeps to adopt him. This brought him under the emperor's *patria potestas*, which made stricter control possible[349]. While the second part of Severy's proposal seems acceptable—the sources do mention Postumus' arrogant and perverse nature[350]—the first is totally inadmissible. The sense in which Tiberius was supposedly a threat to Augustus is completely incomprehensible; combined with conferring on him *tribunicia potestas* and *imperium proconsulare*, his adoption made him the undisputed successor of the princeps. And since succession was near—since Augustus was already sixty-six at the time—I fail to see any reason for Tiberius to be disloyal and act against the princeps in any way, trying to assume power earlier. Nor are there any grounds to assume Augustus had ever feared competition from his closest relatives within the *domus Augusta*; he regularly entrusted them with the most important public functions, including in particular military command, and granted them honours otherwise reserved only for himself. That certainly indicates great trust he placed in members of his family.

A still different track is investigated in Sajkowski, who believes one of Augustus' motives for adopting Agrippa was his deeply ingrained sense of familial ties[351]; through adoption, the princeps was also able to fully control the young man, submitting him to his paternal power. Thus, Sajkowski goes here in roughly the same direction Severy does. Sajkowski also sees that adoption in terms of Augustus' policy of presenting the public with two candidates to succession, only one of whom would actually succeed him. There were allegedly two such pairs during his reign; the first made of Gaius and Lucius Caesar, the second, after their unexpected death, of Tiberius and Agrippa Postumus[352]. The first two reasons for the adoption pointed out by Sajkowski seem acceptable, but the last idea needs to be verified, as it only seems valid as regards the young Caesars, both of whom Augustus had consistently presented as the major candidates to succession. In the latter case, only Tiberius was ever publicly presented as the emperor's political successor; as I have indicated above, no such steps were taken regarding the young Agrippa.

349 Severy 2003, 190.
350 Vell. Pat. 2, 112, 7; Tac. *Ann.* 1, 3, 4; Suet. *Aug.* 65, 1; Cass. Dio 55, 32, 1.
351 Already pointed out earlier by Birch (1981, 446).
352 Sajkowski 2006, 372.

To sum up, of the motives listed above Augustus could have had for adopting Agrippa Postumus, I consider his intention to subject the young man to his *patria potestas* the most likely; the adoptions of Tiberius and Germanicus carried out in AD 4 clearly show the princeps meant not only to settle the issue of succession, but also to bring all the more important male members of the *domus Augusta* under his paternal authority. As a result, a unified family was formed with Augustus as its *pater familias*[353]. Nor do I think adopting Postumus means the question of succession was not unambiguously settled in Tiberius' favour by AD 4. While as the other son of the princeps the adopted Agrippa had the same right to inherit from Augustus as Tiberius did, having the two "imperial" powers conferred on the latter was a clear sign to everybody that he would be the next princeps. It is also telling that the expression *rei publicae causa* apparently used by Augustus during Tiberius' *adrogatio* did not feature in Postumus' adoption process, which indicates it was predominantly a private matter[354]. Furthermore, Augustus intended, as I wrote above, for imperial authority to pass from Tiberius to Germanicus, and then to a son of Germanicus, which clearly shows the princeps saw no room for Agrippa in his succession plans. In that context, Cassius Dio's commentary on the adoptions in question is eloquent:

> Τὸν Τιβέριον καὶ ἐποιήσατο καὶ ἐπὶ τοὺς Κελτοὺς ἐξέπεμψε· τὴν ἐξουσίαν αὐτῷ τὴν δημαρχικὴν ἐς δέκα ἔτη δούς· Καὶ μέντοι καὶ αὐτὸν ἐκεῖνον ὑποπτεύσας πῃ ἐκφρονήσειν καὶ φοβηθεὶς μὴ καὶ νεοχμώσῃ τι· τὸν Γερμανικόν οἱ τὸν ἀδελφιδοῦν καίτοι καὶ αὐτῷ υἱὸν ἔχοντι ἐσεποίησε· Κἀκ τούτων ἐπιθαρσήσας ὡς καὶ διαδόχους καὶ βοηθοὺς ἔχων [...][355].

> and not only adopted Tiberius, but also sent him out against the Germans, granting him the tribunician power for ten years. Yet suspecting that he also would lose his poise somehow or other, and fearing that he would begin a rebellion, he made him adopt his nephew Germanicus, though Tiberius had a son of his own. After this he took courage, feeling that he had successors and supporters [...][356].

He correctly observes that those adoptions gained Augustus new successors and consolidated the reigning dynasty. It is telling that Dio only mentions the adoptions of Tiberius and Germanicus here, without a word of Agrippa

353 The only member of the imperial family not under Augustus' *patria potestas* was Tiberius Claudius Drusus, Germanicus' brother and, later, emperor.

354 Vell. Pat. 2, 104, 1–2. See also Severy 2003, 190.

355 Cass. Dio 55, 13, 2–3

356 Translated by E. Cary (Loeb Classical Library, 83).

Postumus' adoption. In my opinion, that is yet another argument for his role in the new dynastic order having been marginal[357].

The events which followed directly after Agrippa's adoption fully confirm this thesis. In AD 5, he officially donned the toga of manhood[358]. From Cassius Dio we know that this did not result in him receiving the honours and privileges that had earlier fallen to his elder brothers' lot, which no doubt indicates his standing in the *domus Augusta* was, in spite of the adoption, incomparable to that of Gaius and Lucius, and that the princeps did not intend to introduce Agrippa onto the political scene[359]. Moreover, in AD 6, Augustus made him abdicate (undergo an *abdicatio*) and be exiled to Surrentum. One year later, he was by decree of the Senate sentenced to exile for life to Planasia (the modern island of Pianosa), his property confiscated and included in the *aerarium militare*[360].

There are basically two views present in the scholarly literature as to the consequences these sanctions had for Postumus' future standing. According to the first, the *abdicatio* invalidated the earlier adoption, the most important result being Agrippa's exclusion from the *gens Iulia* and from under Augustus' *patria potestas*. Another result was supposedly a return to the *nomen gentile* he had had before the adoption. If that is true, the effects of the *abdicatio* were close to those of the procedure of *emancipatio* provided for by Roman law[361]. The second theory holds abdication merely involved temporarily rejecting or expelling a son, without causing him to break his ties to his *gens* completely, and that he remained under his father's *patria potestas*. On that view, *abdicatio* was a preventive action available to the *pater familias*, whose primary purpose was to bring an unruly son onto the right path, and Augustus applied the measure first of all to control the difficult young man. Scholars who subscribe to this theory believe it was only the sentence of a lifelong exile imposed in a *senatus consultum* that

---

357 *Contra* Mlasowsky (1996, 339), who assumes that after his adoption Postumus was second in line to political succession after Tiberius.

358 Kienast (1982, 120) dates that event to AD 5; Severy (2003, 196), to 6.

359 Cass. Dio 55, 22, 4; Linderski 1995, 377. I want to stress that we have no imperial coins dedicated to Agrippa Postumus; all we have are a few provincial emissions, minted in Corinth and Apamea in Bithynia among other places, dated to AD 4–6. See *RPC* I 1141; Mlasowsky 1996, 322–327. That is in sharp contrast with the way Gaius and Lucius had been honoured on their respective occasions of the same type.

360 Plin. *HN* 7, 150; Suet. *Aug.* 65, 1; 65, 4; *Tib.* 15, 2; Tac. *Ann.* 1, 3, 4; 1, 6, 2; Cass. Dio 55, 32, 2. See also Hohl 1935, 350; Minto 1947, 3–10.

361 Levick 1972b, 674–697; Birch 1981, 450; Corbier 1995, 187; Linderski 1995, 392; Bleicken 1998, 647; Cogitore 2002, 179; Sajkowski 2006, 371; Levick 2010, 187.

fundamentally changed his legal status[362]. They suggest the punishment used against Postumus was *deportatio*, which automatically deprived the convict of his civil rights, entailing exclusion from the *familia Caesaris* and the expiration of Augustus' *patria potestas* over him[363]. It would be difficult to unequivocally determine which side of the debate is correct. I think arguments could be found for either position, but there is no point in launching detailed legal analyses, as the whole discussion boils down to establishing when and how exactly Agrippa's adoption was cancelled, and scholars do agree ultimately that Postumus lost his status as a son of Augustus. Ascertaining whether that happened in AD 6 due to the *abdicatio*, or one year later when he was exiled for life, does not seem all that important.

As Suetonius aptly observed, expelling Postumus from the Caesar family and his exile ultimately confirmed Tiberius' future succession[364]; from then on, he was the only legitimate successor and the main heir to Augustus' property. Ancient authors list several reasons which may have caused Agrippa's exile. Velleius Paterculus and Suetonius mention the young man's perverse nature and his many faults, reputedly increasing in number as he got older, which finally caused Augustus' patience to run out[365]. In addition, Tacitus implies it was Livia who persuaded the princeps into taking this step in order to secure the succession for Tiberius[366]. Cassius Dio tells us another reason for Agrippa's fall: alongside his recalcitrance was the large number of his critical comments aimed at Augustus, demanding the return of property which used to be his natural father's[367]. It would be hard to determine with certainty which of the reasons found in the sources caused young Agrippa's exile directly, but each of them seems likely.

In his interesting paper dealing with the adoptions of AD 4, Birch also points out the political aspect of Postumus' fall and exile. Namely, he claims the exile may have been connected to the tense political situation in Rome in AD 6 following the outbreak of the great anti-Roman uprising in Pannonia and Dalmatia. The sources do in fact mention the great panic the news of that revolt apparently caused[368]. In Birch's opinion, under those circumstances there was more activity

362 Hohl 1935, 350 note 1; Jameson 1975, 287–314; Severy 2003, 196–197.

363 See especially Jameson 1975, 303–309.

364 Suet. *Tib.* 15, 2.

365 Vell. Pat. 2, 112, 7; Suet. *Aug.* 65, 1, 4.

366 Tac. *Ann.* 1, 3, 4.

367 Cass. Dio 55, 32, 1–2.

368 See Vell. Pat., 2, 110, 6; Suetonius (*Tib.* 16, 1) considered that the rebellion the most terrible war since the Punic Wars.

from opposition circles centred on Plautius Rufus and L. Aemilius Paullus, the husband of Augustus' granddaughter Julia. Frustrated with his subordinate position in the imperial family and dismissal from any public functions, which had to be particularly painful in the context of the successful careers of his natural father and brothers, the young Agrippa might have been quite easily drawn into the ranks of this opposition[369]. It was then involvement on the side of Augustus' political enemies that supposedly doomed him to his fate[370]. Birch's hypothesis is certainly interesting, but it bears stressing there is no direct evidence for it in the sources.

Tacitus and Cassius Dio quote a rumour suggesting that a few months before his death, Augustus visited Planasia in order to see Agrippa, and during the meeting they were reconciled, which gave rise to speculation that the princeps intended to recall Postumus from exile and make him his successor[371]. Needless to say, we cannot be certain the episode actually took place, but I do not find it very likely[372]. Firstly, the story may, again, reflect the literary tradition of hostility towards Tiberius, aimed at discrediting him and demonstrating Augustus had doubts until the end about whether he should succeed him. Secondly, we know that in AD 13 the princeps made his choice of the future successor final by prolonging Tiberius' tribunician powers for another ten years and conferring a special *imperium* on him[373]. It is improbable that Augustus, who had always acted rationally, should have suddenly changed his mind and relied on the completely inexperienced Agrippa. Thirdly, his return to Rome could have certainly caused bitter conflict between him and Tiberius, which the elderly emperor must have preferred to avoid. And finally, it seems if the princeps had in fact wanted to restore Postumus to favour, he would not have passed him over in his last will.

369 Apart from the passage in Dio quoted above, echoes of that frustration and criticism regarding Augustus can be found in Suetonius (*Aug.* 51, 1), who mentions a certain Junius Novatus, who apparently published Agrippa's supposed letters, containing numerous accusations aimed at the princeps. Of course, there is no certainty Postumus was the real author; nor do we know whether the letters were circulated before or after his exile. Cf. Jameson 1975, 301.

370 Birch 1981, 449–451; 455. Another scholar to point to the connection between Agrippa's fall and the political situation brought about by the Pannonian war is Kienast (1982, 119–120), who believes one result of Agrippa's exile was the conspiracy of Aemilius Paullus uncovered in AD 8.

371 Tac. *Ann.* 1, 5, 1–2; Cass. Dio 56, 30, 1.

372 Modern scholars disagree on the matter. See, among others, Syme 1958, 306, 688; Corbett 1974, 94; Jameson 1975, 310; Syme 1978, 149–151.

373 More on this subject in section 1. 5. 5.

1.5.4 Ara Providentiae Augustae

The most important result of the adoptions of AD 4 was that a new hierarchy formed within the *domus Augusta* reflected in a new order of succession too. Tiberius was now first in line, with Germanicus second and Drusus the Younger third[374]. The princeps intended those adoptions, as well as the marriages arranged shortly afterwards, of Germanicus to Agrippina and Drusus to Livilla, to ensure the continuation of the dynasty and to keep the imperial succession safely within the *gens Iulia* for three generations to come[375].

Most likely it is with these adoptions that we should connect the construction of the special altar, *Ara Providentiae Augustae*, which was placed *in Campo Agrippae*, very close to the *Ara Pacis*[376]. It is generally accepted the monument was erected to celebrate Augustus' foresight after the death of Gaius and Lucius Caesar by adopting Tiberius and designating him his successor, and so ensuring the continuity of the dynasty[377]. A different opinion can be found in the article of Duncan Fishwick, who does not believe the dedication of that altar should be seen only in terms of the adoptions of AD 4. Rather, he thinks the intention of the Senate was to honour the princeps for the providence he showed regarding designating a future successor earlier in his reign by consistently preparing first Agrippa, then the young Caesars and finally Tiberius for that role. Thus, in his opinion, the monument commemorated the full scope of Augustus' succession

374 This order of succession can also be confirmed by the arrangement of the statuary group on the honorific arch in Ticinum (modern Pavia) constructed to celebrate the *domus Augusta*, dated to the years AD 7–8. In this case the crucial element appears to be the arrangement of the statues of the several members of the imperial family relative to the statue of Augustus central to the whole group. According to Sandro De Maria's reconstruction (1988, 249), directly to the right of the princeps (the right being the more prestigious side) were the images of Tiberius, followed by Germanicus, then Drusus the Younger and Germanicus' eldest son Nero Julius Caesar. On Augustus' left there was a statue of Livia, and next to her, the statues of the decesased Gaius and Lucius Caesar followed by that of Germanicus' younger son Drusus Caesar, and of Claudius, the future emperor. Of that monument, only honorific inscriptions survive. See *CIL* V 6416. For information on the Ticinium arch, see esp. De Maria 1988, 249–250; Roehmer 1997, 57–59; for the most recent interpretation of the way the several members of the imperial family were depicted on the arch, see Seager 2013, 42–43.

375 Cf. Birch 1981, 444; Schrömbges 1986, 160; Corbier 1995, 190; Severy 2003, 190.

376 On the subject of the altar's location, see Zanker 1999, 145 (fig. 114); Fishwick 2010, 251.

377 See Barrett 1989, 68; Mlasowsky 1996, 346; Rose 1997, 34; Severy 2003, 190–191; Cox 2005, 252.

policy so far[378]. However, he fails to convince; in the *AFA* fragments discovered in the 1970s and dated to AD 38, it is listed that a cow was sacrificed on 26th June at the *Ara Providentiae Augustae*[379]. I am convinced that this indicates there was a strict connection between the altar and Tiberius' adoption in particular, which was carried out on 26th June[380]. That interpretation is also borne out by the information in the *Fasti Amiternini*, already mentioned above, that a public holiday was instituted to commemorate Tiberius' *adrogatio*. Unfortunately, we do not know exactly when the Senate decided to have the altar raised, or when it was consecrated[381].

It is probably this altar that can be seen on a series of bronze sesterces and asses produced by the senatorial mint in Rome between AD 22 and 30. On the obverse of the sesterces there is Augustus seated with an altar at his feet, the legend being DIVUS AUGUSTUS PATER. There reverse has the lettering TI CAESAR DIVI AUG F AUGUST P M TR POT XXIIII, and the signature SC[382]. On the asses, the obverse has Augustus' head wearing the *corona radiata*, the legend the same as on the sesterces, while the reverse shows an altar between the signature SC and the letters PROVIDENT, which make identifying the altar possible[383].

---

378 Fishwick 2010, 253–258.

379 See Scheid–Broise 1980, 218, 224; 232–236; Hurlet 1997, 485 note 295.

380 The idea of some historians, that the foundation of the altar ought to be linked to Sejanus' fall, seems mistaken too. According to that theory, *providentia* would have meant care for the emperor's safety, "providence" protecting Tiberius from a coup supposedly planned by that influential Praetorian prefect. For a discussion of that view and specific references to literature, see Sajkowski 2001, 160–161.

381 The earliest mention of that altar is to be found in the text of the *SCPP* (ll. 82–84), edited on 10th December AD 20. Not that it means the monument could not have been erected earlier. Sarah E. Cox (2005, 254) believes the decision to build that altar was taken during the Senate session on 17th September AD 14, when a number of other honours for the newly dead Augustus were voted on. She also thinks the most likely dedication date for the altar to be 26th June AD 16, an anniversary of Tiberius' adoption. However, that seems unconvincing to me; it would have been unlikely for ancient authors, particularly Tacitus, who lists a number of posthumous honours conferred on the dead princeps by the Senate, not to mention the distinction of such prestige. Rather, there is more credibility to the claim made by Fishwick (2010, 252), who supposes the construction was decided on when Augustus was still alive and finished shortly before his death as well.

382 *RIC* I^2 *Tib.* 49; Cox 2005, 256.

383 *RIC* I^2 *Tib.* 80–81; Cox 2005, 255.

The fact the Senate commemorated the adoptions of AD 4 by erecting a monument where public sacrifices were to be made, indicates the commissioners intended to stress the special importance that this move of Augustus had for the future of the state. Owing to *providentia Augustae*, imperial power was to remain in the *domus Caesarum* for another few generations, which guaranteed the *res publica* would be stable and safe.

1.5.5 Tiberius as Augustus' Successor and *collega imperii*

Tiberius' adoption and simultaneously his being conferred with "imperial" prerogatives fundamentally changed his standing within the *domus Augusta*. Those two moves effectively made him the emperor's successor and co-regent[384]. Of course, as in Agrippa's case and so in Tiberius', the co-regency was introduced only formally, while in fact, the state was still ruled by the one princeps. In other words, granting Tiberius the two most vital imperial powers did not institute a double principate in the strict sense of those words.

Rome's poor military situation on the Rhine and Danube fronts meant that almost throughout his co-regency with Augustus (which spanned the period from AD 4 to 14) Tiberius was busy conducting difficult military campaigns, first in Germania (AD 4–6), then in Pannonia and Dalmatia (AD 6–9) and again on the Rhine (AD 10–12)[385]. His successes in this field, especially in the suppression of the dangerous uprising of the Pannonian and Dalmatian tribes and normalizing the situation in Germania after Varus' defeat, won him the reputation of an excellent commander and massive popularity among the soldiers, for whom military talent was among the most important characteristics of a future princeps[386]. With the prospect of Tiberius' intended succession on the horizon, that was quite significant.

Tiberius' changed status in the imperial family was reflected in a new public image, as illustrated by the numismatic material. After Tiberius' adoption, depictions of him began to appear on official coin emissions, where he is presented as Augustus' co-regent and future successor. In that context, one specific series

384 Tacitus (*Ann.* 1, 3, 3) uses the term *collega imperii* to refer to Tiberius.

385 For information on Tiberius' military activity there, see esp. Koestermann 1953, 345–378; Timpe 1967, 285–288; Kienast 1982, 303–307; Welwei 1986, 132–136; Bernecker 1989, passim; Wolters 1989, 27–30; Gruen 2008, 176–178; 183–186.

386 Velleius Paterculus (2, 111, 2; 120, 1) with his typical exaggeration terms Tiberius *praesidium ultimum rei publicae* and *perpetuus patronus Romani imperii*. See also Woodman 1977, 161; 204–205.

of asses is of interest, produced in the senatorial mint in Rome and dated to AD 10–11. On the obverse, the asses have Tiberius' face with the legend TI CAESAR AUGUST F IMPERAT V; on the reverse, there is only the legend PONTIFEX TRIBUN POTESTATE XII and the signature, SC[387]. One striking feature of this series is the fact that Tiberius' portrait and his official titulature were placed on the obverse, which until then had been Augustus' sole privilege when official emissions were concerned, and no other member of the imperial family had had the honour before[388]. What is more, before then all coins coming out of the imperial and senatorial mints, if they showed members of the *domus Augusta* other than the princeps, they depicted him too; on the series in question, however, Tiberius is alone.

Relevant coins were also issued by the imperial mint in Lugdunum. One such group is made of aurei and denarii dated to AD 13 and 14, whose obverse has Augustus' head wearing the laurel crown with the legend CAESAR AUGUSTUS DIVI F PATER PATRIAE, while the reverse shows Tiberius with the lettering TI CAESAR AUG F TR POT XV[389]. The series presumably commemorated the renewal of his tribunician powers in AD 13[390]. Another group contains dupondii and sesterces dated to AD 9–14. The obverse of one of those series shows Tiberius' head in the laurel crown, the legend being TI CAESAR AUGUSTI F IMPERAT

387 *RIC* I^2 *Aug.* 469; *HCC* I *Aug.* 120; Sutherland 1951, 76.

388 See Sutherland 1951, 76; Wallace-Hadrill 1986, 83; Vout 2013, 62. Now, we do have senatorial as series featuring Agrippa in a *corona rostrata* on the obverse, with the legend M AGRIPPA L F COS III, while the reverse has an image of Neptune, but it is unlikely they were minted during Augustus' principate. The dating of those coins is controversial. Some scholars suppose their emission only began under Tiberius and lasted until the beginning of Claudius' principate, but their claim is not very convincing, as the only link between Agrippa and Tiberius was the latter's ex-wife Vipsania Agrippina, whom he had divorced long before he became emperor. Others date the coins only to Caligula's times. For a list of various dating suggestions, see *RIC* I p. 101; *RIC* I^2 p. 89; Roddaz 1984, 607–610; Carter, Metcalf 1988, 145–147; Barrett 1989, 251; Sear 2000, 358 (no. 1812); Ziółkowski 2007, 467–468. One argument for dating them to Caligula's reign could be the fact at the time similar coins with an image of Agrippa in the *corona rostrata* and the same legend were minted in Caesaraugusta. See *RPC* I 381, 386. Thus through those emissions, Caligula would have commemorated his grandfather's great military achievements. Consequently, Suetonius' information (*Calig.* 23, 1) that that emperor despised Agrippa for his lowly birth does not seem very credible.

389 *RIC* I^2 *Aug.* 225–226; *HCC* I *Aug.* 227–228.

390 More on that below.

V, whereas on the reverse there is the famous altar dedicated to Roma and Augustus, built in 12 BC in Lugdunum by Drusus the Elder[391].

Many emissions relating to Tiberius were also minted in the provinces of the Empire, whose inhabitants used them as a way of honouring Augustus' "new" son and future successor, at the same time demonstrating their loyalty and commitment to the imperial family[392].

It ought to be stressed here that the clear majority of the coins bearing Tiberius' image were only minted after AD 4, no doubt a result of his inclusion in the Julian family and his corresponding advancement in the hierarchy of the *domus Augusta*. Preserved emissions dated to before his adoption are only sporadic. Actually, where so-called official minting is concerned, all we have is one emission, and an uncertain one at that[393]. The trends in provincial minting were similar[394].

An important role in the endorsement of Tiberius, especially in military circles, was played by *phalerae*, the medals used to reward legionaries for their service. Dietrich Boschung assumes such *phalerae* bearing the armoured bust of Tiberius were distributed in large numbers in the army between AD 4 and 14[395], and the assumption seems logical, although we cannot be completely certain the medals in question, the so-called type VI in Boschung's classification, do depict Tiberius. Various types of *phalerae* with images of the members of the imperial family did originate under the Julio-Claudian dynasty and were very popular among soldiers, who wore them on diverse ceremonial occasions, expressing their loyalty to the reigning family[396], but that does not guarantee the identification of the persons depicted on them suggested in the scholarly literature is correct.

---

391 *RIC* I² *Aug.* 235, 236ab, 240; *HCC* I *Aug.* 237–238; Sutherland 1951, 76; Kuhoff 1993a, 65.

392 We know of such emissions e.g. from Spain (from Tarraco and Caesaraugusta), Africa (from Leptis Minus) and Macedonia (from Thessalonica). See *RPC* I 215, 330, 789, 791, 1565.

393 See *RIC* I² *Aug.* 164–165. The lack of a proper legend means we cannot be sure the coins show Tiberius with Drusus the Elder. I have already written on that coin series above.

394 The few emissions recorded there include coins minted in Gades, which can probably be explained by the fact Tiberius was the patron of that town. See *RPC* I 88–91.

395 Boschung 1987, 226–228. Detailed iconographic analysis of the medals ibid., 232–234.

396 Boschung 1987, 193–195; 227.

Another direct result of Tiberius' adoption and designation as successor was the appearance of many honorific statues dedicated to him throughout the Empire. Examples include statues funded in Luna in Italy, Athens, or Arsinoe in Egypt. In Luna, the statue of Tiberius was placed in the local theatre next to those of Germanicus and Augustus, whose image was central to the group[397]. In Athens, Tiberius' statue was placed in a most prestigious location, namely in front of the western façade of the Parthenon, where it was an integral part of a larger statuary group including images of Augustus, Germanicus and Drusus the Younger. The arrangement of the statues reflected the order of succession established after AD 4, with Tiberius on the emperor's right and Germanicus on his left, Drusus' the Younger role in the new succession order indicated by the fact his statue was placed on the edge of the group next to Tiberius'[398]. From extant inscriptions, we know that the last statuary group was erected by decree of the Athenian assembly[399]. In Arsinoe, the statue of Tiberius most likely stood in the local amphitheatre next to those of Augustus and Livia[400]. All three statuary groups mentioned are dated to the period from AD 4 to 14 and seen as connected to Tiberius' adoption.

According to the *Fasti Praenestini*, on 23rd October AD 12, Tiberius held his second triumph awarded for earlier successes on the Pannonian-Dalmatian front[401]. It was one of the many rewards granted to him in AD 9 in return for suppressing a dangerous rebellion of the tribes there. We also know it was the second time Tiberius gained the title of *imperator*, and the Senate voted to have a triumphal arch erected for him in Pannonia. The same honours were conferred

---

397 Rose 1997, 93–94 (no. 19).

398 A similar hierarchy within the *domus Augusta* after AD 4 is reflected in the iconographic programme of the Ticinium arch; see above.

399 Rose 1997, 138 (no. 68).

400 Rose 1997, 188–189 (no. 129).

401 Degrassi 1963, 134–135; Vell. Pat. 2, 121, 2; Suet. *Tib.* 20. Mlasowsky (1996, 315) observed Tiberius' second triumph took place exactly on the day Octavian had had his great victory at Philippi fifty-three years before, and did not believe that a coincidence. Rather, he thought it was a way to emphasize the idea that Tiberius' successes against the barbarians, which ensured the Empire its security, had the same importance as Octavian's victory over Caesar's killers, which had made the Republic stable. While the two dates are in fact the same, Mlasowsky's view seems erroneous; I do not see that much connection between a victory in a civil war half a century earlier and presenting one's future successor as the conqueror of barbarian tribes and the promise of the Empire's lasting might, especially with the German scholar mistakenly dating both those events to 23rd December.

on Augustus[402]. However, because of the mourning in Rome after Varus' defeat, the triumph did not take place directly after Tiberius' return from the Pannonian campaign in AD 9. Suetonius writes that only a much more modest ceremony was held then: Tiberius entered Rome on foot, dressed in a *toga praetexta* and with a laurel crown on his head and went to the Campus Martius to ascend, in the presence of standing senators, a specially constructed tribunal, where together with Augustus he was seated between two consuls[403]. Thus the triumph proper was only held three years later, after Tiberius' return from Germania.

Thanks to Velleius Paterculus, and especially to Suetonius, we have a fairly detailed account of that ceremony[404]. Velleius personally took part in it. From both those authors we know the people other than Tiberius who held special places in the triumphal procession were his legates, rewarded with the *ornamenta triumphalia*. Therefore, it seems to make sense to deduce Germanicus was foremost among them, since he had first seen combat during the Pannonian-Dalmatian campaign[405]. What is more, the most important chieftains of the conquered tribes were paraded in the triumph. Interestingly enough, not all of them were subsequently executed, as was the case after most triumphs, because Suetonius mentions one of the leaders of the Pannonian rebellion, a man by the name of Bato, was generously rewarded by Tiberius and then settled in Ravenna. That was supposed to be repayment of sorts, since during the war in Pannonia Bato had let Tiberius and his units withdraw from unfavourable positions. Suetonius also informs us the triumph was presided over by Augustus in person, and before heading for the Capitoline, where each triumphal procession had its climax, Tiberius paid obeisance to the princeps and dedicated his victories to him. The ceremony was crowned by a feast thrown for the Roman plebs, who also received three hundred sesterces per head on the occasion. In the light of the source material cited we can conclude the ceremony contained all the most important elements traditionally present in most Roman triumphal processions.

No doubt Tiberius' second triumph should also be seen in terms of Augustus' dynastic policy, since it was a perfect opportunity to introduce the future princeps to the inhabitants of Rome. Presenting Tiberius as a conqueror of dangerous barbarian tribes and the man responsible for Rome's greatest military successes

402 Suet. *Tib.* 17, 1; Cass. Dio 56, 17, 1. Alas, we have no data on what the arch looked like or how it was decorated. Neither do we know where exactly it was built.

403 Suet. *Tib.* 17, 2.

404 Vell. Pat. 2, 121, 3; Suet. *Tib.* 20.

405 See Bellemore 2013, 82.

Fig. 11. Denarius, Lugdunum, AD 13–14. Obverse: an image of Augustus wearing a laurel wreath; legend: CAESAR AUGUSTUS DIVI F PATER PATRIAE. Reverse: an image of Tiberius in a triumphal quadriga, holding in his hands a laurel branch and a *sceptrum*; legend: TI CAESAR AUG F TR POT XV (*RIC* I² *Aug.* 222).

was to reinforce the opinion widely held by the public that he fully deserved to soon take Augustus' place. Tiberius' victories meant the gods favoured him, which in turn guaranteed the Empire would prosper and be stable under his reign[406].

It is probably Tiberius' second triumph that was commemorated on the aurei and denarii issued in the Lugdunum mint from AD 13 to 14. The obverse of those emissions shows Augustus' head in a laurel wreath and the legend CAESAR AUGUSTUS DIVI F PATER PATRIAE; the reverse has Tiberius in a triumphal quadriga holding a laurel branch and *sceptrum*, the attributes of the *triumphator*, with the legend TI CAESAR AUG F TR POT XV[407]. (fig. 11)

Some scholars suppose the image on one of the two silver skyphoi discovered in Boscoreale near Pompeii also refers to that triumph and victories of Tiberius[408].

406 That aspect of Tiberius' triumph was pointed out by Hickson 1991, 129–130; Beard 2007, 296.

407 *RIC* I² *Aug.* 221–224; Holtzhausser 1918, 22–23; Mlasowsky 1996, 313–315; Vout 2013, 69. *Contra* Kuttner 1995, 153, who unconvincingly connects that coin emission to Tiberius' first triumph in 7 BC.

408 See Zanker 1999, 229. For a detailed analysis of the vessels, see Kuttner 1995, passim. Still, that book needs to be applied carefully due to a number of mis-dated events

Fig. 12. A silver skyphos, Boscoreale (Pompeii), after AD 12. A depiction of Tiberius' triumph (?).

The image on the first vessel depicts the moment of sacrifice before a war expedition and a triumphal procession with a quadriga in its centre, the figure in it identified as Tiberius. The chariot also bears two images of Victory holding a shield. (fig. 12) The message and themes of the scenes of the first skyphos are related to the pictures on the other cup. It is generally assumed the main character in those is Augustus. In the first scene, the princeps is shown seated on a *sella curulis* in the company of lictors and soldiers, receiving the obeisance of barbarians humiliating themselves before him. (fig. 13) In the other, Augustus is again seated on a curule chair, while the goddess Venus places a statuette of Victory on the globe he holds, making him forever victorious. To one side of the image, the Genius of the Roman People holds a horn of plenty and Roma places her foot on enemy weapons, while to the other, Mars leads the personifications of

from Augustus' principate. For instance, the author insists on dating Octavian's triple triumph to 27 BC (*sic!*), when in fact it is common knowledge it had taken place two years earlier, while Tiberius' departure for Rhodes, which took place in 6 BC, she dates to 4 BC. See Kuttner 1995, 85, 147–148, 150, 173, 177, 195.

Fig. 13. A silver skyphos, Boscoreale (Pompeii), after AD 12. An image of Augustus receiving barbarians' tribute.

the conquered provinces towards Augustus[409]. The ideological message of those images was very clear. They showed Augustus as the unquestioned ruler of the world, whose reign, supported by the most important Roman gods, guaranteed universal security and might of the state, whereas Tiberius was depicted as his major aide and military second-in-command, who with his victories confirmed he would become a worthy successor.

Zanker supposes that the picture cycle on the skyphoi may reflect the images from a lost victory monument erected by a decision of the Senate in order to celebrate and commemorate Tiberius' second triumph[410]. A similar opinion can be found in the work of Ann L. Kuttner, who believes the iconographic model which inspired the manufacturers of the skyphoi had been the relief sculptures decorating a public monument constructed on the occasion of Tiberius' triumph, probably the basis of a honorific column with Augustus' statue on top, perhaps placed in the Forum Iulium. Unlike Zanker, this scholar thinks the monument

409 See Kuttner 1995, 94–98; Zanker 1999, 230–231.

410 Zanker 1999, 229. See also Kleiner 1997, 377–380.

was built after Tiberius' first triumph, which took place in 7 BC[411], but that is all speculation. First, we do not know exactly when the cups were made[412], and so in which period to look for their possible iconographic model. Second, we have no data on the type of monument involved. And third, there is no actual certainty any such monument even existed, as ancient authors are silent about the Senate voting to have one built in Rome in connection with a triumph of Tiberius. In fact, according to Cassius Dio, the only material commemoration of Tiberius' victories was a triumphal arch, but that was to be erected somewhere in Pannonia[413].

Another group of scholars see allusions to Tiberius' second triumph in the scene shown on the famous *gemma Augustea*[414]. It is generally supposed the cameo was engraved c. AD 10[415]. The top tier depicts Augustus seated in the company of the goddess Roma, holding in his right hand the *lituus*, which here stands for the highest military authority[416]. Right behind the emperor we can see the personified provinces, pacified and flourishing, whereas before him, Tiberius descends from a triumphal quadriga, with a young soldier in front of it, usually identified as Germanicus. The *lituus* in the emperor's hand indicates Tiberius' victories were all won under his auspices. In the bottom part of the gem, Roman legionaries are shown setting up a tropaeum with tied-up prisoners of war sitting underneath. On the right, personifications of the provinces lead more barbarians towards the tropaeum[417]. (fig. 14) Of course, we cannot reject out of hand the notion the scene on the cameo is about Tiberius' victories on the Pannonian-Dalmatian front and the triumph he was awarded for those successes, but considering Roman art was fundamentally not documentary, which I have already mentioned above, I would be more inclined to see the images on the *gemma Augustea* as symbolic rather than alluding to any specific events of Augustus' times. In my opinion, the scenes primarily highlighted the special role of the *domus Augusta* as the guarantor of

411 Kuttner 1995, 151–153; 193–197. Thus the scene depicting a triumphal procession, found on one of the skyphoi, refers to Tiberius' first triumph.

412 Their dating is uncertain. Some even believe they were only made during Claudius' reign. See Zanker (1999, 349), who reviews various scholars' opinions on that subject.

413 See above.

414 While other historians believe the image in the gem refers to Tiberius' first triumph of 7 BC. See Balbuza (2005, 81), who reviews the opinions present in scholarship.

415 Zanker 1999, 232–233; Hölscher 2011, 68; Havener 2016, 222. *Contra* Meyer (2000, 73–80), who dates the gem to Claudius' times.

416 Zanker 1999, 232–233; Havener 2016, 224.

417 For a description of the images on the cameo gem, see e.g. Zanker 1999, 232–234; Meyer 2000, 59–80; Havener 2016, 222–224.

Fig. 14. The *gemma Augustea*, c. AD 10, Tiberius' triumph (?).

Rome's permanent military success, which in turn could ensure the stability and power of the Empire.

In AD 13, Augustus ultimately confirmed Tiberius' future succession. By decree of the Senate, confirmed additionally by the people, Tiberius received *imperium aequum* relative to that of the princeps in all the provinces of Rome, meaning from then on his *imperium* was *maius* compared to those of all other governors and military commanders throughout the Empire[418].

418 Vell. Pat. 2, 121, 1; Suet. *Tib.* 21, 1. See also Timpe 1962, 28, 47; Parsi 1963, 47; Levick 1999, 63; Sawiński 2005, 31; Gruen 2005, 50; Stevenson 2013, 137. Some scholars date the decision to AD 12; so e.g. Dettenhofer 2000, 204.

At the same time, Tiberius' *tribunicia potestas* was prolonged, presumably by another ten years[419]. Based on indirect information provided by the sources, we can surmise he was also granted *imperium consulare*, the third of the legal pillars supporting the authority of the princeps; namely, in the *Res gestae* Augustus mentions that in AD 14 he carried out another census of citizens, which required an exercise of consular powers, and that Tiberius was his *collega* in that endeavour[420]. That information is further confirmed by Suetonius' account, according to which in AD 13 Tiberius was granted the right to carry out such a census with the princeps, a motion submitted by the consuls[421]. Conferring those powers made Tiberius' position *de iure* equal to that of Augustus, so formally speaking, his future succession was fully prepared.

Tiberius' smooth succession was also supposed to be secured by personal decisions taken by the emperor regarding posts in the public administration and the army. Kienast has demonstrated that after adopting his stepson, Augustus appointed Tiberius' trusted supporters to all major offices[422], and similar moves took place in the military. In AD 13, the general command of the eight legions stationed on the Rhine was given to Germanicus[423]. The Danubian legions were in the care of Quintus Junius Blaesus, an uncle of Sejanus, whose ties with Tiberius were close[424]. The Syrian army was commanded by Quintus Caecilius Metellus Silanus, whose daughter was betrothed to Nero Julius Caesar, Germanicus' eldest son[425]. In Spain, the army was led by M. Aemilius Lepidus, whose daugther was in turn betrothed to Germanicus' younger son, Drusus Caesar[426]. Owing to those moves, at the moment of Augustus' death, all the major military forces of the Empire were in the hands of people closely related to the imperial family[427].

419 Cass. Dio 56, 28, 1. See also Kienast 1996, 77; Severy 2003, 205.
420 *Mon. Anc.* 8, 4. See Brunt, Moore 1967, 51–52; Cooley 2009, 143.
421 Suet. *Tib.* 21, 1. Levick 1999, 63.
422 See Kienast 1982, 122.
423 Tac. *Ann.* 1, 31, 2.
424 Tac. *Ann.* 1, 16, 2.
425 Tac. *Ann.* 2, 43, 2.
426 Vell. Pat. 2, 125, 5; Tac. *Ann.* 6, 40, 3.
427 See Syme 2002, 437–438.

2 Tiberius

2.1 Germanicus and Drusus the Younger as Candidates to Succession

2.1.1 Public Presentation and Honorifics

At the moment Tiberius took over as princeps, Germanicus and Drusus, being the new emperor's sons, became first in line to the succession. The fact Germanicus was an adoptive son of Tiberius, while Drusus was his natural son, bore no weight in that context; they both had identical informal rights to the succession. From the very start of his reign, Tiberius saw to it both his potential successors gained proper experience governing the state by entrusting them with diverse military and administrative tasks. In this regard, he consistently continued the dynastic policy of Augustus, who, as I have demonstrated, used that method to prepare his intended successors to rule. While Germanicus had acquired his first military experience during Augustus' principate, holding important functions in the army, Drusus was completely inexperienced in that matter[1]. Directly after Augustus' death the new princeps kept his predecessor's decisions in force, retaining Germanicus as the commander-in-chief of the army in Germania and conferring on him the *imperium proconsulare*[2]. The successes achieved during the campaigns conducted on the Rhine front between the years 14 and 16 won Germanicus the affection and respect of the soldiers, whose support was a crucial element in the context of his possible succession[3]. The command in Germania also earned him a number of prestigious honours. In AD 15, before the campaign was even over, Germanicus was granted the title of *imperator*, conferred on him at Tiberius' instigation[4]. In the same year, the Senate

---

1 See above.

2 Tac. *Ann.* 1, 14, 3. See also Sawiński 2005, 32–33.

3 For information on Germanicus' imilitary campaigns on the Rhine in the years 14–16, see esp. Koestermann 1957, 429–479; Timpe 1968, passim; Gallotta 1981, 293–316; Lehmann 1991, 79–96; Sawiński 2005, 65–71; Rivière 2016, 189–233.

4 Tac. *Ann.* 1, 58, 5–6. From Augustus' day on the imperatorial acclamation became in fact reserved for the princeps and for members of the *domus Augusta*. The breakthrough in that regard came in 29 BC, when Octavian would not allow M. Licinius Crassus to receive the title of *imperator* for his military successes in the Balkans. See Cass. Dio 51, 25, 2. From then on, the decision as to granting that honour ultimately belonged to the emperor, who could override the army on the matter. For example

voted him a triumph and the construction of a triumphal arch, which was to rise near the temple of Saturn in the Forum Romanum[5]. Germanicus' triumph took place on 26th May AD 17, as Tacitus meticulously noted. We further know from Tacitus that it included all the most important elements typical of triumphal processions. Among others, spoils were displayed during the ceremony as well as paintings of scenery in which battles had been fought in Germania and of the fighting itself. Germanicus' children participated too[6]. Moreover, in Strabo we read famous German chieftains and members of their families were displayed in the procession[7].

No doubt the ceremony was a splendid occasion to reintroduce to the public a major candidate to the succession, returned to Rome after four years in the glory of a conqueror of the Germans and avenger of Varus' defeat, since he had recovered the standards Varus had lost[8]. As Severy aptly noted, Germanicus presented himself "as the perfect imperial heir endowed with both military and familial authority."[9] It is worthy of note Germanicus was the second member of the *domus Augusta* (after Tiberius) to hold a triumph after 19 BC, when Augustus *de facto* reserved that honour for the emperor. Still, unlike Tiberius' second triumph, the ceremony was not about officially displaying the designated successor, since at that stage Tiberius had not unambiguously picked one of his sons to succeed him. Tacitus adds that on the occasion of that triumph the emperor had three hundred sesterces paid out to every member of the plebs in Germanicus'

from Dio (54, 33, 5) we know Augustus forbade to have that title conferred on Drusus the Elder in 11 BC, even though the army had already hailed him *imperator*. From Tiberius' principate we also have one case of a man receiving it who was not part of the imperial family: in 22, the emperor allowed Junius Blaesus to be acclaimed *imperator* for his successes in the war against Tacfarinas. As Tacitus (*Ann.* 3, 74, 4) points out, Blaesus was the last commander from outside the *domus Augusta* to receive that honour. See also Vell. Pat. 2, 125, 5; Maxfield 1981, 103; Griffin 1984, 19; Schumacher 1985, 219.

5 Tac. *Ann.* 1, 55, 1; 2, 41, 1. See also Timpe 1968, 44–46; 50–51; Syme 1979, 321–323; Hurlet 1997, 174–176. For information on the arch, see Sawiński 2014, 122–125.

6 Tac. *Ann.* 2, 41, 2–3; Vell. Pat. 2, 129, 2; Suet. *Calig.* 1, 1; Rose 1997, 24; Hurlet 1997, 179–180.

7 Strab. 7, 1, 4.

8 This was the way Germanicus' achievements were described in the text of the *TS* (fr. I, 13–15).

9 Severy 2003, 226.

name[10]. The intention was no doubt to secure Tiberius' potential successor the affection and support of the people of Rome.

Germanicus' triumph and his victories on the Rhine were commemorated with a series of dupondii, most often dated to the reign of Caligula, who referred to his father's achievements quite often on coins minted during his rule. The obverse of the dupondii shows Germanicus in a quadriga, wearing the military cloak (the *paludamentum*) and holding a *sceptrum* in his left hand. The triumphal chariot bears an image of Victory, the scene complemented by the legend GERMANICUS CAESAR. On the reverse, one can see Germanicus wearing armour with an eagle (*aquila*) in his left hand, with the legend SIGNIS RECEPT DEVICTIS GERM SC[11]. (fig. 15) Thus the reverse highlights one of this commander's most important successes of the German campaign, namely the recovery of the standards lost by Roman legions due to the defeat at the battle of the Teutoburg Forest in AD 9[12].

Images on the scabbard of the so-called Sword of Tiberius, discovered in Germany, probably also refer to Germanicus' victories and provide us with important information on this commander's public image. It is supposed the sword and scabbard were made some time after AD 16, and the interpretation most widespread in scholarship identifies the characters depicted in one of the scenes on the scabbard with Tiberius and Germanicus[13]. The princeps is shown in the style of Jupiter enthroned, his left hand resting on a shield labelled FELICITAS TIBERII. In front of him stands Germanicus, giving him a *victoriola* (a statuette of Victory) and so dedicating his victories to the emperor. In the background, there are images of Mars Ultor and of Victory, who holds a shield with the label VICTORIA AUGUSTI. (fig. 16) In other words, Germanicus was presented as Tiberius' most important commander, who had proven he was a worthy candidate to the throne in the future with his military success. The deities appearing in the image extended their patronate to the victories of the *domus Augusta*, and their support meant the reign of Tiberius and his future successors would continue the period of might and stability of the Empire initiated by Augustus' principate[14].

---

10 Tac. *Ann.* 2, 42, 1.

11 *RIC* I^2 *Cal.* 57; *HCC* I *Cal.* 37.

12 There are mentions of Germanicus recovering the eagles in Tacitus (*Ann.* 1, 60, 3; 2, 25, 1–2), Cassius Dio (57, 18, 1) and the *TS* (fr. I, 13–14).

13 Another interpretation exists, which suggests the scene is Tiberius handing an image of Victory to Augustus seated on a *sella curulis*. See Vout 2013, 69.

14 Schrömbges 1986, 186–187; Mlasowsky 1996, 337–338; Rose 1997, 24; Zanker 1999, 234–235.

Fig. 15. Dupondius, Rome, Caligula's times (?). Obverse: a depiction of Germanicus in the triumphal quadriga wearing a military cloak (*paludamentum*), holding a *sceptrum* in his left hand; legend: GERMANICUS CAESAR. Reverse: a depiction of Germanicus in armour with an eagle (*aquila*) in his left hand; legend: SIGNIS RECEPT DEVICTIS GERM SC (*RIC* I² *Cal.* 57).

Shortly after Germanicus' return from Germania, before the end of AD 17, he was sent on a new mission to the East and granted special powers. By decree of the Senate, additionally confirmed by the people, he gained an *imperium proconsulare* which was *maius* in relation to the powers of other governors and covered all the eastern provinces (*transmarinae provinciae*)[15]. From the *Senatus Consultum de Cn. Pisone patre*, however, we know it had to be *minus* compared to Tiberius'[16]. Other than inspecting the eastern provinces, the aim of the

15 Vell. Pat. 2, 129, 3; Joseph. *AJ* 18, 54; Tac. *Ann.* 2, 43, 1; 3, 12, 1; Suet. *Calig.* 1, 2; *TS* fr. I, 15; *SCPP* ll. 30–36. For information on the extent and nature of Germanicus' *imperium*, see Weingärtner 1969, 33–46; Hennig 1972, 349–359; Lebek 1991b, 103–124; Hurlet 1997, 181–197; Girardet 2000, 219–227; Sawiński 2007, 223–224.

16 *SCPP* ll. 35–36: *dum in omni re maius imperium Ti. Caesari Aug(usto) quam Germanico Caesari esset.*

Fig. 16. The so-called Sword of Tiberius, after AD 16. A detail featuring Tiberius enthroned, with a commander (probably Germanicus) handing his Victory to him.

mission was to solve the Armenian-Parthian problem. Just as it had been for Gaius Caesar, Germanicus' trip to the East was a great occasion to introduce a major candidate for the succession to the inhabitants of those provinces[17]. After reaching Greece early in AD 18, Germanicus assumed his second consulship, an event which gained extra splendour from the fact that Tiberius became the other consul. Although the princeps only held the office for a month, it was still

17 For a discussion of Germanicus' eastern mission, see e.g. Koestermann 1958, 331–375; Pani 1987, 1–23; Hurlet 1997, 198–208; Rivière 2016, 277–338.

certainly a great honour for Germanicus[18]. Nonetheless, Thomas E. Wiedemann goes too far when he claims in that way the emperor clearly designated him as his successor[19]. Regulating the situation in Armenia by setting a pro-Roman ruler on the throne brought Germanicus further honours. Tacitus tells us that in AD 19 the Senate voted for him to be awarded an ovation for this and for an honorific arch to be constructed near the temple of Mars Ultor in the Forum of Augustus[20].

Unlike his adoptive brother, Drusus the Younger only ascended to his first important public offices after Tiberius came into power. As I have indicated above, during Augustus' principate he had held no military commands and his only office had been a quaestorship. Augustus had favoured Germanicus, because he chose him for Tiberius' future successor. In AD 15, Drusus assumed his first consulship[21]. From Tacitus and Cassius Dio we know that in this year he put on gladiatorial games for the inhabitants of Rome, in both his own name and that of Germanicus[22]. The purpose of such undertakings was to win both prospective successors the affections of the Roman plebs. Two years later, Drusus received his first command, in Illyria[23], the scope of which probably also included Raetia, Noricum and Pannonia, where he was to consolidate Roman influence and have control over the situation in neighbouring Germania. In all likelihood he was granted an *imperium proconsulare* in connection with that task[24]. Tacitus says one of Tiberius' main reasons for dispatching his son to the Danube front was his concern that Drusus should gain military experience and support of the army there[25]. In AD 19, Drusus gained the right to hold an ovation for his achievements in Illyria, just as Germanicus did. The Senate also decided to have an honorific arch built for him near the monument that was decreed in honour of his brother at the same time[26].

The question arises which of his sons Tiberius intended to succeed him in the future. Tacitus says the issue resulted in two rival factions coming

---

18 Tac. *Ann.* 2, 53, 1; Degrassi 1952, 8; Schrömbges 1986, 163; Kienast 1996, 78; 80.

19 Wiedemann 2008, 210. Namely I am assuming that while Germanicus was alive, Tiberius did not designate either son as his successor. More on this below.

20 Tac. *Ann.* 2, 64, 1. For information on the arch, see Ganzert 1997, 193–206; Sawiński 2014, 125.

21 Tac. *Ann.* 1, 14, 3; 55, 1; Degrassi 1952, 7; Kienast 1996, 82.

22 Tac. *Ann.* 1, 76, 3; Cass. Dio 57, 14, 3. See also Rogers 1943, 100, 115.

23 On that campaign, see Shaw 1990, 172–199, among others.

24 See Kienast 1996, 82; Levick 1999, 130; Sawiński 2005, 36; 76.

25 Tac. *Ann.* 2, 44, 1.

26 Tac. *Ann.* 2, 64, 1. For the arch, see Sawiński 2014, 125–126.

into being at the imperial court, one supporting Germanicus and the other, Drusus. According to Tacitus, the princeps tended to prefer his natural son, resenting Germanicus, who in turn had the support of the Roman plebs for that reason[27]. Considering the blood-relation between Tiberius and Drusus, this attitude of the princeps might seem comprehensible, but taking into account the *cursus honorum* of Tiberius' two sons during the early years of his principate, we have no grounds for claiming that the emperor did actually favour Drusus as his future successor. What is more, it is possible to establish with certainty that Germanicus won more prestigious honours during this time, such as a triumph or the extraordinary *imperium* in the East. On that basis, Schrömbges deduces that the internal hierarchy of the *domus Augusta* and the succession order set up by the adoptions of AD 4 remained unchanged at the beginning of Tiberius' reign. He believes the princeps stuck to Augustus' dynastic policy, endorsing Germanicus as his future successor[28], but in my opinion his view is debatable. Granted, Germanicus' advancement was faster than that of Drusus, and more impressive. However, it would seem that Drusus' inexperience suffices to explain that fact; Tiberius' younger son was not sufficiently prepared to undertake more responsible tasks. As Tacitus writes, this was the reason the emperor decided to entrust the eastern mission to Germanicus[29], and so I am inclined to accept his opinion that while Germanicus was alive, Tiberius had not unequivocally decided which of his sons would succeed him[30].

The notion that the brothers had the same standing in the *domus Augusta* during Tiberius' reign and were treated as equal candidates to the succession is borne out by coin series featuring them and statuary groups erected in their honour. One illustration is provided by the asses minted in the Spanish provinces (in Tarraco and Italica), dated to AD 14–19. On the obverse of one of the emissions, we see Tiberius' head and the legend TI CAESAR DIVI AUG F PONT MAX IMP; on the reverse, Germanicus' and Drusus' heads facing each other with the legend CUT DRUSUS GERMANICUS CAESARES. The other series has Tiberius' face on the obverse, the legend being IMP TI CAESAR AUGUSTUS PON MAX. On the reverse, Germanicus and Drusus are shown as armoured commanders with spears in their right hands, and the legend is

27 Tac. *Ann.* 2, 43, 5–6.

28 Schrömbges 1986, 161–162; 168; so Seager 2013, 57.

29 Tac. *Ann.* 2, 43, 1.

30 Tac. *Ann.* 3, 56, 3.

GERMANICUS CAESAR DRUSUS CAESAR[31]. Mlasowsky supposes the coins from Italica may have alluded to the military successes of the two brothers in Germania and Pannonia; he also observes that the two series make use of an iconographic pattern applied earlier, on the coins Spanish mints produced in honour of Gaius and Lucius Caesar[32].

It ought to be stressed here we have no official emissions, as they are called, from Tiberius' principate dedicated to Germanicus[33], and in Drusus' case they only appear in AD 22[34]. Mlasowsky believes that could have resulted from Tiberius concentrating more on strengthening his position as the new princeps and consolidating his influence in the early years of his rule, rather than on strongly presenting and endorsing his possible successor[35], but he is utterly unconvincing. As the first official coins bearing the image of the successor designate were only minted in AD 22, we would have to assume the preparatory work took Tiberius nearly nine years. Now, I do not think the princeps could have needed that much time to consolidate his reign, especially as his succession had been prepared before Augustus' death; rather, I think this was a consequence of Tiberius not having resolved which son would succeed him until Germanicus' death. Therefore, there was also no need to mint official emissions presenting one of them as the successor. It is no accident that images of Drusus the Younger only make an appearance on this category of coins after he was publicly designated as successor[36]. One can see here an analogy to Tiberius himself, whose portrait and titulature only made it onto official coins after Augustus designated him[37].

Many honorific statues dedicated to both brothers were constructed throughout the Empire, as had been the case with Gaius and Lucius Caesar.

---

31 *RPC* I 68; 232; Mlasowsky 1996, 331–333. Emissions dedicated to Tiberius' sons were also minted in the East. See e.g. *RPC* I 2367; 2992.

32 Mlasowsky 1996, 332–333.

33 The first official emissions depicting Germanicus were only minted after his death, under Caligula. The aforementioned dupondii commemorating his victories on the Rhine and the related triumph may serve as an example. While the editors of the first edition of the *RIC* (I p. 101; p. 108 no. 36) connected the production of those coins to Tiberius, in the revised edition of the corpus they are already classified as minted during Caligula's reign (*RIC* I^2 *Cal.* 57). Their dating is similar in *HCC* I *Cal.* 37, among other sources.

34 See below.

35 Mlasowsky 1996, 334.

36 See Meise 1966, 16.

37 See above.

In the East, we know of such foundations in Olympia, Palmyra and Lindos on Rhodes, among other places. In Olympia, the statues of Germanicus and Drusus were raised by decree of the local authorities, as we learn from the extant dedicatory inscription. The brothers were celebrated on it as *euergetai*. In Rose's opinion, the statuary group in question may have commemorated Germanicus' participation in the famous Olympian games of AD 17[38]. Unfortunately, we have no data on where the statues stood.

In Palmyra, statues of Germanicus and Drusus were placed next to a statue of Tiberius, first in the courtyard of the local temple to Bel, from which they were later moved to the cella. That statuary cycle was funded by Minucius Horatius Rufus, the legate of *legio X Fretensis*, one of the legions stationed in Syria[39].

In Lindos, the statues of the brothers were put next to those of Tiberius and the godlike Augustus on the Acropolis there. Just like the two emperors, present and deceased, they were both commemorated as *euergetai*. From the preserved dedicatory inscription we know the whole group was erected by decree of the assembly of Lindos[40].

All the foundations discussed above have been linked to Germanicus' mission to the East, but it should be noted that the honours granted him by the inhabitants of those provinces in each case provided the impulse to honour Drusus in the same way, even though he had never visited those parts. That is quite understandable, seeing how he had the same status within the *domus Augusta* and the same right to imperial succession. Under the circumstances, only honouring Germanicus would have been a major *faux pas*, which the local authorities must have been fully aware of. A clear analogy can be seen here with the earlier honorifics for Gaius and Lucius Caesar as Augustus' intended successors[41].

38 Rose 1997, 25; 146–147 (no. 79). Still, such a terse statement might call for some commentary, since it appears to imply Germanicus participated in those games as a spectator or contestant. However, we know that was not possible; Tacitus (*Ann.* 2, 53, 1) indicates quite clearly he only appeared in Greece early in AD 18, having first visited Drusus in Dalmatia. See also Halfmann (1986, 168–169). Even though an inscription from Olympia funded by M. Antonius Pisanus (*IvO* 221) lists Germanicus as the winner in a quadriga race during the Olympic Games of AD 17, it absolutely does not follow that he took an active part in that competition or was even present in the audience: according to the Olympic standards, victory in contests of that kind fell to the owner of the team rather than the charioteer. See Miller 2006, 77.

39 Rose 1997, 189 (no. 130); Boschung 2002, 108.

40 Rose 1997, 154–155 (no. 89).

41 See above.

In the West, an interesting statuary group dedicated to Tiberius' sons was erected in Mediolanum Santonum in Gaul. In it, the statues of Germanicus and Drusus flanked the statue of Tiberius. Rose supposes they were the decoration of an arch which acted as a gate leading onto a bridge. The cycle was funded by Gaius Julius Rufus, a priest in the cult of Roma and Augustus in Lugdunum, and the sculptures are dated to AD 18–19[42].

Some scholars suppose Germanicus and Drusus also received the honorary title of *princeps iuventutis*, which was from Augustus' day on the sole privilege of prospective successors[43], but this is all guesswork. Unlike in the case of Gaius and Lucius Caesar, where epigraphic, numismatic and literary sources clearly attest to them receiving that honour, for Tiberius' sons we have no certain evidence for that[44]. I suspect that if Germanicus and Drusus had been awarded that prestigious title, the fact would have been noted in inscriptions dedicated to them and on coins[45].

Germanicus' unexpected death during his stay in Syria in AD 19 made Drusus first in line to the succession[46]. In the text of the *Senatus Consultum de Cn. Pisone patre*, we read the servile Senate consoled Tiberius after his death and expressed the hope that Drusus, now the only successor, would enjoy special

---

42 Rose 1997, 130 (no. 56); Boschung 2002, 151.

43 See Meise 1966, 17–18; Schrömbges 1986, 169; Shaw 1990, 64–66; Lebek 1993, 105 note 35; Kienast 1996, 80. Bellemore (2013, 81 note 12) supposes they were granted the title already in AD 9, while Rivière (2016, 70) assumes Germanicus received it as early as AD 4, shortly after his adoption by Tiberius. *Contra* Lott 2012, 14.

44 Ovid (*Ponto*, 2, 5, 41) does call Germanicus *iuvenum princeps*, but that is probably mere *licentia poetica*. I suspect he was influenced by the case of Gaius and Lucius Caesar, who had received the same title before formally as Augustus' prospective successors. Considering Germanicus was widely perceived as a major candidate to succession after Tiberius, Ovid may have simply thought he held that high prestige title as well.

45 In this case, as in a few others, the *ex silentio* reasoning would seem solid to me, since for Gaius and Lucius Caesar, Nero, and later Titus and Domitian the title does feature on coins dedicated to them. See e.g. *RIC* I² *Aug*. 205–207; *Claud*. 75, 78; *RIC* II *Vesp*. 23–27.

46 *TS*. fr. I, 35–38; Tac. *Ann*. 2, 83, 2; Suet. *Calig*. 1, 2. The circumstances of Germanicus' death are not completely clear. Ancient authors suggest he was poisoned at the orders of the then governor of Syria, Gnaeus Calpurnius Piso, who supposedly acted at Tiberius' instigation. See Tac. *Ann*. 2, 69–72; Suet. *Tib*. 52, 3; *Calig*. 2; Cass. Dio 57, 18, 10. Of course we are unable to ultimately discern the truth of the matter, but the reports on the emperor's part in the assassination seem unreliable. Whatever the facts of the matter, Piso was made the scapegoat of the whole case and officially charged with insubordination to a superior, insulting a member of the reigning dynasty and

protection of the gods, since the future of the state depended on him[47]. Soon after Germanicus died—Tacitus says the mourning period had not long ended—Drusus' wife Livilla gave birth to twins, Tiberius Julius Caesar and Germanicus Julius Caesar. Tacitus reports that this event was widely seen as weakening the *domus Germanici*[48], and there can be no doubt his comment is correct. The birth of Drusus' sons meant an important change in the order of succession, involving pushing Germanicus' sons into the background as possible successors. At that point, Drusus was first in line to succeed Tiberius, followed by his sons, and only then by the descendants of Germanicus. Drusus' *cursus honorum* after AD 19 and the way his public image was shaped both confirm this. In 20 he held an ovation, which had been granted to him one year earlier for his successes in Illyria[49], and in the following year he held his second consulship. His colleague in the office was Tiberius, who however resigned from the function after three months so that Drusus could the better continue gaining experience administering the state as the sole consul[50]. Robert Rogers assumes that holding a joint consulship with the emperor meant Drusus was thereby officially designated his successor[51], but I have to disagree; I believe this only happened one year later, when Drusus was awarded tribunician powers. According to Cassius Dio, the fact the other consul was the princeps was commonly considered a bad sign for Drusus, since all the men with whom Tiberius had shared consulships before, that is P. Quinctilius Varus, Cn. Calpurnius Piso and Germanicus, had died in dramatic circumstances[52].

---

contributing to his death. Rather than wait for the trial to end, he committed suicide. There is an extensive account of Piso's trial in the text of the *SCPP* (ll. 23–125) and in Tacitus (*Ann.* 3, 12–18). The trial has also been the subject of many penetrating inquiries by modern scholars. See primarily Eck, Caballos, Fernandéz 1996, passim; Eck 1997, 128–145; Griffin 1997, 249–263; Lebek 1999, 183–211; Talbert 1999, 89–97.

47 *SCPP* ll. 125–132. See also Seager 2013, 51, 56.

48 Tac. *Ann.* 2, 84, 1–2; Kienast 1996, 83. For the date of birth of Drusus' sons, see Shaw 1990, 214–216.

49 Tac. *Ann.* 3, 11, 1; 19, 3; *CIL* XIV 244; Rogers 1943, 125; Sawiński 2005, 91. Germanicus was granted that honour as well at the same time (see above), but never held the ovation, as he died before it could happen. See *TS.* fr. I, 17–18.

50 Tac. *Ann.* 3, 31, 1–2; Suet. *Tib.* 26, 2; Rogers 1943, 126–127; Degrassi 1952, 8; Kienast 1996, 78; 82.

51 Rogers 1943, 130.

52 Cass. Dio 57, 20, 1–2.

Drusus' career doubtless reached its crowning point when the Senate granted him the *tribunicia potestas* in AD 22[53]. The importance of that event for his standing in the *domus Augusta* is indicated by Tacitus' words:

> Tiberius [...] mittit litteras ad senatum quis potestatem tribuniciam Druso petebat. id summi fastigii vocabulum Augustus repperit, ne regis aut dictatoris nomen adsumeret ac tamen appellatione aliqua cetera imperia praemineret. Marcum deinde Agrippam socium eius potestatis, quo defuncto Tiberium Neronem delegit ne successor in incerto foret. sic cohiberi pravas aliorum spes rebatur; simul modestiae Neronis et suae magnitudini fidebat. quo tunc exemplo Tiberius Drusum summae rei admovit, cum incolumi Germanico integrum inter duos iudicium tenuisset. sed principio litterarum veneratus deos ut consilia sua rei publicae prosperarent, modica de moribus adulescentis neque in falsum aucta rettulit. esse illi coniugem et tres liberos eamque aetatem qua ipse quondam a divo Augusto ad capessendum hoc munus vocatus sit. neque nunc propere sed per octo annos capto experimento, compressis seditionibus, compositis bellis, triumphalem et bis consulem noti laboris participem sumi[54].

> Tiberius [...] sent a letter to the senate desiring the tribunician power for Drusus. This phrase for the supreme dignity was discovered by Augustus; who was reluctant to take the style of king or dictator, yet desirous of some title indicating his pre-eminence over all other authorities. Later, he selected Marcus Agrippa as his partner in that power, then, on Agrippa's decease, Tiberius Nero; his object being to leave the succession in no doubt. In this way, he considered, he would stifle the misconceived hopes of other aspirants; while, at the same time, he had faith in Nero's self-restraint and in his own greatness. In accordance with this precedent, Tiberius then placed Drusus on the threshold of the empire, although in Germanicus' lifetime he had held his judgment suspended between the pair. Now, however, after opening his letter with a prayer that Heaven would prospect his counsels to the good of the realm, he devoted a few sentences, free from false embellishments, to the character of the youth — "He had a wife and three children; and he had reached the age at which, formerly, he himself had been called by the deified Augustus to undertake the same charge. Nor was it in haste, but only after eight years of trial, after mutinies repressed, wars composed, one triumph, and two consulates, that he was now admitted to share a task already familiar"[55].

To Tacitus, granting Drusus those powers was tantamount to officially designating him Tiberius' successor. Importantly, the princeps only took that decision after Germanicus' death. Also from Tacitus we learn that Tiberius recommended his son to the Senate, as was appropriate, justifying the grant of *tribunicia potestas* with his experience in political and military matters. The passage quoted above

53 Rogers 1943, 130–131; Meise 1966, 15–16; Schrömbges 1986, 166; Levick 1999, 158.

54 Tac. *Ann.* 3, 56, 1–4.

55 Translated by C. H. Moore (Loeb Classical Library, 249).

means the fact that Drusus had male issue was another important reason he had received those powers, a fact of considerable importance in the context of his prospective succession, as it guaranteed the dynasty would be stable for at least two more generations[56]. One can agree with Kornemann that the grant of *tribunicia potestas* also made Drusus legally the emperor's co-regent, except that unlike Tiberius he did not have an *imperium maius*, but it is difficult to accept Kornemann's claim that Drusus' ascension to the rank of Tiberius' *collega imperii* was synonymous with introducing a double principate. The scholar rests his claim mostly on Tacitus' turn of phrase (*Ann.* 3, 57, 1), since he does refer to Tiberius' son as *princeps*[57]. However, this passage must not be taken literally; rather, I am convinced it is purely rhetorical. Furthermore, Tacitus' usage in this case is incongruent with Drusus' actual standing. His position still differed from that of Tiberius, both legally and, especially, in practice[58]. Consequently, claiming we can speak of "Doppelprinzipat" being in existence from AD 22 is in my opinion unjustified.

Unfortunately, we do not know exactly when Drusus began to perform his tribunician duties. Rogers and Kienast suppose the Senate conferred those powers on him in March or April, while Barrett assumes it took place precisely on 23rd April, but they all reject the possibility that it should have coincided with the renewal of Tiberius' *tribunicia potestas* in June or July of the same year[59].

Tacitus recounts the Senate decided to celebrate Drusus' designation as successor by raising temples, altars, honorific arches and statues. In addition, Quintus Haterius reportedly suggested the decree granting Drusus Tribunician powers be carved in the curia with golden letters, although it is hard to determine with certainty which of those honours were actually voted through, since we know Tiberius did not accept all the proposals of the Senate. Tacitus' account shows that he rejected Haterius' idea, at any rate[60].

Public designation of Drusus as successor was commemorated with numerous coin emissions, both official and provincial. As regards the so-called official minting, we possess series of dupondii, asses and sesterces produced in the mint in Rome and dated to AD 22–23. The obverse of the dupondii shows *Pietas* personified, *capite velato* and wearing a diadem, with the legend PIETAS; the

56 See Hurlet 1997, 534–535.

57 Kornemann 1930, 42–43.

58 Cf. also my comments on Agrippa's status during Augustus' principate; see above.

59 Rogers 1940, 457–459; id. 1943, 132; Kienast 1996, 82; Barrett 1989, 17.

60 Tac. *Ann.* 3, 57, 1–2; 59, 2; see also Rogers 1943, 131–132.

Fig. 17. Dupondius, Rome, AD 22–23. Obverse: an image of *Pietas capite velato* and wearing a diadem; legend: PIETAS. Reverse: legend: DRUSUS CAESAR TI AUGUSTI F TR POT ITER; centrally, the signature: SC (*RIC* I² *Tib.* 43).

reverse has the legend DRUSUS CAESAR TI AUGUSTI F TR POT ITER, with the signature SC in the centre[61]. (fig. 17) Ascribing to Drusus *pietas*, which since Augustus' day had been, alongside *virtus*, *iustitia* and *clementia*, one of the four cardinal virtues of a good princeps, highlighted his special suitability for taking over as emperor in the future[62]. The obverse of the asses has Drusus' face with the legend DRUSUS CAESAR TI AUG F DIVI AUG N, and there is PONTIF TRIBUN POTEST ITER on the reverse, accompanied by the signature SC[63]. (fig. 18) I ought to stress here that Drusus was the second designated successor whose image made it to the obverse of an official coin series; the first to receive the honour was Tiberius after he was designated Augustus' successor. That fact is important, since from the reign of the first princeps on, only the emperor had the right to display his face on the obverse of official coins. It is also worth noting that on the first of those emissions, Drusus was not merely depicted as the son of the current princeps (*Tiberii filius*), but also as a relative of Augustus (*Augusti nepos*), which was of major importance for the legitimization of his future

61 *RIC* I² *Tib.* 43; Mlasowsky 1996, 340; 342; Cox 2005, 256.

62 Those four virtues were listed on the famous shield (*clipeus virtutis*) dedicated to Augustus by the Senate and the people in 27 BC. See *Mon. Anc.* 34, 2; Schrömbges 1986, 167; Mlasowsky 1996, 344.

63 *RIC* I² *Tib.* 45; Mlasowsky 1996, 341–342.

Fig. 18. As, Rome, AD 22–23. Obverse: a portrait of Drusus; legend: DRUSUS CAESAR TI AUG F DIVI AUG N. Reverse: the legend, PONTIF TRIBUN POTEST ITER, and the signature, SC (*RIC* I[2] *Tib*. 45).

succession. The third group of coins connected to Drusus is made of sesterces, whose obverse has the heads of two boys facing each other, sticking out of horns of plenty (*cornucopiae*), with a caduceus in between, while the reverse contains the legend DRUSUS CAESAR TI AUG F DIVI AUG N PON TR POT II and, again, the signature SC[64]. (fig. 19) Meise assumes the obverse of that emission depicts Drusus' sons, Germanicus Caesar and Tiberius Caesar Gemellus, both born in AD 19, and he bases this identification on the fact that both boys are shown wearing the bulla, which Roman youth traditionally stopped wearing after they donned the *toga virilis*. Thus, he argues, the images cannot be of Germanicus' sons, since at the time that this series was minted they were already wearing their togas of manhood[65]. His interpretation is solid, but I believe there is a stronger argument to be made for the boys being Drusus' sons, namely the legend on the reverse, which invokes him directly. After all it is unlikely that an emission dedicated to Drusus should have contained the images of his nephews when he had sons of his own. The message expressed by the iconographic motifs

64 *RIC* I[2] *Tib*. 42; Sutherland 1951, 96; Mlasowsky 1996, 343.

65 Meise 1966, 7–8. That identification of characters on the obverse has been accepted by other scholars; see e.g. Lacey 1979, 34; Schrömbges 1986, 168; Mlasowsky 1996, 347; Rose 1997, 28; Severy 2003, 225–226.

Fig. 19. Sestertius, Rome, AD 22–23. Obverse: heads of two boys facing each other, emerging from horns of plenty (*cornucopiae*) with a caduceus between them. Reverse: the legend, DRUSUS CAESAR TI AUG F DIVI AUG N PONT TR POT II and the signature, SC (*RIC* I^2 *Tib*. 42).

on the sesterces in question is extremely interesting though. The horn of plenty and the caduceus stand for good fortune and prosperity; they were already in use with that meaning in Hellenistic and Republican minting. Here, they refer to the birth of the sons of the designated successor and grandsons of the ruling princeps, an event of considerable importance for preserving the stability and continuity of the dynasty, and so for the safety and power of the Empire. Thus the upcoming reign of Drusus and then his sons was presented as a harbinger of *felicitas temporum*. Interestingly, the iconographic pattern applied would be repeated in the minting of future emperors on the occasion of the births of new members of the reigning dynasty[66].

A similar message can be read from coins minted at the time in the provinces. Let emissions from Tarraco in Spain and from Cyrenaica serve as examples. The first of those shows Tiberius' head with the legend TI CAES AUG PONT MAX TRIB POT, while on the reverse one can see the facing heads of Drusus and Livia (the emperor's mother) and the legend is DRUSUS CAES TRIB POT IUL AUGUSTA[67]. The Cyrenaican coins, on the other hand, have Drusus' face on the obverse, with the legend ΔΡΟ(Υ)ΣΟΣ ΚΑΙΣΑΡ ΑΥΤΟ(Υ)ΣΤΟΥ ΥΙΟΣ and with

66 Meise 1966, 12–14; Mlasowsky 1996, 347–348; Hurlet 1997, 535.

67 *RPC* I 233; Mlasowsky 1996, 348–349.

a *lituus* and a *simpulum* placed next to him as the symbols of his priesthoods. The reverse has the heads of Drusus' sons, also facing each other, and the legend ΤΙΒ ΓΕΡ ΚΑΙΣΑΡΕΣ[68].

No doubt all the series discussed above reflect Tiberius' succession policy following Germanicus' death, and they indicate the princeps intended to be succeeded by Drusus, and eventually by Drusus' sons. This analysis of numismatic material demonstrates clearly that during the period in question, Germanicus' descendants were treated as secondary candidates to the succession[69].

Images found on various iconographic relics of the period correspond well with the message of the monetary emissions discussed above. One good example may be the image on a glass medal, a fragment of which was discovered in Xanten in Germany. The characters depicted there are identified as Drusus and his sons. Above the two boys' heads there is a six-pointed star, indicating that they were meant to be seen as the Dioscuri. From epigraphic evidence we know that they were worshipped as such in the East. For example, we have such evidence from Ephesus, where the existence is attested of a priest of Tiberius Caesar and Germanicus Caesar as the new Dioscuri (νέων Διοσκόρων Δρούσου Καίσαρος υἱῶν). The analogy is clearly to how Gaius and Lucius Caesar had been honoured before, and Germanicus and Drusus the Younger after them, likewise identified with the Dioscuri, clearly demonstrating the twins were seen as future successors[70].

Drusus and his sons are also seen in the characters depicted on *phalerae*, the military decorations which played an important role in endorsing members of the imperial family, and prospective successors in particular, in military circles. Three types of such medals discovered in Germania are dated to Tiberius' reign, specifically to the years 19–23. The first of those, type A, shows the bust of a man in armour, whereas type B has the same bust in between the heads of two children, and type C has three children instead. (fig. 20) Following Andreas Alföldi's identification, Meise thinks all three types show Drusus the Younger, with his sons added in type B and then his daughter Julia in type C[71], although not all scholars fully agree. In type C, some see the images of Germanicus and three of

68 *RPC* I 946–947.

69 See Meise 1966, 17.

70 Meise 1966, 17–18; Rose 1997, 28; 175–176 (no. 116).

71 Meise 1966, 18–19.

Fig. 20. *Phalerae* with a putative image of Germanicus with his children, Kunsthistorisches Museum, Vienna.

his children[72], while others believe them to be depictions of emperor Claudius with his son Britannicus and his daughters[73], but of course the problem cannot be ultimately solved and any proposed answers may be at best hypothetical.

Drusus' unexpected death in September of 23, which the ancient authors agree was caused by a poisoning orchestrated by his wife Livilla and the influential Praetorian prefect Sejanus, destroyed Tiberius' succession plans[74]. Shortly afterwards one of the twins, Germanicus Julius Caesar, died as well[75]. As Drusus' other son was only four, Tiberius had to look for a new candidate to succession.

2.1.2 Posthumous Honours

The early deaths of both of Tiberius' sons provided the Senate, the equites, the Roman plebs and the inhabitants of the provinces with a good opportunity to demonstrate their loyalty to the reigning dynasty, which found expression in the

72 See e.g. Rose 1997, 24, who accepts Alföldi's identification of the characters shown in type B. See Rose 1997 (Plate 18).

73 So e.g. Boschung 1987, 248–251.

74 Tac. *Ann.* 4, 8, 1–2; Suet. *Tib.* 62, 1; Cass. Dio 57, 22, 1–2; Rogers 1943, 145; Kienast 1996, 82; Levick 1999, 158; 161.

75 Vell. Pat. 2, 130, 3; Tac. *Ann.* 4, 15, 1; Kienast 1996, 83.

many prestigious posthumous honours conferred on the deceased. We know the Senate's first response to the news of Germanicus' demise was instituting public mourning (*iustitium*), which according to the *Fasti Ostienses* was declared on 8th December AD 19, and was to remain continuously in force until Germanicus' bones were laid to rest in the Mausoleum of Augustus. During the mourning, all official work was suspended, with temples and public baths closed, and all celebrations forbidden[76].

Some other members of the imperial family had died away from Rome and then their bodies were transported to the capital for the funeral ceremony, but the first part of Germanicus' funeral took place in Antioch. The reason for this was probably the climate in the East. The hot weather prevalent in Syria in October (Germanicus died on 10th October) made it necessary to burn the corpse quickly to stop it from decomposing. From the sources we know the funeral was not overly ostentatious. The corpse was displayed publicly in the local forum and then cremated[77]. Germanicus' remains were subsequently carried by ship to Brundisium. Tiberius dispatched two Praetorian cohorts there to serve as the escort for the conduct on its way to Rome. During the procession to the city, the urn holding the bones was alternately carried by military tribunes and centurions, and the conduct was preceded by lictors, who held their *fasces* pointed at the ground as a sign of mourning. The inhabitants of the Italian towns it passed through made funeral sacrifices to Germanicus. In Tarracina it was joined by Drusus the Younger, by the future emperor Claudius, and by Germanicus' children. They all accompanied it to Rome, where it was solemnly greeted by the Senate and consuls[78]. The ceremony of laying the bones in the Mausoleum took place towards the end of March of AD 20. Soldiers in full armour stood guard, officials attended without the insignia of their power and the plebs were present, divided by tribe[79]. In his account of the burial, Tacitus points out how modest it was. He writes that the ceremony differed fundamentally from those held earlier for other members of the *domus Augusta*. To expose the contrast, he adduces the

---

76 *Fasti Ostienses* (Bargagli–Grosso 1997, 23); Tac. *Ann.* 3, 6–7; *TH* ll. 54–55; Weinstock 1966, 892–893; Versnel 1980, 541–618; Fraschetti 1988, 867–889; Galsterer 2000, 174, 182; Lott 2012, 252. From Tacitus (*Ann.* 2, 82, 3) we learn that even before public mourning was declared, the Roman plebs suspended all their activities and left the public spaces, locking themselves indoors. The people's spontaneous reaction to Germanicus' death is also mentioned by Suetonius (*Calig.* 6, 1–2).

77 Tac. *Ann.* 2, 73, 1–4; Cass. Dio 57, 18, 9; *TS* fr. I, 35–36.

78 Tac. *Ann.* 3, 1–2.

79 Tac. *Ann.* 3, 4, 1.

example of Drusus the Elder, stressing the fact that in Germanicus' case, there were no songs or laudatory speeches and no images of the dead man before the bier either. In the historian's opinion, that was proof of Tiberius' insincerity and dislike of his adoptive son[80]. Tacitus' judgement is certainly biased and requires critical verification, since from the *Tabula Siarensis* we know Tiberius read the verse (*carmen*) in a Senate session in which he praised Germanicus' virtues and service to the state. Its text was then supposedly carved in bronze and displayed in public[81]. It seems the *carmen* presented by the emperor before the Senate may have been a replacement for a *laudatio funebris*, traditionally given during public funerals[82]. The *libellus* Drusus read in the Senate in his brother's honour must have carried a similar message[83], and it is possible it played the role of a second funeral speech, traditionally given during the funeral rites of the members of the imperial family, beginning with Octavia's *funus*[84]. It was certainly somewhat novel that those eulogies were read in the Senate rather than in the Forum Romanum, as was practised until then. With that in mind, the lack of *laudationes* during the Mausoleum ceremony stressed by Tacitus seems understandable. Omission of certain elements encountered in the funerals of other members of the imperial family may also be explained by the fact that Germanicus' last rites were not strictly speaking a full *funus publicum*. A major part of his funeral, during which the body was displayed publicly and then burnt, had taken place in Antioch, and Tacitus mentions that a few laudatory speeches had been given there[85]. Thus, the ceremony of laying Germanicus' bones in the Mausoleum may well have differed in nature from the earlier funeral rites of Marcellus, Agrippa, Drusus the Elder or Lucius Caesar[86], since the model of burying a member of the imperial family established by then did not fit Germanicus' circumstances, with his corpse already cremated. The same problem had come up before with Gaius Caesar, whose body had also probably been cremated away from Rome[87]. In this context, the differences outlined above seem reasonable and should not be seen as evidence for Tiberius' ill will.

---

80 Tac. *Ann.* 3, 5, 1–2.

81 *TS* fr. II, col. b, 11–17. See also Flower 1996, 248–250.

82 See Schillinger-Häfele 1988, 73–81; Wesch-Klein 1993, 23; Lott 2012, 230.

83 *TS* fr. II, col. b, 18–19; Schillinger-Häfele 1988, 80.

84 See Cass. Dio 54, 35, 4–5.

85 Tac. *Ann.* 2, 73, 1. Perhaps one of them by Nero Caesar, Germanicus' eldest son, provided of course he was in Antioch at the time.

86 See Wesch-Klein 1993, 23.

87 See above.

Detailed information on the posthumous honours granted Germanicus by the Senate can be found in the *Tabula Siarensis*, the *Tabula Hebana* and Tacitus[88], although, as I have already indicated above, when working with the text of the *Tabula Siarensis* we largely rely on hypothetical reconstructions for the missing fragments.

Honorific arches (*iani*) were one extremely prestigious posthumous honour voted through by the Senate. They were to be constructed in Rome, in Syria and on the Rhine, that is, those places in the Empire which had a special connection to Germanicus' work[89].

The arch in Rome

Tabula Siarensis fr. I, ll. 9–21 (ed. Sánchez–Gutiérrez 1999, 52; 54)

9 Placere uti ianus marmoreus extrueretur in circo Flaminio pe[cunia publica, posi-]
10 tus ad eum locum, in quo statuae divo Augusto domuique Augus[tae publicae positae es-]
11 sent ab G(aio) Norbano Flacco, cum signis devictarum gentium in a[ngulis tituloque]
12 in fronte eius iani, senatum populumque Romanum id monum[entum aeternae dedi-]
13 casse memoriae Germanici Caesaris, cum i{i}s Germanis bello superatis et [deinceps]
14 a Gallia summotis receptisque signis militaribus et vindicata fraud[ulenta clade]
15 exercitus p(opuli) R(omani), ordinato statu Galliarum, proco(n)s(ul) missus in transmarinas pro[vincias]
16 in conformandis iis regnisque eiusdem tractus ex mandatis Ti(berii) Caesaris Au[g(usti), dato re-]
17 ge Armeniae, non parcens labori suo, priusquam decreto senatus [ovans urbem ingre-]
18 deretur, ob rem p(ublicam) mortem obisset; supraque eum ianum statua Ger[manici Caesaris po-]
19 neretur in curru triumphali et circa latera eius statuae D[rusi Germanici patris ei-]
20 us, naturalis fratris Ti(berii) Caesaris Aug(usti) et Antoniae matris ei[us et Agrippinae uxoris et Li-]
21 viae sororis et Ti(berii) Germanici fratris eius et filiorum et f[iliarum eius;]

It was pleasing that a marble arch should be built at public expense in the circus Flaminius, set at that place where the statues for the divine Augustus and the statues for the *domus Augusta* had been set up at public expense by Gaius Norbanus Flaccus, decorated with representation of conquered peoples in the corners and with an inscription on the front of the arch skating that the senate and people of Rome had dedicated this monument to the eternal memory of Germanicus Caesar because, after he had

88 The relevant *senatus consulta* on honouring Germanicus were passed at two different sessions, on 16th and 19th December. Eventually they were promulgated as a single *senatus consultum* though. See *TS* fr. II, col. b, 20–31; Lebek 1992, 66–77; Heinemann 2007, 79.

89 Tac. *Ann.* 2, 83, 2; *TS* fr. I, 9; 22; 26.

> conquered the Germans in war and driven them out from Gaul and recovered the lost military standards and avenged the dishonest defeat of an army of the Roman people and arranged the affairs of the Gauls, and after he had then been sent as proconsul to the overseas provinces to also arrange them and the kingdoms of that same area according to the orders of Tiberius Caesar Augustus, and after he installed a new king of Armenia, not sparing in his own labor and before he could return to the city victorious be decree of the senate, he died on behalf of the state; and (they directed) that on top of this arch should be placed a statue of Germanicus Caesar in a triumphal chariot and that at his sides should be placed statues of his natural father Drusus Germanicus, brother of Tiberius Caesar Augustus, and of his mother Antonia and his wife Agrippina and his sister Livia and his brother Tiberius Germanicus and his sons and daughters[90].

The first of the *iani* dedicated to Germanicus was to be built *in circo Flaminio*[91], not an accidental location, since the traditional route of the triumphal processions passed through the Circus Flaminius[92]. This would mean the purpose of the monument was to commemorate Germanicus' triumph of AD 17. That district of Rome also contained a number of structures closely connected to the imperial family, such as the Porticus Octaviae or the statue group dedicated to Augustus and the *domus Augusta* by Gaius Norbanus Flaccus (consul in AD 15), mentioned in the *Tabula Siarensis*[93]. The Theatre of Marcellus, another structure built in honour of a member of the reigning family, was also located near the Circus Flaminius.

The text of the inscription informs us the attic of the arch was to hold a complex statuary group: a central statue of Germanicus in a triumphal quadriga, flanked by his parents Drusus and Antonia, his wife Agrippina, his brother Tiberius Germanicus (the later emperor Claudius), and his sons and daughters. In spite of certain allusions to Germanicus' triumph, such as depicting him in a quadriga or making use of representations of the conquered peoples, the decoration of the *ianus* only referred to it indirectly, since it also aimed to reinforce the image of a model family whose members ought to be imitated in the collective

---

90 Translated by Lott 2012, 89, 91.

91 On a marble third-century map of Rome (the *Forma Urbis Romae*), the monument is located between the Porticus Octaviae and the Theatre of Marcellus, a location generally accepted by historians. See Castagnoli 1984, 330–331; Lebek 1991a, 67 note 36; *LTUR*, 1, 1993, 94–95 (Rodríguez Almeida s.v. *Arcus Germanici in Circo Flaminio*); Zanker 1999, 150 (fig. 118).

92 For information on the route taken by triumphal processions, cf. esp. Coarelli 1988, 362–437; Beard 2007, 92–105, 335 (the map).

93 *TS* fr. I, 10–11. On the subject of that statuary group, see Flory 1996, 287–306; Severy 2003, 219–220.

consciousness[94]. In other words, Germanicus was depicted as an exemplary *pater familias*. With the numerous progeny depicted on the arch, he more than fulfilled the recommendations of Augustus' marital legislation. It was no accident that during public spectacles the emperor showcased Germanicus surrounded by his children, so as to encourage the people to follow in his footsteps[95]. A special part in the *domus Augusta* fell to women, which was why the arch was to bear the statues of Antonia the Younger, Agrippina the Elder and Livilla. As the wives and mothers of consecutive generations of successors, the latter two guaranteed the smooth transmission of imperial power within the ruling family.

As another important element, the decoration of the *ianus* included the *signa* of the peoples defeated as a result of Germanicus' campaign. Rose supposes these may have been both military standards and images of vanquished barbarians. They were probably displayed as part of a relief sculpture on the monument[96]. In addition, the arch bore an inscription listing Germanicus' achievements in Gaul, Germania and the East, that is, all his most important services to the state.

The arch in the East
Tabula Siarensis fr. I, ll. 22–26 (ed. Sánchez-Gutiérrez 1999, 54)

22 Alter ianus fieret in montis Amani iugo, quod est in [finibus provinciae Syriae, sive qui]
23 alius aptior locus Ti(berio) Caesari Aug(usto) principi nostro [videretur in iis regionibus quarum]
24 curam et tutelam Germanico Caesari ex auctori[tate huius ordinis ipse mandasset;]
25 item statua eius poneretur et titulus conve[niens rebus ab eo gestis fronti eius iani in-]
26 sculperetur.

and that a second arch should be built on the ridge of mount Amanus in Syria or in some other place, if any other location within the areas that he had assigned to the care and protection of Germanicus Caesar in accordance with the will of the senate should seem more appropriate to Tiberius Caesar Augustus our *princeps*; and likewise that a statue of him should be set up there and an inscription assembling the deeds of Germanicus Caesar should be inscribed on the front of the arch[97].

Another arch was to stand in the mountain range of Amanus on the border between Cilicia and Syria, or perhaps in some other place in the East related to Germanicus' actions. The Senate left the choice of the spot to the emperor. The monument was probably constructed in a pass on the main route from Cilicia

94 See Lebek 1991a, 67–68.
95 Suet. *Aug*. 34, 2.
96 Rose 1997, 110. Cf. also Castagnoli 1984, 331.
97 Translated by J. B. Lott 2012, 91.

to Syria, that is, on a busy road[98]. The sources contain no details regarding the decoration of that *ianus*; all we know is that a statue of Germanicus was to be put on top. Lebek supposes the commander was shown in a triumphal chariot, the same as on the Roman arch[99]. The eastern monument also had an inscription on it commemorating Germanicus' most important achievements. Perhaps, as Lott supposes, its contents was similar to those on the arch *in Circo Flaminio*[100], but since this *ianus* was in the Eastern part of the Empire, it was most likely in Greek[101].

The arch in Germania
Tabula Siarensis fr. I, ll. 26–34 (ed. Lott 2012, 90)

26 tertius ianus vel ap[ud ripam Rheni vel prope eum tumulum fieret]
27 quem Druso, fratri Ti(beri) Caesaris Aug(usti), pr[imo sua sponte excitare coepisset totus exerci-]
28 tus, deinde permissu divi Aug(usti) perf[ecisset, supraque eum ianum statua Germanici Cae-]
29 saris constitueretur recipientis[signa militaria a Germanis; et praeciperetur Gal-]
30 lis Germanisque qui citra Rhen[um incolerent, quorum civitates iussae essent ab divo]
31 Aug(usto) rem divinam ad tumulu[m Drusi facere ut eodem loco facerent publice alterum simi-]
32 le sacrificium parentant[es quotannis eo die quo Germanicus Caesar decessisset]
33 et cum esset in ea region[e, ubi is tumulus est, exercitus et hiberna ageret nata-]
34 li Germanici Caesar[is, is eo die decurreret per eum ianum qui ex hoc s(enatus) c(onsulto) factus esset;]

and that a third arch should be either placed on the bank of the Rhine or next to the burial mound which the whole army had first begun of its own accord to build for Drusus the brother of Tiberius Caesar Augustus and then had completed with the permission of the Divine Augustus; and that on this arch should be set a statue of Germanicus Caesar receiving back the military standards from the Germans; and that the Gauls and Germans who live on this side of the Rhine, whose communities had been ordered by the divine Augustus to conduct cult at the burial mound of Drusus, should be ordered to make a second similar public sacrifice, giving funeral offerings annually on that day on which Germanicus Caesar had died; and that when the army should be in the area of the burial mound of Drusus and be in winter quarters on the birthday of Germanicus

98 Lebek 1987, 140–141; Lott 2012, 221–222.
99 Lebek 1991a, 69.
100 Lott 2012, 222.
101 Lebek 1987, 142.

> Caesar, it should parade trough the arch constructed in accordance with this decree of the senate[102].

From Tacitus, we know that the third arch was to be built on the Rhine[103], although he does not specify where exactly. Unfortunately, the text of the *Tabula Siarensis* is badly damaged in the parts dealing with its placement and the rites held there, so that we are reduced to speculation on that matter. In the light of the reconstruction of that part of the text proposed by Lebek, which is generally accepted in scholarship, it was erected in what is today Mainz, near Drusus' cenotaph (the *tumulus Drusi*)[104] and presumably formed the entrance to the cult precinct centred on that symbolic tomb[105].

The arch was reportedly crowned with a statue of Germanicus taking the standards of legions back from the Germans. That decoration of the Rhine *ianus* was therefore primarily intended to glorify Germanicus and etch into the memories of posterity that thanks to his achievements it had been possible to wipe away the shame of Varus' defeat, restoring Rome's prestige in Germania. The arch commemorated one of Germanicus' most important successes on the Rhine, especially from the army's perspective: the loss of the standards was perceived as a dishonour, so recovering them had enormous psychological significance for the soldiers. Considering this aspect of the whole affair, it seems likely that an arch flaunting the triumph of Rome and humiliation of barbarians may have stood somewhere by the road which led from the legions' camp (Mainz-Kästrich) to Drusus' cenotaph, that is, in another spot that was widely frequented, particularly by the legionaries stationed there. That would have had considerable importance for strengthening the loyalty of the Rhine army to the imperial family and for improving the morale of the soldiers. Erecting the *ianus* near the *tumulus Drusi*, where representatives of Gaulish and Germanic tribes gathered yearly to sacrifice to Drusus and Germanicus, also helped reinforce the belief in Rome's omnipotence among the locals[106]. Although the *Tabula Siarensis* provides no information on a dedicatory inscription on the German *ianus*, we can be quite certain it existed. That assumption finds confirmation in Tacitus, who mentions that all three arches voted on by the Senate after Germanicus' death were to bear

---

102 Translated by J. B. Lott 2012, 91.

103 Tac. *Ann.* 2, 83, 2.

104 Lebek 1987, 147; Lebek 1989a, 57–62.

105 Bellen 1989, 78; Herz 2001, 106, 108.

106 On that subject, see esp. Bellen 1984, 385–396.

signs informing their reader of his accomplishments[107]. In any case, it is difficult to picture such a commemorative monument without an accompanying inscription[108].

From both the *Tabula Siarensis* and Tacitus' text, we also learn two sepulchral monuments were to be constructed to commemorate Germanicus in the province of Syria: one in the forum in Antioch, where his body had been cremated, and the other on the spot of his death (*Epidaphne*). It is supposed the former of those, called a *sepulchrum* by Tacitus, was a cenotaph similar to that built by Limyrians after Gaius Caesar's death; the other, referred to by Tacitus as a *tribunal*, possibly a monumental sarcophagus[109].

The Senate also took decisions on the proper celebration of the anniversary of Germanicus death (which fell on 10th October)[110]:

***Tabula Siarensis* fr. II, col. a, ll. 1–14 (ed. Sánchez-Gutiérrez 1999, 60–62)**

1 [...Utique a(nte) d(iem) VI id(us) Oct(obres) quotannis apud eam ara]m, quae es-
2 [set ante tumulum, quo ossa illata essent Germanici Caesaris publice i]nferiae Manibus
3 [eius mitterentur per magistros sodalium] Augustalium p[ullis] amictos togis, quibus eo-
4 [rum ius fasque esset habere e]o die sui coloris togam, eodem ritu sacricfici quo
5 [publice inferiae mitterentur] Manibus G(ai) et L(uci) Caesarum cippusque aeneus prope eum
6 [tumulum poneretur, inque eo hoc s(enatus)c(onsultum)] similiter incideretur ut ea s(enatus) c(onsulta) incisa essent quae
7 [in G(ai) et (Luci) Caesarum honorem facta] essent neve quid eo die rei seriae publice agere
8 [tur per magistratus p(opuli) R(omani eosve qui i(ure) d(icundo) p(raerunt) in] municipio aut colonia c(ivium) R(omanorum) aut Latinorum neve eo
9 [die quae convivia publica post] hac neve quae nuptiae c(ivium) R(omanorum) fierent aut sponsalia ne-

107 Tac. *Ann.* 2, 83, 2.

108 For more on arches posthumously granted Germanicus by the Senate, see Sawiński 2014, 126–133 (ibid. the essential literature).

109 Tac. *Ann.* 2, 83, 2; *TS* fr. I, 35–38. Unfortunately, the sections of the *Tabula Siarensis* which contained information on those structures are preserved in fragments. See Sánchez-Gutiérrez 1999, 164–178; Lott 2012, 223–224.

110 That date of Germanicus' death is listed in the *Fasti Antiates Ministrorum Domus Augustae* (Degrassi 1963, 209).

10 [ve quis pecuniam creditam ab alio] sumeret alive daret neve ludi fierent aut
11 [aliud quod spectaculum eo die e]deretur. (*vacat*) Utique ludi Augustales scaenici
12 [qui a(nte) d(iem) VI id(us) Oct(obres) --- antehac commit]ti solerent, ut a(nte) d(iem) V non(as) committerentur qua
13 [commissionis mutatione pridie] eum diem, quo Germanicus Caesar extinctus
14 [esset, celebraretur extremus] dies ludorum scaenicorum [...]

Annually on October 10 at that altar which is in front of the burial mound where the bones of Germanicus Caesar have been interred the officers of the Augustal Brotherhood, with those of them veiled in black togas that can legally and rightly wear on uncolored toga on that day, should publicly offer sacrifices to his shades in the same manner of sacrifice in which sacrifices are made publicly to the shades of Gaius and Lucius Caesar; and that a bronze marker should be placed near the burial mound and this senate decree inscribed on it just as the senate decrees passe in honor of Gaius and Lucius Caesar were inscribed; and that the magistrates of the Roman people and those who have jurisdiction in a town or colony of Roman citizens or of Latins should not conduct in public any important business on that day, nor should any public banquets be held on that day, nor should any marriages of Roman citizens nor betrothals happen, nor should anyone borrow money from another nor lend it, nor should any games happen nor any other sort of show be given on that day; and that the theatrical Augustal Games, which previously were held on October 10, should be begun on October 3 so that, because of this change of date, the last day of the theatrical shows should fall on the eve of the death of Germanicus [...][111].

***Tabula Hebana* ll. 57–61 (ed. Crawford 1996, 519–521)**

57 [(sextum) id(us) Oct(obres) quo die Germanicus Caes(ar) defun -]
58 ctus est templa deor(um) inmortalium quae in urbe Roma{m} prop{r}iusue urbem [Romam passus (mille) sunt erunt quot annis]
59 clausa sint idque ut ita fiat ii qui eas aedes tuendas redemptas habent h[abebunt curent; utiq(ue) eodem die magistri]
60 sodalium Augustalium qui quoq(ue) anno erunt inferias ante tumulu[m divi Augusti manibus Germanici Cae-]
61 saris mittendas curent [...].

and that annually on October 10, the day on which Germanicus Caesar died, the temples of the immortal gods which are, or will be, in the city of Rome or within one mile of the city should be closed, and those who have or will have the contracts for looking after these temples should see to it that this happen; and that on that same day the officers of the Augustan Brotherhood in office that year should see to it that funeral sacrifices are given to the shades of Germanicus Caesar in front of the tomb of the divine Augustus [...][112].

111 Translated by J. B. Lott 2012, 93.
112 Translated by J. B. Lott 2012, 113.

On that day, the members of the college of *sodales Augustales*, wearing mourning togas, were supposed to offer sacrifices *(inferiae)* to the Manes of Germanicus at a special altar raised in front of the Mausoleum of Augustus. All public speeches of Roman officials were cancelled throughout the Empire, and games were forbidden, as were theatre shows and public feasts. Roman citizens could not perform marriages or betrothals, and the *ludi Augustales,* regularly held from 5th till 12th October, were split in two. Beginning from AD 20, the first part was to last from 3rd October until 9th, ending on the eve of the anniversary of Germanicus' death, while part two, comprised of chariot races, was to take place on 12th October in the *Circus Maximus*[113]. Also in the *Tabula Hebana* we read on the successive anniversaries of Germanicus' death temples were to be closed in Rome and its vicinity[114]. Moreover, the *Tabula Siarensis* provides the information that an appropriate ceremony was to be held on the Rhine near Drusus' cenotaph, with representatives of Gaulish and German tribes settled on the Roman bank sacrificing to the deceased[115].

Statues were another way to posthumously honour Tiberius' dead son, and included some erected by the decision and at the cost of the people of Rome (the *plebs urbana*). Still, we do not know their exact number or locations, only that they depicted Germanicus in the triumphal robe and were supposedly placed in the most important places in Rome. The pedestal of each bore an inscription stating the statues had been dedicated by the *plebs urbana*[116]. In the temple of Concord (the *aedes Concordiae*), two ivory statues of Germanicus on horseback were to stand next to the images of Gaius and Lucius Caesar. They would later be displayed publicly on various occasions, including during the *ludi Victoriae Caesaris*[117].

Just as had been the case with Gaius and Lucius Caesar, Germanicus' name was included in the song of the Salii, one of the Roman religious sodalities. Five further voting centuries received his name, to go with the ten already bearing the names of Augustus' sons[118].

---

113 See Lebek 1988b, 59–71; Lebek 1990, 101; Sánchez–Gutiérrez 1999, 211–214; Lott 2012, 227.

114 *TH* ll. 57–59.

115 *TS* fr. I, 29–32. However, we cannot be certain whether the sacrifice was to be made on the anniversary of Germanicus death or birth. On that subject, see esp. Bellen 1984, 385–396; Lebek 1989a, 67–72; Sánchez–Gutiérrez 1999, 156–158; Herz 2001, 104–107.

116 *TS* fr. II, col. b, 7–10; Lott 2012, 229.

117 *TS* fr. II, col. c, 2–11. See Lebek 1988a, 256–265; Sánchez–Gutiérrez, 1999, 268–274.

118 See Lott 2012, 241–243.

Tabula Hebana **ll. 4–7 (ed. Crawford 1996, 519–521)**

4 utiq(ue) Sali carminibus suis nomen Germanici Caesa[ris pro ho-]
5 norifica memoria int<e>rponant, qui honos C(aio) quoq(ue) et L(ucio)Cae- sarib(us) fratr(ibus) Ti(beri) Caesaris Aug(usti) habitus est; [vacat]
6 utiq(ue) ad (decem) centur(ias) Caesarum quae de co(n)s(ulibus) pr(aetoribus) destinandis suffragium ferre solent adiciantur (quinque): centuri[ae que quae]
7 primae (decem) citabuntur C(ai) et L(uci) Caesar(um) appellentur, insequen<t>es (quinque) Germanici Caesaris

and that the Salian priests should include the name of Germanicus in their hymns for the sake of his honored memory, an honor which has also been observed for Gaius and Lucius Caesar, the brothers of Tiberius Caesar Augustus; and that to the ten centuries of Caesars which regularly cast a vote about destining consuls and praetors, five more should be added; and the first ten centuries which are called forward to vote should be called the centuries of Gaius and Lucius Caesar and the following five called those of Germanicus Caesar[119].

Moreover, the *Tabula Hebana* and Tacitus both say that during the *ludi Augustales*, in all theatres in Rome, among the chairs taken by the priests of the godlike Augustus empty *sellae curules* were to be set, decorated with oak-leaf wreaths, in memory of Germanicus having been a *flamen Augustalis* himself. Placing those chairs there emphasized his crucial role in that cult and highlighted his rank in it, superior to that of the other *sodales Augustales*[120]. The prestige of his priesthood may be indicated by the fact that after his death it was to be reserved only for members of the *gens Iulia*[121].

Tabula Hebana **ll. 50–52 (ed. Crawford 1996, 519–521)**

50 utiq(ue) ludis Augu[stalibus cum sedilia sodalium]
51 ponentur in theatris sellae curules Germanici Caesaris inter ea ponantur cu[m coronis querceis in memoriam]
52 eius sacerdoti [...]

and that during the Augustal Games, when benches of the Brotherhood are placed in the theaters, a curule chair of Germanicus Caesar with oak garlands should be placed among them in his remembrance [...][122].

119 Translated by J. B. Lott 2012, 107.

120 *TH* ll. 50–52; Tac. *Ann.* 2, 83, 1. See also Calabi 1954, 213–214; Weinstock 1957, 144–154; Lott 2012, 250–251.

121 Tac. *Ann.* 2, 83, 1; under Tiberius, that function was held by Drusus the Younger, and after his death, Nero Caesar, Germanicus' eldest son. See Sajkowski 2001, 41; 45–46.

122 Translated by J. B. Lott 2012, 113.

> Honores, ut quis amore in Germanicum aut ingenio validus, reperti decretique: ut nomen eius Saliari carmine caneretur; sedes curules sacerdotum Augustalium locis superque eas querceae coronae statuerentur [...][123].

> Affection and ingenuity vied in discovering and decreeing honours to Germanicus: his name was to be chanted in the Saliar Hymn; curule chairs surmounted by oaken crowns were to be set for him wherever the Augustal priests had right of place[...][124].

Several honours were also granted to Germanicus by the equites. During the solemn mounted parade which was primarily an important festival of equestrian youth, the riders now followed an image of Germanicus. Moreover, the seat row in Roman theatres where young equites sat was named after him[125].

This overview of Germanicus' posthumous honours proves that they did not differ all that much from those granted earlier to other deceased members of the imperial family, especially Gaius and Lucius Caesar; in fact, in some respect they were greater.

Drusus the Younger was later posthumously honoured in an equally spectacular way. From Cassius Dio and Tacitus we know his corpse was displayed in public on the rostra in the Forum Romanum. That is also where two *laudationes* were made, first by Tiberius in the name of the state, the other for the family by Nero Caesar, Drusus' son-in-law and Germanicus' eldest son[126]. The ceremony also drew splendour from a procession during which masks of the most outstanding ancestors of the Julio-Claudian family were displayed, as well as masks of certain legendary figures from Rome's past, such as the kings of Alba Longa, Aeneas or Romulus[127].

The large majority of Drusus' posthumous honours copied those conferred earlier on Germanicus, as is clearly indicated by Tacitus[128]; on that basis we can assume they included honorific arches as well. The assumption may be confirmed by the inscription which held the text of the *senatus consultum* passed after his death, fragments of which have been found in Rome[129]. Unfortunately, that part

123 Tac. *Ann.* 2, 83, 1.

124 Translated by C. H. Moore (Loeb Classical Library, 249).

125 Tac. *Ann.* 2, 83, 4; see Lebek 1993, 106–107.

126 Tac. *Ann.* 4, 12, 1; Cass. Dio 57, 22, 4a; in contrast to Tacitus, Dio (57, 22, 4) has Tiberius give the funeral speech in Drusus' honour in the Senate.

127 Tac. *Ann.* 4, 9, 2. See Flower 1996, 243; 253–254.

128 Tac. *Ann.* 4, 9, 2: "memoriae Drusi eadem quae in Germanicum decernuntur".

129 See Lebek 1989b, 83–84. Just as before in Germanicus' case, now the text of Drusus' honorific decree was probably engraved on bronze tablets placed around Rome and vital places in the Empire.

of the inscription which presumably contained information on the arches to be built for Drusus, has been mostly lost, meaning we are again forced to settle for guesswork. In Lebek's opinion, one of the arches was to be constructed in Rome and have Drusus' statue in a quadriga on top, with an inscription detailing his achievements on the attic[130]. Another such arch was likely erected in Illyria, that is, a region to which Drusus had been dispatched as an imperial envoy. According to Lebek's reconstruction, that monument was also to be crowned by Drusus' statue in a quadriga, with Tiberius' statue next to it and an inscription commemorating the dead man's deeds[131].

Tacitus also mentions that Drusus received many other honours which had not made an appearance with Germanicus[132]. Lebek supposes one of them was a gilt mounted statue funded by the equites, which was to be publicly displayed during the Lupercalia (that is, on 15th February). Just like the other honours granted Drusus and earlier Germanicus by the equestrian order, such as including their images in the mounted parade or naming certain rows of seats in Roman theatres after them, this one, too, was meant to stress the two successors' close connection to the *ordo equester*, and in particular to equestrian youth[133]. However, with the sources silent on the subject, it is impossible to determine what other honours Tacitus meant.

Germanicus and Drusus received posthumous honours in the provinces too. For an example, let us look to Lepcis Magna in Proconsular Africa, where Tiberius' sons were celebrated with a complex statuary group. The statues of both brothers in a triumphal quadriga were placed on a raised platform in front of the local temple to Augustus and Roma. On both their sides, there were statues of Augustus, Agrippina the Elder, Livilla, Antonia the Younger, Vipsania Agrippina and Claudius (the later princeps). (fig. 21) The composition was most likely modelled on the images decorating Germanicus' and Drusus' posthumous arches in Rome[134], so we can assume that the impulse for funding the monument lay in the decrees of the Senate on posthumous honours for the brothers, which were promulgated in all the major towns of the provinces. The statuary cycle was probably created shortly after Drusus' death[135].

---

130 Lebek 1989b, 89, 91.

131 Lebek 1989b, 86–90; Lebek 1991a, 54–55, 71.

132 Tac. *Ann.* 4, 9, 2.

133 Lebek 1993, 97–99.

134 See above.

135 On the subject of that statue group, see esp. Trillmich 1988b, 51–60; Rose 1997, 182–184 (no. 125); Boschung 2002, 14–18.

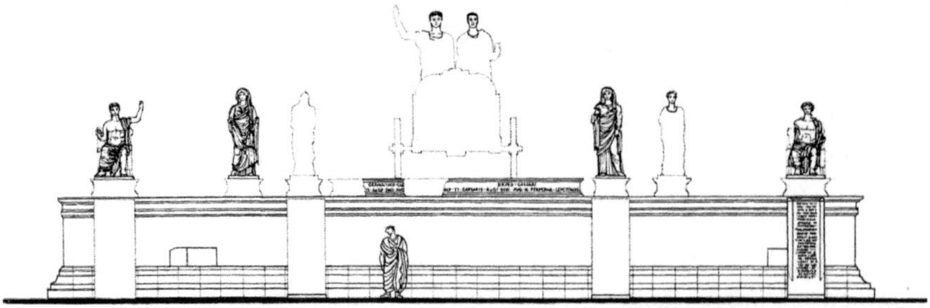

Fig. 21. A reconstruction sketch of a statuary group from Leptis Magna. In the centre, Germanicus and Drusus the Younger in the triumphal quadriga, flanked by members of the imperial family.

The posthumous honours awarded Germanicus and Drusus the Younger discussed in this section are further proof the two of them had the same standing in the *domus Augusta* and were treated as equal candidates to the succession. Importantly, these honours were similar to those conferred earlier on Gaius and Lucius Caesar, or even exceeded them. This was mostly the result of there being a certain tradition in place regarding posthumous honorifics for members of the imperial family, a tradition which reached a climax of its development during Tiberius' principate. The deaths of Germanicus and Drusus also affected the shape of the official state calendar, as numerous prohibitions and instructions were included that regulated the proper way of commemorating them on the anniversaries of their deaths, and were meant to remind the people of the Empire of the dramatic moments in the life of the reigning dynasty and to foster loyalty towards the *domus Augusta*. Regulations of this kind demonstrate that under Tiberius the imperial family fully became "a state institution," as Severy aptly put it[136].

2.2 Germanicus' Sons as Potential Successors

Drusus the Younger's death seriously complicated the succession after Tiberius, as all his grandsons, who were the primary candidates, were too young and inexperienced politically to take over in case the emperor died anytime soon. Neither could any of them replace Drusus as co-regent at that point. Since in AD

136 Severy 2003, 231.

23 Tiberius Gemellus was only four, Tiberius had to give up for the time being on any plans to make a natural descendant of his successor. Under these new circumstances, the princeps had to consider Germanicus' sons first as potential successors. The eldest, Nero Julius Caesar, was seventeen[137]. In AD 20, he had officially donned the toga of manhood, which was celebrated with a special financial allowance to the plebs (a *congiarium*), and was introduced to the Senate. At the same time, he gained the right to run for quaestorship five years before the normally prescribed time and was included in the college of *pontifices*[138]. Shortly afterwards Tiberius married him to his granddaughter Julia, Drusus' daughter[139]. The dynastic nature of that marriage seems obvious; we may assume its more significant goals included securing the stability and permanence of the dynasty in the generations to come. Any sons that this couple may have had could also have been taken into account as potential successors[140].

Three years later Germanicus' second son, Drusus Julius Caesar, also put on the *toga virilis* and received all the same honours his elder brother had[141]. After Drusus the Younger had died, the two brothers became primary candidates to the succession, as is clearly stressed by Tacitus. Apparently, thanks to Germanicus' memory their new status caused widespread enthusiasm[142]. One important characteristic which in the eyes of the Roman public opinion particularly predisposed Germanicus' sons to succeed the current emperor one day was that they were both direct descendants of Augustus[143]. In both Tacitus and Cassius Dio we read that Tiberius introduced them both to the Senate before Drusus was even buried, indicating that he saw them as his potential successors. On the same occasion, he recommended them to the senators' care[144]. Soon after, Nero Caesar gave his first serious public speech. It was also him that gave the second *laudatio funebris* (that is, other than Tiberius) at Drusus' funeral[145].

There is some evidence of a shift towards Germanicus' sons being seen at the time as primary candidates to the succession in the coin emissions dedicated to

137 It is generally accepted in scholarship that he was born in AD 6. See Kienast 1996, 81.
138 Tac. *Ann.* 3, 29, 1; Suet. *Tib.* 54, 1; Cass. Dio 57, 18, 11; Barrett 1989, 17; Mlasowsky 1996, 353.
139 Tac. *Ann.* 3, 29, 4.
140 See Corbier 1995, 184–185.
141 Tac. *Ann.* 4, 4, 1; Suet. *Tib.* 54, 1; Mlasowsky 1996, 354.
142 See Tac. *Ann.* 4, 12, 2; 15, 3; 59, 3.
143 Seager 2013, 56.
144 Tac. *Ann.* 4, 8, 3–5; Cass. Dio 57, 22, 4a. See also Meise 1966, 20–21.
145 Cass. Dio 57, 22, 4a = Zon.11, 2.

them minted in the provinces from AD 23 on[146]. Nero and Drusus were shown on them with Tiberius, whose image was put on the obverse. We have such coins from Caesaraugusta in Spain, among other places, where asses and semisses were minted in honour of the brothers. The obverse of the asses showed Tiberius in a laurel wreath with the legend TI CAESAR DIVI AUGUSTI F AUGUSTUS, while the reverse had Nero and Drusus sitting on curule chairs and the legend was CCA DRUSUS CAESAR NERO CAESAR[147]. On the semisses, the obverse has Tiberius' head, the legend the same as on the asses; on the reverse, one can see the heads of Germanicus' two eldest sons facing each other, whereas the legend is NERO CAESAR DRUSUS CAESAR II VIR CCA[148]. It is assumed that those emissions commemorated the authorities of this town conferring on the two brothers the honorary positions of *duoviri*[149]. Mlasowsky pointed out the way Nero and Drusus Caesar were presented on those coins corresponded to the style used earlier for Gaius and Lucius Caesar, and for Germanicus and Drusus the Younger, two pairs of prospective successors[150]. Coin emissions from Colonia Iulia Tingi in Mauretania provide another example of provincial coins minted in honour of Germanicus' sons. Those have Drusus Caesar's head on the obverse with the legend DRUSUS and Nero Caesar's portrait on the reverse with the legend NERO and the signature of the colony, IUL TIN[151]. The question arises of to what extent the coin series listed here reveal information on Tiberius' succession plans in this period. I believe we can with considerable certainty accept that they do reflect changes in the dynastic order and the hierarchy of the *domus Augusta*, which took place after Drusus the Younger died. It was no accident that images of Germanicus' sons only appeared on coins after AD 23. On the other hand, it behoves us to remember those emissions were not official: neither the imperial nor the senatorial mint produced any coins during that time featuring those two boys[152]. As I have mentioned above, it was those official

146 I here accept the dating of those emissions as proposed by the editors of the *RPC* (I 865) and Mlasowsky (1996, 356).

147 *RPC* I 342; Mlasowsky 1996, 356.

148 *RPC* I 343; Mlasowsky 1996, 356.

149 See Mlasowsky 1996, 357. We know Germanicus' sons were also honoured in this way by the inhabitants of Carthago Nova in Spain. See *RPC* I 179–181 and the commentary on that emission (*RPC* I p. 92).

150 Mlasowsky 1996, 357.

151 *RPC* I 865.

152 See Meise 1966, 9. Official emissions dedicated to Nero and Drusus Caesar only appear during Caligula's reign, when the senatorial mint in Rome produced a series

emissions that played the crucial role in creating the public image of prospective successors and could have told us more about Tiberius' succession plans in that period.

It should also be noted that other than the coins mentioned above we have little evidence for honours granted Nero and Drusus Caesar in the provinces, in sharp contrast to the earlier honorifics of first Gaius and Lucius Caesar, and then Germanicus and Drusus the Younger. What is more, Rose points out that when it comes to Nero and Drusus Caesar, we only have a few confirmed cases of the inhabitants of Italy and the provinces honouring them with statues—another sharp contrast to the previous practice regarding those members of the imperial family that Augustus and Tiberius had designated as successors[153]. Rather, the ardour of the provinces seems to remain in direct proportion to the degree all those young men were celebrated in Rome itself. We do know that while after Drusus' death Tiberius officially presented Germanicus' sons in the Senate as potential successors, he never followed up with more concrete actions which could have considerably accelerated their *cursus honorum*, preparing the ground for the eventual succession of one of them. As I have mentioned above, the two brothers merely gained the right to run for quaestorship early, when they assumed their togas of manhood, but that was their only privilege in terms of speeding up their political careers, not a situation that could be explained by their young age. After all, Gaius and Lucius Caesar had been designated consuls at fourteen, and at eighteen Gaius was given an important military command in the East. Clearly, after Drusus' death Tiberius showed much restraint choosing his future successor. Unlike Augustus, who immediately created a new order of succession through a series of successive adoptions after his sons' death, Tiberius never adopted any of his grandchildren, leaving the question of the succession open.

Tacitus tells us that the prospect of one of Germanicus' sons potentially succeeding Tiberius worried Sejanus, who saw in them both a threat to his own political plans[154]. With the sources terse and mutually contradictory, we are not able today to precisely reconstruct the successive stages of Sejanus' actions, which ultimately led to the exile and death of Nero and Drusus Caesar and their mother

---

of dupondii in their honour, which was a way for Caligula to commemorate his tragically dead brothers. See *RIC* I^2 *Cal.* 49.

153 Rose 1997, 31.

154 Tac. *Ann.* 4, 12, 2–3.

Agrippina the Elder[155]. It is especially controversial whether the fall of Germanicus' family took place before or after Livia's death.

According to Tacitus, the open assault on Germanicus' wife and her eldest son started only after Tiberius' mother died in AD 29, since neither Tiberius nor Sejanus dared act so radically against Germanicus' family while she was alive[156]. There is contradictory evidence to be found in Pliny the Elder's account, which mentions the trial of the popular knight Titus Sabinus, a follower of Germanicus and Agrippina, sentenced *ex causa Neronis Germanici filii*. Pliny says the trial was held during the consulship of Appius Junius Silanus and P. Silius Nerva, that is, in AD 28, implying the fall of Germanicus' eldest son took place before the death of Julia Augusta[157]. Pliny's version is supported by Suetonius, who writes that after his mother's banishment the young Caligula lived with his great-grandmother Livia[158]. Velleius Paterculus' account, too, may indicate Agrippina and Nero Caesar fell out of favour before her death[159].

With such discrepancies in the sources, it is impossible to definitively resolve the issue. On the one hand we have reasons to believe the fall of Germanicus' family happened while Livia was still alive, possibly as early as AD 27, since Tacitus places Titus Sabinus' trial at the very beginning of Silanus and Nerva's consulship (that is, of the year AD 28)[160]. If, as Pliny would have it, we should see a connection between his conviction and Nero Caesar's affair, Nero would have had to be exiled in the previous year. Additionally, both Tacitus and Suetonius report the *laudatio funebris* at Julia Augusta's funeral was given by Caligula, which may indicate his elder brothers were already in disgrace by then[161]. On the other hand, if one were to limit oneself to Tacitus' account, one could conclude that Sejanus' plotting against Agrippina and her eldest son began when Livia was still alive, but the attack in the open which brought about both of their exiles only happened after she died[162].

Be that as it may, in either AD 27 or 29 Agrippina and Nero Caesar were officially charged in front of the Senate and sentenced to exile, to the islands of

155 Unfortunately book five of Tacitus' *Annals*, which contained his account of these events, only survives in fragments.

156 Tac. *Ann.* 5, 3, 1.

157 Plin. *HN* 8, 145.

158 Suet. *Calig.* 10, 1.

159 Vell. Pat. 2, 130, 4.

160 Tac. *Ann.* 4, 68, 1.

161 Tac. *Ann.* 5, 1, 4; Suet. *Calig.* 10, 1.

162 See Tac. *Ann.* 4, 67, 3–4; 5, 3, 1.

Pandateria and Pontia, respectively. Nero was also declared to be an enemy of the state (or *hostis*)[163]. Soon after, although the precise date is unknown, Drusus Caesar shared his elder brother's fate, and was sent back by Tiberius from Capri to Rome. He, too, was decreed *hostis* by the Senate, to be incarcerated under the Palatine[164]. Then in AD 31 Nero Caesar was either starved to death or forced to commit suicide. Two years later, Agrippina and Drusus died under similar circumstances[165], and Tiberius ordered the birth date of Agrippina to be considered *nefastus*[166]. It is difficult to establish with precision the role Sejanus had in those events, but I do not think the princeps was manipulated by him in this case. If he had been, then after Sejanus' fall in AD 31 Agrippina and Drusus would most likely have been recalled from exile and restored to favour; instead, they were killed at Tiberius' unmistakable command, at which time the prefect had been dead for two years himself. Perhaps Suetonius is correct when he claims that Tiberius used Sejanus to remove Germanicus' sons from the succession game by means of his plotting, making it easier for his natural grandson Tiberius Gemellus to take over as emperor in the future[167].

2.3 Sejanus: Co-regent or Potential Successor?

Just how far Sejanus' political ambitions reached, and what plans Tiberius had regarding his prefect, is a separate question. Sejanus' move against Germanicus' sons, who were widely perceived as primary candidates to the succession, after Drusus the Younger's death, demonstrates he aimed quite high. In contrast to Tacitus[168], however, I do not believe Sejanus desired the purple. Rather, I share Barrett's opinion that due to his equestrian origins, he realized his chances of becoming princeps were slim. It seems more probable that he counted on becoming a temporary regent for one of Tiberius' grandsons after the emperor died[169]. His plans to marry Livilla, Drusus the Younger's widow, might argue in

163 Tac. *Ann.* 5, 3–5; Suet. *Tib.* 54, 2; *Calig.* 7; 10, 1; Barrett 1989, 24; Kienast 1996, 81; Levick 1999, 169.

164 Suet. *Tib.* 54, 2; *Calig.* 7; Cass. Dio 58, 3, 8; Schrömbges 1986, 177; Barrett 1989, 26; Kienast 1996, 81.

165 Tac. *Ann.* 6, 23, 2; 25, 1–3; Suet. *Tib.* 53, 2; 54, 2; Kienast 1996, 81.

166 Suet. *Tib.* 53, 2.

167 Suet. *Tib.* 55.

168 Tac. *Ann.* 4, 2–3; 12, 2–4.

169 See Barrett 1989, 18. On the other hand, it is difficult to say if Tiberius considered it possible.

favour of this assumption. Tacitus mentions that in AD 25 Sejanus asked Tiberius for permission to marry her[170]. Now that marriage would in fact have made it possible for him to join the imperial family; besides, as Livilla's husband and the guardian of her son, Tiberius Gemellus, he could have ruled in his name, should Gemellus have succeeded Tiberius, until the boy had reached the appropriate age[171]. Marrying Livilla would have straightaway made Sejanus Gemellus' champion, while eliminating Germanicus' descendants from the succession race. Considering Gemellus was much younger than Agrippina's sons, Sejanus could have expected a long regency if Gemellus were to become Tiberius' successor. Tacitus reports Tiberius was actually quite cautious regarding Sejanus' request: his response was non-committal and involved a number of arguments against the match[172]. We do, however, have a mention in Cassius Dio, transmitted by Zonaras, indicating Tiberius agreed to a marriage between Sejanus and Julia, the daughter of Drusus the Younger and Livilla. Still, as no other sources confirm that information, we do not know whether in the end the marriage was made[173].

Sejanus' political career no doubt reached its crowning point during the consulship he shared with Tiberius in AD 31. The honour was exceptional, as before him the only people to be the emperor's colleagues in that office were Germanicus and Drusus the Younger, both intended successors. After Sejanus stepped down as consul in May of that year, he was granted an *imperium proconsulare*. The Senate also decreed that he and Tiberius would hold a consulship together every five years[174]. The question needs to be addressed here of whether all that promotion meant he had been chosen as the princeps' future successor. Actually, nothing in our sources answers that question in the affirmative; in fact, Suetonius says Tiberius elevated Sejanus to the highest honours not out of affection, but rather in return for his help in getting rid of Germanicus' sons, which in turn was supposed to secure the succession for Tiberius Gemellus[175]. Meanwhile, from Cassius Dio we learn that the emperor meant for Caligula to succeed him, which was in that historian's opinion indicated by the fact that Germanicus' youngest

---

170 Tac. *Ann.* 4, 39, 1–4.

171 See Pistellato 2013, 215.

172 Tac. *Ann.* 4, 40, 1–7. However, E. Meise (1969, 57–60) supposes the marriage was ultimately made.

173 Cass. Dio 58, 9 (= Zonaras 11, 2). See also Meise 1969, 57–59.

174 Tac. *Ann.* 6, 8, 3; Suet. *Tib.* 65, 1; Cass. Dio 57, 20, 2; 58, 4, 3–4; 7, 4; Degrassi 1952, 10; Schrömbges 1986, 173; Barrett 1989, 26.

175 Suet. *Tib.* 55.

son was included in the college of *pontifices*[176]. Moreover, both authors go so far as to claim that regaling Sejanus with such prestigious honours was merely meant to lull him into a false sense of security, as the princeps was going to curtail his influence soon, suspecting him as he did of preparing a coup d'état[177]. Of course, we cannot rule out the possibility their accounts reflect a tradition hostile to Sejanus, formed after his fall, which calls for some caution regarding those reports. However, having taken into account the possible bias of the sources, I do not think the honours Sejanus received in AD 31 prove Tiberius had picked him for his successor; it does not seem likely the emperor would have wished to appoint someone from outside the *domus Caesarum*, thereby passing over his own grandsons[178].

The related question of whether the princeps intended to make the prefect his *collega imperii*, on the other hand, is harder to answer with certainty. Their shared consulship, granting Sejanus proconsular powers and the intention to add tribunician powers to those, mentioned in Suetonius[179], might support such an assumption. On the other hand, it may have all been just a smokescreen meant to lull Sejanus into letting his guard down, just as Suetonius and Cassius Dio suggest; after all, we do not know when exactly the princeps stopped trusting his prefect and decided to do away with him for good.

2.4 Gaius Caligula or Tiberius Gemellus? The Problem of the Succession During the Final Years of Tiberius' Rule

After the murders of Nero Caesar and Drusus Caesar, the circle of primary candidates to the succession included Germanicus' youngest son Gaius Caesar, and Drusus the Younger's son Tiberius Gemellus[180], both grandsons of Tiberius. At that time, considering their respective ages, Gaius' chances were greater. His first public appearance was the *laudatio funebris* he gave at Livia's funeral in AD 29[181]. Two years later, he assumed the toga of manhood. It is worth noting the

---

176 Cass. Dio 58, 8, 1.

177 Suet. *Tib.* 65, 1; Cass. Dio 58, 4, 1–3.

178 That is confirmed by Tacitus (*Ann.* 6, 46, 2), who reports that when thinking on choosing a successor towards the end of his rule, Tiberius unambiguously rejected the possibility that he might pass on the throne to someone from outside the dynasty, on which see below.

179 Suet. *Tib.* 65, 1.

180 Suet. *Calig.* 12, 1; Schrömbges 1986, 177.

181 Tac. *Ann.* 5, 1, 4; Suet. *Calig.* 10, 1.

event took place on Capri, where Tiberius had resided since 26. Still, Suetonius tells us that no ceremony of the kind that had been held for Germanicus' elder sons accompanied this event[182]. It is also striking that Caligula only started wearing the *toga virilis* at the age of eighteen, which makes it obvious Tiberius did not particularly care about speeding up his political career or preparing him for the role of the princeps; intended successors normally received the *toga virilis* shortly after their fourteenth birthday, at the earliest age a young Roman man could. At the same time, they would also be granted a number of prestigious honours and designated for the highest public offices, which they would later assume outside of the traditional *cursus honorum*[183].

Not long after assuming the *toga virilis*, Gaius became a *pontifex*[184]. To Suetonius, that was proof of the emperor's high regard and a sign Gaius might be able to succeed him. Cassius Dio's tone is similar, that is, he believes that with this decision the emperor implied he saw Germanicus' son as his future successor[185]. In my opinion, both their assessments go too far, as they overestimate the importance of that appointment to Caligula's standing. From Augustus' day, a large majority of male members of the imperial family joined the ranks of that college, not all of them possible successors. For instance, in 15 BC that honour fell to Tiberius; at some point before AD 11, to Drusus the Younger[186]—and in neither case was there a connection to designating the successor, since they were both minor candidates to the succession at the time they received those nominations. What is more, Cassius Dio says Sejanus and his son both became *pontifices* at the same time Caligula did[187]. Therefore, it is difficult to treat these nominations as being evidence of Tiberius' succession policy.

In AD 33, Gaius was designated for quaestorship, an office he assumed in the same year, and got the right to run for the other magistracies five years before

182 Suet. *Calig.* 10, 1; see also Kornemann 1930, 46; Schrömbges 1986, 177; Barrett 1989, 27; Kienast 1996, 85; Levick 1999, 175–176; Winterling 2011, 37.

183 This had been the case with Gaius and Lucius Caesar, and would later be the case with Nero, who assumed the *toga virilis* at the age of thirteen; see below.

184 Suet. *Calig.* 12, 1; Cass. Dio 58, 8, 1; Schrömbges 1986, 177; Mlasowsky 1996, 361; Kienast 1996, 85; Levick 1999, 176. It is not certain though whether Gaius was also made an augur, as Suetonius recounts (*Calig.* 12, 1). Barrett (1989, 27; 260 note 43) points out that no epigraphic sources attest to Gaius becoming a member of the college of augurs before his ascent to the throne.

185 Suet. *Calig.* 12, 1; Cass. Dio 58, 8, 1.

186 See Kienast 1996, 76, 82.

187 Cass. Dio 58, 7, 4.

the prescribed ages. Nonetheless, Cassius Dio notes that Tiberius did not let the Senate vote through any more honours for his grandson, arguing they could spoil him too much[188]. It is also Cassius Dio who informs us that, due to the memory of Gaius' father, the honours granted him met with huge enthusiasm of the Roman plebs[189]. Importantly, the quaestorship was the only office Caligula held during Tiberius' reign; it is also telling he was not given any military command or officially introduced to the legions. All that shows Tiberius' restraint when endorsing Gaius as his future successor, just as he had when it came to his elder brothers. His actions regarding Tiberius Gemellus were similar. While the youth was seventeen at the moment of Tiberius' death, he had not donned the *toga virilis* by then or received any major privileges or honours, except for becoming an augur[190].

It is also significant that we have no official coin emissions featuring either Gaius or Gemellus from the time of Tiberius' rule to reflect his succession plans during the last stage of his reign. All we have are the two provincial series dated to the years 32–37, minted in Carthago Nova and Caesaraugusta in Spain, which we can see as connected to Gaius. The former commemorated him receiving the honorary title of *quinquennalis* from that town, while the circumstances surrounding the second are unclear. Perhaps, but only perhaps, Tiberius' two grandsons are also depicted on another local series, this one minted in Corinth[191]. However, contrary to Mlasowsky, I do not believe the drachmas minted towards the end of Tiberius' principate in Caesarea in Cappadocia, one series of which showed Augustus and Germanicus, while the other featured Tiberius and Drusus, had anything to do with endorsing Gaius and Tiberius Gemellus as future successors[192]. Since the coins in question bore neither the images of Tiberius' grandsons nor any legend naming them, it is hard to imagine the audience of their message should be able to guess they heralded Gaius' and Gemellus succession in the future. In my view, if the minter's intention had

188 Cass. Dio 58, 23, 1; Barrett 1989, 31; Kienast 1996, 85; Winterling 2011, 42; Wiedemann 2008, 219.

189 Cass. Dio 58, 8, 2.

190 Barrett (1989, 39) supposes that this was because despite his age, Gemellus was not mature enough. In my opinion, the reason lay more in Tiberius' restraint regarding the public endorsement of his grandsons. As I have pointed out above, Caligula only donned the toga of manhood after he was eighteen. Gemellus' augurship is not quite clear either, as we do not know when he assumed that function. See Kienast 1996, 83.

191 *RPC* I 182–184; 362–364; 1171; Mlasowsky 1996, 366.

192 Mlasowsky 1996, 365.

been, as Mlasowsky suggests, to stress the two young men's rights to succession by alluding to their famous ancestors, they would have made it onto the coins as well.

Now to move on to the central issue of this section, namely which of his grandsons Tiberius ultimately intended to succeed him, it should be noted the problem is not an easy one to solve, since the ancient authors have preserved many different opinions on the subject. Flavius Josephus recounts that the princeps preferred Gemellus for that role as his natural descendant, but in the end he went against his own wishes and chose Gaius, following a sign sent him by the gods:

> Ὁ δὲ Τιβέριος Εὐόδῳ πρόσταγμα ποιησάμενος κατὰ τὴν ὑστεραίαν ὑπὸ τὴν ἕω εἰσαγαγεῖν τοὺς παῖδας εὔχεται τοῖς πατρίοις θεοῖς σημεῖόν τι πρόφαντον αὐτῷ δεῖξαι περὶ τοῦ τὴν ἡγεμονίαν διαδεξομένου, σπεύδων μὲν τῷ υἱεῖ τοῦ παιδὸς αὐτὴν καταλιπεῖν, μεῖζον δὲ δόξης τε καὶ βουλήσεως τῆς αὐτοῦ πεπιστευκὼς τοῦ θεοῦ τὸ ἐπ' αὐτοῖς ἀποφανούμενον. οἰώνισμα δ' οὖν αὐτῷ προύκειτο, εἰς ἐκεῖνον ἥξειν τὴν ἡγεμονίαν, ὃς ἂν κατὰ τὴν ἐπιοῦσαν ἀφίκοιτο πρότερος πρὸς αὐτόν. ταῦτα διανοηθεὶς πέμπει παρὰ τοῦ υἱωνοῦ τὸν παιδαγωγὸν κελεύων ὑπὸ πρώτην ὥραν ἄγειν τὸν παῖδα ὡς αὐτόν, καταμελήσεσθαι στρατηγίας τὸν θεὸν ὑπολαμβάνων: ὁ δ' ἀντεψήφιζεν αὐτοῦ τὴν χειροτονίαν. ὁ μὲν δὴ ταῦτ' ἐνθυμησάμενος, ἐπεὶ τάχιστα ἡμέρα ἦν, κελεύει τὸν Εὔοδον εἰσκαλεῖν τῶν παίδων τὸν παρόντα πρότερον. ἐξελθὼν δ' ἐκεῖνος καὶ τὸν Γάιον πρὸ τοῦ δωματίου καταλαβὼν[...] Τιβέριος δὲ ὡς θεᾶται Γάιον, τότε πρῶτον εἰς ἐπίνοιαν ἐλθὼν τοῦ θείου τῆς ἐξουσίας καὶ τὴν κατ' αὐτὸν ἡγεμονίαν παντελῶς ἀφῃρημέν ἐπικυροῦν οἷς ψηφίσαιτο δυνάμεως ἐκεῖθεν αὐτῷ μὴ παραγενομένης, πολλὰ δὴ κατολοφυράμενος αὐτὸν μὲν τοῦ ἐφ'οἷς προβουλεύσειε κυροῦν ἀφῃρημένου τὸ κράτος, Τιβέριον δὲ τὸν υἱωνόν, ὡς τῆς τε Ῥωμαίων ἀρχῆς ὁμοῦ διαμάρτοι[...] καίπερ δὲ συντεταραγμένος τῇ παρὰ δόξαν τῆς ἀρχῆς εἰς οὓς οὐκ ἤθελεν περιόδῳ, ἄκων δὲ καὶ μὴ βουλόμενος φησὶ γοῦν πρὸς τὸν Γάιον:'ὦ παῖ, καίπερ μοι συγγενεστέρουΤιβερίου ἢ κατὰ σὲ ὄντος δόξῃ τε τῇ ἐμαυτοῦ καὶ τῷ ὁμοψήφῳ ἐπ' αὐτῇ τῶν θεῶν σοὶ φέρων ἐγχειρίζω τὴν Ῥωμαίων ἡγεμονίαν[193].
>
> But when Tiberius had given order to Euodus to bring the children to him the next day in the morning, he prayed to his country gods to show him a manifest signal which of those children should come to the government; being very desirous to leave it to his son's son, but still depending upon what God should foreshow concerning them more than upon his own opinion and inclination; so he made this to be the omen, that the government should be left to him who should come to him first the next day. When he had thus resolved within himself, he sent to his grandson's tutor, and ordered him to bring the child to him early in the morning, as supposing that God would permit him to be made emperor. But God proved opposite to his designation; for while Tiberius was thus contriving matters, and as soon as it was at all day, he bid Euodus to call in that child which should be there ready. So he went out, and found Caius before the

193 Joseph. *AJ.* 18, 211–219.

door […] As soon as Tiberius saw Caius, and not before, he reflected on the power of God, and how the ability of bestowing the government on whom he would was entirely taken from him; and thence he was not able to establish what he had intended. So he greatly lamented that his power of establishing what he had before contrived was taken from him, and that his grandson Tiberius was not only to lose the Roman empire by his fatality, but his own safety also […]Now although he was disordered at this unexpected revolution of the government to those for whom he did not intend it, he spake thus to Caius, though unwillingly, and against his own inclination: "O child! although Tiberius be nearer related to me than thou art, I, by my own determination, and the conspiring suffrage of the gods, do give and put into thy hand the Roman empire" […][194].

Cassius Dio, on the other hand, writes that the princeps was more inclined towards Caligula, because Gemellus was underage and there was some suspicion of his illegitimacy:

[…] καὶ διότι καὶ τὸν Γάιον ὁ Τιβέριος ἱερέα ἀποδείξας ἐπῄνεσε, καί τι καὶ ὡς διάδοχον αὐτὸν τῆς μοναρχίας ἕξων ἐνεδείκνυτο[195].

[…]there was also the fact that Tiberius, after appointing Gaius priest, praised him and gave some indications that he intended to make him his successor to the throne[196].

[…] καὶ τὸν Γάιον ταμίαν μὲν οὐκ ἐν τοῖς πρῶτον ἀπέδειξεν, ἐς δὲ δὴ τὰς ἄλλας ἀρχὰς πέντε ἔτεσι θᾶσσον τοῦ καθήκοντος προβιβάσειν ὑπέσχετο, καίτοι καὶ τῆς γερουσίας δεηθεὶς ὅπως μήτε πολλαῖς μήτ΄ ἀκαίροις τιμαῖς αὐτόν, μὴ καὶ ἐξοκείλῃ ποι, ἐπαίρῃ. Εἶχε μὲν γὰρ καὶ τὸν Τιβέριον τὸν ἔκγονον· ἀλλ΄ ἐκεῖνον μὲν διά τε τὴν ἡλικίαν (ἔτι γὰρ παιδίον ἦν) καὶ διὰ τὴν ὑποψίαν (οὐ γὰρ ἐπιστεύετο τοῦ Δρούσου παῖς εἶναι) παρεώρα, τῷ δὲ δὴ Γαΐῳ ὡς καὶ μοναρχήσοντι προσεῖχε, καὶ μάλισθ΄ ὅτι τὸν Τιβέριον καὶ ὀλίγον χρόνον βιώσεσθαι καὶ ὑπ΄ αὐτοῦ ἐκείνου φονευθήσεσθαι σαφῶς ἠπίστατο[197].

Besides doing all this, he appointed Gaius quaestor, though not of the first rank, and promised to advance him to the other offices five years earlier than was customary, despite the fact that he had requested the senate not to make the young man conceited by numerous or premature honours, for fear he might go astray in some way or other. He also had a grandson by the name of Tiberius, but him he disregarded both on account of his age (he was still a mere child) and on account of the suspicion that he was not the son of Drusus. He therefore cleaved to Gaius as his successor in the monarchy, the more so as he felt sure that Tiberius would live but a short time and would be murdered by Gaius himself[198].

194 Translated by W. Whiston (Perseus Collection, Greek and Roman Materials).
195 Cass. Dio 58, 8, 1.
196 Translated by E. Cary (Loeb Classical Library, 175).
197 Cass. Dio 58, 23, 1–2.
198 Translated by. E. Cary (Loeb Classical Library, 175).

Then there is Suetonius, who claims Tiberius originally meant to secure the succession for his natural grandson and to that end used Sejanus to eliminate Nero Caesar and Drusus Caesar, which would have paved Gemellus' way to imperial power. Then supposedly after the prefect's fall he lost his enthusiasm for the young man, again suspecting that he was not Drusus' son[199]:

> Aelium Seianum; quem ad summam potentiam non tam benivolentia provexerat, quam ut esset cuius ministerio ac fraudibus liberos Germanici circumveniret, nepotemque suum ex Druso filio naturalem ad successionem imperii confirmaret[200].

> This man he had advanced to the highest power, not so much from regard for him, as that he might through his services and wiles destroy the children of Germanicus and secure the succession for his own grandson, the child of his son Drusus[201].

> Sed avum meum narrantem puer audiebam, causam operis ab interioribus aulicis proditam, quod Thrasyl<l>us mathematicus anxio de successore Tiberio et in verum nepotem proniori affirmasset non magis Gaium imperaturum quam per Baianum sinum equis discursurum[202].

> But when I was a boy, I used to hear my grandfather say that the reason for the work, as revealed by the emperor's confidential courtiers, was that Thrasyllus the astrologer had declared to Tiberius, when he was worried about his successor and inclined towards his natural grandson, that Gaius had no more chance of becoming emperor than of riding about over the gulf of Baiae with horses[203].

> Quod nisi eum et mors praevenisset et Thrasyllus consulto, ut aiunt, differre quaedam spe longioris vitae compulisset, plures aliquanto necaturus ac ne reliquis quidem nepotibus parsurus creditur, cum et Gaium suspectum haberet et Tiberium ut ex adulterio conceptum aspernaretur[204].

> And had not death prevented him, and Thrasyllus, purposely it is said, induced him to put off some things through hope of a longer life, it is believed that still more would have perished, and that he would not even have spared the rest of his grandsons; for he had his suspicions of Gaius and detested Tiberius as the fruit of adultery[205].

---

199 Tiberius might have given up on an original intention of making Gemellus his successor as a result of rumours that the young man was the issue of an affair between Sejanus and Livilla, circulated after the prefect's fall. Perhaps the princeps also changed his attitude to his natural grandson as a result of the intrigue of Macro, who supported Gaius. See Barrett 1989, 38.

200 Suet. *Tib*. 55.

201 Translated by J. C. Rolfe (Loeb Classical Library, 31).

202 Suet. *Calig*. 19, 3.

203 Translated by J. C. Rolfe (Loeb Classical Library, 31).

204 Suet. *Tib*. 62, 3.

205 Translated by J. C. Rolfe (Loeb Classical Library, 31).

And then, according to Tacitus, the princeps took a long time pondering the choice of his successor. He preferred Gemellus as his natural relative, but there was a major obstacle in the form of Gemellus' young age. The argument in favour of Gaius, on the other hand, was supposedly his popularity among the people, although Tacitus also claims that in turn resulted in Tiberius resenting him. Tacitus adds that the emperor considered Claudius as a possible successor as well, but gave up on the idea because of Claudius' mental infirmity. For the sake of Augustus' memory, however, Tiberius rejected the option of handing the imperial power over to a person from outside the reigning dynasty. Ultimately, the weary princeps did not resolve the issue of succession, deciding to trust fate instead:

> Gnarum hoc principi, eoque dubitavit de tradenda re publica, primum inter nepotes; quorum Druso genitus sanguine et caritate propior, sed nondum pubertatem ingressus, Germanici filio robur iuventae, vulgi studia, eaque apud avum odii causa. etiam de Claudio agitanti, quod is composita aetate bonarum artium cupiens erat, imminuta mens eius obstitit. sin extra domum successor quaereretur, ne memoria Augusti, ne nomen Caesarum in ludibria et contumelias verterent, metuebat: quippe illi non perinde curae gratia praesentium quam in posteros ambitio. mox incertus animi fesso corpore consilium, cui impar erat, fato permisit [...][206].

> This the emperor knew; and he hesitated therefore with regard to the succession—first between his grandchildren. Of these, the issue of Drusus was the nearer to him in blood and by affection, but had not yet entered the years of puberty: the son of Germanicus possessed the vigour of early manhood, but also the affections of the multitude—and that, with his grandsire, was a ground of hatred. Even Claudius with his settled years and aspirations to culture came under consideration: the obstacle was his mental instability. Yet, if a successor were sought outside the imperial family, he dreaded that the memory of Augustus — the name of the Caesars — might be turned to derision and to contempt. For the care of Tiberius was not so much to enjoy popularity in the present as to court the approval of posterity. Soon, mentally irresolute, physically outworn, he left to fate a decision beyond his competence [...][207].

As the sources cited above demonstrate, ancient historians themselves do not agree on whom Tiberius finally saw as his successor, and indicate he hesitated between his two grandsons until the end of his rule. Only Josephus writes that

206 Tac. *Ann.* 6, 46, 1–3.
207 Translated by J. Jackson (Loeb Classical Library, 312).

ultimately the emperor designated Caligula as the next princeps, but his account is contradicted by that of Tacitus, who clearly informs his reader that Tiberius never unequivocally designated a successor. Personally, I am inclined to accept Tacitus' version, whose correctness may be supported by a passage in Suetonius regarding Tiberius' last will, which states both grandsons were indicated there as equal heirs[208].

Sajkowski disagrees; based on Suetonius' and Cassius Dio's accounts, he believes after getting rid of Sejanus, Tiberius definitively saw Caligula as his future successor. In his opinion, the prefect's fall made the emperor hostile towards Gemellus as Sejanus' protégé, naturally resulting in his attitude towards Germanicus' youngest son also changing, so that the princeps began to prepare him for the succession. Sajkowski also highlights the special role of Antonia the Younger, Caligula's grandmother, who supposedly actively backed his interests: by revealing Sejanus' plotting, she helped Caligula become Tiberius' successor in the end[209]. In my view, Sajkowski's claims are quite questionable. First, some ancient historians (including Flavius and Tacitus) clearly imply the princeps favoured Gemellus, who was his natural grandson. Second, it ought to be stressed that Sejanus' fall did not strengthen Caligula's position in any noticeable way. It is enough to say, as I have above, that he only ascended to his first office, notably a relatively insignificant quaestorship, two years after the prefect's death, and that was the only magistracy he held under Tiberius. Bearing the swift advancement of Augustus' intended successors in mind, one should not see Caligula's *cursus honorum* as indicative of Tiberius planning to make him his successor. Third, we have no official coin emissions bearing images of Gaius, and—as I have already mentioned a few times—those played an important part in endorsing and creating the public image of planned successors. Thus I do not think we have sufficient evidence to suppose that after Sejanus' fall Tiberius prepared Caligula to succeed him, and neither can we determine how Antonia the Younger ultimately contributed to her grandson's imperial accession, if she did at all. Still, I think other factors proved decisive; see below.

It is worth inquiring here why the emperor never resolved the question of the succession; I think this fact was connected to the suspicions, mentioned by Suetonius and Cassius Dio, that Tiberius Gemellus might not be legitimate. I suppose if the princeps had been convinced Gemellus was actually his

208 Suet. *Tib.* 76.
209 Sajkowski 1994, 49–61.

grandson, he would have made him his successor and Caligula would have been murdered like his brothers before him. Indicating both grandsons in his last will as equal heirs (and so presumably equal-footed candidates to the succession) meant that, realistically speaking, Caligula's chances in the endgame were higher, a topic to which I shall return below.

2.5 Tiberius' Last Will and the Issue of "Doppelprinzipat"

Based on the provisions of Tiberius' last will, some ancient authors—namely Philo of Alexandria, Suetonius and Cassius Dio—suggest that in the end he decided to institute a co-regency of Caligula and Tiberius Gemellus[210]:

> συναγαγὼν τοὺς ἐν τέλει "βούλομαι μὲν ἔφη τὸν γένει μὲν ἀνεψιὸν εὐνοίᾳ δὲ ἀδελφόν, ἑπόμενος καὶ τῇ τοῦ τετελευτηκότος Τιβερίου γνώμῃ, κοινοπραγεῖν τῆς αὐτοκρατοῦς ἐξουσίας· ὁρᾶτε δὲ καὶ αὐτοὶ νήπιον ἔτι ὄντα κομιδῇ καὶ χρῄζοντα ἐπιτρόπων καὶ διδασκάλων καὶ παιδαγωγῶν [...]"[211].

> Having summoned the chief officials he said, "In accordance with the will of the deceased Tiberius I wish the imperial authority to be shared by him who is my cousin by birth but my brother by affection, though you see yourselves that he is still a mere child and needs guardians and teachers and tutors"[212].

> ingressoque urbem, statim consensu senatus et irrumpentis in curiam turbae, inrita Tiberi voluntate, qui testamento alterum nepotem suum praetextatum adhuc coheredem ei dederat, ius arbitriumque omnium rerum illi permissum est[213].

> When he entered the city, full and absolute power was at once put into his hands by the unanimous consent of the senate and of the mob, which forced its way into the House, and no attention was paid to the wish of Tiberius, who in his will had named his other grandson, still a boy, joint heir with Caligula[214].

> Περὶ μὲν οὖν τοῦ Τιβερίου ταῦτα παραδέδοται, διεδέξατο δὲ αὐτὸν ὁ Γάιος ὁ τοῦ Γερμανικοῦ καὶ τῆς Ἀγριππίνης παῖς, ὃν καὶ Γερμανικὸν καὶ Καλιγόλαν, ὥσπερ εἶπον, ἐπωνόμαζον. Ἐκεῖνος μὲν γὰρ καὶ τῷ Τιβερίῳ τῷ ἐγγόνῳ τὴν αὐταρχίαν κατέλιπεν· ὁ δὲ δὴ Γάιος τὰς διαθήκας αὐτοῦ ἐς τὸ συνέδριον διὰ τοῦ Μάκρωνος ἐσπέμψας ἀκύρους ὑπό τε τῶν ὑπάτων καὶ ὑπὸ τῶν ἄλλων τῶν προπαρεσκευασμένων οἱ, ὡς καὶ

210 *Contra* Barrett (1989, 39), who believes rather than focusing on legal nuance, those authors meant to demonstrate Caligula's aspirations to rule independently were unfounded.

211 Philo. *Leg.* 4, 26.

212 Translated by F. H. Colson (Loeb Classical Library, 379).

213 Suet. *Calig.* 14, 1.

214 Translated by J. C. Rolfe (Loeb Classical Library, 31).

παραφρονήσαντος, ἐποίησεν, ὅτι παιδίῳ, ᾧ μηδὲ ἐσελθεῖν ἐς τὸ βουλευτήριον ἐξῆν, ἄρχειν σφᾶς ἐπέτρεψε[215].

These are the stories, then, that have been handed down about Tiberius. His successor was Gaius, the son of Germanicus and Agrippina, who was also known, as I have stated, by the names of Germanicus and Caligula. Tiberius, to be sure, had left the Empire to his grandson Tiberius as well; but Gaius sent his will to the senate by Macro and caused it to be declared null and void by the consuls and the others with whom he had arranged matters beforehand, on the ground that the testator had not been of sound mind, as shown by the fact that he had permitted a mere boy to rule over them, who did not yet possess the right even to enter the senate[216].

The perspective in these sources has also been adopted by certain modern-day scholars. One of the first of these was Kornemann, for whom making the two grandsons equal heirs in the will meant the princeps wanted a "double principate" to be introduced after his death, apparently following in Augustus' footsteps in this regard. For Kornemann, this was one more argument in favour of the claim he consistently made, namely that most Roman *principes* were guided in their actions by the notion of "Doppelprinzipat."[217]

Contrary to the opinions of a subset of ancient historians and modern scholars following them, I find it unlikely that Tiberius should have had any such plans. First, there is nothing to that effect in either Josephus Flavius or, more importantly, Tacitus, who clearly states the princeps took no decisions at all regarding the succession after his death. Second, all the actions relevant to the succession policy taken by Tiberius during the last years of his principate evidently show he did nothing to prepare Tiberius Gemellus for possibly becoming anybody's co-regent, let alone an independent successor.

So, how should the provisos of the will be understood? From a formal point of view, they only mean the emperor made Gaius and Gemellus his equal heirs in the private sphere. Still, as I have mentioned a few times, such heirs were also perceived as primary candidates to one's political legacy, which in this case meant the imperial purple. In this context, we can assume that with his will Tiberius indicated that both young men were his *potential* successors, without deciding which of them it should be. This interpretation fits well with the opinion of

215 Cass. Dio 59, 1, 1–2.

216 Translated by. E. Cary (Loeb Classical Library, 175).

217 Kornemann 1930, 47–48. Similar opinions have been expressed by Mlasowsky (1996, 362), Levick (1999, 210) and Bauman (2003, 162), among others, who stress primarily the political message of Tiberius' will, pointing out that his provisions clearly prove he intended a future co-regency of Caligula and Gemellus. *Contra* Yavetz 1999, 166.

Tacitus cited earlier—that the princeps never completely resolved the issue of succession.

Another question that needs to be asked here is what Gemellus' chances were, realistically, of being chosen to rule. While Tiberius did informally designate him as the other successor, I doubt he could have made it. Unlike Gaius, who officially began his public career during Tiberius' rule, Gemellus had not even donned the toga of manhood by then. It is also unlikely that he had any significant political followers who would have supported his candidacy to the throne[218]. Quite regardless of Caligula's seniority, his strongest asset in the succession race was doubtless the fact that he was a son of the widely popular Germanicus, and a natural great-grandson of Augustus on his mother's side. Such family connections particularly predisposed him to taking over from Tiberius as emperor, especially in the eyes of the urban plebs and the army[219]. I think the princeps was perfectly aware of these assets of Caligula and his lack of a decision regarding the succession was *de facto* equivalent to consenting to Germanicus' son becoming the next emperor.

218 They were probably quite few. See Timpe 1962, 58; Mlasowsky 1996, 362.

219 Tacitus (*Ann.* 6, 46, 1) mentions Caligula's great popularity among the Roman plebs, which he enjoyed precisely because he was a son of Germanicus.

3 Caligula

3.1 Tiberius Gemellus as Caligula's Intended Successor?

Shortly after Caligula's accession, Gemellus assumed the *toga virilis* and was adopted by the new princeps. He also received the title of *princeps iuventutis* and was admitted into the college of the *Fratres Arvales*[1]. The only author to provide us with any information on that adoption, beyond the fact that it took place, is Philo. According to his account, the most important officials in the state were present, and the emperor gave a speech in which he justified his decision by claiming it was necessary for him to take care of the underage and inexperienced youth[2]. Since Tiberius Gemellus was *sui iuris*, the procedure applied was *adrogatio*, the same as in the case of the adoptions of AD 4[3]. It is worth noting that in this case the age difference between the adopter and adoptee was very small: only seven years. Moreover, Caligula failed to fulfil one of the formal requirements for this adoption procedure, as he was not yet sixty[4]. Of course, that did not pose a problem. Presumably nobody would have dared accuse the new princeps of violating the legal norm[5].

The question arises of whether we can consider that adoption as a sign Caligula saw Gemellus as a future successor. In fact, I do not think we have enough evidence for this. Rather, there is much to suggest the *adrogatio* in question should not be seen in terms of Caligula's succession policy at all[6]: at the time, the new princeps was only twenty-five and on the threshold of his reign, which means he was in the position to expect he might in the near future have a son who could succeed him after his death. Therefore, it would have made little sense for Caligula to definitively settle the matter of the succession right at the beginning of his rule[7]. In addition to this, the sources make no mention of Gemellus receiving any privileges on the occasion of the adoption and the assumption of

1 Suet. *Calig.* 15, 2; Cass. Dio 59, 1, 3; 8, 1; Barrett 1989, 67; Kienast 1996, 83; Lindsay 2009, 200; Boruch 2010, 42; Winterling 2011, 50.
2 Philo. *Leg.* 4, 26–27.
3 See Kunst 2005, 57–58; 180.
4 See Prevost 1949, 40.
5 The situation was similar when Tiberius adopted Germanicus, as he had not been sixty either.
6 *Contra* Ehrhardt 1978, 52.
7 Similarly Barrett 1989, 68.

the *toga virilis* which might have made it easier for him to embark on a political career and sped up his *cursus honorum*, which proves the princeps had no interest in his cousin and adoptive son gaining experience and preparing for the role of a possible successor. It is also telling that we have no official coins with images of Gemellus from Caligula's principate, and neither did the adoption echo loudly around the provinces. There are no provincial coin series celebrating him and only few cases of honouring him with statues[8].

In that case, why did Caligula decide to adopt Gemellus? According to Philo, his intentions were insincere, and the main purpose of the adoption was to deprive the young man of independent agency and to completely control him by subjecting him to Caligula's *patria potestas*. In that way, the princeps neutralized his greatest rival in the struggle for the throne[9]. Philo's opinion is no doubt correct, although the *adrogatio* may have served other purposes as well. I suspect Caligula may have wanted to dispel the bad impression left by invalidating Tiberius' last will, the results of which included primarily depriving Gemellus of the right to his grandfather's political legacy. Seen in that light, the adoption of Gemellus would have been a clever public image gambit, meant to show the new princeps did treat the young man as his potential successor and had no intention of cutting him out. Or, as some scholars suggest, it may have been a nod of sorts towards Gemellus' supporters and friends, assuming he had some, whose political ambitions were tied to his succession[10]. Later events demonstrated that this was all smoke and mirrors which Caligula dismantled as soon as his position as the new emperor was solid, because a few months after the adoption Gemellus was either murdered or forced to commit suicide at Caligula's orders[11]. Philo reports the direct reason for eliminating Gemellus was his alleged participation

8 We do have such foundations from *Velleia*, *Augusta Emerita* and *Lepcis Magna*, but the statues in honour of Gemellus erected in those cities were integral parts of larger statuary groups dedicated to the reigning dynasty. See Rose 1997, 121–123 (no. 50); 132–133 (no. 60); 182–184 (no. 125); Boruch 2010, 43.

9 Philo. *Leg.* 5, 28. That purpose of the adoption is also highlighted by modern scholars. Prevost (1949, 42–43) claimed Caligula adopted Gemellus so he could have him killed easily later on, based on the *ius vitae necisque* he would have over him as a result of the *patria potestas*. See also Lindsay 2009, 201; Boruch 2010, 42.

10 Timpe 1962, 74; Boruch 2010, 42.

11 Philo. *Leg.* 4, 23; Suet. *Calig.* 23, 3; Cass. Dio 59, 8, 1. It is assumed it happened late in 37 or during the early months of the following year. See Barrett 1989, 75; Kienast 1996, 83; Boruch 2010, 42. The *terminus ante quem* in this case is 24th May 38, the date under which the *AFA* says C. Caecina Largus was co-opted into the college to replace Gemellus. See Scheid 1998, 30 (ll. 34–36).

in a conspiracy aimed at killing Caligula, but he doubts Gemellus could have actually been involved in a coup at his age[12]. Cassius Dio adds that the emperor's excuse for having the younger man murdered was that during Caligula's illness Gemellus supposedly prayed for his cousin's death, hoping for a swift succession[13]. It is of course hard to be certain if Gemellus was in fact involved in an assassination conspiracy, or if one even existed, but in my opinion both those things are rather improbable. Significantly, there are no such suggestions in authors other than Philo, who actually doubts Gemellus was part of a conspiracy. It seems more likely the accusation was merely a convenient excuse to have him killed.

Some scholars suppose that after Gemellus' murder Caligula also cancelled his earlier adoption[14], a theory potentially confirmed by epigraphical sources, since a sepulchral inscription dedicated to Gemellus has been found near the Mausoleum of Augustus where he features as Drusus' son: *Ti. Caesar Drusi Caesaris f./hic situs est*[15]. That is also the way he is posthumously referred to in the *AFA*[16].

3.2 Julia Drusilla and Marcus Lepidus in the Princeps' Succession Plans

In Suetonius, we read that during the grave illness Caligula came down with in October of 37, he designated his beloved sister Drusilla as both the heiress of his private property and his political successor (*heredem quoque bonorum atque*

12 Philo. *Leg.* 4, 23.

13 Cass. Dio 59, 8, 1.

14 See e.g. Boruch 2010, 42–43.

15 *CIL* VI 892 = ILS 172. The exact spot of Gemellus' burial is unknown. Barrett (1989, 75) supposes his remains were deposited in the Mausoleum of Augustus, while Kienast (1996, 83) believes the young man was interred in the *Campus Martius*, where the corpse was burnt.

16 Scheid 1998, 30 (l. 34). According to Boruch (2010, 42–43), one piece of evidence indicating that Gemellus' *adrogatio* was annulled is his burial, modest for a son and intended successor of the emperor, but the argument is not convincing. I believe that in Gemellus' case the lack of a sumptuous funeral and posthumous honours resulted not so much from any cancellation of his adoption as from the fact he had fallen out of favour and was sentenced to death for supposedly planning an attempt on the emperor's life; it would have been almost inconceivable for Caligula to honour with a public funeral a member of the dynasty officially executed for conspiring against the incumbent princeps.

imperii aeger instituit)[17], in a passage somewhat difficult to interpret. While Roman custom made it possible for women to inherit property, it is hard to imagine how Drusilla could have been appointed Caligula's political successor. Nor does it seem likely the princeps counted on the Senate and the army accepting a female emperor. Thus personally I doubt the veracity of that passage in Suetonius. Rather, I believe the historian meant for Caligula's alleged intention to make a woman princeps to be further proof of the young emperor's extreme eccentricity, along with his plan to appoint a horse consul[18], fitting in perfectly with Suetonius' image of Caligula as insane. Some scholars are of the opinion that in the event of the emperor's death Drusilla was only meant to inherit his property, while the throne would have fallen to her husband Marcus Aemilius Lepidus[19]; a possible scenario provided that Drusilla was already Lepidus' wife during her brother's illness. The problem, however, is that she might not have been, since it is supposed the marriage was made no earlier than AD 38[20].

This a good moment to take a closer look at Marcus Lepidus and consider what role he was supposed to play in Caligula's succession plans. Cassius Dio writes that the princeps was close with his brother-in-law, who reportedly took part in Caligula's most debauched sexual orgies. The same author recounts Caligula granted Lepidus the dispensation which made it possible for him to run for every magistracy five years before the age prescribed by the law, as well as promised he would make Lepidus his successor[21]. There is evidence for Drusilla's husband's role having been special, in the form of a statue of him erected in the Sebasteion in Aphrodisias next to the statues of members of the imperial family: Agrippina the Elder, Germanicus and most likely Livia. In that way, the inhabitants of the city celebrated Lepidus becoming part of the reigning family[22]. Modern scholars are of the opinion that with Gemellus' murder and Caligula not having a son, Lepidus became the primary candidate for the succession[23], and that view seems to be correct. No doubt at that stage the princeps could have seen in Drusilla's husband a potential successor who could take over in case of his unexpected death, although that was a temporary solution. I do not believe Caligula could

---

17 Suet. *Calig.* 24, 1. Barrett 1989, 81–82; Bauman 2003, 161–162; Boruch 2010, 48.

18 On the subject of that episode, see Suet. *Calig.* 55, 3.

19 See Boruch 2010, 48.

20 See Kienast 1996, 87; Bauman 2003, 162. Cassius Dio (59, 11, 1) mentions the marriage while reporting on events which took place in 38.

21 Cass. Dio 59, 22, 6–7; Barrett 1989, 81.

22 Barrett 1989, 82; Rose 1997, 36; 164 (no. 104).

23 See Ehrhardt 1978, 52; Griffin 1984, 26; Barrett 1989, 81; Mlasowsky 1996, 370.

have intended to make Lepidus his successor in the long run; he was young and might have had a son at any moment, which would have completely changed his succession plans.

Drusilla's death in June of AD 38 loosened Lepidus' ties to the ruling dynasty, pushing the prospect of his succession away[24]. Perhaps the loss of his old position did encourage him to take part in an assassination plot aimed at Caligula, into which the emperor's other sisters, Agrippina the Younger and Julia Livilla, were also dragged. Either way, in 39 he was officially charged by the princeps with working on a coup d'état, and sentenced to death. On the occasion of his execution, the Praetorians received gratuities, and at the temple of Mars Ultor three swords were offered which had supposedly been used in the assassination attempt[25].

24 Kienast 1996, 87; Mlasowsky 1996, 370.

25 Suet. *Calig.* 24, 3; Cass. Dio 59, 22, 6–8. See also Barrett 1989, 106–109; Mlasowsky 1996, 371; Boruch 2010, 52–53.

4 Claudius

4.1 Britannicus as the Primary Successor

The fact Caligula never settled the issue of the succession caused the Praetorian Guard to take matters in their own hands after his death. They handed the throne over to Claudius, the assassinated emperor's uncle[1]. Several days after Claudius was made emperor, his son was born and named Tiberius Claudius Germanicus, from AD 43 on popularly called Britannicus in celebration of his father's conquest of Britain[2]. The birth of a successor right at the beginning of a new emperor's reign was an extremely important event, especially in the context of ensuring the stability of the dynasty and continued transfer of imperial power within it. It is supposed it is to Britannicus' birth that we should connect the emission of sesterces and asses minted in Rome and dated to the years 41–42. Their obverse has a portrait of Claudius with the legend TI CLAUDIUS CAESAR AUG PM TR P IMP PP, whereas the reverse shows *Spes*, the female personification of hope, with a bunch of flowers in her right hand, while with her left, she lifts her dress off the ground, with the legend SPES AUGUSTA and the signature SC. Some scholars believe the coins were meant to express the new princeps' hope for his newly born son's succession and continued reign of the dynasty[3], an acceptable interpretation but only speculative; after all, the coins bear no legend referring to Britannicus, which would allow us to connect them to his birth with certainty.

Cassius Dio says the Senate was going to celebrate Britannicus' birth by granting him the title *Augustus*, but Claudius forbade it[4], whereas from Suetonius we know the princeps introduced his son to the army and the people many times during games while he was yet an infant, trying to win their support for him as his prospective successor[5].

As could be expected, the birth of a future successor resonated loudly in the provinces as well. One of the most prestigious ways in which Britannicus was celebrated by the inhabitants there involved honorific statues of him placed next

1 I discuss the process of Claudius' ascent to imperial power in more detail in Chapter Eight.

2 Cass. Dio 60, 12, 5; 22, 2; Kienast 1996, 93.

3 *RIC* I[2] *Claud.* 99; Sutherland 1951, 131–132; Levick 1990, 55; Mlasowsky 1996, 372–373, 375; Boruch 2010, 74.

4 Cass. Dio 60, 12, 5.

5 Suet. *Claud.* 27, 2.

to the images of his parents and sisters throughout the Empire. Examples include foundations in Arnae in Lycia, Ilium and Alexandria. In Arnae, the statue of Britannicus was displayed between the statues of Claudius and Messalina. The statuary group, made at the instigation of the local Council and Assembly, is dated to between AD 44 and 48[6]. In Ilium, the statue of Britannicus joined those of his sisters Antonia and Octavia; perhaps the group stood near the local Buleuterion. From its foundation inscription we know the decision to set it up was taken by the local authorities. It is assumed that those statues of Claudius' children were erected between AD 41 and 49. Later, after the princeps adopted Nero, his statue was added[7]. Information on the statuary group in Alexandria, on the other hand, comes from a papyrus containing Claudius' answer to the petition sent to him by the Alexandrians, asking the emperor for permission to raise statues in their city in honour of the ruling family. The text tells us that Claudius agreed to have a complex statuary group set up in Alexandria, including the statues of his mother Antonia, himself, Messalina, Britannicus, Antonia and Octavia. It is supposed the whole cycle was put in place shortly after AD 41[8].

Right after Britannicus' birth, coins began to be minted in the provinces reflecting the hierarchy within the imperial family before the year 49. One interesting example is made of the asses and didrachms produced in Patras in Achaia and in Caesarea in Cappadocia. The obverse of the former series, dated to AD 42–43, has Claudius' image and the legend TI CLAUDIUS CAESAR AUG GERM(ANICUS). The reverse shows Britannicus' image between the heads of his sisters Antonia and Octavia emerging from horns of plenty, and the legend is LIBERIS AUG COL AAP[9]. The obverse of the Caesarean didrachm, dated to 46–48, there is the image of the emperor's wife Messalina and the legend MESSALINA AUGUSTI, while the reverse shows Britannicus and Octavia facing each other and holding hands in a *dextrarum iunctio* with Antonia to one side, holding a horn of plenty. That image bears the legend OCTAVIA BRITANNICUS ANTONIA[10]. (fig. 22) The obverse of another Caesarean emission, this one dated to AD 48, one can see Britannicus' portrait and the legend ΚΛΑΥΔΙΟΣ ΚΑΙΣΑΡ ΒΡΙΤΑΝΝΙΚΟΣ; the reverse has images of Antonia and Octavia, again holding horns of plenty, and the legend ΚΑΙΣΑΡ ΕΤ Η ΟΚΤΑΟΥΙΑ ΑΝΤWΝΙΑ[11]. All

---

6 Rose 1997, 170 (no. 108); Boschung 2002, 153, 157 (I, no. 65).

7 Rose 1997, 178–179 (no. 120).

8 Rose 1997, 185–188 (no. 128).

9 *RPC* I 1255; Mlasowsky 1996, 375; Rose 1997, 41.

10 *RPC* I 3627; Mlasowsky 1996, 375; Rose 1997, 41.

11 *RPC* I 3656.

Fig. 22. Didrachm, Caesarea, AD 46–48. Obverse: an image of Messalina; legend: MESSALINA AUGUSTI. Reverse: Britannicus and Octavia facing each other and holding hands (*dextrarum iunctio*); to the side, Antonia, holding a horn of plenty; legend: OCTAVIA BRITANNICUS ANTONIA (*RPC* I 3627).

these coin series unambiguously stressed that the reign of the current dynasty guaranteed the stability and prosperity of the state. It is worth pointing out the message was expressed partly by means of the iconographic pattern featuring *cornucopiae* as a motif, applied earlier on coins minted when Drusus the Younger was designated Tiberius' successor and when his sons were born[12].

It ought to be stressed here that while we have quite a lot of provincial emissions for Britannicus from the beginning of Claudius' reign[13], there are no extant official coins celebrating him. The only exception could be the asses and sesterces mentioned above, those with the motif of *Spes Augusta*, provided of course that they should in fact be seen in connection with Britannicus' birth. Boruch supposes the situation may have been a consequence of Claudius' *moderatio*, since during the early years of his rule he showed considerable restraint endorsing his son[14], a

12 See above.

13 Other than the coins from Patras and Caesarea mentioned here, we also have emissions from Alexandria (*RPC*, I, 5135), Tomi (*RPC*, I, 1834) and Cyzicus (*RPC*, I, 2248), among others.

14 Boruch 2010, 72–73.

supposition supported to an extent by Cassius Dio, who writes that the princeps consistently did not allow Britannicus to receive overly spectacular honours[15].

To sum up, it can be said that during the early years of Claudius' reign, Britannicus was the emperor's unquestioned and only successor. That only changed in AD 50, when the princeps adopted the son of his new wife Agrippina, which remade the whole hierarchy of the imperial family and the succession order in place so far.

4.2 Gnaeus Pompeius and Lucius Silanus: the Emperor's Sons-in-law as Possible Successors?

There remains as a separate issue the question of whether Gnaeus Pompeius or Lucius Junius Silanus could have possibly succeeded Claudius. In AD 41, the former married the emperor's elder daughter Antonia, while the latter was betrothed to the younger daughter, Octavia[16]. Although Britannicus, being the emperor's son, was the primary candidate to succession, he could not have assumed the purple had Claudius died before he came of age. Because of this, the princeps needed to consider his sons-in-law, both the one he already had and the one he would soon get, in his dynastic calculations. In AD 41, both were vigintiviri. In the following year, they acted as urban prefects during the *Feriae Latinae*, and in AD 44 they received the special dispensation which let them run for every magistracy five years before the customary age[17]. These honours indicate that Pompeius and Silanus held important places in the imperial family at the time. Still, I would not treat these privileges, in either case, in terms of the emperor endorsing his intended successors; rather, they were a form of him honouring his current and future sons-in-law. What were the chances then for either of them to actually become a future princeps? I believe the only way that could have happened would be if Claudius had died before Britannicus reached the age which would have made it possible for him to rule independently. If such were the case, one of the sons-in-law might have taken over and Britannicus would have stood little to no chance to come into his father's political legacy[18]: it is unlikely either Pompeius or Silanus would have been content to remain "temporary" regents while Claudius' son was underage[19].

---

15 Cass. Dio 60, 12, 5.

16 Cass. Dio 60, 5, 7; Ehrhardt 1978, 59, Levick 1990, 58; Kienast 1996, 92, 99.

17 Cass. Dio 60, 5, 8; Ehrhardt 1978, 60; Levick 1990, 58.

18 See Ehrhardt 1978, 67.

19 That was an entirely different situation from the one we know from Augustus' times, when the princeps chose Marcus Agrippa as a potential *quasi*-regent for

4.3 Britannicus or Nero? The Problem of Succession During the Final Years of Claudius' Rule

The fall and execution of Claudius' third wife Messalina in AD 48, and his marriage to Germanicus' daughter Agrippina the Younger one year later, powerfully influenced the emperor's succession policy during the last years of his reign. It was no accident that Agrippina was chosen. As Augustus' great-granddaughter, she was a very attractive match for Claudius, who was himself not part of the Julian family. It needs to be emphasized here that theirs was the first marriage between an uncle and niece, not a practice encountered in Roman society before, as marriages of this kind were forbidden and seen as a dishonour (*incestum*)[20].

The emperor's new wife had a son, Lucius Domitius Ahenobarbus, from her first marriage to Gnaeus Domitius Ahenobarbus, consul in AD 32[21]. Consequently Britannicus, until then the only successor, gained a rival to succeed Claudius in the future, since it must have been obvious to all that the ambitious Agrippina would do her best to see her son on the throne. We know Lucius Domitius' first public presentation was before he became the emperor's stepson. In Tacitus and Suetonius we read that in AD 47 he and Britannicus both took part in the riding competition of *lusus Troiae*, with Tacitus noting the audience responded to Agrippina's son's performance with more enthusiasm, in his opinion primarily because he was descended from Germanicus. Knowing the future course of events, Tacitus treats the behaviour of the Roman plebs as a foreshadowing of Nero's reign[22]. In AD 49, shortly after Claudius' marriage to Agrippina, Domitius was betrothed to Octavia, the younger of the emperor's daughters[23]. Before this happened, the princeps had cancelled her betrothal to the Junius Silanus mentioned above, who was also excluded from the senatorial order and removed from praetorship. On the day that Claudius married Agrippina, Silanus committed suicide[24]. According to Tacitus, Domitius' engagement to Octavia meant his

---

Agrippa's own natural sons, Gaius and Lucius Caesar until they came of age, which I discuss above.

20 Tac. *Ann.* 12, 5–7. Suet. *Claud.* 26, 3; 39, 2; Cass. Dio 61, 31, 6. On that marriage, see e.g. Griffin 1984, 29; Levick 1990, 69–70; Treggiari 1991, 112; Barrett 1996, 100–102; Bauman 2003, 180.

21 Kienast 1996, 94.

22 Suet. *Ner.* 7, 1; Tac. *Ann.* 11, 11, 2; 12, 1.

23 Tac. *Ann.* 12, 9, 1–2; Cass. Dio 61, 31, 8; Griffin 1984, 29; Kienast 1996, 99; Bauman 2003, 180; Krüger 2012, 24–25.

24 Tac. *Ann.* 12, 4, 1–3; 12, 8, 1; Levick 1990, 71.

standing in the imperial family became the same as Britannicus'[25], but in my opinion that is anachronistic, as Tacitus' assessment does not reflect Domitius' actual significance at that moment. For now, he was still only the emperor's stepson and future son-in-law, while Britannicus remained Claudius' only son and so his primary successor.

This only changed after the princeps adopted Domitius, no doubt a breakthrough moment in that latter's life[26]. From the *AFA* we know it took place on 25th February AD 50[27]. Ancient historians report that Claudius took the decision under the influence of Agrippina, who, Cassius Dio claims, had full control of the emperor from the moment she became his wife. Tacitus recounts the person who ultimately persuaded Claudius was the freedman Pallas, who convinced him that adopting Domitius would strengthen the reigning family. Tacitus meticulously stresses Pallas had in turn been influenced by the emperor's new wife[28]. In other words, both historians treat Agrippina as the prime mover behind the adoption in question[29].

Since Domitius had no *pater familias* above him, the procedure was *adrogatio*, the same as when Tiberius adopted Germanicus, or when Caligula adopted Tiberius Gemellus. And because the princeps already had a son of his own, the adoption of Domitius needed to have proper justification (a *iusta causa adrogandi*)[30]. In such cases, it was usually the *pontifices* who issued an opinion. Of course it is difficult to imagine the emperor, who was the *pontifex maximus*, might not have been given the approval of the other members of the college he presided over. Domitius' *adrogatio* was further sanctioned by the Senate and finally by the Comitia (with a *lex curiata*)[31]. From that moment on, Agrippina's son was officially *Nero Claudius Drusus Germanicus Caesar*[32]. The adoption of Nero significantly changed the order of succession as it had stood until then.

---

25 Tac. *Ann.* 12, 9, 2.

26 Joseph. *AJ.* 20, 150; Tac. *Ann.* 12, 25, 1; Suet. *Claud.* 27, 2; *Ner.* 7, 1.

27 Under 25th February 59 we find a mention of sacrifices to be made to Jupiter, Juno and Minerva on a successive anniversary of Claudius adopting Nero. See Scheid 1998, 67 (ll. 58–60).

28 See Tac. *Ann.* 12, 25, 1; Cass. Dio 60, 32, 1–2.

29 On the way Tacitus' and Cassius Dio's narratives frame Agrippina's role as regards Claudius' succession moves, see Ginsburg 2006, 22–35.

30 Suetonius (*Claud.* 39, 2) harshly criticizes Claudius for adopting his stepson, even though he had a natural son of his own.

31 Tac. *Ann.* 12, 26, 1; 12, 41, 3. See also Prevost 1949, 39–41; Barrett 1996, 112–113; Lindsay 2009, 201–202; Krüger 2012, 25.

32 Kornemann 1930, 54; Levick 1990, 71; Barrett 1996, 113; Kienast 1996, 96.

Certainly it meant Britannicus gained a serious rival, as from that point Nero was a legitimate successor, just like Claudius' natural son. However, he was older than Britannicus, which made his actual chances for becoming the next princeps higher, in particular should Claudius die before his natural son reached the proper age to rule independently[33]. Nonetheless, Nero's greatest asset was no doubt the fact he was a natural descendant of Augustus and a grandson of Germanicus on his mother's side, which also gave him a handicap for a potential succession race against Britannicus.

Nero's adoption also turned out to be a good occasion to honour his mother. From Tacitus and Cassius Dio we know Agrippina received the prestigious title of *Augusta*[34]. Significantly, it was the first time that this happened to the current emperor's spouse[35]. Judith Ginsburg pointed out the fact that Nero's adoption and his mother's receiving the title occurred at the same time, hardly an accident; the purpose of the title was to emphasize her standing, not simply as the emperor's wife, but also the mother of his future successor[36].

Another extremely important moment in Nero's career was assuming the toga of manhood, which he did in AD 51, although the exact date is unknown. Traditionally ceremonies of this kind were scheduled on the Liberalia, that is on 17th March[37], but in Nero's case it probably happened earlier. We do know he was designated for consulship on 4th March[38], and it seems unlikely he would not have donned the *toga virilis* before[39]. Tacitus correctly comments that the ceremony of Nero receiving his toga of manhood took place too early[40]; after all, he was not yet fourteen, which was the minimum age at which young Roman men

33 Similarly Ginsburg 2006, 25, who is correct to emphasize that in spite of there being no legal regulations to guarantee the succession of the elder of the emperor's sons, after his adoption by Claudius, due to his age Nero was in actual fact treated as the primary candidate to the throne.

34 Tac. *Ann.* 12, 26, 1; Cass Dio 61, 33, 2a.

35 See Levick 1990, 71; Barrett 1996, 108. Livia only received that honour after Augustus' death (Suet. *Aug.* 101, 2; Tac. *Ann.* 1, 8, 1), and in Messalina's case Claudius refused to grant it (Cass. Dio 60, 12, 5).

36 Ginsburg 2006, 71.

37 Levick 1990, 73; Barrett 1996, 116.

38 That is the date given in the *AFA* (Scheid 1998, 67, ll. 65–67). See also Kornemann 1930, 55; Griffin 1984, 29; Kienast 1996, 96; Barrett 1996, 116.

39 At any rate, Tacitus' account (*Ann.* 12, 41, 1) clearly indicates he received that honour precisely on the occasion of assuming the toga of manhood.

40 Tac. *Ann.* 12, 41, 1: *Ti. Claudio quintum Servio Cornelio Orfito consulibus virilis toga Neroni maturata quo capessendae rei publicae habilis videretur.*

could receive their *toga virilis*[41]. I must emphasize no other member of the imperial family had ever received this honour so early[42]. It is also certainly no accident that Nero's celebration coincided with Claudius' fifth consulate, which gave the ceremony extra splendour. A clear analogy can be seen to the years 5 and 2 BC, when Augustus made a point of assuming consulship in order to grant more splendour to the ceremonies of Gaius and Lucius Caesar receiving their togas[43].

Nero's entry into "adulthood" was commemorated with appropriate gratuities paid out to the Praetorian Guard (the *donativum*) and the plebs of the city of Rome (the *congiarium*). The lad was also officially introduced to the Praetorian Guard, and then the Senate[44], and circus games were held. Tacitus stresses Nero took part in them wearing triumphal garb (the *toga picta*) like an *imperator*, in sharp contrast to Britannicus' merely boyish outfit (the *toga praetexta*). For the historian, it was an extremely clear sign meant to let the public opinion know who would succeed Claudius[45]. Rose rightly observed Nero's that presentation during those games meant that realistically, his standing in the imperial family was stronger than Britannicus'[46]. Bauman claims Agrippina's son was granted the right to participate in the triumphal garb in the future in all games held in his honour[47], but this claim is purely hypothetical; no sources mention Nero receiving such a privilege and we cannot say whether he wore the *toga picta* during any later celebrations in his name.

In connection with Nero assuming the toga of manhood, Tacitus lists a few prestigious honours awarded him by the Senate:

---

41 However, Levick (1990, 72–73), against Tacitus, suggests Nero was already of the right age for that, pointing out that since he was born on 15th December 37, in 51 he was in his fourteenth year. Even so, the Roman historian's commentary (that Nero received the toga prematurely), and the earlier cases of Gaius and Lucius Caesar indicate Romans only donned the *toga virilis* after they were fourteen. See also Griffin 1984, 29; Rose 1997, 42; Shotter 2005, 13.

42 Later, the same would happen with Commodus and Caracalla, who likewise received the toga of manhood before their fourteenth birthdays. See Koestermann 1967, 177; Kienast 1996, 147.

43 Degrassi 1952, 14; Levick 1990, 72; Barrett 1996, 116–117; Osgood 2011, 229.

44 Tac. *Ann.* 12, 41, 1–2; Suet. *Ner.* 7, 2.

45 Tac. *Ann.* 12, 41, 2: *et ludicro circensium, quod adquirendis vulgi studiis edebatur, Britannicus in praetexta, Nero triumphali veste travecti sunt: spectaret populus hunc decore imperatorio, illum puerili habitu, ac perinde fortunam utriusque praesumeret.* See also Ginsburg 2006, 27.

46 Rose 1997, 42.

47 Bauman 2003, 181.

> Et Caesar adulationibus senatus libens cessit ut vicesimo aetatis anno consulatum Nero iniret atque interim designatus proconsulare imperium extra urbem haberet ac princeps iuventutis appellaretur[48].
>
> The Caesar yielded with pleasure to the sycophancies of the senate, which desired Nero to assume the consulship in the twentieth year of his age, and in the interval, as consul designate, to hold proconsular authority outside the capital and bear the title Prince of the Youth[49].

The first item on the list is designating the youth for consulship, an office he was to hold in his twentieth year (that is, at the age of nineteen). Since he was born in December of 37, most likely he was meant to assume that consulship at the beginning of AD 57[50]. Thus from AD 51 he had the status of *consul designatus*. Another honour was an *imperium proconsulare*, valid out of the city of Rome (*extra urbem*) and granted until he assumed the consulship. Importantly, in that case the *imperium* had no connection to any specific mission in the provinces[51]. On top of these, the equites gave him the prestigious title of *princeps iuventutis*, which since Augustus' day had been conferred on prospective successors. At the same time, Nero was admitted into all of Rome's major priestly colleges, a fact confirmed by both epigraphic and numismatical sources[52].

The honours Nero received on the assumption of the *toga virilis* show great similarities to those conferred earlier, on analogous occasions, on Gaius and Lucius Caesar. The common points included receiving the title of *princeps iuventutis* and the designation for consulship before the age of twenty, with all the previous steps of the *cursus honorum* omitted. Conferring an *imperium proconsulare* on a thirteen-year-old, on the other hand, had had no precedent; no other Roman had ever been granted such powers at such a young age. All

48 Tac. *Ann.* 12, 41, 1.

49 Translated by J. Jackson (Loeb Classical Library, 312).

50 So e.g. Griffin 1984, 29; Levick 1990, 73; Bauman 2003, 180; Shotter 2005, 13. *Contra* Kienast (1996, 96), Wiedemann (2008, 242), who erroneously assume Nero was to become consul in AD 58.

51 Parsi (1963, 47) believes that away from Rome that *imperium* was equal to that of Claudius, as had been the case with Tiberius, whose power equalled that of Augustus in the provinces (see above), but the sources do not confirm this opinion. Wiedemann's (2008, 242) claim that Nero's *imperium* would only be valid within Italy is unfounded as well.

52 *CIL* VI 921 = *ILS* 222; *RIC* I^2 *Claud.* 76–77. See also Levick 1990, 73; Barrett 1996, 117–118; Kuhoff 1993a, 69; Krüger 2012, 26. In this context, Boruch's (2010, 81) statement that coins are the only evidence of that is erroneous.

those honours go to prove that at that moment Agrippina's son was treated as the major candidate to the succession. Britannicus, who received no honours at the time, as Cassius Dio emphasizes, was clearly in his shadow[53]. Nor can there be any doubt that Nero's endorsement as the intended successor, at the expense of Claudius' natural son, resulted largely from the determined actions of Agrippina, who aimed to ensure her son would reign[54].

To celebrate the onset of Nero's public career, the imperial and senatorial mints in Rome produced several interesting coin series, including aurei, denarii, sesterces and dupondii, basically all of them dated to the years 51–54. The first group is made up of coins bearing Nero's image on the obverse, which can be divided into two series. The first of those comprises coins with the legend NERO CLAUD CAES DRUSUS GERM PRINC IUVENT, their reverse showing a *simpulum*, a *lituus*, a tripod and a *patera*—that is, the symbols of the major priestly colleges—with the legend SACERD(OS) COOPT(ATUS) IN OMN(IA) CONL(EGIA) SUPRA NUM(ERUM) EX SC[55]. (fig. 23) On the one hand, that emission commemorated admitting Agrippina's son to the four most important Roman priestly colleges, and on the other, it highlighted his *pietas* towards the gods, one of the constitutive virtues of a princeps[56]. The obverse of the other series bears the legend NERONI CLAUDIO DRUSO GERM COS DESIGN instead, with a spear and shield on the reverse and with EQUESTER ORDO PRINCIPI IUVENT written on the shield[57]. (fig. 24) Those coins marked an extremely important moment in Nero's career: his designation as consul and the grant of the prestigious title of *princeps iuventutis*[58]. Moreover, the emission is evidence for him having received a silver shield and spear from the equestrian order, in the way Gaius and Lucius Caesar had. It is worth pointing out that Nero was the third intended successor (after Tiberius and Drusus the Younger) whose portrait was put on the obverse of official coins. However, it was also the first time that happened with the obverse of imperial coins; in the case of Tiberius and Drusus, the series had been senatorial.

---

53 Cass. Dio 61, 32, 5.

54 See Corbier 1995, 189–190; Bauman 2003, 181.

55 *RIC* I² *Claud.* 76–77, 107; *HCC* I *Claud.* 40–41; Sutherland 1951, 146; Mlasowsky 1996, 382–383.

56 See Mlasowsky 1996, 384.

57 *RIC* I² *Claud.* 78–79, 108; *HCC* I *Claud.* 42–43; Sutherland 1951, 146; Mlasowsky 1996, 382–383.

58 Barrett 1996, 117.

Fig. 23. Aureus, Rome, AD 51–54. Obverse: an image of Nero; legend: NERO CLAUD CAES DRUSUS GERM PRINC IUVENT. Reverse: images of a *simpulum*, a *lituus*, a tripod and a *patera*; legend: SACERD(OS) COOPT(ATUS) IN OMN(IA) CONL(EGIA) SUPRA NUM(ERUM) EX SC (*RIC* I^2 *Claud.* 76).

Fig. 24. Aureus, Rome, AD 51–54. Obverse: an image of Nero; legend: NERONI CLAUDIO DRUSO GERM COS DESIGN. Reverse: images of a spear and shield, labelled EQUESTER ORDO PRINCIPI IUVENT (*RIC* I^2 *Claud.* 78).

Fig. 25. Denarius, Rome, AD 51–54. Obverse: a portrait of Agrippina as Ceres, wearing a crown of ears of corn (the *corona spicea*); legend: AGRIPPINAE AUGUSTAE. Reverse: Nero's head; legend: NERO CLAUD CAES DRUSUS GERM PRINC IUVENT (*RIC* I² *Claud.* 75).

The second group comprises coins where Nero's image was put on the reverse. The denarii are of particular interest here, the obverse bearing a portrait of Agrippina as Ceres in the *corona spicea*—a crown of ears of corn—and the legend AGRIPPINAE AUGUSTAE. The reverse has Nero's head and the legend NERO CLAUD CAES DRUSUS GERM PRINC IUVENT[59]. (fig. 25) The originality of this series lies in one and the same coin bearing the images of the empress, who was the mother of the presumed successor, and of the successor himself, which was somewhat novel in official minting[60]. Still another series contains aurei and denarii with Claudius in a laurel wreath on the obverse, the legend being TI CLAUD CAESAR AUG GERM PM TRIB POT PP, while the reverse has a depiction of Nero and the legend NERO CLAUD CAES DRUSUS GERM PRINC IUVENT[61]. (fig. 26) It is supposed those two series may have been paid out to the Praetorian Guard as the *donativum* on the occasion of Nero putting on the *toga virilis*[62]. As indicated above, that episode is mentioned in both Tacitus and Suetonius.

59 *RIC* I² *Claud.* 75; Mlasowsky 1996, 382–383.

60 Barrett 1996, 116–117; Rose 1997, 42; Ginsburg 2006, 72.

61 *RIC* I² *Claud.* 82–83.

62 Sutherland 1951, 144; Rose 1997, 238 note 57.

Fig. 26. Aureus, Rome, AD 51–54. A portrait of Claudius wearing a laurel wreath; legend: TI CLAUD CAESAR AUG GERM PM TRIB POT PP. Reverse: an image of Nero; legend: NERO CLAUD CAES DRUSUS GERM PRINC IUVENT (*RIC* I^2 *Claud.* 82).

Mlasowsky observed that the construction on coins of the public image of Nero as the future successor made use of iconographic patterns similar to those already created under Augustus and employed in the succession propaganda of the time[63]. Since those patterns were well understood by most, this is quite comprehensible. All the coins described above distinctly reflect the new succession order which formed after the adoption of Nero, now the primary candidate to succession. It is striking there is no Britannicus on any official emissions from that period[64], a phenomenon not at all explicable by the fact of his still being a child. First, we know that images of Gaius and Lucius Caesar, and after of the sons of Drusus the Younger, made it onto official coins even before these young men assumed their togas of manhood. And second, we know that many provincial emissions dedicated to Britannicus were first minted only a few years after his birth[65]. The message of the numismatic sources cited above is clear then. They confirm what we know from literary sources: that Claudius' natural son was very much overshadowed by Nero from the moment the latter was adopted by the princeps[66].

63 Mlasowsky 1996, 382.

64 See Kuhoff 1993a, 68–69.

65 See above.

66 It also ought to be emphasized that after Nero's adoption statues of him began to appear in statuary groups erected in celebration of the imperial family in Rome and

I must point out here that a different picture is painted by provincial coins from the period, where both of Claudius' sons are shown as equal candidates to the succession. Let me illustrate this with two emissions produced in Corinth and Sinope[67]. The obverse of the Corinthian asses, dated to 50–51, has Claudius' face and the legend TI CLAUDIUS CAESAR. The reverse shows Nero and Britannicus in togas, facing each other. The latter holds a globe in his hand, while Nero rests a hand on it. The image bears the legend NE BR. Also on the reverse there are the names of the duumviri of the colony[68]. Now in Mlasowsky's opinion that emission shows Britannicus as the primary successor and future princeps, whereas Nero is only presented as his possible helper in administering the Empire; Mlasowsky points out it was no accident the younger brother was shown in a toga; rather, it was supposed to stress his maturity and readiness to take over public duties in the near future[69]. However, I find Rose's interpretation more convincing: both youths are shown as equal successors and future partners in wielding the imperial power[70].

Other interesting images can be found on coins minted in Sinope as well, but dated to 51–52. On the obverse of these, one can see Nero's and Britannicus' faces with the legend NER CLAUD CAES CLAUD BRITTAN CAE. The reverse has a caduceus between two horns of plenty[71]. This choice of iconographic motifs emphasized that succession of one of Claudius' sons meant continued prosperity for the Empire under the reign of new members of the ruling dynasty.

Although provincial coins show both sons of the emperor as equal candidates to the throne, I do not believe this is sufficient evidence to question the claim

---

Italy. The dynastic monument placed on the *via Lata* right next to the triumphal arch built in Claudius' honour to commemorate his conquest of Britain may serve as an example. It was most likely dedicated in AD 51, and from the preserved dedicatory inscriptions we know it included statues of Claudius, Antonia, Germanicus, Agrippina the Younger, Nero, Britannicus and Octavia. See Rose 1997, 42, 113–115 (no. 42). In Italy statues of Nero were added to existing statue groups dedicated to the reigning family, e.g. in *Rusellae* and *Velleia*. See Rose 1997, 42, 116–118 (no. 45); 121–126 (no. 50). Those monuments obviously reflect changes in the dynastic order caused by Nero's adoption and his elevation to the standing of a successor of Claudius.

67 We also know of coins dedicated to Nero and Britannicus originating in Pergamum (*RPC* I 2371), Laodicea (*RPC* I 2915–2916) and Hierapolis (*RPC* I 2971–2972).

68 *RPC* I 1182. We also have another emission from Corinth with the same image on the reverse, but with Agrippina on the obverse. See *RPC* I 1183–1184.

69 Mlasowsky 1996, 381.

70 Rose 1997, 43.

71 *RPC* I 2132.

made above: namely that after his adoption it was Nero who was endorsed as Claudius' successor, since on this issue the literary sources and official coin series are absolutely clear. In this context, a mere handful of provincial emissions, originating in the eastern parts of the Empire at that, cannot—in my opinion—overturn the general picture. One may well wonder why in this case the message of provincial coins diverges from what the official emissions tell us. Griffin thinks the reason might be that the people of the provinces were not up to date with the events in Rome relating to Nero's endorsement[72], a view that fails to convince me. After all, hitherto the inhabitants of the provinces had been rather familiar with the hierarchy within the imperial family and quickly responded to changes in the order of succession[73]. I find Rose's point of view more justified; namely, Rose believes the situation was the result of a tradition, strong in the provinces, that both sons of the incumbent emperor ought to be honoured in similar ways, even if one of them, Nero in that case, in fact had a better position. In his opinion, the point of reference here is the manner in which Gaius and Lucius Caesar, and later Germanicus and Drusus, had been celebrated[74].

Another important moment of Nero's career was doubtless his marriage to Claudius' daughter Octavia, which took place in AD 53[75]. Cassius Dio reports that before it took place, the emperor first had her adopted out into another family[76], so that legally speaking she was no longer his daughter[77]. The reason for this was that, according to Roman law, marriages between siblings were forbidden, and as we know since Nero's adoption in AD 50 Octavia had been formally his sister.

The role Agrippina played in securing her son's succession is a separate question. Josephus' diagnosis is apt, as he writes that it was due to her machinations that

---

72 Griffin 1984, 29.

73 Proven for example by the ways Tiberius was honoured in the provinces after he was adopted by Augustus and designated as his successor; see above.

74 Rose 1997, 42–43.

75 Joseph. *AJ*. 20, 150; Tac. *Ann*. 12, 58, 1; Suet. *Ner.* 7, 2.

76 Cass. Dio 61, 33, 2[2]. Kienast (1996, 99) supposes she was included in the *gens Octavia*, but his claim is quite groundless; he is incorrect to consider the *cognomen Octavia*, which Claudius' daughter had had since birth too, her new *nomen gentile*, to have been used only after the adoption mentioned in Cassius Dio. Thus, with the sources silent, we cannot tell which Roman *gens* she was placed in before her marriage to Nero.

77 See Kornemann 1930, 54; Prevost 1949, 41–42; Griffin 1984, 29–30; Barrett 1996, 135; Bauman 2003, 180; Shotter 2005, 13. Hugh Lindsay (2009, 201) on the other hand supposes Octavia may have gone through an *emancipatio*, which included a change of *gens* among its consequences, but that is another suggestion unconfirmed by any sources.

Nero ended up becoming emperor[78]. I have already mentioned that it was mostly in response to her prompting that Claudius decided to adopt Nero. From Tacitus we know that shortly afterwards Agrippina brought about important personnel changes in the Praetorian Guard, persuading the princeps to recall two of its prefects, L. Lusius Geta and P. Rufrius Crispinus, because as former followers of Messalina they supported Britannicus' candidacy to the throne. S. Afranius Burrus, a loyal henchman of Agrippina, was nominated in their place. Officers known for sympathizing with Britannicus were also removed from the Guard[79]. Cassius Dio in turn recounts that during Claudius' illness, with which he probably came down in AD 53, Agrippina intensely canvassed for support for her son among the Roman plebs, presenting him as the future emperor. He also writes that she tried to convince the princeps to officially proclaim Nero his successor before the Senate and the people, so he could take over smoothly in the event of Claudius' death[80].

Suetonius and Cassius Dio both claim that Claudius came to resent Agrippina and Nero towards the end of his reign, because she was too insistent about working on her son's succession. According to these authors, the princeps regretted his decision to adopt Nero and wished he had not favoured him at his own son's expense. Supposedly, for these reasons he was going to grant Britannicus the toga of manhood in the near future and prepare him for the succession. However, the ambitious Agrippina saw to it that his plans failed by having the emperor poisoned[81].

Of course, we cannot definitively determine whether Claudius did in fact have such intentions, as speculation is all we have in this matter, but personally I do not find it likely[82]. Nero had been consistently prepared for the succession since

78 Joseph. *AJ*. 20, 153.

79 Tac. *Ann*. 12, 41, 2; 42, 1. See also Timpe 1962, 95–96; Ginsburg 2006, 28.

80 Cass. Dio 61, 33, 9–10. Timpe (1962, 98 note 1) considers that information false, but I find his scepticism unjustified. Considering Agrippina's earlier actions, consistently aimed at securing Nero's succession, such behaviour during Claudius' illness seems highly likely for her.

81 Suet. *Claud*. 43, 44, 1–2; Cass. Dio 61, 34, 1–2. Suggestions that Claudius was poisoned at the instigation of Agrippina, apparently out of fear the princeps would pass Nero over and designate Britannicus as his successor, can also be found in Flavius Josephus (*AJ*. 20, 148; 151) and Tacitus (*Ann*. 12, 66, 1–2).

82 A similar opinion is expressed by some scholars. Thomas A. Dorey (1966, 155) assumes such rumours were spread by Agrippina to get back at Nero after she lost influence, while Levick (1990, 76) supposes they were circulated by supporters of Britannicus. Barett (1996, 146) is equally sceptical regarding such suggestions of the sources.

his adoption in AD 50 and there is no evidence to indicate Claudius changed his succession plans in the last months of his rule. It is especially striking that ultimately the emperor had not decided to grant Britannicus his *toga virilis* even though, as our authors clearly state, at some point he had meant to. In February of 54 the boy was thirteen years old and virtually capable of receiving that privilege, as proven by the earlier example of Nero, who had put on his toga when only slightly older[83]. On the occasion, Agrippina's son had also received a number of prestigious honours, the purpose of which was to accelerate his political career. Still, in Britannicus' case the emperor never took that step, even though it could have strengthened his position vis-à-vis Nero a great deal and let him join the final race for imperial power. We also know that during the last years of his reign the princeps took no actions to endorse his natural son as a potential successor, such as introducing him to the legions or the Praetorian Guard, followed by distributing appropriate gratuities. And finally, we must not forget that both the authors cited above were active after Nero's rise to power, which means their accounts may reflect echoes of the literary tradition unfriendly to Nero, in which he became emperor against the will of the previous princeps and at the expense of his natural son. Thus we ought to retain some caution regarding their opinions.

83 Granting Nero the toga of manhood at such a young age was in fact a unique event, since we know before him young men only gained the privilege after they were fourteen years old (for which see above), but it did constitute a precedent. Therefore there was nothing to say Britannicus could not assume the *toga virilis* early, just as his adoptive brother had.

5 Nero

Nero becoming princeps meant that after Claudius the imperial power now passed back to a natural descendant of Augustus; the new emperor was related to him on the distaff side. While Nero ruled for almost fourteen years, he never chose a possible successor during that time. I hardly think that was because he had no interest in the matter; rather, the reason was that he did not have a son, or else a close relative who could have been prepared for the succession. Tacitus says the young princeps very much wanted to sire a male heir[1]. To that end, he embarked on three marriages. His first marriage took place when Claudius was still emperor: Nero wed Claudius' daughter Octavia[2]. Their union remained childless, and this apparently gave Nero an excuse to divorce her, which he did in AD 62. Soon after, Octavia was charged with adultery, exiled and, on Nero's orders, murdered[3].

Several days after that divorce, the princeps married Poppea Sabina[4]. Early in AD 63, this new wife gave birth to a daughter, Claudia. The emperor is said to have responded enthusiastically. The baby and her mother both received the titles of Augusta on the occasion. However, the girl died a few months after she was born. It is worth mentioning the Senate officially deified her[5]. Two years later, Poppaea was pregnant again, but this time, there was no birth, because, as the ancient authors report, during one of their fights Nero kicked his wife in the abdomen and as a result, she died. Regretting his temper, he granted Poppaea a public funeral and her embalmed body was laid to rest in the Mausoleum of Augustus[6].

After Poppaea's death, Nero quickly picked a new candidate to be his spouse. From Suetonius' account we know he intended to marry Antonia, Claudius' other daughter[7]. If she were to give birth to a son, Nero's future successor would have the blood of both the Julii and the Claudii. Corbier believes the princeps

---

1 Tac. *Ann.* 16, 6, 1–2.

2 See above.

3 Tac. *Ann.* 14, 60, 1–5; 63, 1–2; Suet. *Ner.* 35, 1–2; Cass. Dio 62, 13, 1. According to Tacitus and Suetonius, the accusation of adultery was completely baseless.

4 Tac. *Ann.* 14, 60, 1; Suet. *Ner.* 35, 3; Cass. Dio 62, 13, 1. See also Griffin 1984, 98–99; Kienast 1996, 96, 99.

5 Tac. *Ann.* 15, 23, 1–3; Suet. *Ner.* 35, 3; Griffin 1984, 103; Kienast 1996, 100.

6 Tac. *Ann.* 16, 6, 1–2; Suet. *Ner.* 35, 3.

7 Suet. *Ner.* 35, 4.

also hoped that the marriage would rehabilitate him in the eyes of the public, dispelling the bad impression left by his banishing and killing Octavia, who had been very popular[8]. In the end, however, the marriage fell through, because Antonia refused, and as a result was murdered on the emperor's orders[9]. Towards the end of his reign, Nero undertook one more attempt at siring a male child by marrying Statilia Messalina. However, this marriage, made in AD 66, did not provide the princeps with a son either[10].

During the years of his reign Nero did not have a son. Even so, he took no steps to solve the issue of the future succession in some other way. With no male issue of his own, one of his options was to adopt and designate his stepson Rufrius Crispinus, Poppaea's son from her first marriage. Instead, he had him murdered; the excuse being that Crispinus had pretended to be the emperor during a game[11]. The episode makes it clear that Nero only ever intended to be succeeded by a son of his own. Since in the end he had waited in vain, the issue of the succession remained unsettled until the end of his rule. Thus with Nero's death, after a nearly hundred-year-long reign, the Julio-Claudian dynasty died out.

8 Corbier 1995, 187. Tacitus (*Ann.* 14, 60, 4–5; 61, 1) and Suetonius (*Ner.* 35, 2) both write that Octavia was very popular, especially with the Roman plebs.

9 Suet. *Ner.* 35, 4. Kienast 1996, 93.

10 Suet. *Ner.* 35, 1; see also Griffin 1984, 194; Mlasowsky 1996, 388; Kienast 1996, 97, 100.

11 Suet. *Ner.* 35, 5; Griffin 1984, 196.

Conclusions

The analysis of Augustus' actions relating to the succession policy carried out in Chapter One unambiguously indicates that the emperor's intention was that the throne should in the future pass on to a member of his immediate family, and more precisely to a descendant of his. In that chapter I argued against the opinion, repeated by many historians, that Marcellus and later Agrippa were to be Augustus' successors. Instead, I believe that despite all the honours and prestigious posts lavished on them, their role was merely to help the princeps, who had no son of his own, fulfil his succession plans by siring the future successor. To that end, Augustus gave his only daughter—Julia—in marriage, first to Marcellus, and after his death, to Agrippa. Those moves make it clear that the key figure in Augustus' succession policy during the early years of his rule was Julia rather than her husbands. His dynastic ambitions were fulfilled when Julia and Agrippa had Gaius and Lucius. Their adoption by the emperor in 17 BC was a clear sign to his contemporaries that one of the brothers would be the next princeps. However, the plan to make a natural descendant his direct successor fell through when the Caesars both died and Agrippa Postumus was excluded from the *gens Iulia*. Under the circumstances, the princeps was forced to rely on Tiberius, who was adopted and designated successor in AD 4. The latter move was meant to keep the throne within the *gens Iulia*, even though the successor the princeps appointed was a Julius by adoption rather than by blood. Still, forcing Tiberius to adopt Germanicus in turn means that Augustus' plans for his future successor to be a blood relative of his were only postponed rather than abandoned; I believe his intention was for Germanicus, a relative of Augustus on his mother's side, to follow Tiberius as princeps. The fact Augustus brought about Germanicus' marriage to Agrippina makes it in turn possible to suppose he hoped for imperial power to later pass on into the hands of this couple's son, who would in fact be descended from him.

One of the most important aspects of Augustus' dynastic policy was the public presentation and endorsement of his intended successors, a matter of particular significance in a political regime which formally speaking was not a hereditary monarchy. The princeps certainly took great care to secure them the support of and popularity with the army, regularly entrusting them with prestigious military command, also on vital campaigns. These allowed the men in question to win wartime glory and demonstrate their aptitude for ruling the state. Victories won by members of the *domus Augusta* were also of considerable importance for shaping the soldiers' loyalty towards the reigning dynasty. The missions carried out by the prospective successors in the provinces were also part of their endorsement. On the one hand, they provided a good occasion to introduce them to the inhabitants there, and on the other, they gave the people in the provinces a chance to express their affection for and commitment to the imperial family by honouring its members. Gaius Caesar's eastern mission can be seen as an example of that, as can the planned inspection of the Spanish provinces his brother Lucius was to conduct but did not.

The analysis of the *cursus honorum* of the members of the *domus Augusta* endorsed by Augustus as his successors carried out above proves they were very different from the political careers of those members of the imperial family whose role in Augustus' succession plans were secondary. It ought to be enough to mention Gaius Caesar received an *imperium proconsulare* at eighteen and assumed consulship one year later, skipping all the previous offices, while Tiberius and Drusus the Elder had only held quaestorships at a comparable age. There are also important differences between how Augustus' sons and stepsons were presented to the public, with numismatic evidence being especially telling. Whereas Gaius and Lucius were regularly depicted on numerous emissions, coins bearing the images of Tiberius or Drusus were extremely rare. In Tiberius' case it is no accident the situation changed only after his adoption and designation as successor in AD 4.

I want to stress that in spite of Augustus' intensive actions in the sphere of dynastic policy, conducted practically from the beginning of his rule, the princeps took a very long time to actually designate his political successor. I have above expressed the belief that granting Agrippa tribunician powers in 18 BC should be treated more as raising him to the status of co-regent than as designating him successor as such. In that respect, the year 4 was a breakthrough, since the adoption of Tiberius and the Senate and the people granting him *tribunicia potestas* and *imperium proconsulare* should be considered as his official designation to be Augustus' successor. From then on, the model outlined in Tiberius' case became the traditional method of designating one's successor, used by successive rulers in the principate era.

The analysis of Tiberius' succession policy I carried out in Chapter Two shows that at the beginning of his reign he continued along the line staked out by his predecessor, aimed at keeping the throne within the *domus Augusta*. However, I do not see sufficient evidence to claim that Tiberius saw Germanicus as his future successor, as Augustus had most likely intended;

the honours granted to Drusus the Younger indicate his status in the imperial family was the same as his adoptive brother's, and both were widely treated as equal candidates to the succession. I am convinced that this observation is further confirmed by Tacitus, who in no uncertain terms writes that until Germanicus died, the emperor had not decided which son would succeed him politically, and it was only Germanicus' death that made Drusus the primary successor. In AD 22 he was also officially designated as the future princeps. The procedure applied, which was the Senate conferring *tribunicia potestas* on him, drew on the model of designating the successor and/or co-regent created under Augustus. Drusus' sudden death in the following year ruined Tiberius' succession plans. Unlike Augustus, who after the deaths of Gaius and Lucius Caesar at once proceeded to set up a new order of succession through more adoptions, Tiberius took no concrete steps after AD 23 to find new successors. The circle of potential successors then included primarily Germanicus' sons and Tiberius Gemellus, the emperor's natural grandson. However, the princeps showed great restraint when it came to endorsing any of them as future successors; he did not give them any military functions to carry out, and did not let them receive any overly prestigious honours. Moreover, after reaching the age at which they were difficult to control, Germanicus' elder sons were first imprisoned, and later killed at the emperor's command. Thus after 23, Tiberius' succession policy boiled down mostly to eliminating unwanted potential candidates to the succession and delaying the decision as to who the successor would be. Ultimately, the princeps did not decide this unequivocally until the end of his reign.

In Chapter Three, I put forward the claim that the adoption of Tiberius Gemellus should not be seen as indicative of Caligula's intention to make him his political successor. In my opinion, the point of this move was only to dispel the bad impression resulting from excluding the young man from possible succession by invalidating Tiberius' last will. It could have also been the new emperor's way of incapacitating Gemellus' supporters by making it clear to them that he did see him as his future successor. After the murder of Gemellus, a brief role in Caligula's succession plans fell to Marcus Lepidus, the husband of Caligula's beloved sister Drusilla; Lepidus was seen as an emergency successor in case the princeps died without male issue. Still, after Drusilla's unexpected death, Lepidus was sidelined and soon executed on charges of working on a coup. Overall, it is possible to say that during his short principate Caligula never took any definite steps toward resolving the issue of the succession; I believe that was largely because he lacked a son, whose birth would have made it much easier for him to settle the matter for good. While he was married four times, in the end none of his wives gave him a son[1]. On the other hand, the fact that Caligula never designated a successor could have been simply a consequence of his young age; after all, at the time of his death he was only twenty-nine. Thus, it is no wonder he took no binding decisions regarding the matter.

When analysing Claudius' actions in the field of the succession policy, a pursuit to which I dedicated Chapter Four, we see he followed—as had Tiberius—the precedent established by Augustus, in seeking to pass the throne over to another member of the dynasty. During the early years of Claudius' reign, the primary and virtually only candidate to succession was his natural son Britannicus. His statues appear next to those of Claudius and the most significant members of the imperial family in a number of provinces. There are also images of Britannicus in the company of the emperor, Britannicus' mother Messalina and his sisters on numerous coin emissions produced in provincial mints. The honorifics granted Claudius' son clearly demonstrate he was at the time seen as the only potential successor.

The situation changed radically in AD 49, after Messalina was executed and the princeps married Agrippina the Younger. By adopting her son Lucius Domitius one year later, Claudius changed the order of succession as it had stood until then. At that moment Agrippina's son gained the status of a legitimate successor of the emperor, the same as that of Britannicus. In AD 51, in connection with the assumption of his *toga virilis* Nero was granted a number of prestigious honours, which were meant to speed up his *cursus honorum*. In the same year, the imperial and senatorial mints also began to make coins bearing his image, some of them on the obverse. In striking contrast, we have no such emissions featuring Britannicus, which demonstrates he was overshadowed by his adoptive brother. The prestigious honours awarded Nero after his adoption, some of them unprecedented, are obvious evidence that he was being prepared for the succession. We may accept the perspective of our sources here and see that Nero's promotion at Britannicus' expense was a result of the determined actions of Agrippina, who wanted to ensure it would be her own son that succeeded Claudius; the ancient authors do strongly suggest that after marrying the emperor she came

1 Caligula was married to Junia Claudilla, Cornelia Orestilla, Lollia Paullina and Milonia Caesonia. See Kienast 1996, 86. It is striking that during the four years of his reign he was married three times. The first three of those four marriages were childless and only Caesonia bore him a daughter. Other reasons aside, changing wives so often may have meant the emperor was really determined to have a son who could succeed him. It is also telling that Cassius Dio (59, 23, 7) lists infertility, alongide boredom, as a reason for Caligula divorcing Lollia Paullina.

to control him completely. In this context, it is telling that in his description of Claudius' diverse moves aimed at strengthening Nero's position, Tacitus consistently uses the passive voice, and so indicates who actually "pulled the strings" there. It would be hard to establish with certainty, though, whether towards the end of his rule Claudius did intend to remove Nero from power and designate Britannicus as his successor, as the ancient authors suggest. In my opinion, that is somewhat unlikely, as can be seen, for example, by the emperor's inaction with regard to preparing his natural son for taking over as princeps in the future.

Then under Nero it is hard to identify him taking any clear actions in the sphere of the succession policy at all, other than eliminating Britannicus as a potential rival. Not having a natural son, Nero never settled the matter of succession during his principate, just as Caligula had not before him.

Part Two “The princeps is dead, long live the princeps”: the New Emperors Taking Over

6 Tiberius' Accession

6.1 Augustus' Death and Last Will

As the ancient authors all agree, Augustus died on 19th August AD 14 in Nola in Campania, in the same house where his natural father Octavius had died over seventy years earlier[1]. However, their accounts of the last moments of the first princeps do differ. Velleius Paterculus and Suetonius report that before his death Augustus had a confidential conversation with Tiberius, who, having heard the news of the emperor's health getting worse, had interrupted his trip to Illyria and arrived in Nola. Reportedly during that last meeting, Augustus gave him some final advice on matters of the state:

> Venitur ad tempus, in quo fuit plurimum metus. Quippe Caesar Augustus cum Germanicum nepotem suum reliqua belli patraturum misisset in Germaniam. Tiberium autem filium missurus esset in Illyricum ad firmanda pace quae bello subegerat, prosequens eum simulque interfuturus athletarum certaminis ludicro, quod eius honori sacratum a Neapolitanis est, processit in Campaniam. Quamquam iam motus imbecillitatis inclinataeque in deterius principia valetudinis senserat, tamen obnitente vi animi prosecutus filium digressusque ab eo Beneventi ipse Nolam petiit: et ingravescente in dies valetudine, cum sciret, quis volenti omnia post se salva remanere accersendus foret, festinanter revocavit filium; ille ad patrem patriae expectato revolavit maturius. Tum securum se Augustus praedicans circumfususque amplexibus Tiberii sui, commendans illi sua atque ipsius opera nec quidquam iam de fine, si fata poscerent, recusans, subrefectus primo conspectu alloquioque carissimi sibi spiritus, mox, cum omnem curam fata vincerent, in sua resolutus initia Pompeio Apuleioque consulibus septuagesimo et sexto anno animam caelestem caelo reddidit[2].

> We now come to the crisis which was awaited with the greatest foreboding. Augustus Caesar had dispatched his grandson Germanicus to Germany to put an end to such traces of the war as still remained, and was on the point of sending his son Tiberius to Illyricum to strengthen by peace the regions he had subjugated in war. With the double purpose of escorting him on his way, and of being present at an athletic contest which the Neapolitans had established in his honour, he set out for Campania. Although he had already experienced symptoms of growing weakness and of a change in his health for the worse, his strong will resisted infirmity and he accompanied his son. Parting from him at Beneventum he went to Nola. As his health grew daily worse, and he knew full well

---

1 Vell. Pat. 2, 123, 1–2; Tac. *Ann.* 1, 5, 3–4; Suet. *Aug.* 100, 1; Cass. Dio 56, 30, 5; see also Kienast 1996, 65.

2 Vell. Pat. 2, 123, 1–2.

for whom he must send if he wished to leave everything secure behind him, he sent in haste for his son to return. Tiberius hurried back and reached the side of the father of his country before he was even expected. Then Augustus, asserting that his mind was now at ease, and, with the arms of his beloved Tiberius about him, commending to him the continuation of their joint work, expressed all his readiness to meet the end if the fates should call him. He revived a little at seeing Tiberius and at hearing the voice of one so dear to him, but, ere long, since no care could withstand the fates, in his seventy-sixth year, in the consulship of Pompeius and Apuleius he was resolved into the elements from which he sprang and yielded up to heaven his divine soul[3].

Mox Neapolim traiecit, quanquam etiam tum infirmis intestinis morbo variante; tamen et quinquennale certamen gymnicum honori suo institutum perspectavit et cum Tiberio ad destinatum locum contendit. Sed in redeundo adgravata valitudine tandem Nolae succubuit revocatumque ex itinere Tiberium diu secreto sermone detinuit, neque post ulli maiori negotio animum accommodavit[4].

Presently he crossed over to Naples, although his bowels were still weak from intermittent attacks. In spite of this he witnessed a quinquennial gymnastic contest which had been established in his honour, and then started with Tiberius for his destination. But as he was returning his illness increased and he at last took to his bed at Nola, calling back Tiberius, who was on his way to Illyricum, and keeping him for a long time in private conversation, after which he gave attention to no business of importance[5].

Ac non multo post lege per consules lata, ut prouincias cum Augusto communiter administraret simulque censum a[u]geret, condito lustro in Illyricum profectus est. Et statim ex itinere revocatus iam quidem adfectum, sed tamen spirantem adhuc Augustum repperit fuitque una secreto per totum diem[6].

Since the consuls caused a law to be passed soon after this that he should govern the provinces jointly with Augustus and hold the census with him, he set out for Illyricum on the conclusion of the lustral ceremonies; but he was at once recalled, and finding Augustus in his last illness but still alive, he spent an entire day with him in private[7].

Cassius Dio is more sceptical in that regard. He treats the information of the last-moment meeting between the princeps and his successor to be unreliable, and instead claims Livia had concealed the truth about Augustus' death until Tiberius came to Nola. In order to bring the reader round to his point of view, Dio argues that his version is to be found in the works of most historians, and in those he considers most trustworthy:

3 Translated by F. W. Shipley (Loeb Classical Library, 152).
4 Suet. *Aug.* 98, 5.
5 Translated by J. C. Rolfe (Loeb Classical Library, 31).
6 Suet. *Tib.* 21, 1.
7 Translated by J. C. Rolfe (Loeb Classical Library, 31).

Οὐ μέντοι καὶ ἐκφανὴς εὐθὺς ὁ θάνατος αὐτοῦ ἐγένετο· ἡ γὰρ Λιουία, φοβηθεῖσα μὴ τοῦ Τιβερίου ἐν τῇ Δελματίᾳ ἔτ' ὄντος νεωτερισθῇ τι, συνέκρυψεν αὐτὸν μέχρις οὗ ἐκεῖνος ἀφίκετο. Ταῦτα γὰρ οὕτω τοῖς τε πλείοσι καὶ τοῖς ἀξιοπιστοτέροις γέγραπται· εἰσὶ γάρ τινες οἳ καὶ παραγενέσθαι τὸν Τιβέριον τῇ νόσῳ αὐτοῦ καὶ ἐπισκήψεις τινὰς παρ' αὐτοῦ λαβεῖν ἔφασαν[8].

His death, however, was not immediately made public; for Livia, fearing that as Tiberius was still in Dalmatia there might be some uprising, concealed the fact until he arrived. This, at any rate, is the statement made by most writers, and the more trustworthy ones; but there are some who have affirmed that Tiberius was present during the emperor's illness, and received some injunctions for him[9].

Tacitus' account falls in between the two versions cited above, since he states there is not enough information to settle the matter definitively:

utcumque se ea res habuit, vixdum ingressus Illyricum Tiberius properis matris litteris accitur; neque satis compertum est, spirantem adhuc Augustum apud urbem Nolam an exanimem reppererit. acribus namque custodiis domum et vias saepserat Livia, laetique interdum nuntii vulgabantur, donec provisis quae tempus monebat simul excessisse Augustum et rerum potiri Neronem fama eadem tulit[10].

Whatever the truth of the affair, Tiberius had hardly set foot in Illyricum, when he was recalled by an urgent letter from his mother; and it is not certainly known whether on reaching the town of Nola, he found Augustus still breathing or lifeless. For house and street were jealously guarded by Livia's ring of pickets, while sanguine notices were issued at intervals, until the measures dictated by the crisis had been taken: then one report announced simultaneously that Augustus had passed away and that Nero was the master of the Empire[11].

I share Tacitus' opinion that it is impossible to determine for sure whether such a conversation actually took place. Indeed, if one were to rely on the accounts of Tacitus and Cassius Dio, one should probably consider that unlikely, as both these authors report Tiberius was in Illyria by the time news reached him of Augustus' illness getting worse, and in that case he could have hardly had the time to get to Nola before the emperor's death. On the other hand, were we to accept the version in Velleius Paterculus and Suetonius, who tell us Tiberius had parted ways with Augustus in Beneventum and was only on his way to Illyria when he received the news, then it would be possible for him to arrive in Nola in time.

8 Cass. Dio 56, 31, 1.
9 Translated by E. Cary (Loeb Classical Library, 175).
10 Tac. *Ann.* 1, 5, 3–4.
11 Translated by J. Jackson (Loeb Classical Library, 249).

Livia's behaviour at the time of Augustus' illness and death remains a separate issue. The passages in Tacitus and Cassius Dio quoted above claim she was extremely active then, taking a number of preventive measures meant to secure Tiberius' succession. For a few dozen years the claim has been present in scholarship that the passage in Tacitus, where he describes her actions in the last days of the first princeps' life actually contains veiled allusions to the circumstances under which Hadrian rose to power, and to Plotina's controversial role in the events. The supporters of this idea suggest Tacitus wrote his Livia *in similitudinem Plotinae*, which would have corresponded to a tendency typical of most Roman historians, who regarded the past *sub specie temporis praesentis*. That opinion is primarily based on the belief that the final edition of the *Annals* was made at the beginning of Hadrian's reign[12].

Yet not all scholars accept this point of view. Frank Goodyear, the author of an extensive commentary on Tacitus' *Annals*, thinks the first few books were written before Trajan's death, which would mean Tacitus' description of Augustus' last days and Tiberius' accession cannot have contained any allusions to events connected to Hadrian's ascent to the throne. He also does not suppose that Tacitus would have included any allusions to the controversial circumstances under which Hadrian became princeps; they wouldn't have been comprehensible to his contemporaries and, more importantly, the risk would have been too great. Instead, Goodyear suspects Tacitus might have drawn on Livy at that point in his narrative, specifically Livy's story about Tanaquil, whose determined actions supposedly ensured Servius Tullius would rule as king after Tarquinius Priscus' death[13]. He also considers it possible that Tacitus' account of Augustus' death and Tiberius taking over as princeps has in it certain echoes of Nero's rise to imperial power forty years later. His description of the actions taken by Agrippina the Younger in order to make sure her son would be princeps (*Ann.* 12, 68, 1–3) is extremely similar to his account of Livia's behaviour while Tiberius was taking over after Augustus' death[14].

---

12 See Strack 1933, 52–53 note 58, who was the first to put forward this idea, and especially Syme 1958, 481–482. For a detailed discussion of consenting views, see Temporini 1978, 157–159. For Tacitus' attitude towards Livia, see e.g. Hardy 1976, 14–58; Barrett 2001, 171–175. For an overview of the most important trends in research into Livia, see Olszewski 2003, 366–370. Finally, for innuendo as Tacitus' writing strategy, see the classic paper by Ryberg (1942, 383–404).

13 For an account of the episode, see Liv.1, 41, 1–5.

14 Goodyear 1972, 126–128. On the similarities in the accounts of those two episodes, see also Cattaneo 1958, 476–482.

Goodyear's ideas regarding the events which may have inspired the passages in question are purely speculative; it is also possible that Livia and her actions in the last days of Augustus' life may have been Tacitus' model on which to later base his narrative on the behaviour of Agrippina the Younger while Claudius lay dying. The fact that Tacitus depicted their sons' ascent to the throne in similar ways does not necessarily mean that this is just a literary trope; I believe we have reasons to think Livia did play an active role in Augustus' final days, taking specific steps to make sure her son would rule next[15]. Now Tiberius' succession had been formally prepared in Augustus' lifetime: as I have mentioned previously, it was to be made secure by appointing trusted supporters to all the crucial positions in the army. However, killing Agrippa Postumus, who was Tiberius' most dangerous—if not only—rival to the purple, right after Augustus died, makes it clear that Tiberius did not feel completely safe[16]. In this context, Suetonius' words are especially telling, as he states the news of Augustus' demise was released only after the execution of young Agrippa[17]. Also telling is Tacitus' comment referring to that event as *primum facinus novi principatus*[18]. Taking that aspect of the situation into account and remembering it was the first replacement of an old princeps by a new one, I do not think it was possible for Livia, who was after all present at the dying Augustus' side, not to have had an active part in Tiberius' accession. Her significant actions included, for example, calling her son back to Nola after the princeps' condition deteriorated, as recounted by Tacitus[19].

Tacitus and Cassius Dio tell us that after Augustus died, Tiberius immediately had news of that fact dispatched from Nola to all the armies of the Empire and all the provincial governors[20]. We can only guess that such messages were sent to Rome as well. Shortly after the news reached the capital, the incumbent consuls Sextus Pompeius and Sextus Appuleius swore allegiance to Tiberius (*in verba Tiberii Caesaris iuravere*). Next, they took the same oath from the *praefectus praetorio* and *praefectus annonae*, followed by the Senate, the Praetorian Guard

15 So Hardy 1976, 17–18. Still, his suggestion that Augustus' death created the opportunity for many ambitious people to try and aim for the throne, goes much too far. *Contra* Timpe (1962, 100 note 3), who believes Tacitus ascribed to Livia actions actually taken by Agrippina as Nero took over.

16 I discuss the murder of Postumus in more detail in the next section.

17 Suet. *Tib.* 22.

18 Tac. *Ann.* 1, 6, 1.

19 Tac. *Ann.* 1, 5, 3.

20 Tac. *Ann.* 1, 7, 5; Cass. Dio 57, 2, 1.

and the Roman plebs convoked in assembly by the consuls[21]. An oath of allegiance made by the highest institutions of the state and its most important officials meant that Tiberius had officially been accepted as the legitimate princeps. From Tacitus we also know Germanicus swore in those closest to him—and the "Belgian states" (or, *Belgarum civitates*) subordinate to Rome—to Tiberius' name[22]. Barrett supposes other governors did the same in their respective provinces[23].

Then from Suetonius we learn the final version of Augustus' last will had been made on 3rd April AD 13. Apparently the document was written down in two books and given into the care of the Vestals[24]. It was read out in the first Senate session after the emperor's death[25]. Our sources provide us with a considerable amount of detailed information on the contents. The princeps had indicated two principal heirs to his property, Tiberius (who would inherit "one half and one sixth") and Livia (the remaining third); both were also obliged to accept the titles of *Augustus* and *Augusta*. The second-order heirs were Drusus the Younger, Germanicus and Germanicus' sons, while the third category included the remaining family members, closest friends and befriended monarchs of Rome's satellite kingdoms. There were also appropriate bequests made to the people, the Praetorian and urban cohorts, and to the legionaries[26]. Making Tiberius the main heir meant that, as the new superior of the *domus Augusta*, he also inherited the dead emperor's political capital (or, *statio paterna*), of which the most important aspect was no doubt the political clientele. A special category of clients included the army, sworn in to the emperor's name[27]. Augustus left a disposition for certain definite sums of money to be paid out to the army after his death and, as the main heir, Tiberius was responsible for carrying out the provisions of the

21 Tac. *Ann.* 1, 7, 2; Cass. Dio 57, 3, 2. See also Timpe 1962, 38–40; 65.

22 Tac. *Ann.* 1, 34, 1.

23 Barrett 1989, 54. The assumption seems logical, even though we have no information on the subject in the sources.

24 Suet. *Aug.* 101, 1. On Augustus' will, see primarily Ober 1982, 306–328; Champlin 1989, 154–165.

25 Tac. *Ann.* 1, 8, 1; Suet. *Tib.* 23. We do not know the day, although scholars tend to date that Senate session to early September. See Hohl 1933, 108; Sage 1982–83, 296.

26 Suet. *Aug.* 101, 2; *Tib.* 23; Tac. *Ann.* 1, 8, 1–2; Cass. Dio 56, 32, 1–2.

27 See Dettenhofer 2000, 204. The exceptional character of the relationship between the army on the one hand, and the princeps and the reigning family on the other, was also stressed in a passage of the *SCPP* (ll. 160–165), where the army was shown as a major support of the imperial family. The text clearly states the loyalty and dedication of the soldiers were necessary conditions for the stable rule of the *domus Augusta*, and thus of the security of the whole Empire. See also Seager 2013, 54.

will. It was no accident the funds that the will listed as being meant for the army were to be paid out first. Carrying out Augustus' will quickly in that respect was supposed to win Tiberius the loyalty and affection of the army at the delicate moment of the takeover[28].

The decision about Livia's adoption was among the more interesting clauses of that will. From now on, she was officially to be named Julia Augusta[29]. Corbier supposes that by including the mother of his successor in the *gens Iulia*, the princeps wanted to highlight Tiberius' rights to succession the more[30], but this view is questionable. We do know that in Roman society a man was a member of his natural father's gens, not his mother's, unless he was adopted out or disowned. In the light of Roman law, after his adoption in AD 4, Tiberius was a legitimate son of Augustus and grandson of the godlike Caesar. After Augustus died, virtually nothing could have legitimized his position as the new princeps better than this. Thus I do not think adopting Livia into the Julian gens could have reinforced her son's rights to the succession to any conspicuous extent. I believe two things indicate that his family relationship to Julia Augusta did not significantly help Tiberius legitimize his succession. First, Tacitus and Suetonius both report that he refused the Senate's suggestion for his titulature to include the expression *Iuliae filius*[31]. And second, he did not consent to have his mother deified after her death in 29[32]. The fact *divi Augusti filius* is the only filiation present in Tiberius' official titulature demonstrates the status of the godlike Augustus' son was enough to confirm the legitimacy of his reign. Numerous coin emissions minted during Tiberius' reign are the primary evidence for the importance of that fact to his position[33], so I think that by including his wife among the Julii and giving her the right to the prestigious title of *Augusta*, Augustus mostly intended to confirm the exceptional position she had already held in the imperial family, and the adoption had no connection to Tiberius' succession[34].

---

28 Timpe 1962, 44–45.

29 Vell. Pat. 2, 75, 3; Tac. *Ann.* 1, 8, 1; Hardy 1976, 19; Kienast 1996, 84.

30 Corbier 1995, 186.

31 Tac. *Ann.* 1, 14, 1–2; Suet. *Tib.* 50, 2–3. Suetonius is however wrong to report that the title the Senate offered Tiberius was *Liviae filius*; we do know that after the adoption by Augustus, Livia's name was Julia Augusta. See also Holtzhausser 1918, 39.

32 Suet. *Tib.* 51, 2; Cass. Dio 58, 2, 1.

33 See e.g. *RIC* I^2 *Tib.* 1–10; 23–24; 70.

34 On the significance of the title *Augusta* for Livia's standing, see Ritter 1972, 313–338; Hardy 1976, 19; Flory 1988, 113–125; Kuhoff 1993b, 245–248; Bauman 2003, 131–133.

Other than that, the will contained a clause concerning the other two Julias, Augustus' daughter and granddaughter, who were not to be buried in the Mausoleum of Augustus[35]. The caveat was necessary, because otherwise both had the right to be buried there as members of the *domus Augusta*[36].

The will was in its way complemented by additional books containing Augustus' instruction regarding his funeral (*mandata de funere*), a list of his deeds (*res gestae*) and a report on the condition of the army and public finances (*breviarium totius imperii*)[37]. The former two documents were read out during the same session of the Senate as the princeps' will; the third was made public at a Senate session on 17th September, that is, after Augustus' funeral[38].

6.2 *Recusatio imperii*[39]: Tiberius' Unwillingness to Become Princeps

That second Senate session[40], held after Augustus' funeral, passed a *senatus consultum* which deified the deceased princeps, introduced his cult and resolved that a temple would be built to him. A priestly college of *sodales Augustales* was created to take care of this cult, made up of twenty-one senators plus Tiberius, Drusus the Younger, Germanicus and Claudius. A special role in the cult of the godlike Augustus fell to Germanicus, the first to hold the prestigious office of *flamen Augustalis*, while Julia Augusta became a priestess of that cult, her title being *sacerdos divi Augusti*[41]. In the context of Tiberius' succession, the deification of the first princeps by the Senate was important, as it gave Tiberius' reign

35 Suet. *Aug.* 101, 3.

36 See Linderski 1995, 385–386.

37 Suet. *Aug.* 101, 1; 4; Tac. *Ann.* 1, 11, 4; Cass. Dio 56, 33, 1–3. Suetonius mentions three books; Cassius Dio, four—the fourth supposedly containing Augustus' instructions for Tiberius as his successor on how to govern the state in the future.

38 See Tac. *Ann.* 1, 11, 4. On that subject, see also Hohl 1933, 112–113; Kienast 1982, 124.

39 I understand *recusatio imperii* as a situation in which the person on whom power is bestowed either actually refuses or pretends to refuse, the definition of the term suggested by Ulrich Huttner (2004, 16).

40 Generally, the session is dated to 17th September. See Hohl 1933, 115; Wellesley 1967, 26; Kienast 1982, 124–125; Sage 1982–83, 310–311; Huttner 2004, 128.

41 Vell. Pat. 2, 75, 3; 124, 3; 126, 1; Tac. *Ann.* 1, 10, 8; 54, 1; Cass. Dio 56, 46, 1–3. On Augustus' *consecratio*, see esp. Price 1987, 73–82; Gradel 2002, 261–339. On Livia as Augustus' priestess, see e.g. Bartman 1999, 102–108; Rüpke-Glock 2005, 1113–1114 (no. 2265).

another religious source of legitimacy. From then on, he could officially style himself *divi Augusti filius*, which gave him additional splendour and very much strengthened his *auctoritas*[42].

Next, the senators asked Tiberius to officially confirm he accepted the position of the princeps. However, as all our sources unanimously stress, he refused the purple in an act known as *recusatio imperii*[43]. Tacitus, Suetonius and Cassius Dio all add that Tiberius asked the Senate to lighten his administrative burdens by dividing the state duties into three parts. The first would relate to governing Rome and Italy; the second—commanding the army; and the third—administering the provinces. Reportedly, Tiberius also requested that the Senate choose one of those three departments for him to run. As could be expected, the suggestion was refused. Tacitus says the senators rejected the solution, arguing they were convinced a princeps' powers were indivisible and should be wielded all together by one person[44]. According to the sources, only after the Senate had insisted for a long time did Tiberius eventually consent to ascend to Augustus' vacated position and take over as princeps[45].

My main objective in this section will be to establish what motivated Tiberius to act in this way. All the ancient authors agree that Augustus' successor delayed assuming imperial power, but they list different reasons he may have done so. Velleius Paterculus treats Tiberius' unwillingness to accept the principate as a sign of his modesty, emphasizing Tiberius did not want to take Augustus' place, because he meant to live the life of an ordinary citizen. Finally he agreed to assume the principate, but his motives were not a lust for power or a desire to receive honours, but rather concern for the state—or so Paterculus scrupulously notes. Velleius' Tiberius is a statesman sent by divine providence, whose consent to take over at the helm of the state saved it from a crisis:

> Id solum voce publica dixisse satis habeo: cuius orbis ruinam timueramus, eum ne commotum quidem sensimus, tantaque unius viri maiestas fuit, ut nec pro bonis neque contra malos opus armis foret. Una tamen veluti luctatio civitatis fuit, pugnantis cum Caesare senatus populique Romani, ut stationi paternae succederet, illius, ut potius aequalem civem quam eminentem liceret agere principem. Tandem magis ratione quam

42 See Hohl 1933, 112; Timpe 1962, 47–48; Rose 1997, 22; Levick 1999, 75; Zanker 2005, 28.

43 Ov. *Pont*. 4, 13, 27–28; Vell. Pat. 2, 124, 1–2; Val. Max. 4, 1; Tac. *Ann*. 1, 11–12; Suet. *Tib*. 24, 1; Cass. Dio 57, 2, 1–6.

44 Tac. *Ann*. 1, 11–12; Suet. *Tib*. 25, 2; Cass. Dio 57, 2, 4–6. See also Schrömbges 1992, 298–307; Huttner 2004, 129–130.

45 Vell. Pat. 2, 124, 2–3; Suet. *Tib*. 24, 1–2; Tac. *Ann*. 1, 13, 5.

> honore victus est, cum quidquid tuendum non suscepisset, periturum videret, solique huic contigit paene diutius recusare principatum, quam, ut occuparent eum, alii armis pugnaverant[46].
>
> Suffice it for me to voice the common utterance: "The world whose ruin we had feared we found not even disturbed, and such was the majesty of one man that there was no need of arms either to defend the good or to restrain the bad." There was, however, in one respect what might be called a struggle in the state, as, namely, the senate and the Roman people wrestled with Caesar to induce him to succeed to the position of his father, while he on his side strove for permission to play the part of a citizen on a parity with the rest rather than that of an emperor over all. At last he was prevailed upon rather by reason than by the honour, since he saw that whatever he did not undertake to protect was likely to perish. He is the only man to whose lot it has fallen to refuse the principate for a longer time, almost, than others had fought to secure it[47].

Tacitus, on the other hand, maintains Tiberius' *cunctatio* stemmed from his fear that Germanicus, who enjoyed enormous popularity among the people and had eight legions under his command, would want to reach for the throne himself:

> Nam Tiberius cuncta per consules incipiebat tamquam vetere re publica et ambiguus imperandi [...] Causa praecipua ex formidine ne Germanicus, in cuius manu tot legiones, immensa sociorum auxilia, mirus apud populum favor, habere imperium quam exspectare mallet[48].
>
> For in every action of Tiberius the first step had to be taken by the consuls, as though the old republic were in being, and himself undecided whether to reign or no [...]The chief reason was his fear that Germanicus—backed by so many legions, the vast reserves of the provinces, and a wonderful popularity with the nation—might prefer the ownership to the reversion of a throne[49].

Then there is Suetonius' opinion that Tiberius mostly hesitated because of news that the legions in Pannonia and Germania had rebelled[50]. He must have been especially concerned with the mutiny in the Rhine army, which did not accept him as princeps, putting forward Germanicus' candidacy. Suetonius also lists the subversive actions of Clemens[51] (a slave of Agrippa Postumus) and a coup d'état prepared by L. Scribonius Libo as possible reasons why Tiberius delayed:

46 Vell. Pat. 2, 124, 1–2.

47 Translated by F. W. Shipley (Loeb Classical Library, 152).

48 Tac. *Ann.* 1, 7, 3; 7, 6.

49 Translated by J. Jackson (Loeb Classical Library, 249).

50 On the subject of those mutinies, see, among others, Liechtenhan 1947, 52–67; Schmitt 1958, 378–383; Wilkes 1963, 268–271; Timpe 1968, 27–28; Sordi 1979, 481–495.

51 More on the subject in Paladini 1954, 313–329.

Cunctandi causa erat metus undique imminentium discriminum, ut saepe lupum se auribus tenere diceret. Nam et servus Agrippae Clemens nomine non contemnendam manum in ultionem domini compararat et L. Scribonius Libo vir nobilis res novas clam moliebatur et duplex seditio militum in Illyrico et in Germania exorta est. Flagitabant ambo exercitus multa extra ordinem, ante omnia ut aequarentur stipendio praetoriani[s]. Germaniciani quidem etiam principem detractabant non a se datum summaque vi Germanicum, qui tum iis praeerat, ad capessendam rem p. urgebant, quanquam obfirmate resistentem[52].

The cause of his hesitation was fear of the dangers which threatened him on every hand, and often led him to say that he was "holding a wolf by the ears." For a slave of Agrippa, Clemens by name, had collected a band of no mean size to avenge his master; Lucius Scribonius Libo, one of the nobles, was secretly plotting a revolution; and a mutiny of the soldiers broke out in two places, Illyricum and Germany. Both armies demanded numerous special privileges—above all, that they should receive the same pay as the praetorians. The army in Germany was, besides, reluctant to accept an emperor who was not its own choice, and with the greatest urgency besought Germanicus, their commander at the time, to assume the purple, in spite of his positive refusal[53].

Germanicus, C. Caesaris pater, Drusi et minoris Antoniae filius, a Tiberio patruo adoptatus, quaesturam quinquennio ante quam per leges liceret et post eam consulatum statim gessit, missusque ad exercitum in Germaniam, excessu Augusti nuntiato, legiones universas imperatorem Tiberium pertinacissime recusantis et sibi summam rei p. deferentis incertum pietate an constantia maiore compescuit atque hoste mox devicto triumphavit[54].

Germanicus, father of Gaius Caesar, son of Drusus and the younger Antonia, after being adopted by his paternal uncle Tiberius, held the quaestorship five years before the legal age and passed directly to the consulship. When the death of Augustus was announced, he was sent to the army in Germany, where it is hard to say whether his filial piety or his courage was more conspicuous; for although all the legions obstinately refused to accept Tiberius as emperor, and offered him the rule of the state, he held them to their allegiance. And later he won a victory over the enemy and celebrated a triumph[55].

Finally, Cassius Dio cites various opinions he heard on why Tiberius acted in this way, siding with Suetonius on the most likely one being that he harboured fears caused by the mutiny, and with Tacitus on pointing to the fear of Germanicus, whom the legions on the Rhine loved. Dio also thinks an explanation for Tiberius' *cunctatio* can be found in his personality:

52 Suet. *Tib.* 25, 1–2.

53 Translated by J. C. Rolfe (Loeb Classical Library, 31).

54 Suet. *Calig.* 1, 1.

55 Translated by J. C. Rolfe (Loeb Classical Library, 31).

Ὁ δ᾽ οὖν Τιβέριος ταῦτα τότε ἐποίει τὸ μὲν πλεῖστον ὅτι οὕτω τε ἐπεφύκει καὶ οὕτω προῄρητο, ἤδη δὲ καὶ ὅτι τά τε στρατεύματα, καὶ τὰ Παννονικὰ καὶ τὰ Γερμανικά, ὑπετόπει, καὶ τὸν Γερμανικὸν τῆς τότε Γερμανίας ἄρχοντα καὶ φιλούμενον ὑπ᾽ αὐτῶν ἐδεδίει[56].

Tiberius acted in this way at that time, chiefly because it was his nature to do so and because he had determined upon that policy, but partly also because he was suspicious of both the Pannonian and Germanic legions and feared Germanicus, then governor of the province of Germany and beloved by them[57].

Tacitus and Suetonius both stress that while Tiberius put off officially assuming the principate, he took over all of Augustus' duties straight away after his death, thus behaving as the new princeps in practice. In their opinion, this was because his behaviour was insincere. They see his reluctance merely as a symptom of hypocrisy: a false and sophisticated game.

sed defuncto Augusto signum praetoriis cohortibus ut imperator dederat; excubiae, arma, cetera aulae; miles in forum, miles in curiam comitabatur. Litteras ad exercitus tamquam adepto principatu misit, nusquam cunctabundus nisi cum in senatu loqueretur[58].

Yet, on the passing of Augustus he had given the watchword to the praetorian cohorts as Imperator; he had the sentries, the men-at-arms, and the other appurtenances of a court; soldiers conducted him to the forum, soldiers to the curia; he dispatched letters to the armies as if the principate was already in his grasp; and nowhere manifested the least hesitation, except when speaking in the senate[59].

At Romae nondum cognito qui fuisset exitus in Illyrico, et legionum Germanicarum motu audito, trepida civitas incusare Tiberium quod, dum patres et plebem, invalida et inermia, cunctatione ficta ludificetur, dissideat interim miles neque duorum adulescentium nondum adulta auctoritate comprimi queat[60].

Before the upshot of events in Illyricum was known at Rome, word came that the German legions had broken out. The panic-stricken capital turned on Tiberius: "While with his hypocritical hesitation he was befooling the senate and commons, two powerless and unarmed bodies, meantime the troops were rising and could not be checked by the unripe authority of a pair of boys."[61]

Principatum, quamuis neque occupare confestim neque agere dubitasset, et statione militum, hoc est vi et specie dominationis assumpta, diu tamen recusavit,

56 Cass. Dio 57, 3, 1.
57 Translated by E. Cary (Loeb Classical Library, 175).
58 Tac. *Ann.* 1, 7, 5.
59 Translated by J. Jackson (Loeb Classical Library, 249).
60 Tac. *Ann.* 1, 46, 1.
61 Translated by J. Jackson (Loeb Classical Library, 249).

> impudentissimo mimo nunc adhortantis amicos increpans ut ignaros, quanta belua esset imperium, nunc precantem senatum et procumbentem sibi ad genua ambiguis responsis et callida cunctatione suspendens, ut quidam patientiam rumperent atque unus in tumultu proclamaret: aut agat aut desistat! alter coram exprobaret ceteros, quod polliciti sint tarde praestare, se<d> ipsum quod praestet tarde polliceri. Tandem quasi coactus et querens miseram et onerosam iniungi sibi servitutem, recepit imperium; nec tamen aliter, quam ut depositurum se quandoque spem faceret[62].

> Though Tiberius did not hesitate at once to assume and to exercise the imperial authority, surrounding himself with a guard of soldiers, that is, with the actual power and the outward sign of sovereignty, yet he refused the title for a long time, with barefaced hypocrisy now upbraiding his friends who urged him to accept it, saying that they did not realise what a monster the Empire was, and now by evasive answers and calculating hesitancy keeping the senators in suspense when they implored him to yield, and fell at his feet. Finally, some lost patience, and one man cried out in the confusion: "Let him take it or leave it." Another openly voiced the taunt that others were slow in doing what they promised, but that he was slow to promise what he was already doing. At last, as though on compulsion, and complaining that a wretched and burdensome slavery was being forced upon him, he accepted the Empire, but in such fashion as to suggest the hope that he would one day lay it down[63].

My view is that the reasons provided by those sources fail to completely explain the issue, and that they also need to be critically verified in places. In Velleius Paterculus' case, we have an obvious panegyric in Tiberius' honour. What is more, Paterculus interprets his gesture too literally, by assuming he really meant to refuse the throne. Conversely in Tacitus, Suetonius and Cassius Dio, we hear echoes of a tradition hostile to Tiberius and his principate. Nor do I think mutinies in the legions or fear of Germanicus are a sufficient explanation of why Tiberius was so reluctant to accept the principate[64]. Firstly, we do not know exactly when the mutiny broke out, and especially when the news of it reached Rome[65]. Michael M. Sage, who attempted to determine a precise timeline of events during the first few weeks after Augustus' death, supposes the information that the German legions revolted cannot have reached Rome before 11th September[66],

62 Suet. *Tib.* 24, 1–2.

63 Translated by J. C. Rolfe (Loeb Classical Library, 31).

64 So Levick (1999, 75), who decisively rejects the notion those mutinies could have caused Tiberius' *cunctatio*.

65 The accounts by Velleius Paterculus (2, 125, 1) and Tacitus (*Ann.* 1, 16, 1; 1, 31, 1) might indicate the mutinies in the legions broke out after Tiberius officially assumed his principate, but we have no guarantee they related to the first few weeks of his reign chronologically.

66 Sage 1982–83, 304–306.

and in Levick's opinion the earliest date was actually 17th September. Otherwise, the Senate would not have risked the safety of the delegation sent to Germania shortly before in order to hand him the decree conferring proconsular powers on him, and to offer official condolences on Augustus' death[67].

If we accept the dates suggested by these scholars, it is impossible for the mutiny of the Rhine army to have influenced Tiberius' stance, since from Tacitus' account we know he first expressed his doubts and unwillingness to become princeps during the first session of the Senate convened after Augustus' death (that is, early in September), before anybody in Rome knew about the revolt in Germania[68]. Secondly, even if Tiberius had already known of the mutiny then, which seems very unlikely, I do not think he would have demonstrated indecision in a situation which called for the quick and decisive action of the new ruler. Delaying the official takeover in the face of so many legions mutinying would have been extremely risky. Thirdly, I find it improbable that the Rhine legions did not want to accept Tiberius as the new princeps and proposed Germanicus instead as their candidate to the imperial purple[69]; we must not forget that Tiberius had commanded them for years under Augustus, and led them in a number of successful campaigns, which no doubt won him the loyalty and liking of the units stationed there. Germanicus had only taken over the high command of the German army in AD 13 and had led no campaigns before the mutiny, devoting most of his time to governing the Gaulish provinces[70]. Thus, he hardly could have enjoyed enough authority among the soldiers there at the moment the mutiny broke out that it would have made it possible for him to compete with Tiberius[71], and it is unlikely that after Augustus died the army saw Germanicus as a potential rival of Tiberius for the imperial power[72]. Rather, I am convinced that

67 Levick 1999, 74.

68 Tac. *Ann.* 1, 7, 3; 7, 5. It would appear that the news of the Pannonian legions rebelling had not yet reached Rome. Rogers (1943, 108) suspects that this only happened in the middle of September. *Contra* Toit 1980, 130.

69 Similar scepticism in that regard is expressed by Levick 1999, 247 note 6; Wiedemann 2008, 208. *Contra* Pettinger 2012, 189.

70 Tac. *Ann.* 1, 31, 3; 33, 1; 34, 1; *TS* fr I, 15; Levick 1999, 73. On the nature and extent of Germanicus' powers there, see Sawiński 2005, 32–34; 62.

71 I suspect Germanicus' huge popularity and the respect he enjoyed in the legions, indicated by our authors, were a result of his later activity in Germania between the years 14 and 16. Moreover, Tacitus (*Ann.* 1, 46, 1–2) himself stresses Tiberius was the only person at the time with enough *auctoritas* to rein the rebelling soldiers in.

72 Nor do I think he was seen in that way by the Senate or the Roman plebs. Rather, I believe his contemporaries treated him as Tiberius' future successor, just as Augustus had intended; see above.

the ancient historians arrived at this view by interpreting events with the benefit of hindsight.

Moreover, in the accounts of the mutiny by Tacitus, Suetonius and Cassius Dio, we see a deliberate tendency to depict Tiberius as the unwanted princeps, contrasted with the commonly admired and liked Germanicus[73]. Depicting Germanicus as the favourite of the Rhine army and its candidate to the throne corresponded well with the rumour, repeated by Tacitus and Suetonius, according to which Augustus had intended to make him his direct successor[74]. It should be stressed that the authors in question were also eager to highlight the fact that the rebelling legions gave up on the idea of making Germanicus the emperor only after his determined refusal. In my opinion, this is another example for those authors belittling Tiberius by insisting that the loyalty of his adoptive son was a major reason he was able to take over smoothly[75].

I also do not think the image of an army convinced it could decide who would become the new princeps, conveyed by most of our sources[76], fits the Augustan-Tiberian period, but rather reflects the situation after the Year of the Four Emperors, a consequence of which was the awareness among the legions that they could impose their candidate to the throne on the Empire[77]. Therefore, in the light of the arguments presented above, I consider the information found in most sources—that the Rhine legions were going to acclaim Germanicus princeps—unreliable, and I believe the mutiny in Germania, just like the Pannonian one, had purely a socio-economic basis, resulting from the difficult conditions of service in the legions at the time[78]. The sources do agree that the soldiers mostly

73 See Tac. *Ann.* 1, 31, 1; 35, 3–4; Suet. *Tib.* 25, 2; *Calig.* 1, 1; Cass. Dio 57, 3, 1; 5, 1; 6, 2.

74 Tac. *Ann.* 4, 57, 3; Suet. *Calig.* 1; 4. Sage (1982–83, 321) assumes that tradition, hostile to Tiberius, had its origin during the rule of Caligula, who wanted to add splendour to his own reign by glorifying Germanicus. The many coin emissions commemorating Germanicus' achievements are another piece of evidence for how significant he was to his son. See e.g. *RIC* I^2 *Cal.* 57; 59; as well as Hurley 1991, 1–2; 17; Pettinger 2012, 192 note 36. I have expressed my views on Germanicus' part in Augustus' succession plans above.

75 See Tac. *Ann.* 1, 34, 1–4; 35, 4; 42, 1–4; Suet. *Calig.* 1, 1; Cass. Dio 57, 6, 2. *Contra* Pettinger (2012, 190–191).

76 See Tac. *Ann.* 1, 31, 1; 35, 3; Suet. *Tib.* 25, 2; *Calig.* 1, 1; Cass. Dio 57, 4, 3; 5, 1.

77 In that context, Tacitus' (*Hist.* 1, 4) words are telling; namely, he claims it was only after the overthrow of Nero that the idea arose one could become the princeps away from Rome.

78 Purely economic reasons for the mutiny are highlighted, e.g. by Watson 2014, 14; 93–94. *Contra* Woodman (1977, 228–229), who assumes the revolt of the military in

demanded higher pay, shorter service time and that veterans be let go early. Augustus' death and the resulting takeover were an exceptionally convenient moment for the army to present the new emperor with those demands[79].

Suetonius' suggestion that Tiberius may have delayed because of the seditious actions of Clemens and L. Scribonius Libo should also be rejected, for chronological reasons, since Tacitus tells us that those events only happened in AD 16[80].

The problem of Tiberius' *cunctatio* has also received some interest on the part of modern scholars, who have tried to explain his behaviour in a number of different ways. I shall limit myself here to reviewing only the most important opinions on the matter present in scholarship[81]. In his paper of 1933, now a classic, Ernst Hohl put forward the claim that a major reason why Tiberius delayed assuming the principate was his regard for public opinion. First of all, Tiberius did not want to be seen as the emperor who rose to the throne through behind-the-scenes dynastic arrangements; rather, he wanted to be perceived as a princeps legally appointed by the state (the *res publica*). Hohl follows Tacitus here, who writes that Tiberius feared possible slanderous claims that he only became princeps due to his mother's plotting and his adoption by Augustus[82]. Apparently that was why he put off assuming the emperor's position: he waited for the Senate to officially confer it on him[83]. Hohl's view seems unacceptable to me. First, we know that in AD 13 Tiberius was granted in a *senatus consultum*

---

both Germania and Pannonia was largely political. It should also be emphasized that neither Tacitus (*Ann.* 1, 16, 1) nor Suetonius (*Tib.* 25, 1–2) mention that the legions stationed in Pannonia intended to exert any influence on the appointment of the new princeps. Cassius Dio (57, 4, 3) does report the Pannonian army supposedly threatened Tiberius with a march on Rome and imposing another emperor if he did not grant its demands, but he says nothing of the legions there rejecting Tiberius as princeps in principle, or proposing Germanicus as a competing candidate of their own. Obviously the threat to propose another candidate to the purple was only a form of pressure meant to persuade Tiberius into fulfilling the demands of the mutinied legionaries rather than an actual demand. Therefore it is difficult to understand on what grounds Alisdair G. Gibson (2013, 129) claims that the Danubian legions offered the throne to Germanicus in AD 14.

79 Vell. Pat. 2, 125, 1–2; Tac. *Ann.* 1, 16, 1; 17, 1–6; 31, 1; Suet. *Tib.* 25, 2; Cass. Dio 57, 4, 2. See also Keppie 1998, 169–170; Webster 1998, 142.

80 Tac. *Ann.* 2, 27–31; 39–40. See also Rogers 1943, 115; Wiedemann 2008, 211.

81 For a detailed discussion and a list of literature referring to the subject, see Sage 1982–83, 293; Huttner 2004, 128–148; Pettinger 2012, 162–163.

82 Tac. *Ann.* 1, 7, 7.

83 Hohl 1933, 109–111.

(later confirmed by the Comitia), an *imperium* equal to that of Augustus in all the provinces, and at the same time had his tribunician powers prolonged. Those two grants confirmed his succession in a final manner and made it legitimate, so I do not believe that under the circumstances he could have felt there was anything illegal to his position, having been officially designated as the successor by the Senate and the people. Second, it was the senators themselves who had requested that Tiberius officially assume the principate, which involved the Senate's obvious readiness to pass an appropriate *senatus consultum* ratifying his succession. And yet Tiberius continued to hesitate. Thus Hohl's theory does not clarify the problem.

In Colin Wells's opinion, Tiberius was afraid to take on the burden of power and duties which might have exceeded his abilities. He assumes Tiberius was mostly comfortable as a military commander and felt out of place "among the political intrigue of the court and the Senate." Wells explains his ultimate consent by referring to his sense of duty and obedience to the will of Augustus, who had chosen him to be his successor[84]. A similar tone can be read in Huttner's interesting book dealing with the phenomenon of *recusatio imperii* under the Empire. Huttner sees the reason for Tiberius' behaviour mostly in his inborn dislike of power and honours, supposedly illustrated by his departure for Rhodes in 6 BC and thus giving up on the role of Augustus' co-regent. Both Wells and Huttner assume Velleius Paterculus' perspective on the matter[85].

I do not see solid grounds to accept either scholar's view; Tacitus, Suetonius and Cassius Dio all unambiguously state that after Augustus died, Tiberius took over actual power immediately and willingly, acting as the new princeps in fact if not in name, and only demonstrated indecision when he spoke before the Senate[86]. His political career after AD 4 also argues against any claims of his dislike of being in power. In the time between his adoption and Augustus' death, Tiberius held the highest public offices, and as the ageing emperor's co-regent, he shouldered the greater part of duties involved. There is no evidence in the sources to suggest he was weary of ruling at that time, or had the intention of resigning as Augustus' co-regent. As I have previously mentioned, I rather see his withdrawal to Rhodes as a result of his offended ambition after he had not

84 Wells 2005, 123–124.

85 Huttner 2004, 133–134, 137, 147.

86 Tac. *Ann.* 1, 7, 5; Suet. *Tib.* 24, 1; Cass. Dio 57, 2, 1–2. See Pettinger (2012, 163), who correctly observes Tiberius' first actions after Augustus' death already clearly demonstrated that he had no intention of giving up on the throne.

been designated as successor, while the princeps favoured the young Caesars over him, rather than as a sign of any surfeit of power.

I think we should look at the problem from a different perspective. I suspect Tiberius' actions during the so-called succession debate in the Senate in September of AD 14 may have been inspired by an earlier stance of Augustus, who ostentatiously "resigned" his special prerogatives at the memorable Senate session in January of 27 BC[87]. It is no accident that Ovid writes that by showing restraint regarding assuming the principate, Tiberius equalled his father in virtue, since he only agreed to stay in power after much insistence[88]. Of course we should not assume that either Augustus or Tiberius did intend to actually give up the power they had, but I would not see their behaviour in the Senate purely in terms of a farce or hypocrisy, as some ancient authors put it in Tiberius' case. In his inspiring work on the meaning of various gestures and signs in Roman politics, Egon Flaig noted that already under the Republic a prominent individual who refused prestigious honours need not have meant they did not really want them. Rather, they meant to demonstrate modesty and temperance (*moderatio*), as well as to make those who had conferred the honours in the first place to beg them even more[89]. I think it is in this spirit that we ought to interpret Tiberius' hesitation to take over from Augustus. Thus I do not see his *recusatio imperii* as a symptom of his innate modesty, supposedly demonstrated through a dislike of power and special honours (as Velleius would have it), or as hypocritical deception aimed at the senators (as Tacitus, Suetonius and Cassius Dio all suggest). Rather, I believe it was a deliberate display of *moderatio*—the skill of self-control, one of the most important hallmarks of a good ruler. By showing his restraint in reaching for the honour offered to him, which in that case happened to be the imperial power, Tiberius confirmed that he fully deserved to have it, as per the principle that he who can rule himself will be good at ruling others too. His final

87 The similarity between those two situations has been recently pointed out by Pettinger (2012, 163–166), among others.

88 Ov. *Pont.* 4, 13, 27–28.

89 See Flaig 2013, 117. An example of such behaviour under the Republic is that of Pompey, who would refuse the special powers granted him for the purpose of fighting pirates in 67 BC, even though it was common knowledge he dearly wanted the command. Aulus Gabinius, who first moved for those powers to be granted, explained Pompey's reluctance as a facet of his restrained attitude to power in general, here depicted as a characteristic of a good citizen. For a detailed description of that episode, see Cass. Dio 36, 23–29; for more on Pompey's command against the pirates, see especially Girardet 1992, 181–182; id. 2001, 171–176.

consent to accept the principate from the Senate should also be seen as a demonstration of *moderatio*, as it showed he respected the Senate's expectations[90]. I think that this was the way the senators took it and none of them took seriously the idea that Tiberius might not take over after Augustus.

To sum up, in my opinion the display of *moderatio* under discussion was a result, on the one hand, as I have indicated above, of Tiberius' *imitatio Augusti*[91], and, on the other, of standards established in Republican times, which determined the behaviour expected of those taking part in political life. And according to these, a man in office should have moderation and an ability to control his own desires[92]. I ought to stress here that Tiberius' *moderatio* would later become a frequent theme of his official relations with the Senate[93], and we know the Senate celebrated this attitude of the princeps with a special series of dupondii minted in the early years of his reign. Interestingly, that is the only case of an emperor's *moderatio* being commemorated on coins[94]. Also

---

90 That aspect of an emperor's *moderatio* is highlighted by Pliny the Younger (*Paneg.* 21, 1; 55, 5) as he analyzes Trajan's refusal of the honours granted him by the Senate. In that author's view, the princeps proved his *moderatio* not simply by showing his restraint regarding the honours offered him, but also by finally consenting to accept some of them; Pliny sees this as a sign of Trajan's respect for the Senate. In contrast to this, if the emperor had rejected all the honours offered, it could have been seen as excessive pride. For an interpretation of that episode, see Pigoń 1996, 75. The passage in Tacitus I quote earlier (*Ann.* 1, 7, 7) already indicates Tiberius saw it as important that he should be perceived as a princeps appointed by the Senate.

91 Other occasions are known—than that of 27 BC—when Augustus showed *moderatio* regarding the honours offered him. Two examples may be the princeps rejecting the dictatorship offered him by the people, and then the position of the "overseer of laws and morals" (*curator legum et morum*). See *Mon. Anc.* 5, 1; 6, 1.

92 See Cotton–Yakobson 1985, 503; Pigoń 1996, 72; Olszewski 2011, 345–346.

93 I believe it is in that spirit that we ought to interpret a relevant passage in the *Tabula Siarensis* (fr. I, 5). I rely here on the reconstruction of a missing fragment proposed by Vinko Hinz (1993, 59–63), a reading accepted also by the editors of one of the more important editions of that text. See Sánchez–Gutiérrez 1999, 50, 82–89. For other examples, see Tac. *Ann.* 1, 8, 5; 14, 2; 3, 56, 1. It is worth mentioning that it is to Tiberius that Tacitus refers most of his examples of an emperor's *moderatio*, although he sees such behaviour as nothing but a smoke screen. On Tiberius' *moderatio* in Tacitus' perspective, see especially Christes 1994, 112–135; Pigoń 1996, 76–78. Suetonius' approach to the matter is similar, and he stresses Tiberius only showed moderation early on in his reign. See Suet. *Tib.* 57, 1.

94 See *RIC* I^2 *Tib.* 39–40. It is supposed those emissions commemorated the Senate granting Tiberius a special "shield of moderation". On that emission, see Levick 1975a, 123–137; Pigoń 1996, 76.

importantly, during Tiberius' reign, *moderatio* played an important part in creating the public image, not just of the princeps, but of other members of the imperial family as well[95].

6.3 Tiberius' Official Titulature after Accession

The ancient authors tell us that Tiberius firmly refused the praenomen of *imperator* and the title *pater patriae*, both of which Augustus used to have. According to Dio, only soldiers were allowed to address him as *imperator*. He was also reluctant to accept the title *Augustus*, which he would only use in the correspondence addressed to foreign monarchs[96].

In the case of the first two titles, epigraphic and numismatic sources confirm the version preserved in literature, generally speaking. The praenomen *imperator* and the title *pater patriae* both feature sporadically in Tiberius' titulature, and then only in provincial minting and unofficial inscriptions[97]. That they appeared at all should be ascribed to the initiative of local communities, which wanted to honour Tiberius in that way, and is by no means a sign of those terms being a fixture of the official titulature of Augustus' successor[98]. However, when it comes to the title *Augustus*, we know these ancient historians to be wrong: rather than being used sporadically in letters to kings of other states, it was an integral element of Tiberius' official imperial titulature. Based on the analysis of imperial and senatorial coin emissions, as well as Senate documents from the period, we may posit his full titulature to have been *Tiberius Caesar divi Augusti filius Augustus*[99].

95 Germanicus makes an excellent example. In the *SCPP* (ll. 26–27), his *moderatio* is contrasted with Calpurnius Piso's "savage morals" (*feritate morum*). See also *SCPP* ll. 132–133; 146–147; 167.

96 Suet. *Tib.* 26, 2; 67, 2; Tac. *Ann.* 1, 72, 1; 2, 87; Cass. Dio 57, 2, 1; 8, 1–2. See Timpe 1962, 65.

97 For the praenomen *imperator*, see *RPC* I 64; 849–850; *ILS* 151–152; Cognomen *pater patriae, see RPC* I 294; 754–756; *CIL* V 6416; XI 3085. Cf. also Grant 1950, 43–44; 46–50; Kienast 1996, 77; Levick 1999, 247–248 note 11; Stevenson 2007, 121–122; Syme 2009, 55.

98 Official emissions confirm Tiberius as princeps kept his old *praenomen*. See e.g. *RIC* I² *Tib.* 1–5; 33–40.

99 Cf. e.g. *RIC* I² *Tib.* 1–4; 23–30; 48; 89–90; *TS* fr. I, 4, 16; fr. II, col. b, 11; *SCPP* l. 4. See also Lott 2012, 261.

6.4 *Primum facinus novi principatus*: the Murder of Agrippa Postumus

Another step which was an integral part of Tiberius taking over and securing imperial power was the murder of Agrippa Postumus, his main rival to succession after Augustus died[100]. As Tacitus begins to recount Tiberius' principate, he considers this killing to be the first action of the new reign and suspects it was carried out at the behest of Tiberius and Livia. He does however doubt the veracity of the version according to which the decision that the young Agrippa be eliminated had been taken by Augustus himself, and Tiberius merely delivered that order (*patris iussa*, as he put it before the Senate) to the commander of the guard on Planasia. In Tacitus' opinion, Augustus would never have stooped to assassinating a member of his family, not even for the sake of the state:

> Primum facinus novi principatus fuit Postumi Agrippae caedes, quem ignarum inerumumque quamvis firmatus animo centurio aegre confecit. nihil de ea re Tiberius apud senatum disseruit: patris iussa simulabat, quibus praescripsisset tribuno custodiae adposito, ne cunctaretur Agrippam morte adficere, quandoque ipse supremum diem explevisset. multa sine dubio saevaque Augustus de moribus adulescentis questus, ut exilium eius senatus consulto sanciretur, perfecerat: ceterum in nullius umquam suorum necem duravit, neque mortem nepoti pro securitate privigni inlatam credibile erat, propius vero Tiberium ac Liviam, illum metu, hanc novercalibus odiis, suspecti et invisi iuvenis caedem festinavisse. nuntianti centurioni, ut mos militiae, factum esse quod imperasset, neque imperasse sese et rationem facti reddendam apud senatum respondit[101].

> The opening crime of the new principate was the murder of Agrippa Postumus, who, though off his guard and without weapons, was with difficulty dispatched by a resolute centurion. In the senate Tiberius made no reference to the subject: his pretence was an order from his father, instructing the tribune in charge to lose no time in making away with his prisoner, once he himself should have looked his last on the world. It was beyond question that by his frequent and bitter strictures on the youth's character Augustus had procured the senatorial decree for his exile: on the other hand, at no time did he harden his heart to the killing of a relative, and it remained incredible that he should have sacrificed the life of a grandchild in order to diminish the anxieties of a stepson. More probably, Tiberius and Livia, actuated in the one case by fear, and in the other by stepmotherly dislike, hurriedly procured the murder of a youth whom they suspected and detested. To the centurion who brought the usual military report,

---

100 On this subject, see esp. Hohl 1935, 350–355; Allen 1947, 131–139; Lewis 1970, 165–184; Sordi 1979, 481–495.

101 Tac. *Ann.* 1, 6, 1–3.

> the emperor rejoined that he had given no instructions and the deed would have to be accounted for in the senate[102].

Suetonius' version is very similar in spirit. He is also sceptical that the murder of Agrippa could have followed from Augustus' final instructions. He is most inclined to see it as a personal command of Tiberius, who however never admitted to issuing it, fearing the censure of the public:

> Excessum Augusti non prius palam fecit, quam Agrippa iuvene interempto. Hunc tribunus militum custos appositus occidit lectis codicillis, quibus ut id faceret iubebatur; quos codicillos dubium fuit, Augustus ne moriens reliquisset, quo materiam tumultus post se subduceret; an nomine Augusti Livia et ea conscio Tiberio an ignaro, dictasset. Tiberius renuntianti tribuno, factum esse quod imperasset, neque imperasse se et redditurum eum senatui rationem respondit, invidiam scilicet in praesentia vitans. Nam mox silentio rem obliteravit[103].

> Tiberius did not make the death of Augustus public until the young Agrippa had been disposed of. The latter was slain by a tribune of the soldiers appointed to guard him, who received a letter in which he was bidden to do the deed; but it is not known whether Augustus left this letter when he died, to remove a future source of discord, or whether Livia wrote it herself in the name of her husband; and in the latter case, whether it was with or without the connivance of Tiberius. At all events, when the tribune reported that he had done his bidding, Tiberius replied that he had given no such order, and that the man must render an account to the senate; apparently trying to avoid odium at the time, for later his silence consigned the matter to oblivion[104].

Cassius Dio's tone is similar, again. He does adduce a number of versions of the circumstances of Postumus' death, but clearly favours the opinion that he was executed on Tiberius' command:

> Τὸν μὲν γὰρ Ἀγρίππαν παραχρῆμα ἀπὸ τῆς Νώλης πέμψας τινὰ ἀπέκτεινε· καὶ ἔλεγε μὲν μὴ ἐκ τῆς ἑαυτοῦ προστάξεως τοῦτο γεγονέναι, ἐπηπείλει τε τῷ δράσαντι, οὐ μὴν καὶ τιμωρίαν τινὰ αὐτοῦ ἐποιήσατο, ἀλλ᾽ εἴα τοὺς ἀνθρώπους λογοποιεῖν, τοὺς μὲν ὅτι ὁ Αὔγουστος αὐτὸν ὑπὸ τὴν τελευτὴν ἀπεχρήσατο, τοὺς δ᾽ ὅτι ὁ ἑκατόνταρχος ὁ τὴν φρουρὰν αὐτοῦ ἔχων καινοτομοῦντά τι ἀπέσφαξεν αὐτογνωμονήσας, ἄλλους ὡς ἡ Λιουία, ἀλλ᾽ οὐκ ἐκεῖνος, ἀποθανεῖν αὐτὸν ἐκέλευσεν[105].

> Indeed, he immediately sent from Nola and caused Agrippa to be put to death. He declared, to be sure, that this had not been done by his orders and made threats against the perpetrator of the deed; yet he did not punish them at all, but allowed men to invent

102 Translated by J. Jackson (Loeb Classical Library, 249).
103 Suet. *Tib.* 22.
104 Translated by J. C. Rolfe (Loeb Classical Library, 31).
105 Cass. Dio 57, 3, 5–6.

> their own versions of the affair, some to the effect that Augustus had put Agrippa out of the way just before his death, others that the centurion who was guarding him had slain him on his own responsibility for some revolutionary dealings, and still others that Livia instead of Tiberius had ordered his death[106].

In the light of the accounts quoted above, it is possible to conclude that the ancient historians fundamentally reject the idea that Augustus had anything to do with the execution of Agrippa Postumus, ascribing it rather to Tiberius.

Some modern scholars accept these authors' point of view[107], but there are many historians who claim Agrippa may have been executed in obedience to Augustus' last instructions after all. They point out the pragmatic princeps valued the raison d'état higher than any family sentiment he may have felt in this situation, as he always put the interests of the state (*rei publicae causa*) first, and killing Postumus reputedly ensured Tiberius' smooth succession, preventing potential unrest after his death. In the opinion of these historians, Augustus took the decision to have young Agrippa killed in the final months of his rule, and the relevant orders were given to Sallustius Crispus, a trusted aide of Augustus, who related them to the commander of the guard on Planasia as soon as the princeps had died[108]. Of course, it is not an option we can rule out, but personally I am in this matter inclined to trust the ancient authors and suppose Postumus' execution was done at Tiberius' command. According to the principle of *cui prodest*, Augustus' successor is the prime suspect, because he profited the most from his most dangerous rival being dead. It is also telling that in Velleius Paterculus, who lived at the time of those events, we find no information at all on Postumus' death. I am convinced the pro-Tiberian historiographer was silent on that subject because it was inconvenient for the new emperor.

The extremely swift execution of Agrippa Postumus proves that, in spite of his previous exclusion from the *gens Iulia* and banishment from Rome, as a natural grandson of Augustus he was still too dangerous to be allowed to live. Still, the question automatically arises of whether he had any actual ability to threaten Tiberius' succession. No doubt the most important—indeed the only—asset Agrippa had as Tiberius' potential rival, was the fact he was related to Augustus by blood. However, at the moment of the first emperor's death, he had been in exile for seven years, totally isolated and forgotten. Therefore, I do not suppose

---

106 Translated by E. Cary (Loeb Classical Library, 175).

107 See e.g. Shotter 1971, 1120, 1122; Birch 1981, 456.

108 So e.g. Hohl 1935, 350–355; Béranger 1973, 140; Levick 1999, 65–66; Wiedemann 2008, 202; Syme 2002, 439.

he had any influential supporters who could have advanced his cause. Moreover, the stance of the highest-ranking official, the Senate, the army and the plebs, all of whom swore allegiance to Tiberius directly after Augustus' death, demonstrates that nobody wanted a civil war, so it seems unlikely that Postumus could have threatened the new princeps' position to any significant degree, and I think we should see Agrippa's murder in terms of prevention. We must not forget it was the first change from one princeps to the next, so Tiberius could not afford to take even the slightest risks[109]. Yet the assassination of Postumus is the best proof of the strength of dynastic feelings and the importance of blood ties in the context of the succession struggle.

109 Later emperors of the principate era displayed similar caution. In that context, it would appear apt to quote this statement of Syme (2002, 439): "The arbitrary removal of a rival was no less essential to the Principate than the public conferment of legal and constitutional power".

7 Caligula's Accession

7.1 Tiberius' Death and Caligula's First Actions Intended to Secure the Succession

Tiberius died on 16th March AD 37 in Lucullus' old villa in Misenum without having designated a successor[1]. Ancient authors quote various rumours on the circumstances of his death. In one version, he died of poison applied by Caligula; in others, he was starved or strangled by either Caligula or Macro after he temporarily lost consciousness and then came round again[2]. Generally speaking, present-day historians are sceptical about the suggestion of the sources that Tiberius was murdered[3].

Of course, we cannot be absolutely certain, and I do not believe we have grounds to rule that out entirely. Needless to say, ancient authors' claims that Caligula actively worked to get rid of his predecessor may follow from the tendency those sources have to paint as black a picture of him as possible. On the other hand, we must remember Gaius may have acted from the desire to avenge Agrippina, as well as Nero and Drusus Caesar, for which Tiberius was more to blame than anybody, and active participation in the killing of the man who had prosecuted his mother and brothers could have been a specific sign of his *pietas* towards his closest relatives[4]. The new emperor's first moves after assuming power do indicate he was determined to stress his devotion to his mother and brothers. From Suetonius and Cassius Dio we know he travelled to Pontia and Pandateria, from where the remains of Agrippina and Nero Caesar were brought over to Rome, with the greatest of honours, to be laid in the Mausoleum of Augustus. On the anniversaries of their deaths, solemn sacrifices (*inferiae*) were to be made, and circus games were instituted in Agrippina's honour[5]. Caligula also cancelled all of Tiberius' decrees aimed against his mother and brothers[6], and gave the

---

1 Dio (58, 28, 5) wrongly dates Tiberius' death to 26th March, as Suetonius (*Tib.* 73, 1), Tacitus (*Ann.* 6, 50, 4) and the *Fasti Ostienses* (Bargagli–Grosso 1997, 25) all list 16th March. See also Kienast 1996, 78.

2 For an account of the last moments of Tiberius' life, see Tac. *Ann.* 6, 50, 1–5; Suet. *Tib.* 73, 2; *Calig.* 12, 2; Cass. Dio 58, 28, 3.

3 See. Timpe 1962, 63–64; Barrett 1989, 41, among others.

4 This motivation for Caligula's actions is pointed out by Suetonius (*Calig.* 12, 3).

5 Suet. *Calig.* 15, 1; Cass. Dio 59, 3, 5.

6 Tiberius ordered Agrippina's birthday to be marked as *nefastus*, whereas Nero and Drusus Caesar were declared enemies of the state; see above.

order to destroy the villa in Herculaneum where Agrippina had been imprisoned for a while[7]. According to Suetonius, Caligula made such a display of his reverence for and devotion to his closest family members in order to win popularity with the plebs at the onset of his reign[8].

Some scholars assume the first stage of his takeover had already taken place in Misenum: that on 16th March he was acclaimed emperor by a number of Praetorians who had been there with Tiberius after his departure from Rome[9]. Barrett also believes Gaius was acclaimed new emperor by the fleet units stationed there[10]. In my opinion, this hypothesis is very controversial; first of all it should be stressed that our sources mention no acclamation in Misenum. Naturally arguments from silence need not always be final, but I think if the supposed *acclamatio* really had happened, ancient authors would have been eager to mention it. Meanwhile, all Tacitus has to say is that after receiving the news of Tiberius' death, his entourage and the inhabitants of Misenum congratulated Caligula on his ascent to power, which proves they automatically regarded him as the new emperor[11]. Josephus' account corresponds well with Tacitus'; he reports that right after Tiberius' death, but before the Senate and the people accepted him as the emperor, Caligula behaved exactly like the new princeps, issuing specific orders to officials of even the highest rank. He mentions two letters dispatched by Gaius, to the Senate and to the *praefectus urbi*, in which he notified them of Tiberius' death and his own rise to the throne. The urban prefect was also issued a clear order to release Agrippa, a grandson of Herod the Great, from prison[12]. In other words, both cited passages make it clear that Tiberius' death in fact meant the beginning of the reign of Caligula, who from then on was seen by most subjects of the Empire as the legitimate princeps, and as we can see, no Praetorian acclamation was needed in his case. The situation had been similar before, when Tiberius took over after Augustus and the mere information of that fact was enough for the Senate, officials, Praetorian Guard and the plebs to swear allegiance to him[13].

7 Sen. *Ira*. 3, 21, 5; Cass. Dio 59, 3, 6; Barrett 1989, 61; Rose 1997, 35; Bauman 2003, 158; Boruch 2010, 32–33.

8 See Suet. *Calig*. 15, 1.

9 See Timpe 1962, 64; Barrett 1989, 53; Scheid 1992, 224; Kienast 1996, 85; Levick 1999, 220; Winterling 2011, 46.

10 Barrett 1989, 53.

11 Tac. *Ann*. 6, 50, 4.

12 Joseph. *AJ*. 18, 234–236.

13 On which see above.

Generally it is emphasized that a crucial role in securing Caligula's succession during the early days after Tiberius' death was played by Macro, the influential prefect of the Praetorian Guard, who had replaced Sejanus after his fall in AD 31. It was Macro who ensured that Caligula had the support of, first of all, the Praetorians, and second, provincial governors and legion commanders. There is also the suspicion that it was at his instigation that letters containing the relevant orders were sent out to the most important military commanders[14].

News of Tiberius' death most likely reached Rome on 18th March, the day the Senate officially declared Caligula to be the princeps. We know this from the *AFA*, which under 18th March of 38 and 39 lists sacrifices to be made on the day *C. Caesar Augustus Germanicus a senatu impera[tor appellatus est]*[15]. I agree with the scholars who believe that this only meant the Senate accepted Gaius as the princeps, but did not involve conferring on him the whole range of imperial powers, which only took place after he arrived in Rome ten days later[16]. Even though the sources are silent on this, we may guess that after the Senate declared Caligula the princeps, those high-ranking officials and Senators present in Rome at the time swore an oath of allegiance to the new emperor's name, similar to that mentioned by Tacitus in the context of Tiberius' takeover after Augustus' death[17].

As most of our sources report, the news that Tiberius was dead and replaced by Caligula received an enthusiastic response from the inhabitants of Rome. Suetonius' account is especially eloquent, as he describes the dominant mood of the Roman plebs as being hostile towards the deceased princeps. Reportedly the people demanded that after being brought to Rome, Tiberius' body be cast down the Gemonian Stairs and later thrown into the Tiber. Suetonius also tells us that on his way back to Rome, Caligula was welcomed by the people of the towns that Tiberius' funeral procession passed through. Altars were built in honour of the new emperor and solemn sacrifices made[18].

---

14 Suet. *Calig.* 12, 2; Tac. *Ann.* 6, 50, 4–5; Cass. Dio 59, 1, 2–3; Timpe 1962, 63–64; Barrett 1989, 41, 50, 53. Next to obtaining the support of the Praetorian Guard, ensuring the loyalty of the provincial legates was vital for securing Caligula's succession.

15 Scheid 1992, 225; Scheid 1998, 29 (ll. 8–12); 37 (ll. 12–17).

16 So, among others, Lesuisse 1961a, 420–421; Brunt 1977, 98; Barrett 1989, 53–56; Hurley 1991, 58; Scheid 1992, 224, 231; Wiedemann 2008, 221; Winterling 2011, 46; *contra* Cotton–Yakobson 1985, 498. I discuss this issue in more detail in the next section.

17 See Timpe 1962, 64.

18 Suet. *Tib.* 75, 1; *Calig.* 13.

Gaius arrived in Rome at the end of March, with the procession which carried Tiberius' corpse[19]. Shortly after, the Senate was convened, and according to Suetonius and Cassius Dio joined by representatives of the equites and the plebs[20]. During that meeting, Tiberius' last will was read out, followed by a discussion on holding his funeral ceremony and on his posthumous honorifics[21]. Also during that session, the Senate granted Caligula all the imperial prerogatives[22].

From Suetonius, we know that Tiberius' will indicated another major heir beside Caligula: his other living grandson Tiberius Gemellus[23]. Formally speaking, all that meant was having two heirs to his property and position within the family, but then as I have said more than once before, we know that in Rome the private heir was also treated as the primary candidate to coming into one's political legacy, which in this case constituted the imperial power. Due to the provisions of the will, both grandsons of Tiberius gained the same informal right to the succession[24]. Under those circumstances, Caligula could afford to take no risks, so as Cassius Dio recounts, he acted through Macro to "convince" the senators to cancel the will. According to Dio, the excuse was the notion that Tiberius could not have been sane while drafting the will if he designated as Caligula's co-regent the young and completely inexperienced Gemellus[25]. As I have already stressed above, the episode clearly points to Tiberius' last will

19 According to the *AFA* (Scheid 1998, 29–30, ll. 15–19), on 28th March; under 28th March 38 there is mention of a sacrifice made on the anniversary of the new emperor's arrival (*adventus*) in the capital. In the *Fasti Ostienses*, in turn (Bargagli–Grosso 1997, 25) we read Tiberius' corpse was brought to Rome on 29th March. See also Kienast 1996, 78, 85.

20 Suet. *Calig.* 14, 1; Cass. Dio 59, 6, 1. Scholars disagree on when exactly that Senate session took place. Cotton–Yakobson 1985, 497; Barrett 1989, 56 believe it was 28th March, while Timpe 1962, 65; 70 note 3; Brunt 1977, 98; Scheid 1992, 224 argue 29th, and Levick 1999, 220 assumes 30th.

21 Timpe 1962, 70; Levick 1999, 220.

22 On which below.

23 Suet. *Tib.* 76; see also Schrömbges 1986, 177–178; Mlasowsky 1996, 361. Anthony Barrett (1989, 39–40) suggests the emperor may have hoped to keep his natural grandson safe in this way after his death, but his opinion is utterly unconvincing. I do not think Tiberius, who had himself ordered the elimination of Agrippa Postumus before, could have remained unaware that by designating Gemellus the other, equal heir and thus making him Caligula's principal rival, he sentenced him to death. Therefore his motivations remain unclear.

24 Lesuisse 1961a, 420; Timpe 1962, 57; Barrett 1989, 51.

25 Cass. Dio 59, 1, 1–2.

having a political dimension as well as private ones[26]. Declaring it invalid meant not only Gemellus lost the status of heir to Tiberius' property; so did Caligula. Thus Barrett is correct in his assumption that Gaius cannot have come into Tiberius' funds on the basis of that will; instead, it must have happened "by virtue of his position as princeps."[27] Cancelling that document was an extremely important move in the process of Caligula securing his succession. Importantly, one he decided to make even though the Senate had already officially accepted him as the princeps, which shows the new ruler did prefer to exercise great caution.

Another issue discussed during that particular Senate session was Tiberius' funeral and his posthumous honorifics. From Dio we know that even before arriving at the Senate, the new emperor demanded that his predecessor receive honours identical to those conferred earlier on Augustus, but the senators waited until Gaius made it to the house. Eventually he gave up on the idea and settled for a mere public funeral for Tiberius[28]. When it comes to describing the *funus*, the sources are much more terse than in Augustus' case. Flavius Josephus only remarks the funeral was sumptuous and held according to the Roman customs. There is slightly more information in Suetonius and Cassius Dio, who relate that the corpse was displayed in public, most likely in the Forum Romanum, and the *laudatio funebris* was given by Caligula. Dio stresses the fact that in his speech the new princeps focused mostly on glorifying Augustus and Germanicus, and much less on praising Tiberius. Afterwards the emperor's body was cremated and the remains were laid in the Mausoleum of Augustus[29].

I think if Caligula gave up on his idea to grant Tiberius a number of prestigious posthumous honours and especially did not have the Senate consecrate him, that was because his predecessor mattered little to him when it came to legitimizing his reign. Invoking the memory of Augustus and Germanicus in Tiberius' *laudatio funebris* clearly demonstrates that emphasizing his natural descent from the first princeps and the popular Germanicus was more important to him than

---

26 Philo (*Leg*. 4, 26) also points out that tone of the will.

27 See Barrett 1989, 52.

28 Cass. Dio 59, 3, 7.

29 Joseph. *AJ*. 18, 236; Suet. *Tib*. 75, 3; *Calig*. 15, 1; Cass. Dio 59, 3, 7–8. From the *Fasti Ostienses* (Bargagli–Grosso 1997, 25) we know that Tiberius' funeral was held on 3rd April. While no sources state explicitly that the second emperor's remains were laid in the Mausoleum of Augustus, we have absolutely no reason to assume otherwise. See Barrett 1989, 59, 267 note 46.

concentrating on his family ties to the somewhat unpopular Tiberius[30]. Thus, as Timpe aptly noted, Caligula did not need to bring about Tiberius' deification, which would not have significantly strengthened his *auctoritas* as the new princeps[31]. One can see a sharp contrast to Tiberius' circumstances when taking over in AD 14, as for him the consecration of Augustus was important.

Caligula's next action aimed at ensuring his succession was paying out the gratuities to the Praetorian Guard, the urban cohorts, the *vigiles*, the provincial armies and the plebs in Rome. Dio tells us that after coming to Rome, the new princeps inspected the Praetorian units, accompanied by senators. Apparently each soldier in the Guard received a thousand sesterces, a sum set aside for them in Tiberius' will. It needs to be pointed out that the new emperor paid out those sums in spite of the fact he had earlier invalidated his predecessor's last will. There can be no doubt that this move was meant to win him the affection and loyalty of the Praetorians right at the beginning of his principate. They also received something extra from Caligula's private funds to celebrate his ascent to power[32]. It is supposed that it is in connection with this episode that the sesterces dated to the start of his rule were minted. The obverse of those coins shows Gaius' portrait with the legend C CAESAR AUG GERMANICUS PON M TR POT, and on the reverse one can see the emperor standing on a dais addressing a speech to soldiers below, with the legend ADLOCUT COH[33]. Next, sums provided for by Tiberius' last will were paid out to the soldiers of the other formations listed above, and to the plebs of Rome. They, too, received extra sums from Caligula's private resources[34]. It should be noted that, with Tiberius' will cancelled, all that money was given out purely in the new emperor's name. Such actions were certainly intended to ensure the young princeps would enjoy the support of and popularity among the military and the inhabitants of the capital.

Supposedly Caligula's rise to power caused euphoria in the provinces just as it did in Rome itself. Philo of Alexandria tells us that the Jews in Jerusalem and Alexandria congratulated the new princeps on his rise to power and made solemn sacrifices to celebrate it[35]. Interesting information on the mood prevalent in the provinces then can be found in epigraphical sources. We have at our

---

30 It is enough to consult the coin emissions issued under Caligula to see how important his family connections to Augustus and Germanicus were to him. See e.g. *RIC* I² *Cal.* no. 1–3, 9, 15, 39–41, 57, 59–62. See also Hekster 2015, 166-167.

31 Timpe 1962, 74–75.

32 Cass. Dio 59, 2, 1. See also Suet. *Calig.* 16, 3.

33 *RIC* I² *Cal.* 32; *HCC* I *Cal.* 14; Barrett 1989, 60; Łuć 2011, 231–234.

34 Cass. Dio 59, 2, 2–3.

35 Philo. *Leg.* 32, 231–232; 45, 356.

disposal two inscriptions of considerable length, one from Assos in Asia Minor, the other from Aritium in Hispania Lusitania. From the Assos text we know the inhabitants of that town swore allegiance to Caligula as the new princeps. His rise to power was seen as an extremely joyous event for all of humanity, and the beginning of a new age of happiness in the history of the Empire. A special delegation was also sent to Rome to congratulate the new emperor[36]. The people of Aritium made a similar oath of allegiance a few weeks after his inauguration. From the inscription we learn they vowed to regard as an enemy everyone who acted against the emperor's interest, and declared their readiness to take up arms against any such people on land and sea until they were punished. The text indicates the oath was inspired by Gaius Ummidius Durmius Quadratus, the *legatus Augusti pro praetore* for the province of *Hispania Lusitania*. Barrett supposes he acted on the basis of instructions sent by Macro[37].

While we only know of two oaths sworn by the inhabitants of the provinces after Caligula assumed the principate, we may with considerable confidence assume similar statements of loyalty were made in other cities of the Empire too. Without a doubt, the widespread enthusiasm mentioned earlier which the onset of Caligula's principate caused mostly resulted from his being a son, as Suetonius is right to stress, of the popular and appreciated Germanicus[38]. Therefore, his accession seems to have been generally perceived as a sign of better times coming after the reign of the unpopular Tiberius.

7.2 Granting Caligula Imperial Prerogatives

In Suetonius we read that after Caligula's arrival in Rome, the Senate granted him *ius arbitriumque omnium rerum*, or, literally "the right to decide in all things."[39] The *senatus consultum* was passed at the aforementioned session, which took place towards the end of March. What we have here is a so-called discretionary clause. It gave the emperor an unlimited right to take decisions according to his own judgement, in every area of public life. From a practical point of view, that privilege had already been enjoyed by Augustus, but Caligula was the first princeps to receive it formally. Some scholars see that *senatus consultum* as a model for the later *leges de imperio* and think the sixth clause of the famous *lex de*

36 *IGRR* IV 251. Barrett 1989, 55.

37 *ILS* I 190. Barrett 1989, 54. For the oath of the inhabitants of Aritium, see also Timpe 1962, 64–66.

38 Suet. *Calig.* 13.

39 Suet. *Calig.* 14, 1.

imperio Vespasiani was based directly on it[40]. What is more, at the same session Caligula received all the vital prerogatives of a princeps—the *tribunicia potestas* and the *imperium proconsulare*—and an emperor's titulature[41]: as Cassius Dio writes, after the new ruler came to Rome, the Senate conferred on him in one go all the powers and titles (except that of *pater patriae*) which Augustus had been given successively over his long reign, and some of which Tiberius had not accepted. It would appear that Dio means the same session Suetonius does[42]. The *senatus consultum* which granted Caligula an emperor's full powers was then sanctioned by the people in the Comitia (through the *lex de imperio*). Barrett and Kienast believe that was done on 21st April, that is on the day of the Parilia[43], basing the date primarily on this passage in Suetonius:

> decretum autem ut dies, quo [Caligula] cepisset imperium, Parilia vocaretur, velut argumentum rursus conditae urbis[44].

> It was further decreed that the day on which he began to reign should be called the Parilia, as a token that the city had been founded a second time[45].

Now, their opinion is absolutely unacceptable. First, we know that in the official calendar the Parilia featured as a *dies nefastus*, on which the Comitia could not be convoked[46]. Second, Suetonius only reports that the day when Caligula assumed power would be *named* Parilia, never indicating the event took place *on* the Parilia (which fell on 21st April). If that had been the case, there would have been no need to rename the day, as it had already had that name in the official calendar. And third, I believe Suetonius means not the day the people ratified the Senate's decision to bestow imperial powers on Caligula, but rather the

40 So especially Brunt 1977, 98, 107–115. See also Timpe 1962, 75; Barrett 1989, 56–57; Barrett 1996, 144; Ziółkowski 2004, 412–414.

41 This is a little different in Barrett (1989, 56), who believes the *ius arbitriumque omnium rerum* mentioned by Suetonius already contained in it all the key powers of a princeps.

42 Cass. Dio 59, 3, 2. See also Timpe 1962, 65, 75; Parsi 1963, 84; Brunt 1977, 98; Cotton–Yakobson 1985, 497–498; Barrett 1989, 56. From the *AFA* we know Caligula assumed the title of *pater patriae* on 21st September AD 37. See Scheid–Broise 1980, 224–225, ll. 55–60; 240–242; Barrett 1989, 70; Scheid 1992, 226; Kienast 1996, 85; Stevenson 2007, 122–123. However, just as Tiberius before him, the new emperor did not include the praenomen *imperator* in his official nomenclature. See Lesuisse 1961a, 421. It only sporadically appears in provincial inscriptions See e.g. *ILS* II. 2, 8789, 8792.

43 Barrett 1989, 71–72; Kienast 1996, 85.

44 Suet. *Calig.* 16, 4.

45 Translated by J. C. Rolfe (Loeb Classical Library, 31).

46 See e.g. the *Fasti Antiates Maiores* or the *Fasti Caeretani* (Degrassi 1963, 9; 66).

day on which his principate actually began (the *dies principatus*). Some modern historians suppose that would have been 18th March, when the Senate officially declared him emperor, and it was that day that would from then on be called *Parilia* in the official calendar as well[47]. However, towards the end of his *Life of Caligula*, Suetonius says that princeps reigned for three years, ten months and eight days[48]. Taking into account that Caligula was assassinated on 24th January AD 41, our author obviously considers his *dies principatus* to be 16th March 37, that is, the day Tiberius died.

Therefore everything suggests that 16th March, not 18th, was singled out to be called *Parilia*. It does not seem likely that this involved moving the date of this ancient festival; rather, I think all this meant was extending the name to another day in the official calendar. Suetonius says that it was in this way that the Senate celebrated Caligula as the new founder of Rome. To summarize, we can see that attempts to establish the date when the *lex* in question was passed based on Suetonius' account are doomed to failure. Unfortunately, the *AFA*, which did note the dates of analogous *leges* for some emperors, in this case contain no information on the matter either[49], and so we do not know when the people sanctioned the *senatus consultum* granting Caligula his imperial powers. Formally speaking, there can be no doubt that granting Gaius the full range of an emperor's powers via a *senatus consultum* and having that decision confirmed by the people were the two most important moments of his investiture.

It ought to be stressed here that at the moment when he took over after Tiberius, Caligula's position was fundamentally different from that which his predecessor had enjoyed when taking over after Augustus' death. Firstly, Tiberius' succession had been formally prepared before Augustus died through his adoption and by conferring on him the *tribunicia potestas* and the *imperium proconsulare*, the two key components of imperial power. And secondly, unlike his adoptive grandfather, Caligula had no military achievements under his belt to reinforce his *auctoritas*, especially in the eyes of the army. In that situation his most important asset, which ultimately made him princeps, turned out to be the fact he was a natural great-grandson of Augustus and a son of the popular Germanicus[50].

---

47 See e.g. Weinstock 1971, 191; Hurley 1991, 57, 90.

48 Suet. *Calig.* 59.

49 See Scheid 1992, 227.

50 That fact was then meticulously emphasized on many coin emissions minted during Caligula's reign, where the emperor was styled *divi Augusti pronepos*. See e.g. *RIC* I^2 *Cal.* 40–42; *HCC* I *Cal.* 16, 26–35. See also Hekster 2015, 166-167.

7.3 Caligula and the *recusatio imperii*

While in Tiberius' case all the sources agree that he delayed the assumption of his principate, for Caligula we only find a suggestion of that sort in Cassius Dio. Namely, Dio says at first Gaius refused all the imperial titles and prerogatives, expressing willingness to share his powers with the senators. As we know, Tiberius had likewise suggested handing over some of his public duties to the Senate:

> Δημοκρατικώτατός τε γὰρ εἶναι τὰ πρῶτα δόξας, ὥστε μήτε τῷ δήμῳ ἢ τῇ γε βουλῇ γράψαι τι μήτε τῶν ὀνομάτων τῶν ἀρχικῶν προσθέσθαι[51].

> Thus, he had seemed at first most democratic, to such a degree, in fact, that he would send no letters either to the people or to the senate nor assume any of the imperial titles[52].

> Ἐν μὲν οὖν τῷ ἔτει ἐν ᾧ ὅ τε Τιβέριος ἐτελεύτησε καὶ αὐτὸς ἐς τὴν ἡγεμονίαν ἀντικατέστη, πρῶτον μὲν τοὺς βουλευτάς, παρόντων ἐν τῷ συνεδρίῳ καὶ ἱππέων τοῦ τε δήμου τινῶν, πολλὰ ἐκολάκευσε, τήν τε γὰρ ἀρχὴν κοινώσειν σφίσι καὶ πάνθ᾽ ὅσα ἂν καὶ ἐκείνοις ἀρέσῃ ποιήσειν ὑπέσχετο, καὶ υἱὸς καὶ τρόφιμος αὐτῶν λέγων εἶναι[53].

> In the year that Tiberius died and Gaius succeeded to the rule, he at first showed great deference to the senators on an occasion when knights and also some of the populace were present at their meeting. He promised to share his power with them and to do whatever would please them, called himself their son and ward[54].

Although no other sources mention any reluctance on Caligula's part when it came to assuming the principate, I see no grounds to reject Cassius Dio's account in this case. Hannah Cotton and Alexander Yakobson assume the above passage from Dio refers to Caligula rejecting the imperial powers, in their opinion granted him by the Senate as early as 18th March, since they think the Senate declaring Gaius princeps, which took place on that day, was tantamount to bestowing those powers on him. They also believe Caligula did, however agree to accept them after his arrival in Rome ten days later, when the senators and the urban plebs apparently prevailed upon him to assume the principate and its accompanying prerogatives[55]. I cannot agree with those historians' view; as

51 Cass. Dio 59, 3, 1.

52 Translated by E. Cary (Loeb Classical Library, 175).

53 Cass. Dio 59, 6, 1.

54 Translated by E. Cary (Loeb Classical Library, 175).

55 Cotton–Yakobson 1985, 497–503, a claim accepted also by Huttner (2004, 154 note 19). *Contra* Barrett 1989, 265 note 21; Wiedemann 2008, 221.

I have already indicated, I believe that on 18th March the Senate merely declared Caligula princeps, and only granted him all the relevant powers after he came to Rome[56]. In other words, I think the *recusatio imperii* in question was not so much Caligula's response to the declaration of 18th March, as to him receiving the titles and prerogatives of a princeps during the Senate session in the final days of March, and it is at this session that the situation described by Dio took place. However, I do not suppose Gaius was actually going to refuse the imperial power offered to him; rather, I assume he intended to give another demonstration of *moderatio*, similar to that of Tiberius: in this way, the new princeps wanted to impress the senators on the threshold of his reign.

56 That point of view is generally shared by most scholars; see above.

8 Proclaiming Claudius the Next Princeps

8.1 The Position of the Senate Regarding the Appointment of Caligula's Successor

Caligula's death on 24th January AD 41 in an assassination brought about by a few officers of the Praetorian Guard caused the first succession crisis: the emperor had left no male issue and, not expecting to die so young, had not designated anybody as his successor via adoption either. Importantly, with Caligula the family of *Iulii Caesares* to which all the emperors had so far belonged, died out. Under these circumstances choosing the new princeps was an open question.

From our sources we know that after the assassination the incumbent consuls Gn. Sentius Saturninus and Q. Pomponius Secundus undertook a number of actions intended to prevent possible riots and looting in the city. To this end they deployed soldiers of the urban cohorts on the Capitoline and issued an edict calling on the people and the Praetorians to remain calm, promising tax exemptions and gratuities in return. In order to secure the public finances, the consuls ordered the money moved from the public treasury in the temple of Saturn to the Capitoline[1]. Then they convened the Senate, which probably gathered on the same day Caligula was murdered, that is, on 24th January[2]. The ancient authors report that the debate was heated. Allegedly, some of the senators unambiguously argued for restoring *libertas* (freedom), and at the same time put forward the motion that the name of the Caesars be erased from memory and temples to them destroyed[3]. Others opted for appointing a new princeps. Still, the supporters of preserving monarchy disagreed on who should be the next emperor[4]. Among the potential candidates, Josephus lists primarily Marcus

1 Joseph. *AJ.* 19, 160; Suet. *Claud.* 10, 3; Cass. Dio 59, 30, 3; 60, 1, 1–2.

2 Sources disagree as to where the first Senate session after Caligula's death was held. Josephus now says it was on the Capitoline (*BJ.* 2, 205), now in the Curia in the Forum (*AJ.* 19, 158). Similarly Suetonius (*Calig.* 60; *Claud.* 10, 3), while Dio (60, 1, 1) unambiguously points to the Capitoline Hill. Present-day scholars disagree on the matter as well. Timpe (1962, 84–85 note 4) assumes the Curia, whereas other historians believe it was the Capitoline. See e.g. Ehrhardt 1978, 51; Barrett 1989, 172; Levick 1990, 31. Security concerns would have argued for the Capitoline; we do know aggressive crowds were gathered in the Forum.

3 I suspect the hostile attitude of this group of senators towards the *domus Caesarum* could have resulted from the particularly bad impression Caligula's reign left behind.

4 Joseph. *BJ.* 2, 205; Suet. *Calig.* 60; *Claud.* 10, 3–4; Cass. Dio 60, 1, 1.

Vinicius (husband to one of Caligula's sisters) and Valerius Asiaticus, but their candidacies failed to gain the support of the majority of senators. The same historian writes that eventually both candidates withdrew from the race out of fear for their own lives as well as the desire to avoid fratricidal fighting[5]. Allegedly, the Senate remained in session all day and night, or so Cassius Dio emphasizes, but it still did not take any constructive decisions[6].

All the ancient authors recounting the events after Caligula's assassination agree that some of the senators demanded that *libertas* be restored; Suetonius actually claims initially the whole Senate was unanimous in that regard[7]. It is worth inquiring here what was behind the use of this word. Did those senators explicitly intend to restore the Republic, or did they understand *libertas* in the context of their day the way Tacitus would later, namely as the Senate's unlimited and exclusive right to appoint the new princeps? In Timpe's opinion, they were not hostile towards principate (or, monarchy) as a political system; rather, they opposed the continued reign of the dynasty which had ruled so far. Timpe is convinced that *libertas* meant not bringing back the Republic as such, but rather freeing the state from the tyranny of the Caesar family, which did not involve giving up on appointing a new princeps, unconnected to the old dynasty[8]. Timpe's view does not appear convincing though. Flavius Josephus and Cassius Dio unambiguously treat the senators in question as adherents of a form of government which those authors refer to as "aristocracy" or "democracy." Moreover, Flavius clearly points out that their intention was to restore the old constitution[9], and the speech he cites by Sentius Saturninus, one of the consuls, has a Republican tone and wording. Saturninus speaks out against monarchy in no uncertain terms, contrasting it with rule by the Senate, but has nothing to say regarding a need to appoint a new princeps[10]. The hostile attitude towards some of the senators of the Praetorians and the people, who both came forward as champions of the principate, may also indicate that these senators did intend to restore the Republic[11]. Nothing then indicates they were in favour of preserving the established system, provided the Senate would gain the right to choose each

5 Joseph. *AJ*. 19, 251–253; Barrett 1989, 174–175.

6 Cass. Dio 60, 1, 2.

7 Suet. *Calig*. 60.

8 Timpe 1962, 86–87.

9 Joseph. *BJ*. 2, 205; Cass. Dio 60, 1, 1.

10 Joseph. *AJ*. 19, 166–187. On the subject of this speech, see also Barrett 1989, 174; Levick 1990, 31; Gibson 2013, 108–109.

11 Joseph. *AJ*. 19, 224–225; 227–228; Suet. *Clad*. 10, 4.

successive princeps[12]. There is of course the separate issue of any idea about restoring Republican government being completely utopian. Set against the determined stance of the Praetorian Guard and the people of Rome (on which see below), the notion was absolutely unfeasible.

Since the Senate was not able to decide anything, the initiative passed to the Praetorians, who acclaimed Claudius—the assassinated Caligula's uncle—emperor. When informed of the fact, the senators immediately sent envoys to the Castra Praetoria, calling upon Claudius to subject himself to the Senate and not accept the throne handed him by the soldiers against its will. The envoys expressed the same opinion that had already come up during the first Senate debate after Caligula's murder: that the Senate is the only legitimate institution which can appoint the new princeps[13]. In Josephus, we read Claudius replied in a conciliatory manner, telling them he was mindful of Caligula's fate and was going to rule fairly and in co-operation with the Senate. Despite this declaration, the Senate would not yield, threatening Claudius with military conflict. The threats failed to achieve their intended purpose and Claudius told the senators he would not resign even if blood were to be spilled[14]. This unrelenting attitude stemmed from the fact he had considerable military force at his disposal: the three urban cohorts stationed in Rome had all taken his side[15]. In the end it was possible to avoid a violent solution. The later course of events was largely decided by the stance of the aforementioned *cohortes urbanae*, which, when faced with the prospect of a domestic battle with the Praetorians, abandoned the Senate's cause and went over to Claudius' side[16]. This development finally convinced the senators to declare him princeps, which they did on 25th January[17].

Shortly afterwards Claudius assembled the Senate again. This time, it met on the Palatine Hill. During that session, the Senate conferred on him all the powers and titles of the emperor[18]; Cassius Dio tells us the only one Claudius declined

12 So Hammond (1956, 65), who believes those senators aimed to abolish the principate and restore the republic.

13 Joseph. *AJ*. 19, 229–235; Cass. Dio 60, 1, 4.

14 Joseph. *BJ*. 2, 206–210; *AJ*. 19, 236–246. Josephus reports that the intermediary in Claudius' negotiations with the Senate was the Jewish king Agrippa, who was in Rome at the time. However, he no doubt exaggerates the king's role in the events in question. See Levick 1990, 33.

15 Joseph. *BJ*. 2. 205; 209; *AJ*. 19, 188; 242; Suet. *Claud*. 10, 3. According to Levick's (1990, 31) calculations, they numbered roughly 1,500 soldiers.

16 Joseph. *BJ*. 2, 211–213; Cass. Dio 60, 1, 4.

17 See Timpe 1962, 90; Brunt 1977, 98; Kienast 1996, 90.

18 Joseph. *AJ*. 19, 266; Cass. Dio 60, 1, 4. See also Levick 1990, 33; Osgood 2011, 31.

was the title of *pater patriae*, which he would however later include in his official titulature[19]. Moreover, in Suetonius we read that the new princeps also forbade the title of *imperator* from being used as his new praenomen, as had been the case with Augustus[20], a piece of information confirmed by numismatic sources, among others, which indicate Claudius only used the word as one of his imperial titles[21]. Later on, the *senatus consultum* under discussion here, which bestowed on Claudius the imperial prerogatives, would also be sanctioned by the people in the form of a *lex de imperio*[22], as had been the case with Caligula.

In the same session, the Senate resolved to put to death Cassius Chaerea and the other members of the assassination plot. They were charged not only with breaking the oath of allegiance they had sworn to the previous emperor, but also with the intention to slay Claudius[23]. On the other hand, the senators who after Caligula's assassination had called for restoring the Republic or come forward as candidates for the new princeps, were included in the amnesty. What is more, Cassius Dio recounts that many of the pardoned senators would later receive prestigious offices from the new emperor[24].

During the same session, the Senate wanted to pass a *senatus consultum* on Caligula's *damnatio memoriae*[25]. The sources indicate that in his case it was going

19 Cass. Dio 60, 3, 2. From the *AFA* (Scheid 1998, 45, ll. 3–9) we know this probably happened on 12th January 42. See Kienast 1996, 90; Stevenson 2007, 123–124.

20 Suet. *Claud.* 12, 1; see also Timpe 1962, 92–93; Gibson 2013, 111.

21 See e.g. *RIC* I² *Claud.* 51–54; 61–64; 102, 104.

22 Since between the *senatus consultum* and the *lex* some time had to pass, including at least three market days (*trinum nundinum*). See Brunt 1977, 99; Barrett 1989, 71. Regrettably in Claudius' case, the *AFA* does not list the date the *lex* was passed.

23 Joseph. *AJ.* 19, 268–271; Suet. *Claud.* 11, 1; Cass. Dio 60, 3, 4–5; see also Timpe 1962, 91; Jung 1972, 383; Levick 1990, 35–36; Gibson 2013, 111.

24 Suet. *Claud.* 11, 1; Cass. Dio 60, 3, 5; it is supposed that the reverse legend OB CIVES SERVATOS refers to this amnesty, found on aurei and denarii minted during the first year of Claudius' reign (*RIC* I² *Claud.* 5–6). So e.g. Ehrhardt 1978, 66 note 111; Levick 1990, 39.

25 It ought to be pointed out here that *damnatio memoriae* is a modern term, not found in the ancient sources, and so I use it loosely to refer to various actions taken by ancient Romans to condemn the memory of a person. That is also the sense in which the term is commonly used in the literature. It is also worth stressing that *damnatio memoriae* often contained other elements as well, since depending on the circumstances the Senate took various decisions meant to dishonour the person. For instance, in Mark Antony's case, the senators decided nobody in his *gens* could use the *praenomen* Marcus in the future, and the day of his birth (14th January) would be treated as cursed (*dies vitiosus*). See Cass. Dio 51, 19, 3; *Fasti Verulani* (Degrassi 1963, 159). The package of Senate

to involve removing images of him from public spaces and listing the day of his assassination as a public holiday. However, according to Dio, Claudius did not allow this. The historian says that the new princeps himself merely ordered all of Caligula's images removed from the city by night. Suetonius adds that Claudius nullified all of his predecessor's decrees in a *recissio actorum*[26]. Thus in Caligula's case there was no official *damnatio memoriae*, such as had been instituted for Gnaeus Calpurnius Piso or later for some emperors under the principate, because the Senate never ratified it[27].

To sum up, we can be quite certain that in practice the Senate had no say at all in appointing Claudius to the principate, its role being limited to merely ratifying the candidate imposed on it by the Praetorians and to granting him the full package of an emperor's powers. Therefore, we may consider the Praetorian acclamation the crucial moment in Claudius' accession process[28]. It should also be stressed that after the assassination of Caligula the belief appeared for the first time among senators that the Senate had the exclusive right to appoint the emperor, a result of the line of the *Iulii Caesares* dying out. However, with the loss of the urban cohorts' backing, and with the soldiers of the Praetorian Guard and the Roman plebs determined, it was not possible to make this idea a reality.

8.2 Claudius Hailed Emperor by the Praetorian Guard: an Accident, or a Planned Scenario?

At this point, I would like to take a closer look at the role the Praetorians had to play during the first few days after Caligula's assassination, since it is worth asking the question of whether their choice of Claudius for the new emperor was really purely accidental, as a large majority of ancient sources suggest. Flavius Josephus, Suetonius and Cassius Dio all agree that after Caligula's assassination

---

decrees regarding condemning the memory of Calpurnius Piso, on the other hand, included having all his statues and other images removed from public spaces and a ban on displaying his *imago* during the funerals of Calpurnii. See *SCPP* ll. 75–76; 80–82.

26 Suet. *Claud.* 11, 3; Cass. Dio 60, 4, 5–6. See also Timpe 1962, 92; Barrett 1989, 177–178.

27 It should also be stressed we have few confirmed cases of Caligula's name being erased from inscriptions, most of them from Italy and some of the provinces. In that case they are more likely to have been spontaneous local initiatives rather than directives carried out from above. See Barrett 1989, 178.

28 Some scholars correctly and explicitly treat Claudius' rise to the throne as a "military usurpation" or "military coup", later sanctioned with a *senatus consultum*. So e.g. Parsi 1963, 145; Ehrhardt 1978, 52.

Claudius hid in a room in the imperial palace, where a soldier of the Praetorian Guard happened upon him. He then took Claudius to the Praetorian camp near the *porta Viminalis*, where in spite of his reluctance he was acclaimed princeps[29]. These accounts all indicate that Claudius' *acclamatio* happened as a result of the spontaneous actions of some of the Praetorians. Can we accept this uncritically though? I think we should remain quite cautious in this regard, because there is evidence that the choice of Claudius was anything but simply accidental. It would be a good idea to look at Josephus' account again.

In another passage, he reports the events which took place right after Caligula's death somewhat differently[30]: apparently after assassinating the emperor, the Praetorians gathered to consult together, unanimously decided that appointing a new princeps was necessary, and resolved that Claudius was the best candidate. The plan was put into action immediately as the soldiers abducted Claudius, taking him to their camp and acclaiming him emperor[31]. Now, this passage could in turn indicate that the Praetorians' actions were actually quite pragmatic and their choice of candidate was by no means accidental.

Based on that passage in Flavius Josephus, Helmut Jung claims that Claudius' appointment was a result of deliberate actions by a group of Praetorian officers who had been involved in Caligula's assassination plot, without playing a major role in it. Unlike the main organizers of the assassination, Cassius Chaerea and Cornelius Sabinus, who wanted to eliminate both Claudius and Caligula, those officers saw Claudius as the future princeps and allegedly their position was that of the majority of soldiers of the Guard. In Jung's opinion, it was this group that convoked the meeting mentioned in Flavius at which Caligula's uncle was acclaimed emperor, and the image of Claudius fixed, primarily by Suetonius and Cassius Dio, as being intimidated, indecisive and owing his principate only to a lucky coincidence, may reflect both those authors'—or actually their sources'—dislike of this princeps. Jung also thinks it possible that Claudius was privy to the assassins' plans[32].

Jung's hypotheses are purely speculative, although his general assumption that hailing Claudius emperor was not accidental seems solid. The question immediately arises of what motivated the Praetorians to choose him. In this context,

---

29 Joseph. *AJ*. 19, 212–226; Suet. *Claud*. 10, 1–3; Cass. Dio 60, 1, 2–3.

30 That is most likely a result of Josephus using of multiple sources which differently described the events to do with Caligula's assassination and Claudius' takeover.

31 Joseph. *AJ*. 19, 162–166.

32 Jung 1972, 367–386.

Flavius Josephus' account is again of paramount importance. From his narrative, we know that soldiers of this force were fully convinced appointing a new princeps was necessary from the very moment of Caligula's death, as they considered the option of abolishing the principate unacceptable[33]. Josephus adds that the soldiers did not want any of the leaders of the plot to ascend to the throne, but wanted someone who would owe his principate exclusively to their support. Eventually they decided on Claudius, and Flavius stresses that their main reasons were his family relationship to the previous princeps, his education[34], and the prospect of receiving gratuities. Supposedly, for them it was important that Claudius was the brother of Germanicus, who had been universally liked[35]. Thus Flavius Josephus' account clearly indicates that when choosing Claudius, the Praetorians mostly had the dynastic principle in mind. While not a member of the *domus Caesarum*, he was a close relative of each previous princeps[36]. For the soldiers of the Praetorian Guard this was no doubt an asset no other candidate possessed[37], and their choice means they remained loyal to the dynasty which had ruled until then: in spite of the bad impression Caligula's short reign had left behind, they clearly spoke in favour of this dynastic rule being continued, an attitude which seems quite comprehensible. From the day of Augustus on, the soldiers of that particular force had enjoyed exceptional privileges, and for them the reign of Caesars meant a guarantee of stability. Therefore, we may with considerable confidence deduce that appointing Claudius the new princeps was not

---

33 Joseph. *AJ*. 19, 223–225. Levick (1990, 33) is no doubt correct when she stresses that attitude of the Praetorians stemmed not merely from their hope of receiving generous gratuities from the new emperor, but also from their concern for the future of their force, which was created to guard emperors; restoring the Republic would have questioned the point of the Guard's existence. One can see how hostile the Praetorians were to the notion of abolishing the principate, which some Senators endorsed, in an episode to do wih the consul Pomponius Secundus. Flavius Josephus (*AJ*. 19, 263) recounts that Secundus was almost killed by incensed soldiers for exhorting his listeners to bring back the old freedom.

34 I suppose to most Praetorians this aspect was actually marginally important at best, but the intellect and education of a potential princeps may have mattered to Josephus, who as a member of an important priestly family had been thoroughly educated himself. Thus he highlighted that characteristic as one of the criteria which supposedly guided the Praetorians in their choice of Claudius for emperor.

35 Joseph. *AJ*. 19, 162–166; 223–225. See also Jung 1972, 371; 376–377.

36 Claudius was a son of a niece of Augustus, a nephew of Tiberius and an uncle of Caligula.

37 See Parsi 1963, 145; Griffin 1984, 192; Levick 1990, 33.

an accident but rather a well-thought-out move by a large group of Praetorians acting in their own best interest.

Josephus and Dio both report that Claudius was initially unwilling to accept the position of princeps. Eventually he gave in, if reluctantly[38], but I do not believe he was really going to refuse the imperial power offered him by the Praetorians. After all, Flavius Josephus writes clearly that his manner was all pretence, since in fact he did want to become princeps[39]. Moreover, Claudius must have realized that rejecting the soldiers' decision would have carried immense risks. If another candidate had been appointed, as a person closely related to the old dynasty, he would have been in grave danger. Thus most likely his actions were a conventional gesture of *recusatio imperii*, such as we have already encountered when Tiberius and Caligula rose to power. Still, it should be emphasized that while in the case of those two emperors the show had been held in the Senate, Claudius made his gesture in front of the army[40].

In Flavius Josephus and Suetonius, we read that right after Claudius accepted, the Praetorians swore their allegiance to him. On that occasion, the new princeps ordered that they receive exceptionally high *donativa.* Josephus mentions sums of 5,000 drachmas (or, 20,000 sesterces), while in Suetonius it is 15,000 sesterces. These were the sums paid out to rank and file soldiers; officers received more. Similar gratuities were promised to the legions[41]. To put the amount in perspective, the sums promised the Praetorians were five times their yearly pay[42]. Moreover, Cassius Dio informs us that the Praetorians were to receive a hundred sesterces each on every anniversary of Claudius acclamation[43]. The size of those sums makes clear the importance of the Praetorian Guard in Claudius' ascent to the throne, demonstrated also by the aurei and denarii the minting of which started in Rome immediately after he came to power, and continued for the first few years of his reign. From the iconographic point of view, we can distinguish two types among those coins. The obverse of the first type contains Claudius' image with the legend TI CLAUD CAESAR AUG PM TR P, while the reverse shows the Castra Praetoria and in it, a soldier holding a spear, standing before an eagle (*aquila*). The whole picture is complemented by the legend IMPER

---

38 Joseph. *AJ.* 19, 166; Cass. Dio 60, 1, 3a.
39 Joseph. *AJ.* 19, 166.
40 See Jung 1972, 386; Huttner 2004, 160–163.
41 Joseph. *AJ.* 19, 247; Suet. *Claud.* 10, 4. See also Parsi 1963, 145–146; Barrett 1989, 175.
42 See Łuć 2004, 133–134.
43 Cass. Dio 60, 12, 4.

Fig. 27. Aureus, Rome, AD 44–45. Obverse: an image of Claudius; legend: TI CLAUD CAESAR AUG PM TR P IIII. Reverse: the Praetorian camp, with a soldier in it holding a spear, standing in front of an *aquila*; legend: IMPER RECEPT (*RIC* I² *Claud*. 25).

RECEPT[44]. (fig. 27) The obverse of the second type is the same as of the first, whereas the reverse has a full-body image of Claudius extending his hand to a Praetorian soldier standing opposite. The legend for the scene is PRAETOR RECEPT[45]. (fig. 28) Both those emissions extremely clearly highlighted the decisive role of the Praetorian Guard in Claudius' ascent to the principate. They depicted the Praetorians as loyal allies and a major supporting pillar of the new princeps and the reigning dynasty. Levick supposes the coins in question may have subsequently been used for the payment of the *donativa* promised by Claudius[46].

The Praetorians' choice was readily accepted by the people, who called for the appointment of a new emperor immediately after Caligula's murder, unambiguously speaking out in favour of having the principate continue. Just like the Praetorians, the plebs of Rome were against the prospect of restoring the rule of the Senate, fearing that would bring about the outbreak of a new civil war[47].

---

44 *RIC* I² *Claud*. 7–8; 19, 25–26; *HCC* I *Claud*. 8–9.

45 *RIC* I² *Claud*. 11–12; 23–24; 29. On the subject of those emissions, see e.g. Parsi 1963, 146; Jung 1972, 383 note 65; Osgood 2011, 34–36; Łuć 2011, 234–237; Gibson 2013, 118–125.

46 Levick 1990, 39.

47 Joseph. *AJ*. 19, 228; 254; Suet. *Claud*. 10, 4.

Fig. 28. Denarius, Rome, AD 44–45. Obverse: an image of Claudius; legend: TI CLAUD CAESAR AUG PM TR P IIII. Reverse: an image of Claudius extending his hand to a Praetorian soldier standing opposite; legend: PRAETOR RECEPT (*RIC* I[2] *Claud.* 24).

The choice of Claudius was also fairly smoothly accepted by provincial governors and legion commanders. Suetonius merely writes that the people nearest Galba, then the commander of legions in Germania, encouraged him to try for the throne now that Caligula was dead. However, Galba decided against such a step, for which Claudius repaid him by nominating him to prestigious offices and counting him among his closest friends[48].

8.3 The Problem of Legitimizing Claudius' Succession

At the moment of his appointment to princeps, Claudius' position was no doubt weaker than those of the previous two emperors. Tiberius took over as Augustus' son, and in addition to this, he already had extensive political and military experience by then. Caligula, in his turn, legitimized his principate with his direct descent from Augustus. While until then he had never held any important public functions, as a natural great-grandson of the first princeps and a son of the beloved Germanicus he was accepted as emperor without protest. Unlike the two rulers before him, Claudius could not legitimize his ascent to the throne

48 Suet. *Galb.* 7, 1.

by claiming descent from Augustus. Moreover, just like Caligula, at the time he was made emperor he had practically no experience in politics or the military[49]. For these reasons, right after his ascent he embarked on a number of projects whose purpose was to legitimize and secure his succession. No doubt one important move in that regard was assuming the cognomen *Caesar*, meant to stress that he was a legitimate successor and that his rule would continue those of the emperors before him. From then on, Claudius' official titulature was *Tiberius Claudius Caesar Augustus Germanicus*[50]. It ought to be emphasized here that this was when the cognomen *Caesar*, previously used primarily by men of the *gens Iulia*, became another title of the emperor, next to *Augustus* [51].

As I have already mentioned, Claudius' family ties to the imperial family proved enough of an asset in the eyes of the Praetorians for them to hail him emperor. Therefore, from the very beginning of his reign the new princeps went out of his way to display his connections to the dynasty which had ruled until then. It was no accident that at the onset of his rule the central place fell to Antonia the Younger and to Germanicus; through his mother, who was Augustus' niece, the new emperor could claim to be related to the creator of principate, which mattered a lot for reinforcing his *auctoritas* in the eyes of the public. Shortly after being made emperor, Claudius granted Antonia a number of posthumous honours, including the very prestigious title of Augusta, which she had refused when alive[52]. Many coins were also minted in her honour, such as aurei and denarii, presumably produced in the years 41–45. The obverse shows Antonia wearing the *corona spicea*, with the legend ANTONIA AUGUSTA. On the reverse, Claudius' mother holds a torch in one hand and a horn of plenty in the other, and the accompanying legend is CONSTANTIAE AUGUSTI[53]. Another group of coins is made up by dupondii minted at roughly the same time. The obverse of that series has Antonia's face with the legend ANTONIA AUGUSTA, and on the reverse, a togate Claudius holds a *simpulum*, the legend being TI CLAUDIUS CAESAR AUG PM TR P IMP, with the senatorial signature of SC[54].

---

49 He did become consul in 37, but only held that office for two months. See Suet. *Claud.* 7; Cass. Dio 60, 2, 1; Degrassi 1952, 10. See also Osgood 2011, 30.

50 Timpe 1962, 92–93, 96–97; Griffin 1984, 192; Corbier 1995, 185; Kienast 1996, 90.

51 See Lesuisse 1961b, 271–287; Barrett 1996, 97. From Claudius' reign on, it was also a privilege of the intended successor.

52 Suet. *Claud.* 11, 2; Corbier 1995, 185.

53 *RIC* I² *Claud.* 65–66.

54 *RIC* I² *Claud.* 92. For more on the various emissions dedicated to Antonia, see Trillmich 1978, 17–24, 69–77, 142–177; Kokkinos 2002, 87–104.

Another important link between Claudius and the old dynasty was his brother Germanicus, a member of the *domus Caesarum* through adoption. Suetonius stresses that the emperor made a point of cultivating his memory during his reign[55], a fact expressed through coin emissions. A series of asses and sesterces may serve as an example. On the obverse, we see a portrait of Germanicus with the legend GERMANICUS CAESAR TI AUG F DIVI AUG N, which extremely clearly highlighted his relationship to the godlike Augustus; the reverse had the legend TI CLAUDIUS CAESAR AUG GERM PM TR P IMP PP. Still, the dating of those emissions is uncertain. They were most likely struck between 42 and 50[56].

With no military successes to his name, the new emperor also needed to take care of his image with the army, and to achieve that, he used his father, Drusus the Elder. As early as in AD 41, the mint in Rome began to produce coins commemorating Drusus' military achievements. They included, among others, a series of sesterces whose obverse showed an image of Claudius with the legend, TI CLAUDIUS CAESAR AUG PM TR P IMP PP, while the reverse had an arch crowned with a statue of a rider in gallop, between two tropaea. The whole thing was accompanied by the legend NERO CLAUDIUS DRUSUS GERMAN IMP and the signature SC[57]. (fig. 29) Thus the iconography on the reverse drew on Drusus' successes during his campaign in Germania. It seems highly likely that by bringing up those victories, Claudius wanted to not only posthumously honour his father, but also to win the affection of the army, since we know the legions had held Drusus in high regard, and the memory of his successes was still alive[58].

All of Claudius' actions in the sphere of dynastic policy listed here clearly demonstrate how important legitimizing his reign was to this princeps. That is quite understandable, seeing as he was the first emperor from outside the Julian family, which placed him in a difficult situation right at the start of his rule. He was also aware the Senate only agreed to declare him emperor reluctantly and under pressure from the Praetorians, which may well have made him uncomfortable. Personal changes in the Praetorian Guard were another step he took

55 Suet. *Claud.* 11, 2.

56 *HCC* I *Claud.* 89–91; *RIC* I^2 *Claud.* 105–106.

57 *HCC* I *Claud.* 45. For other emissions dedicated to Drusus, see e.g. *RIC* I^2 *Claud.* 69–74.

58 For the role played by Drusus the Elder in Claudius' dynastic propaganda, see Osgood 2011, 60–62; Hekster 2015, 49–50.

Fig. 29. Sestertius, Rome, AD 41–42. Obverse: an image of Claudius; legend: TI CLAUDIUS CAESAR AUG PM TR P IMP PP. Reverse: an image of an arch with a rider in gallop on top, shown between two trophies; legend: NERO CLAUDIUS DRUSUS GERMAN IMP; signature: SC (*HCC* I *Claud.* 45).

with securing his succession in mind. Even before the Senate officially sanctioned his principate, he had appointed two new prefects, Rufrius Pollio and Catonius Justus. Additionally, soldiers regarded as suspicious were removed from the Praetorian cohorts[59].

59 Joseph. *AJ*. 19, 267; 274; Ehrhardt 1978, 65; Barrett 1989, 175–176.

9 Nero's Succession

9.1 Claudius' Death and Will

Claudius died on 13th October AD 54. Seneca eloquently named the day of his death, *initium saeculi felicissimi*[1]. Most ancient authors unanimously report the princeps was poisoned at the instructions of Agrippina, who was afraid Nero would be excluded from the succession and Britannicus would be designated as the successor. In Tacitus, Suetonius and Cassius Dio, we find detailed descriptions of the way the poison was administered: supposedly mixed in with mushrooms, although the intense retching it caused made it less effective. Therefore, Claudius was given another dose, which was, according to Tacitus, introduced into the body with a special feather used to induce vomiting[2]. Some present-day historians reject the account of the poisoning, believing the emperor died of natural causes, which in their opinion could have been a digestive disease or a heart attack[3]. This is nothing but speculation, although the sceptical approach of these scholars towards the accounts of the circumstances of Claudius' death found in the sources may well be justified, as it is possible those accounts simply reflect a literary tradition hostile towards Agrippina and Nero. Still, in my opinion we are unable to determine whether the princeps died of an illness or from poison, and neither possibility can be ruled out completely.

There remains the problem of the role Agrippina played in the final moments of Claudius' life and in Nero's ascent. According to Tacitus, she locked Britannicus and his sisters in rooms in the palace with guards on all entrances. Moreover, on her command news was spread that the princeps was improving, even though at the time he was probably already dead. As Suetonius informs us, the news of the emperor's death was only shared with the public after a series of actions aimed at securing Nero's succession[4]. Tacitus' account of Agrippina's conduct automatically

1 Sen. *Apocol.* 1.

2 Tac. *Ann.* 12, 66–67; Suet. *Claud.* 44, 2–3; Cass. Dio 60, 34, 2–3. Only Flavius Josephus (*AJ.* 20, 148) points out that only *some* historians report the version in which Claudius is poisoned.

3 For an overview of different opinions on the causes of Claudius' death, see Barrett 1996, 142, 289 note 166.

4 Tac. *Ann.* 12, 68, 1–3; Suet. *Claud.* 45. Scholars suppose delaying the official announcement of Claudius' death was mostly caused by the need to take the steps intended to win Nero the Praetorian Guard's support and to prepare his acclamation by the soldiers of that force. See Hammond 1956, 65–66; Timpe 1962, 100; Koestermann 1967, 227.

brings to mind his own passage describing Livia's actions as Augustus lay dying and Tiberius took over the purple[5]. Thus, we should inquire whether Nero's mother really did play an active part in those events, or perhaps all we have here is a literary trope with Agrippina as a *dux femina* taking decisions that were crucial for the Empire. Obvious similarities between the narratives on Livia and Agrippina aside, I believe we have no reasons to doubt Nero's mother did play a major role in ensuring her son's succession, as had Augustus' wife before her. Taking into account that the transfer of power is always a delicate moment in monarchy, especially in a monarchy with no formal principles of inheriting the throne and no laws regulating the succession, as well as the fact Nero had a potential rival in Britannicus, Agrippina's foresight appears fully understandable.

From our sources, we know that the Senate granted the dead princeps a public funeral and posthumous honours the same as those Augustus had received before. Claudius' body was first put on public display in the Forum, where Nero gave the *laudatio funebris,* already as the new princeps; Tacitus reports that the speech had been composed by Seneca. A few days later, the corpse was moved to the Campus Martius in a solemn procession, accompanied by magistrates, senators, equites and Praetorians, and there cremated. The remains were then laid in the Mausoleum of Augustus. No doubt the greatest posthumous honour bestowed on Claudius was his deification. Agrippina became a priestess of his cult (*flaminica divi Claudii*), and Nero was co-opted into the collegium of *sodales Augustales*, which looked after the cult of deceased emperors and members of their families[6]. It is worth stressing that this was the second deification of a dead emperor, after Augustus. It was also important for Nero himself, who from then on could style himself *divi filius*, which considerably shored up his *auctoritas* as the new princeps[7].

One extremely interesting question, which has given rise to much scholarly debate, is that of Claudius' will. In Suetonius, we read that the princeps drew it up a few months before his death and it bore the seals of all the magistrates[8]. Alas, ancient historians share no details of its contents with us the way they do

---

5 See above.

6 Tac. *Ann.* 12, 69, 3; 13, 2, 3; 3, 1; Suet. *Claud.* 45; *Ner.* 9; Cass. Dio 60, 35, 2. For a reconstruction of the several stages of Claudius' funeral, see Levick 1990, 78; Barrett 1996, 147.

7 We possess numerous coin emissions attesting that Nero considered it very important to highlight his divine filiation. For official ones, see *RIC* I², *Ner.* 1–2; 6. For provincial ones, see e.g. *RPC* I, 3631; 3635; 3647 (Caesarea); 4122–23 (Antioch). On that subject see also Hekster 2015, 50-51.

8 Suet. *Claud.* 44, 1.

for Augustus and Tiberius. Tacitus merely recounts that after Claudius' death the Senate confirmed the Praetorians' choice of Nero for princeps, implying that decision went against the provisions of the previous emperor's last will. For that reason, once Nero had been declared princeps, it was decided the will would not be read out lest that should incite riots among the people of Rome[9]. It is also telling that when referring to Nero, Tacitus uses the word *privignus* (*step-son*), trying to point out his rights to succession were lesser than those of Britannicus, who was Claudius' natural son. This, however, is an obvious anachronism, as from the moment of his adoption Agrippina's son had the same rights to succession as Britannicus did:

> inlatusque castris Nero et congruentia tempori praefatus, promisso donativo ad exemplum paternae largitionis, imperator consalutatur, sententiam militum secuta patrum consulta, nec dubitatum est apud provincias [...] testamentum tamen haud recitatum, ne antepositus filio privignus iniuria et invidia animos vulgi turbaret[10].

> Nero was carried into the camp; and, after a few introductory words suited to the time, promised a donative on the same generous scale as that of his father, and was saluted as Imperator. The verdict of the troops was followed by the senatorial decrees; nor was any hesitation evinced in the provinces. [...] His will, however, was not read, lest the preference of the stepson to the son should leave a disquieting impression of injustice and invidiousness upon the mind of the common people[11].

In Suetonius' version, on the other hand, the striking part is that the mention of Claudius drawing up a will comes right after the information that in the end he intended to designate Britannicus as his successor. Suetonius unambiguously implies the provisions of the will were not in Nero's best interest:

> Sub exitu vitae signa quaedam nec obscura paenitentis de matrimonio Agrippinae deque Neronis adoptione dederat, siquidem commemorantibus libertis ac laudantibus cognitionem, qua pridie quandam adulterii ream condemnarat, sibi quoque in fatis esse iactavit omnia impudica, sed non impunita matrimonia; et subinde obvium sibi

---

9 I think Griffin (1984, 244 note 88) misinterprets the passage, since she believes Tacitus' text indicates it was Nero whom the will designated as the main heir and successor. I think if the passage meant this, keeping the text of the will secret would have made no sense, as the Senate would have followed Claudius' intentions in declaring Nero the emperor, and not reading out the will, which after all confirmed the Senate's choice, would have been irrational. Rather, in my opinion the passage is interpreted correctly by Barrett (1996, 145). For a commentary on that section in Tacitus, see also Koestermann 1967, 230–231.

10 Tac. *Ann.* 12, 69, 2–3.

11 Translated by J. Jackson (Loeb Classical Library, 312).

Britannicum artius complexus hortatus est, ut cresceret rationemque a se omnium factorum acciperet; Graeca insuper voce prosecutus: ὁ τρώσας ἰάσεται. Cumque impubi teneroque adhuc, quando statura permitteret, togam dare destinasset, adiecit: ut tandem populus R. verum Caesarem habeat. non multoque post testamentum etiam conscripsit ac signis omnium magistratuum obsignavit[12].

Towards the end of his life, he had shown some plain signs of repentance for his marriage with Agrippina and his adoption of Nero; for when his freedmen expressed their approval of a trial in which he had the day before condemned a woman for adultery, he declared that it had been his destiny also to have wives who were all unchaste, but not unpunished; and shortly afterwards meeting Britannicus, he hugged him close and urged him to grow up and receive from his father an account of all that he had done, adding in Greek, "He who dealt the wound will heal it." When he expressed his intention of giving Britannicus the gown of manhood, since his stature justified it though he was still young and immature, he added: "That the Roman people may at last have a genuine Caesar." Not long afterwards he also made his will and sealed it with the seals of all the magistrates[13].

Cassius Dio's account is similar in tone, although he explicitly claims Nero destroyed the will and disowned Britannicus:

Νέρων οὖν τάς τε διαθήκας τοῦ Κλαυδίου ἠφάνισε καὶ τὴν ἀρχὴν πᾶσαν διεδέξατο, τόν τε Βρεττανικὸν καὶ τὰς ἀδελφὰς αὐτοῦ διεχρήσατο[14].

And thus Nero, having first destroyed the will of Claudius and having succeeded him as master of the whole Empire, put Britannicus and his sisters out of the way[15].

All the authors quoted above clearly suggest that the provisions of the will were unfavourable to Nero, as in their opinion he was not named as the main heir in it. On this basis, most modern scholars assumed the princeps listed both sons as equal heirs in the will, and the content was not revealed so that Nero could take over as emperor smoothly. They believe the situation was the same as with Tiberius' will, which named both his grandsons as equal heirs[16]. Based on Suetonius' account, some scholars also consider it possible that the will actually named Britannicus as the main heir[17]. However, personally I think we should be cautious regarding these ancient reports. Their suggestions of Claudius' will

12 Suet. *Claud.* 43; 44, 1.

13 Translated by J. C. Rolfe (Loeb Classical Library, 38).

14 Cass. Dio 61, 1, 2.

15 Translated by E. Cary (Loeb Classical Library, 176).

16 So e.g. Timpe 1962, 104; Levick 1990, 78; Barrett 1996, 145–146; Bauman 2003, 187.

17 See e.g. Koestermann 1967, 230, who also lists various views on the contents of the will.

being unfavourable to Nero correspond well with the rumours spread by those historians suggesting that towards the end of his reign the emperor intended to cut Nero out and make Britannicus his successor, which was supposedly the reason he was poisoned. I have already suggested that these may be echoes of a tradition hostile to Agrippina's son, according to which he became princeps illegally, against the previous emperor's will and at the expense of his natural son[18]. Such a tradition may have formed later, as a result of Nero's rule being evaluated negatively. Thus I believe, based on the source accounts available, nothing certain can be said about the contents of Claudius' will, and any discussion of the matter is purely speculative.

9.2 The Successive Stages of Nero's Rise to the Purple

In Nero's case, the sources make it possible to fairly accurately recreate the several stages of his imperial accession, as alongside the reports of historians we have the information preserved in the *AFA*. We know that the process began with the Praetorian acclamation, which took place on 13th October, that is, on the day of Claudius' death. Nero was first introduced to the cohort on duty in the palace, and next carried to the Praetorian camp near the *Porta Viminalis*, where soldiers of this force declared him the new princeps and swore allegiance to him. There, Nero gave a speech before the Praetorians and promised them *donativa* identical to those paid out by Claudius when he was made princeps[19]. Erich Koestermann is probably right when he claims that in Nero's case we can distinguish two *salutationes*, one in the imperial palace and the other in the Castra Praetoria[20]. Tacitus highlights the large part played in the events by Burrus, the prefect who won Nero the Praetorians' support, while Josephus claims other active roles were played by the Praetorian tribunes and some of the freedmen. The care taken was justified, since Tacitus' account may indicate initially some of the Praetorians wavered, keeping Britannicus in mind. Still, eventually they accepted the choice of the majority[21].

The second stage of Nero's imperial investiture unfolded in the Senate, where he arrived straight from the Praetorian camp. In the Curia he gave another speech, composed, as Cassius Dio meticulously stresses, by Seneca. The speech impressed the senators so much that they decided to have the text engraved on

18 See above.

19 Tac. *Ann.* 12, 69, 1–2; Suet. *Ner.* 8; Cass. Dio 61, 3, 1.

20 Koestermann 1967, 228–229.

21 Tac. *Ann.* 12, 69, 1; Joseph. *AJ.* 20, 152.

a silver shield. From then on, each pair of consuls would be expected to read it out when assuming their office[22]. Tacitus and Suetonius report that during this session the Senate granted Nero the package of imperial titles and powers. The new emperor refused only one of them, the title of *pater patriae*, being too young for it[23]. At this point, we should ask what this grant actually involved, since we know Nero already possessed one of the most important imperial prerogatives, that is *imperium proconsulare*, conferred on him in 51. I fully agree with Peter Brunt, who believes that after Nero's rise to the principate, the Senate merely extended his *imperium* so that it would be *maius* relative to the powers of all the governors and military commanders throughout the Empire, and would remain in force after he crossed the *pomerium*. After such modifications, Nero's *imperium* had the same nature as those of all previous *principes* beginning with Augustus[24].

It remains disputable whether at the same session the Senate granted the new princeps *tribunicia potestas*. Based on a mention in the *AFA*, some scholars believe that only happened on 4th December, nearly two months after Nero was declared emperor[25]. I am more convinced by the view proposed by Brunt, who thinks that the Senate had already granted Nero the prerogatives on 13th October, that is during the session convoked immediately after Claudius' death, whereas on 4th December the people only ratified the *senatus consultum*[26]; after all, it is not very credible that Nero should have gone without the most important imperial prerogative for almost two months after being acclaimed as the princeps. Thus the information found in the *AFA* under 4th December of the years 57 and 58, of sacrifices to be made *ob tribunic(iam) potestatem Neronis Claudi Caesaris Aug(usti) Germanici*[27], presumably refers not so much to Nero first receiving tribunician powers, as to the people sanctioning in the Comitia the earlier *senatus consultum* which granted him the whole package of imperial powers, and the expression *ob tribuniciam potestatem* used in the text should not

22 Suet. *Ner.* 8; Cass. Dio 61, 3, 1. See also Parker 1946, 46.

23 Tac. *Ann.* 12, 69, 2; Suet. *Ner.* 8. See also Hammond 1956, 66; Timpe 1962, 103; Levick 1990, 78; Barrett 1996, 144.

24 Brunt 1977, 99.

25 So e.g. Koestermann 1967, 229; Scheid 1992, 232; Kienast 1996, 97; Barrett 1996, 144; Krüger 2012, 33. Unfortunately, we have no solid data that would let us determine when Nero himself saw the first day of his tribunician powers to be. See Griffin 1984, 244 note 91.

26 Brunt 1977, 99.

27 Scheid 1998, 66 (ll. 20–21).

be understood literally. Rather, it simply reflects the superiority of tribunician powers (Tacitus' *summum fastigi vocabulum*) over the other prerogatives of the princeps[28], which is why it was this particular power that got mentioned in the *AFA* fragment quoted above, in the context of the Comitia law ratifying the Senate's grant of the full package of an emperor's powers.

Timpe supposes that after the Senate announced Nero was to be princeps, all the magistrates, senators and the people swore allegiance to the new emperor before the consuls[29]. This assumption is quite well founded, except that any such oath would rather have been sworn directly before Nero, who was after all present in Rome at the time of his appointment; the situation was quite different from when Tiberius was taking over, but was away from Rome and in his absence the consuls swore in the Praetorian Guard, Senate, plebs and the other magistrates to his name.

The last stage of Nero's accession to the purple involved ratification by the people. As mentioned above, the *AFA* indicate the relevant *lex de imperio* was passed on 4th December[30]. As Barrett was correct to observe, the formal process of Nero's rise to the principate was then complete[31].

Tacitus recounts that Nero's ascent was also smoothly accepted in the provinces, which should be understood to mean that the provincial governors, military commanders, legions and populace also swore allegiance to the new emperor[32]. Barrett suggests the relevant letters were sent out to governors and client kings, informing them of Nero's succession at Agrippina's behest[33], a supposition possibly confirmed by Cassius Dio's account where one reads that Nero's mother was extremely active early on in his reign, and her activity included correspondence with governors and monarchs of allied states[34].

To summarize, it is possible to see it was the backing of the Praetorian Guard which proved decisive for Nero's ascent to the throne, just as it had for Claudius. The Senate and the people merely sanctioned the earlier Praetorian acclamation, granting the new emperor the package of prerogatives. The fact that after Claudius' death Nero went straightaway to the Praetorian camp rather than the

28 See Parsi 1963, 129; Barrett 1989, 71. We have no evidence to assume the people ratified granting Nero an *imperium proconsulare* at separate Comitia.

29 Timpe 1962, 103.

30 See Scheid 1992, 227; Scheid 1998, 66 (ll. 20–21).

31 Barrett 1996, 144.

32 Tac. Ann. 12, 69, 2. See also Timpe 1962, 103 note 2; Levick 1990, 78.

33 Barrett 1996, 143.

34 Cass. Dio 61, 3, 2.

Senate, shows that gaining the support of soldiers from this force was crucial in the context of his takeover.

It is also worth considering what ultimately caused Nero, and not Britannicus, to become the next princeps. In my opinion, several factors were responsible. It seems to me the most significant one was the fact that Nero was a natural descendant of Augustus and a grandson of Germanicus, which was of considerable importance to the Roman public. It also mattered that he was older than his adoptive brother, who had not yet donned the toga of manhood. Moreover, at the moment of Claudius' death, Nero had proconsular powers, which was one of the two major prerogatives of a princeps. Since his adoption he had also been consistently endorsed as the future successor.

9.3 Eliminating Potential Rivals in the Struggle for Imperial Power

As Tacitus writes, the first crime of the new principate was the murder of M. Junius Silanus, the proconsul of Asia, carried out on Agrippina's orders and without Nero's knowledge[35]. According to Tacitus, the main reason for killing him, other than Agrippina's dislike of him, was that he was related to Augustus: just like Nero, Silanus was descended directly from the first princeps, which caused a section of the Roman plebs to see him as a serious rival of Nero. The example of Silanus perfectly demonstrates how important family ties to Augustus were to the assessment of a candidate's suitability for the purple. Tacitus emphasizes that this element was of particular importance under the Julio-Claudian dynasty[36]. Of course, the question remains of whether Silanus had any chance to threaten Nero's succession; in my opinion this is unlikely. As the proconsul of Asia, he had no military force to support him, while right after Claudius' death Nero was hailed as emperor by the Praetorians, who swore allegiance to him, with the acclamation confirmed by the Senate on the very same day. Provincial armies made similar declarations of loyalty, so I do not think anybody could have put forward Silanus as a possible candidate to the throne. Not that there is any evidence to indicate Silanus himself aspired to this. Thus I am inclined to treat his

35 Tac. Ann. 13, 1, 1. Similarly Cassius Dio (61, 6, 4–5), who thinks the assassination was commissioned by Agrippina; *contra* Pliny (*HN* 7, 58), who thinks Nero was responsible. Still, the opinions of Tacitus and Dio seem more reliable, seeing how Agrippina was such a major player when her son was taking over as emperor.

36 Tac. *Ann.* 13, 1, 1–2.

assassination as a pre-emptive strike of sorts, rather than as a step taken to eliminate an actual threat.

No doubt Nero's most significant—actually his only—rival to the throne was Britannicus, who as Claudius' son had the same rights to the succession as his adoptive brother[37]. Tacitus' account indicates that the motivation behind Britannicus' assassination lay in the actions of Agrippina, who felt aggrieved by Nero gradually curtailing her influence and began to canvass for support for Britannicus. Supposedly she publicly spread the idea that as the previous emperor's natural son, he deserved the imperial power more than the adopted Nero. Concerned, the princeps decided to get rid of his brother, who was murdered shortly before his fourteenth birthday, that is, early in AD 55[38]. The ancient authors tell us that Nero employed Locusta, a poisoner known for her skill. Even so, the first attempt to poison Britannicus failed. Only the second succeeded, made during a feast, when cold water containing strong poison was added to his hot drink. The official cause of death given was an epileptic attack[39]. According to Tacitus and Suetonius, Britannicus' body was cremated in haste, the bones buried in the Campus Martius without ceremony[40]. Tacitus reports a large part of the public regarded Britannicus' murder as justified, reasoning that it was committed in the best interest of the state, namely to prevent a potential conflict between the brothers as they fought for power[41].

Not all scholars accept the sources' account that Britannicus was poisoned. Barrett considers it possible that he did die of a strong epileptic attack, basing his theory on Cassius Dio's account (61, 7, 4), which informs the reader of livid stains which came out on the corpse after death. According to Barrett, the only poison capable of producing such results is strychnine, unknown in antiquity,

---

37 Cassius Dio (61, 1, 1–2) does suggest Britannicus deserved the throne more, as Claudius' natural son, but we know that in Roman society an adopted son had the same rights as a natural one.

38 Tac. *Ann.* 13, 14, 2; 15, 1. See also Kienast 1996, 93.

39 Joseph. *AJ.* 20, 153; Tac. *Ann.* 13, 15–16; Suet. *Ner.* 33, 2–3.

40 Tac. *Ann.* 13, 17, 1; Suet. *Ner.* 33, 3. Britannicus' funeral is presented somewhat differently in Cassius Dio (61, 7, 4), who reports the body was first displayed publicly in the Forum, with heavy rain washing off the gypsum with which Nero had the corpse covered in order to mask the livid stains caused by the poison. From Suetonius (*Tit.* 2) we know the emperor Titus, brought up with Britannicus, honoured him posthumously with two statues placed on the Palatine: one pedestrian, of gold, the other mounted, of ivory.

41 Tac. *Ann.* 13, 17, 1.

although death caused by a strong epileptic attack is in fact accompanied by such staining[42]. I would find it difficult to verify the medical arguments adduced by Barrett in favour of his claim, but it seems to me that drawing such conclusions based merely on a mention in Dio may be misleading. Of course, we cannot completely rule out the possibility of death by natural causes; the authors cited above might have been promulgating a tradition hostile to Nero. On the other hand, eliminating one's potential rival(s) to the throne was a move frequently encountered during imperial takeovers under the principate: suffice it to remember the earlier removal of Agrippa Postumus by Tiberius or of Tiberius Gemellus by Caligula. Therefore, personally I believe that in Britannicus' case we can see the same mechanism at work.

42 Barrett 1996, 171–172.

Conclusions

Taking over imperial power from a predecessor was no doubt among the most delicate moments during the reign of the Julio-Claudian dynasty, and under the principate in general. That was a consequence of there being no specific legal acts regulating the principles of succession or the manner of appointing a new princeps. The analysis conducted in Part Two of this book demonstrates that until the moment of Claudius' accession, the death of one emperor automatically entailed the onset of another's rule. That was the case with Tiberius and Caligula, who behaved as sovereign monarchs and were treated as such by the Roman public immediately after the deaths of their predecessors, without having to wait for their succession to be confirmed by the Senate and the people. Only in the case of Claudius, who did not belong to the family of *Iulii Caesares*, did the problem arise of who ought to choose the next princeps. Ultimately, the decision fell to the Praetorians, and in spite of its initial reluctance, the Senate had to accept their choice.

We may see Nero's ascent to power as a breakthrough in shaping the mechanisms of appointing a new princeps, as in his case for the first time we encounter a formalization of the imperial accession. Its first stage was the Praetorian acclamation, complete with the oath of allegiance to the new emperor's name. Next, their decision was sanctioned by the Senate, which bestowed on Nero the package of imperial powers. Finally, the third stage of accession involved the people passing a *lex* to ratify the earlier *senatus consultum*. That pattern would be repeated, with certain modifications, with successive future emperors of the principate period.

The most important criterion taken into account when appointing a new emperor during the Julio-Claudian period was the way he was related to the previous princeps, as well as whether he was a relative of Augustus. The latter factor no doubt played an important part in the appointments of Caligula and Nero, who legitimized their respective ascents to the throne with direct descent from the initiator of principate. The dynastic principle also proved decisive in the appointment of Claudius, who was closely related to all the previous emperors.

Another factor of importance whenever a new emperor took over was his predecessor's consecration. In the period in question that happened twice: in AD 14 when Tiberius had Augustus deified, and in 54 when the Senate deified Claudius. Consequently, Tiberius and Nero were able to style themselves *divi filii*, which considerably raised their *auctoritas* early on in their reign and was of importance for legitimizing their succession.

One characteristic feature present in all the Julio-Claudian takeovers, except that of Claudius, was the elimination of potential rivals to the succession. Such was the first step taken by Tiberius after his ascent, as he ordered the assassination of Agrippa Postumus, who as a natural descendant of Augustus could not be allowed to live. Caligula and Nero each behaved in similar ways after they rose to the throne. A few months into his reign, Caligula ordered the murder of Tiberius Gemellus, who was a natural grandson of Tiberius and so had the same rights to the throne he did. Nero on the other hand got rid of Britannicus, Claudius' natural son, and so his most dangerous rival to the throne.

In Closing

In the famous speech attributed by Tacitus to Galba, the dynastic principle pursued by Augustus in his succession policy as he chose successors from among the members of his own *domus*, is contrasted with choice via adoption of the best candidate, whose qualifications matter more than his birth[1]. Tacitus' diagnosis of Augustus' succession policy is no doubt correct. What is more, it applies equally well to the later Julio-Claudian emperors: the analysis of the succession policies followed by the emperors of that dynasty, carried out in Part One of this book, unambiguously indicates that when choosing their future successors, they were mostly guided by the dynastic principle. Namely, the first men to be taken into account as potential successors were any descendants of the given princeps, natural or adoptive, followed by other relatives, provided they were members of the reigning dynasty. As a result, imperial power was transferred solely within the *domus Augusta*, and Rome came, as Tacitus aptly put it, under one family's hereditary rule (*unius familiae quasi hereditas*)[2].

Endorsing and publicly presenting the intended successors, which was meant to ensure they would be popular among various groups within Roman society, was an important part of the succession policy of Julio-Claudian emperors, and particularly important in an autocracy in which imperial power was not formally hereditary. Coins were without any doubt the most significant means to that end. It is no accident that throughout the rule of the Julio-Claudian dynasty, the only male members of the dynasty featured on official coin emissions were the princeps, his prospective successors and co-regents. Tiberius may serve as a good example here, as his images only appear in imperial minting after his designation as Augustus' successor in AD 4. In turn, under Claudius only Nero had that honour, endorsed as he was as the future successor after his adoption. Again, in this context it is telling that we possess no such emissions with Britannicus, who was overshadowed by his adoptive brother.

One occasion for the emperor to publicly introduce his prospective successor(s) to the inhabitants of Rome was the ceremony of putting on the toga of manhood *(toga virilis)*, usually held in the Forum Romanum or the Forum of Augustus. On the occasion of those celebrations, circus games were held and gifts of money distributed, mostly to the *plebs urbana*. This is what happened, for

1 Tac. *Hist.* 1, 15–16.

2 Tac. *Hist.* 1, 16.

instance, when first Gaius and Lucius Caesar, and later Nero entered adulthood. Actions of this kind were an important part of winning one's prospective successors popularity with the people of Rome.

Another excellent occasion for presenting the intended successors to the people was provided by triumphs, which from the time of Augustus were virtually reserved for the princeps and his closest relatives. During the reign of the Julio-Claudian dynasty, we encounter such a situation twice: first in AD 12[3], when Tiberius was allowed a triumph for his victories on the Pannonian-Dalmatian front, and then five years later when Germanicus held his for his victories on the Rhine. Presenting Tiberius and Germanicus as victorious generals whose military successes ensured the safety and stability of the Empire was meant to win them the support and favour of the Roman public.

The one social group whose support was vital to the intended successors was the army, the main supporting pillar of the principate. Entrusting candidates to the succession with commands in significant military campaigns, something we encounter during all of Augustus' reign and at the start of Tiberius', gave them an opportunity to gain wartime glory and, with it, the affection and loyalty of the army. Moreover, publicly announcing military successes considerably increased their *auctoritas* and confirmed their talent for ruling the Empire. Tiberius' military missions in Germania and Pannonia are a good example, as are Germanicus' on the Rhine or Drusus the Younger's in Illyria. Another important part in endorsing the intended successors among the legions was played by medals (*phalerae*) bearing their images, with which the deserving legionaries were rewarded. Those were very popular among the soldiers, who wore them during various ceremonies to stress their loyalty towards the reigning dynasty.

The analysis of the *cursus honorum* of the prospective successors I carried out in Part One shows they differed fundamentally from the political careers of those members of the imperial family who were secondary candidates to the succession; the intended successors received special dispensations, based on which they could hold the most prestigious magistracies with lightning speed. The cases of Gaius Caesar and Nero can both be illustrative: Augustus' adopted son assumed consulship before he was twenty and without holding the previous offices first. Nero in turn was designated for consulship as a thirteen-year-old (he was supposed to hold it after he turned nineteen), acquiring the *imperium*

---

3 While Tiberius held his first triumph already in 7 BC (see above), that had hardly any connection to any endorsement of an intended successor, as he was a secondary candidate to the succession at the time.

proconsulare at the same time. In contrast, Drusus the Elder had only held a quaestorship by the age of twenty.

It should be emphasized that the inhabitants of the provinces were quite familiar with the dynastic plans of the several emperors and were able to react quickly to changes in the order of succession. It is no accident that coins depicting Tiberius and honorific statues dedicated to him only begin to appear en masse in the provinces after the death of Gaius and Lucius, and Tiberius' adoption by Augustus. Before then, the practice was sporadic. A similar tendency can be observed in the case of Nero, who began to receive such honours after Claudius adopted him. Inhabitants of the provinces also responded briskly to important events in the successors' lives, as indicated by the stances of the authorities of Sardis and Messene, who decided that the day Gaius Caesar donned the *toga virilis* and was designated consul would be a public holiday in that city. It was a way of expressing affection and loyalty towards the ruling family.

An important place in the dynastic policies of the Julio-Claudian dynasty fell to women, who were a significant element in the *domus Augusta*. Such important women included Julia, Agrippina the Elder and Livilla. As wives and as the mothers of the next generation of successors, they guaranteed that the dynasty would remain stable and power would be transmitted within its bounds. There were also times when women had a decisive influence over the choice of the successor, the best example being of course Agrippina the Younger, whose determined actions ended up bringing about Nero's succession.

Even though during the principate no laws or other legal acts regulated the mechanism of succession or of appointing the successor, we can say that in practice a pattern began to form of designating one in Augustus' reign, which would then be repeated by future emperors. The first stage involved adopting the candidate chosen, and was put into use when the princeps had no son of his own. In the eyes of Roman society, the adopted man or boy would then become the rightful successor. As Béranger aptly put it, succession through adoption was a substitute for succession through kinship[4]. The second stage was the Senate and the people conferring *imperium proconsulare* and *tribunicia potestas*, the two most important components of imperial power, on the candidate, although it ought to be stressed that neither proconsular nor tribunician powers in themselves entailed being designated as the successor: it was one thing to grant *imperium proconsulare* to Gaius Caesar in 1 BC or later to Germanicus in AD 17, and another to confer it on Tiberius in AD 13. In the first two cases, the purpose of the

4 Béranger 1973, 138.

imperium was to enable certain specific military and diplomatic missions in the East, whereas in Tiberius' case granting him powers equal to those of Augustus in all the provinces (as that was what his *imperium maius* amounted to) had no connection to a mission, being instead indicative of bestowing one of two crucial imperial powers on an intended successor, which was synonymous with formally preparing his succession in advance. I have also tried to show there was a difference of nature between granting *tribunicia potestas* to Agrippa in 18 and 13 BC, and granting the same powers to Tiberius in AD 4. I believe the former case was not strictly speaking about designating a successor, but merely a co-regent who would have temporarily ruled in the event of Augustus' death until one of his adoptive sons reached the age when he could reign on his own, while the latter case was about designating not just a co-regent, but primarily the future successor.

I should point out that during the whole reign of the Julio-Claudian dynasty a successor was only officially designated twice: first in AD 4 when Augustus designated Tiberius to succeed him, and then in 22, when Tiberius in his turn publicly designated Drusus the Younger. In the latter case the succession fell through, as Drusus died early. In this context, it is worth emphasizing the formal presence of the Senate and the people in the procedure of designating the successor: the Senate would grant the intended successors *imperium proconsulare* and *tribunicia potestas*, and the people sanctioned the grant. Thus the prerogatives which made the foundation of each emperor's power were not automatically inherited by his successor, being instead conferred on him by the most important Republican institutions, although the fact remains that the actual decision on that was taken solely by the princeps, with the Senate merely doing his will.

The Senate and the people also had a formal part to play in the new emperor's investiture, by bestowing on him the imperial powers if he had not obtained them while the previous princeps was alive. Under those circumstances, the role of the people was limited to passing the *lex* ratifying the earlier *senatus consultum*. That is the way things went for Caligula, Claudius and Nero, who had only had proconsular powers; only Tiberius had received the full package of imperial prerogatives before Augustus' death.

Augustus' successors saw the importance of legitimizing their power. For Tiberius' position, his adoption by the first princeps was no doubt crucial; being Augustus' son was enough legitimacy when it came to his succession. After Augustus' consecration, Tiberius could also style himself *divi filius*, which additionally strengthened his *auctoritas* in the eyes of Roman society. Augustus was also an important source of legitimacy for the reigns of Caligula and Nero, both of whom were able to demonstrate a family relationship to the first princeps.

Being naturally descended from him made them predestined for the throne, so to speak. In Nero's case, being the son of the previous emperor was an extra element which helped confirm the legitimacy of his ascent, while for Claudius, the legitimizing factor involved the family ties between him and each emperor before him. From a formal point of view, the most important aspect of the legitimization of each of those successions, however, was having it ratified by the Senate and the people, a consideration of particular importance for a monarchy which wanted to be officially regarded as a "restoration" of the Republic.

It should also be stressed that the situation of the emperors who came after Augustus was at the moment of their takeover fundamentally different for each of them. Tiberius was the only one who had the full package of imperial powers at the moment of his predecessor's death, making his succession already secure on the formal side of things. As Augustus' *collega imperii* of many years, he had massive military and political experience, too. In contrast, Caligula and Claudius were both *privati* at the moment of their predecessors' deaths, and totally unfamiliar with the art of ruling the Empire. Nero's position was still different, as at the moment of Claudius' death he had the status of *consul designatus*, as well as an *imperium proconsulare*, that is, one of the two pillars of an emperor's power. Still, because of his young age, he had no political or military experience, unlike Tiberius at an analogous point.

Finally, it ought to be pointed out that under the Julio-Claudian dynasty a deeply rooted conviction formed in Roman society that members of the Caesar family had a special right to rule the Empire, and Augustus' natural descendants in particular. This belief became a decisive factor for the ascents of Caligula and Nero. The situation after Caligula's death is the best example of loyalty towards the reigning dynasty: the Praetorians and the Roman plebs then clearly spoke in favour of its continued rule and against the plans of some of the senators, who meant to bring back the Republic. Another noteworthy point is that until Nero's principate we encounter no serious usurpers to threaten the position of Augustus' successors. It is telling that when L. Furius Scribonianus, a governor of Dalmatia, tried to rise up against Claudius in 42, he failed because of the behaviour of the legions, which ultimately refused to be used against the emperor. It took Nero's unpopular rule, and nearly fourteen years of it too, for the loyalty towards the *domus Caesarum* to crumble. As a result, governors of the western provinces rebelled against Nero and acclaimed Galba the new princeps, and the events that started in this way eventually culminated in Nero being overthrown and the first imperial dynasty coming to an end.

Appendix: The *dies principatus* of the Julio-Claudian Emperors

The term *dies principatus* means the first day of a given emperor's principate. For example, it is used in that sense by Suetonius and Tacitus, when they refer to the beginning of Vespasian's reign[1]. It is generally assumed its meaning is similar to that of the expression *dies imperii*, which can also mean the inauguration day of a specific emperor's principate[2]. However, it should be stressed that *dies imperii* is largely a technical term referring primarily to the moment somebody began to hold a specific *imperium*. In that context, Augustus' *dies imperii* would be 7th January 43 BC, when the Senate first conferred *imperium* on the young Caesar[3]. Thus for the first princeps, the *dies imperii* and the *dies principatus* fall on two different dates. The same is the case with Tiberius and Nero, who also each received their first *imperium* before assuming the throne. Since my objective here is to determine the moment the ancients considered to be the start of each princeps' reign, in order to avoid misunderstandings, I shall use the term *dies principatus*.

It is not easy to accurately establish the *dies principatus* of the several emperors of the first dynasty, primarily because of the nature of our sources, since for some of them the ancient authors cite differing reign lengths and thus they date the first day the emperors held the throne differently.

The first discrepancies appear in the ancient historians' writings with regard to attempts to determine Augustus' *dies principatus*, as Flavius Josephus counts duration second triumvirate into the time of his reign[4], while Cassius Dio dates the beginning of Augustus' principate to 2nd September 31 BC, that is, to his victory at Actium, which paved the way to his independently ruling over the Empire[5]. Of course, the way Dio dates the onset of Augustus' reign makes more sense than the way Josephus does; even so, I believe we may symbolically date his inauguration to 13th January 27 BC, when he received the prestigious title of *Augustus* from the Senate, which would then become a synonym for *the princeps*.

1 Suet. *Vesp.* 6, 3; Tac. *Hist.* 2, 79, 1.
2 On that subject see esp. Parsi 1963, 127–128; 130–132.
3 See the *Fasti Praenestini* (Degrassi 1963, 113); Kienast 1996, 61.
4 Joseph. *AJ.* 18, 32.
5 Cass. Dio 56, 30, 5.

In Tiberius' case, scholars propose several moments when his principate may have officially commenced, most of them assuming it was 17th September, the day of the Senate session which deified Augustus. Supposedly it was then that Tiberius eventually accepted the position of the princeps[6]. Other historians suppose it only happened in October, after the mutiny of the legions on the Rhine and the Danube was pacified[7]. Others still argue for as early as the first few days of September[8]. The first option could be supported by the accounts of Velleius Paterculus and Tacitus, which indicate Tiberius stopped resisting and agreed to assume the principate after the Senate passed the *senatus consultum* deifying Augustus[9]. The second possibility on the other hand might follow from the information to be found in Josephus, who reports Tiberius was in power for twenty-two years, five months and three days, thus dating his *dies principatus* to 13th October[10]. The third option is the least likely one, since no sources confirm it.

Based on Cassius Dio's report, it is possible to put forwards one more possible date of Tiberius' inauguration day. Dio claims that emperor reigned for twenty-two years, seven months and seven days. Considering he also dates Tiberius' death to 26th March 37, it follows that he thinks his principate started on 19th August, that is, on the day Augustus died[11]. I find Dio's way of dating the start of Tiberius' reign the most reasonable. Formal considerations aside, I believe that in the eyes of Roman society, Tiberius became a legitimate princeps immediately after Augustus' death, as indicated by, among other things, the oath of allegiance sworn to him as the new princeps by the Senate, the army and the Roman plebs as soon as the news was officially announced[12]. In this context, formally confirming Tiberius' succession with a *senatus consultum* and Tiberius himself officially accepting the principate were fairly unimportant to the general public. In either case, we know from Tacitus that right after Augustus died, Tiberius acted *par excellence* as the new princeps, convening the Senate and issuing orders to the Praetorians and to the commanders of legions[13].

---

6 See Hohl 1933, 112, 115; Flach 1973, 552–569; Kienast 1982, 124–125; id. 1996, 77; Huttner 2004, 128.

7 So e.g. Sage 1982–1983, 309–311.

8 See Wellesley 1967, 23–30.

9 Vell. Pat. 2, 124, 3; Tac. *Ann.* 1, 10–13.

10 Joseph. *AJ.* 18, 224.

11 Cass. Dio 58, 28, 5.

12 Tac. *Ann.* 1, 7, 2.

13 Tac. *Ann.* 1, 7, 5.

As in Tiberius' case, determining Caligula's *dies principatus* is something of a problem. Our sources disagree again. In the text of the *AFA*, there is mention of sacrifices made on every anniversary of the day the Senate declared Caligula princeps[14], and in the light of that document we could date the start of his reign to 18th March AD 37[15], but Suetonius recounts Gaius ruled for three years, ten months and eight days, thus setting his *dies principatus* on 16th March instead, that is, the day of Tiberius' death[16]. Then there is Cassius Dio, who reports Caligula's reign lasted three years, nine months and twenty-eight days, identifying 27th March of the same year as the first day of his principate[17]. Based on this calculation, Donna Hurley concludes that Dio considers Gaius' principate to have commenced on the day the Senate granted him the package of imperial prerogatives after he came to Rome from Misenum[18]. However, from the *AFA* we know that Caligula only entered the capital on 28th March, and the Senate gathered to grant him his powers one or two days later[19]. Despite this minor chronological inaccuracy (which probably stems from Dio's error), it seems that Dio does consider that particular Senate session to have been the inauguration of Caligula's principate (or at least his sources did). Apparently, for him the most important part of Gaius' accession was the *senatus consultum*, which conferred on him the package of an emperor's powers.

With the sources differing so widely, it is difficult to pinpoint the moment Caligula himself would have treated as his *dies principatus*. The account by Josephus cited above indicates that immediately after Tiberius' death Gaius in fact behaved as the new princeps, sending letters to the Senate from Misenum informing them he had assumed the imperial power[20]. The passage implies that for Caligula the day his predecessor died was also the first day of his own rule. As I have mentioned above, this moment is also considered the beginning of Caligula's principate in Suetonius.

Establishing Claudius' *dies principatus* is much less controversial. Suetonius considers it to be the day Caligula was assassinated, that is, 24th January AD 41[21]. This corresponds well with the accounts of Flavius Josephus and Cassius Dio,

---

14 Scheid 1998, 29 (ll. 8–12); 37 (ll. 12–17).

15 So e.g. Kienast 1996, 85.

16 Suet. *Calig*. 59. In his commentary on Suetonius, Hurley (1991, 57, 321) incorrectly calculates that the historian dates Caligula's *dies imperii* to 18th March.

17 Cass. Dio 59, 30, 1.

18 Hurley 1991, 57.

19 See above.

20 Joseph. *AJ*. 18, 234–235.

21 Suet. *Claud*. 11, 3.

who report that Claudius reigned for thirteen years, eight months and twenty days, also identifying 24th January as the beginning of his rule[22]. Thus, it would appear that the authors in question regard the day of Caligula's death as Claudius' *dies principatus*, and so I believe we can with considerable certainty assume Caligula's successor also considered his principate to have started on that day rather than on 25th January, when the Senate declared him princeps[23].

Without a doubt, determining the onset of Nero's principate is the least difficult, since the *AFA* provides us with data on sacrifices made yearly on 13th October *ob imperium Neronis Claudii Caesaris Aug. Germanici*, that is, on the occasion of him rising to imperial power[24]. Since this was the day Claudius died and the two most important events of Nero's investiture took place, that is to say, he was hailed by the Praetorians and declared princeps by the Senate, we may with certainty take the date of 13th October AD 54 to be his *dies principatus*[25].

---

22 Joseph. *AJ*. 20, 148; *BJ*. 2, 248; Cass. Dio 60, 34, 3.

23 See also Timpe (1962, 90), Brunt (1977, 98), who stress Claudius may have seen as his *dies principatus* the Praetorian acclamation, which took place on the same day Caligula was killed. Another argument for that lies in the fact that the Senate only reluctantly and under Praetorian pressure accepted Claudius as the new princeps. Thus it is unlikely he saw that moment as his *dies principatus*.

24 Scheid 1992, 225; id. 1998, 65 (ll.10–11); 71 (ll. 49–50). It ought to be emphasized in this context the term *imperium* refers not to the *imperium proconsulare* granted Nero as one of the emperor's two powers, but to imperial power in general. See Parsi 1963, 130.

25 See also Griffin 1984, 244 note 91; Kienast 1996, 96.

List of Figures

Bibliography

Sources

Literary Sources

Appianus (**App.**), *Bellorum civilium*, edd. P. Viereck, A. G. Roos, Leipzig 1905 (Bibliotheca Teubneriana).

Appian, *Roman History*, vol. III - IV: *The Civil Wars*, Books 1-3.26; 3.27-5, translated by H. White, Cambridge, MA 1913 (Loeb Classical Library, 4, 5).

Cassius Dio (**Cass. Dio**), *Historia Romana*, Bd. 2, ed. U. Ph. Boissevain, Berlin 1898.

Cassius Dio, *Roman History*, vol. VI-VIII (Books 51-70), translated by E. Cary, H. B. Foster, Cambridge, MA 1917, 1924, 1925 (Loeb Classical Library, 83, 175, 176).

Cicero (**Cic.**), *In Marcum Antonium orationes Philippicae XIV*, ed. P. Fedeli, Leipzig 1982 (Bibliotheca Teubneriana).

Cicero, *Philippics*, vol. I-II (1–6; 7–14), translated by D. R. Shackleton Bailey, revised by J. T. Ramsey, Cambridge, MA 2010 (Loeb Classical Library, 189, 507).

Consolatio ad Liviam (**Cons. ad Liv.**), ed. J. Amat, Paris 1997 (Les Belles Lettres).

Flavius Josephus (**Joseph.**), *Antiquitates Judaicae*, ed. B. Niese, Berlin 1892.

Flavius Josephus, *De bello Iudaico*, ed. B. Niese, Berlin 1895.

Florus (**Flor.**), *Epitome of Roman History*, translated by E. S. Forster, Cambridge, MA 1929 (Loeb Classical Library, 231).

Livy (**Liv.**), *History of Rome*, vol. I (Books 1-2), translated by B. O. Foster; vol. XII (Books 40-42), translated by E. T. Sage, A. C. Schlesinger; vol. XIII (Books 43-45), translated by A. C. Schlesinger, Cambridge, MA 1919, 1938, 1951 (Loeb Classical Library, 114, 332, 396).

Orosius (**Oros.**), *Historiae adversus paganos*, ed. M. P. Arnaud-Lindet, Paris 1990.

Ovidius (**Ov.**), *Ars amatoria*, ed. R. Ehwald, Leipzig 1907 (Bibliotheca Teubneriana).

Ovidius, *Epistulae ex Ponto*, ed. A. L. Wheeler, Cambridge 1939.

Philo (**Philo.**), *On the Embassy to Gaius*, translated by F. H. Colson, Cambridge, MA 1962 (Loeb Classical Library, 379).

Plinius Maior (**Plin.**), *Historia naturalis*, ed. A. Ernout, Paris 1949–1985.

Pliny the Younger (**Plin.**), *Letters*, vol. II (Books 8-10), *Panegyricus*, translated by B. Radice, Cambridge, MA 1969 (Loeb Classical Library, 59).

Plutarchus (**Plut.**), *Vitae parallelae*, vol. I-IV, ed. K. Ziegler, Leipzig 1915–1973 (Bibliotheca Teubneriana).

Polybius (**Polyb**.), *The Histories*, vol. VI (Books 28-39), *Fragments*, translated by S. D. Olson, W. R. Paton, revised by F. W. Walbank, Ch. Habicht, Cambridge, MA 2012 (Loeb Classical Library, 161).

Res gestae divi Augusti (**Mon. Anc.**), ed. J. Scheid, Paris 2007 (Les Belles Lettres).

Seneca (**Sen.**), *Apocolocyntosis*, edd. W. H. D. Rouse, M. A. Litt D, London 1913.

Seneca, *Moral Essays*, vol. I–II, translated by J. W. Basore, Cambridge, MA 1928, 1932 (Loeb Classical Library, 214, 254).

Strabo (**Strab.**), *Geographica*, edd. W. Aly, E. Kirsten, F. Lapp, Bonn 1968–1972.

Suetonius (**Suet.**), *De vita Caesarum libri VIII*, ed. M. Ihm, Stuttgart 1993 (Bibliotheca Teubneriana).

Suetonius, *Lives of the Caesars*, vol. I-II, translated by J. C. Rolfe, Cambridge, MA 1914 (Loeb Classical Library, 31, 38).

Tacitus (**Tac.**), *Annales*, ed. E. Koestermann, Leipzig 1965 (Bibliotheca Teubneriana).

Tacitus, *Histories (Books 1-3)*, translated by C. H. Moore, Cambridge, MA 1925 (Loeb Classical Library, 111).

Tacitus, *Annals (Books 4-6, 11-12)*, translated by J. Jackson, Cambridge, MA 1937 (Loeb Classical Library, 312).

Tacitus, *Annals (Books 13-16)*, translated by J. Jackson, Cambridge, MA 1937 (Loeb Classical Library, 322).

Tacitus, *Historiae*, ed. R. Til, Heidelberg 1963.

Tacitus, *Histories (Books 4-5), Annals (Books 1-3)*, translated by C. H. Moore, J. Jackson, Cambridge, MA 1931 (Loeb Classical Library, 249).

Valerius Maximus (**Val. Max.**), *Facta et dicta memorabilia*, ed. R. Combès, Paris 2003.

Velleius Paterculus (**Vell. Pat.**), *Historia Romana*, ed. W. S. Watt, Sttutgart, Leipzig 1988 (Bibliotheca Teubneriana).

Velleius Paterculus, *Compendium of Roman History. Res Gestae Divi Augusti*, translated by F. W. Shipley, Cambridge, MA 1924 (Loeb Classical Library, 152).

Epigraphic Sources

Bargagli B., Grosso C., 1997, *I Fasti Ostienses. Documento della storia di Ostia*, Roma (cited as **Bargagli–Grosso 1997**).

Corpus Inscriptionum Graecarum, vol. I–IV, Berolini 1828–1877 (cited as **CIG**).

Corpus Inscriptionum Latinarum, Berolini 1963– (cited as **CIL**).

Degrassi A., 1963, *Inscriptiones Italiae*, XIII. 2, *Fasti anni Numani et Iuliani*, Roma (cited as **Degrassi 1963**).

Dittenberger W., Purgold K., 1896, *Die Inschriften von Olympia*, Berlin (cited as **IvO**).

Eck W., Caballos A., Fernandéz F., 1996, *Das senatus consultum de Cn. Pisone Patre*, München (cited as **SCPP**).

Inscriptiones Graecae, Berolini 1873– (cited as **IG**).

Inscriptiones Graecae ad res Romanas pertinentes, ed. R. Cagnat et al., vol. I–IV, Paris 1901–1927 (cited as **IGRR**).

Inscriptiones Latinae selectae, ed. H. Dessau, vol. I–III, Berolini 1892–1916 (cited as **ILS**).

Lott J. B., 2012, *Death and Dynasty in Early Imperial Rome. Key Sources, with Text, Translation, and Commentary*, Cambridge (cited as **Lott 2012**).

Roman Statutes, ed. M. H. Crawford, vol. I, Bulletin of the Institute of Classical Studies, Supplement 64, London 1996 (cited as **Crawford 1996**).

Rowe G., 2002, *Princes and Political Cultures: The New Tiberian Senatorial Decrees*, Ann Arbor (cited as **Rowe 2002**).

Sánchez A., Gutiérrez O., 1999, *Tabula Siarensis: Edición, Traducción y Comentario*, Pamplona (cited as **TS**).

Scheid J., 1998, *Commentarii fratrum arvalium qui supersunt: les copies épigraphiques des protocoles annuels de la confrérie arvale (21 av. – 304 ap. J.-C.)*, Roma (cited as **Scheid 1998**).

Numismatic Sources

Roman Imperial Coins in the Hunter Coin Cabinet University of Glasgow, I: *Augustus to Nerva*, ed. A. S. Robertson, London–Glasgow–New York 1962 (cited as **HCC**).

Roman Provincial Coinage, I: *From the Death of Caesar to the Death of Vitellius (44 BC–AD 69)*, eds. A. Burnett, M. Amandry, P. P. Ripollès, London 1992 (cited as **RPC**).

Sear D. R., 2000, *Roman Coins and Their Values*, I: *The Republic and the Twelve Caesars 280 BC–AD 96*, London (cited as **Sear** 2000).

The Roman Imperial Coinage, I: *Augustus to Vitellius*, eds. H. Mattingly, E. A. Sydenham, London 1968.

The Roman Imperial Coinage, I²: *From 31 BC to AD 69*, ed. C. H. V. Sutherland, London 1984 (cited as **RIC I²**).

The Roman Imperial Coinage, II: *Vespasian to Hadrian*, eds. H. Mattingly, E. A. Sydenham, London 1968.

Commentaries on Literary Sources

Brunt P. A., Moore J. M., 1967, *Res gestae divi Augusti*, Oxford.

Cooley A. E., 2009, *Res gestae divi Augusti: Text, Translation, and Commentary*, Cambridge.

Goodyear F. R. D., 1972, *The Annals of Tacitus*, vol. I, *Annals I, 1–54*, Cambridge.

Holtzhausser C. A., 1918, *An Epigraphic Commentary on Suetonius's Life of Tiberius*, Philadelphia.

Hurley D. W., 1991, *A Historical and Historiographical Commentary on Suetonius' "Life of Caligula"*, Columbia University (Diss.).

Koestermann E., 1967, *Cornelius Tacitus – Annalen*, Bd. III, Buch 11–13, Heidelberg.

Rich J. W., 1990, *Cassius Dio: The Augustan Settlement (Roman History 53 – 55.9)*, Warminster.

Seif K. P., 1973, *Die Claudiusbücher in den Annalen des Tacitus*, Mainz (Diss.).

Swan P. M., 2004, *The Augustan Succession: An Historical Commentary on Cassius Dio's Roman History Books 55-56 (9 B.C. – A.D. 14)*, Oxford.

Woodman A. J., 1977, *Velleius Paterculus. The Tiberian Narrative (2.94–131)*, Cambridge.

Woodman A. J., 1983, *The Caesarian and Augustan Narrative (2.41–93)*, Cambridge.

Woodman A. J., Martin R. H., 1996, *The Annals of Tacitus: Book* 3, Cambridge.

Literature

Akveld W. F., 1961, *Germanicus*, Groningen.

Alföldi A., 1970, *Die monarchische Repräsentation im römischen Kaiserreiche*, Darmstadt (third ed.).

Allen W., 1947, "The Death of Agrippa Postumus", *TAPhA* 78, 131–139.

Ameling W., 1994, "Augustus und Agrippa: Bemerkungen zu PKöln VI 249", *Chiron* 24, 1–28.

Baar M., 1990, *Das Bild des Kaisers Tiberius bei Tacitus, Sueton und Cassius Dio*, Stuttgart.

Badian E., 1980, "Notes on the Laudatio of Agrippa", *CJ* 76, 97–107.

Badian E., 1982, "Crisis Theories and the Beginning of Principate", [in:] *Romanitas – Christianistas: Untersuchungen zur Geschichte und Literature der römischen Kaiserzeit, J. Straub zum 70. Geburstag gewidmet*, hrsg. von G. Wirth, Berlin–New York, 18–41.

Balbuza K., 2005, *Triumfator. Triumf i ideologia zwycięstwa w starożytnym Rzymie epoki cesarstwa* ("The Triumphator: Triumph and the Ideology of Victory in Ancient Rome under the Empire"), Poznań.

Barrett A. A., 1989, *Caligula: The Corruption of Power*, London–New York.

Barrett A. A., 1996, *Agrippina: Sex, Power, and Politics in the Early Empire*, London.

Barrett A. A., 2001, "Tacitus, Livia, and the Evil Stepmother", *RhM* 144, 171–175.

Barrett A. A., 2002, *Livia: First Lady of Imperial Rome*, New Haven–London.

Bartman E., 1999, *Portraits of Livia. Imaging the Imperial Women in Augustan Rome*, Cambridge.

Bauman R. A., 2003, *Women and Politics in Ancient Rome*, London–New York.

Beard M., 2007, *The Roman Triumph*, Cambridge–Massachusetts–London.

Bellemore J., 2013, "The Identity of Drusus: The Making of a Princeps", [in:] *The Julio-Claudian Succession: Reality and Perception of the 'Augustan Model'*, ed. A. G. G. Gibson, Leiden–Boston, 79–94.

Bellen H., 1984, "Das Drususdenkmal apud Mogontiacum und die Galliarum Civitates", *JRGZ* 31, 385–396.

Bellen H., 1989, "Der römische Ehrenbogen von Mainz-Kastel: *Ianus Germanici aut Domitiani?*", *AKB* 19, 77–84.

Bernecker A., 1989, *Die Feldzüge des Tiberius und die Darstellung der unterworfenen Gebiete in der 'Geographie des Ptolemaeus'*, Bonn.

Béranger J., 1939, "L'hérédité du principat: Note sur la transmission du pouvoir impérial aux deux premiers siècles", *REL* 17, 171–187 [= Béranger J., 1973, "Principatus. Études de notions et d'histoire politiques dans d'Antiquité gréco-romaine", eds. F. Paschoud, P. Ducrey, Genéve, 137–152].

Béranger J., 1953, *Recherches sur l'aspect idéologique du principat*, Basel.

Béranger J., 1959, "Diagnostic du principat: l'empereur romain, chef de parti", *REL* 37, 151–170.

Bianchi E., 2006, "La politica dinastica di Caligola", *Mediterraneo antico. Economie, società, culture* 9, 597–630 (non vidi).

Birch R. A., 1981, "The Settlement of 26 June A.D. 4 and its Aftermath", *CQ* 31, 443–456.

Bleicken J., 1998, *Augustus: Eine Biographie*, Berlin.

Borchhardt J., 1974, "Ein Kenotaph für Gaius Caesar", *JDAI* 89, 217–241.

Boruch W., 2010, *Studies in the History of the Julio-Claudian Dynasty*, Toruń.

Borzsák I., 1969, "Das Germanicus-Bild des Tacitus", *Latomus* 28, 588–600.

Boschung D., 1987, "Römische Glasphalerae mit Porträtbüsten", *BJ* 187, 193–258.

Boschung D., 2002, *Gens Augusta: Untersuchungen zu Aufstellung, Wirkung und Bedeutung der Statuengruppen des julisch-claudischen Kaiserhauses*, Mainz.

Bowersock G. W., 1984, "Augustus and the East: The Problem of Succession", [in:] *Caesar Augustus: Seven Aspects*, eds. F. Millar, E. Segal, Oxford, 169–188.

Brandt H., 1995, "Marcellus «successioni praeparatus»? Augustus, Marcellus und die Jahre 29–23 v. Chr.", *Chiron* 25, 1–17.

Bringmann K., 1977, "*Imperium proconsulare* und Mitregentschaft im frühen Prinzipat", *Chiron* 7, 219–238.

Brunt P. A., 1977, "Lex de imperio Vespasiani", *JRS* 67, 95–116.

Calabi I., 1954, "Sugli onori postumi a Germanico. Due note alla *Tabula Hebana*", *PP* 9, 212–214.

Carter G., Metcalf W., 1988, "The Dating of M. Agrippa Asses", *NC* 148, 145–147.

Castagnoli F., 1984, "L'Arco di Germanico in Circo Flaminio", *ArchClass* 36, 329–332.

Castritius H., 1982, *Der römische Prinzipat als Republik*, Husum.

Cattaneo E., 1958, "Sul parallelismo degli episodi della morte di Augusto e di Claudio negli Annali di Tacito", *RIL* 92, 476–482.

Champlin E., 1989, "The Testament of Augustus", *RhM* 132, 154–165.

Christes J., 1994, "Tacitus und die *moderatio* des Tiberius", *Gymnasium* 101, 112–135.

Ciaceri E., 1934, *Tiberio, successore di Augusto*, Milano (non vidi).

Coarelli F., 1988, *Il Foro Boario: dalle origini alla fine della repubblica*, Roma.

Cogitore I., 2002, *La légitimité dynastique d'Auguste à Néron à l'épreuve des conspirations*, Rome.

Cohen D., 1991, "The Augustan Law on Adultery: The Social and Cultural Context", [in:] *The Family in Italy from Antiquity to the Present*, eds. D. Kertzer, R. Saller, New Haven, 109–126.

Corbett J. H., 1974, The Succession Policy of Augustus, *Latomus* 33. 1, 87–97.

Corbier M., 1991a, "Constructing Kinship in Rome: Marriage and Divorce, Filiation and Adoption", [in:] *The Family in Italy from Antiquity to the Present*, eds. D. Kertzer, R. Saller, New Haven, 127–144.

Corbier M., 1991b, "Divorce and Adoption as Roman Familial Strategies", [in:] *Marriage, Divorce and Children in Ancient Rome*, ed. B. Rawson, Oxford, 47–78.

Corbier M., 1995, "Male Power and Legitimacy through Women: The Domus Augusta under the Julio-Claudians", [in:] *Women in Antiquity. New Assessments*, eds. R. Hawley, B. Levick, London–New York, 178–193.

Cotton H. M., Yakobson A., 1985, "Caligula's Recusatio Imperii", *Historia* 34. 4, 497–503.

Cox S. E., 2005, "The Mark of the Successor: Tribunician Power and the Ara Providentia under Tiberius and Vespasian", *NAC* 24, 251–270.

Crawford M., 1983, "Roman Imperial Coin Types and the Formation of Public Opinion", [in:] *Studies in Numismatic Method Presented to Philip Grierson*, ed. C. N. L. Brooke, Cambridge, 47–64.

Dąbrowa E., 1998, *The Governors of Roman Syria from Augustus to Septimius Severus*, Bonn.

Degrassi A., 1952, *I fasti consolari dell'impero romano dal 30 avanti Cristo al 613 dopo Cristo*, Roma.

De Maria S., 1988, *Gli archi onorari di Roma e dell'Italia romana*, Roma.

Dettenhofer M. H., 2000, *Herrschaft und Widerstand im augusteischen Principat: Die Konkurrenz zwischen Res Publica und Domus Augusta*, Stuttgart.

De Visscher F., 1964, "La politique dynastique sous le règne de Tibère", *Synteleia* 5, Arangio-Ruiz, Napoli, 54–65.

Dorey T. A., 1966, "Claudius und seine Ratgeber", *Das Altertum* 12, 144–155.

Drinkwater J., 2013, "Nero Caesar and the Half-Baked Principate", [in:] *The Julio- Claudian Succession: Reality and Perception of the 'Augustan Model'*, ed. A. G. G. Gibson, Leiden–Boston, 155–173.

Eck W., 1995, "Plebs und Princeps nach dem Tod des Germanicus", [in:] *Laeders and Masses in the Roman World. Studies in Honor of Zvi Yavetz*, eds. I. Malkin, Z. W. Rubinsohn, Leiden–New York–Köln, 1–10.

Eck. W., 1997, "Die Täuschung der Öffentlichkeit. Der Prozess gegen Cnaeus Calpurnius Piso im Jahre 20 n. Chr." [in:] *Grosse Prozesse der römischen Antike*, eds. U. Manthe, J. von Ungern-Sternberg, München, 128–145.

Eck W., 2007, *The Age of Augustus*, Oxford (second edition).

Eder W., 1990, "Augustus and the Power of Tradition: The Augustan Principate as Binding Link between Republic and Empire", [in:] *Between Republic and Empire. Interpretations of Augustus and his Principate*, eds. K. Raaflaub, M. Toher, Berkeley–Los Angeles, 71–122.

Ehrenberg V., Jones A. H. M., 1976, *Documents Illustrating the Reigns of Augustus and Tiberius*, Oxford.

Ehrhardt C., 1978, "Messalina and the Succession to Claudius", *Antichthon* 12, 51–78.

Fantham E., 2006, *Julia Augusti: The Emperor's Daughter*, London–New York.

Fishwick D., 2010, "Agrippa and the Ara Providentiae at Rome", *ZPE* 174, 251–258.

Flach D., 1973, "Die Regierungsanfang des Tiberius", *Historia* 22, 552–569.

Flaig E., 2013, *Zrytualizowana polityka. Znaki, gesty i władza w starożytnym Rzymie* (= *Ritualisierte Politik. Zeichen, Gesten und Herrschaft im Alten Rom*, Göttingen 2003), translated by L. Mrozewicz, A. Pawlicka, Poznań.

Flory M. B., 1988, "The Meaning of *Augusta* in the Julio-Claudian Period", *AJAH* 13. 2, 113–138.

Flory M. B., 1996, "Dynastic Ideology, the Domus Augusta, and Imperial Women: A Lost Statuary Group in the Circus Flaminius", *TAPhA* 126, 287–306.

Flower H. I., 1996, *Ancestor Masks and Aristocratic Power in Roman Culture*, Oxford.

Fraschetti A., 1988, "La Tabula Hebana, la Tabula Siarensis e il iustitium per la morte di Germanico", *MEFRA* 100, 867–889.

Fraschetti A., 1990a, *Roma e il principe*, Bari.

Fraschetti A., 1990b, "Augusto e la "laudatio" di Agrippa", [in:] *Il bimillenario di Agrippa*, a cura di A. Ceresa Gastaldo, Genova, 83–98.

Fullerton M. D., 1985, "The Domus Augusti in Imperial Iconography of 13-12 B.C.", *AJA* 89, 473–483.

Galinsky K., 1981, "Augustus' Legislation on Morals and Marriage", *Philologus* 125, 126–144.

Galinsky K., 1996, *Augustan Culture: An Interpretive Introduction*, Princeton.

Galinsky K., 2012, *Augustus: Introduction to the Life of an Emperor*, Cambridge.

Gallotta B., 1981, "Germanico oltre il Reno", *Acme* 34, 293–316.

Gallotta B., 1987, *Germanico*, Roma.

Galsterer H., 2000, "Die Trauer der Städte um verstorbene Prinzen in der frühen Kaiserzeit", [in:] *La commemorazione di Germanico nella documentazione epigrafica*, a cura di A. Fraschetti, Roma, 173–187.

Ganzert J., 1984, *Das Kenotaph für Gaius Caesar in Limyra: Architektur und Bauornamentik*, Tübingen.

Ganzert J., 1997, "Zu den Ehrenbögen für Germanicus und Drusus auf dem Augustusforum: «…arcus circum latera templi Martis Ultoris…»," *MDAI(R)* 104, 193–206.

Gibson A. G. G., 2013, "All Things to All Men": Claudius and the Politics of AD 41, [in:] *The Julio-Claudian Succession: Reality and Perception of the 'Augustan Model'*, ed. A. G. G. Gibson, Leiden–Boston, 107–132.

Ginsburg J., 2006, *Representing Agrippina: Constructions of Female Power in the Early Roman Empire*, Oxford–New York.

Girardet K. M., 1992, "Imperium und *provinciae* des Pompeius seit 67 v. Chr.", *CCG* 3, 177–188.

Girardet K. M., 2000, "Imperium 'Maius': Politische und verfassungsrechtliche Aspekte. Versuch einer Klärung", [in:] *La Révolution Romaine après Ronald Syme. Bilans et Perspectives*, éd. par A. Giovannini, Vandoeuvres–Geneve, 167–236.

Girardet K. M., 2001, "Imperia und provinciae des Pompeius 82 bis 48 v. Chr.", *Chiron* 31, 153–209.

Göbl R., 1978, *Antike Numismatik*, Bd. I, München.

Gradel I., 2002, *Emperor Worship and Roman Religion*, Oxford.

Grant M., 1950, *Aspects of the Principate of Tiberius. Historical Comments on the Colonial Coinage Issued outside Spain*, New York.

Grant M., 1952, *Roman Coins as Propaganda*, *Archaeology* 5, 79–85.

Grant M., 1954, *Roman Imperial Money*, Edinburgh.

Grant M., 1990, "Agrippa's Coins", [in:] *Il bimillenario di Agrippa*, a cura di A. Ceresa Gastaldo, Genova, 9–17.

Gray E. W., 1970, "The Imperium of M. Agrippa: A Note on P. Colon. inv. nr. 4701", *ZPE* 6, 227–238.

Grenade P., 1961, *Essai sur les origines du principat: investiture et renouvellement des pouvoirs impériaux*, Paris.

Griffin M., 1984, *Nero. The End of a Dynasty*, London.

Griffin M., 1997, "The Senate's Story", JRS 87, 249–263.

Gruen E. S., 2005, "Augustus and the Making of the Principate", [in:] *The Cambridge Companion to the Age of Augustus*, ed. K. Galinsky, Cambridge, 33–51.

Gruen E. S., 2008, "The Expansion of the Empire under Augustus", [in:] *The Cambridge Ancient History* 10: *The Augustan Empire 43 B.C. – A.D. 69*, eds. A. Bowman, E. Champlin, A. Lintott, Cambridge (second edition), 147–197 (online edition).

Halfmann H., 1986, *Itinera principum. Geschichte und Typologie der Kaiserreisen im römischen Reich*, Stuttgart.

Hammond M., 1933, *The Augustan Principate in Theory and Practice during the Julio-Claudian Period*, Cambridge.

Hammond M., 1956, "The Transmission of the Powers of the Roman Emperor from the Death of Nero in A.D. 68 to that of Alexander Severus in A.D. 235", *MAAR* 24, 63–133.

Hardy L. B., 1976, *The Imperial Women in Tacitus' "Annals"*, Indiana University (Diss.).

Haselberger L., 2007, *Urbem Adornare: Die Stadt Rom und Ihre Gestaltumwandlung unter Augustus/Romes Urban Metamorphosis under Augustus* (English translation of the main text by Alexander Thein), Portsmouth.

Haslam M. W., 1980, "Augustus' Funeral Oration for Agrippa", *CJ* 75, 193–199.

Havener W., 2016, *Imperator Augustus. Die diskursive Konstituierung der militärischen persona des ersten römischen princeps*, Stuttgart.

Heinemann A., 2007, "Eine Archäologie des Störfalls. Die toten Söhne des Kaisers in der Öffentlichkeit des frühen Prinzipats", [in:] *Archäologie und Geschichte* 12, hrsg. von F. Hölscher, T. Hölscher, Heidelberg, 41–109.

Heintschel-Heinegg A., 1954, *Untersuchungen zum Regierungsantritt der römischen Kaiser von Tiberius bis Commodus*, Wien (non vidi).

Hekster O., 2015, *Emperors and Ancestors. Roman Rulers and the Constraints of Tradition*, Oxford.

Hennig D., 1972, "Zur Ägyptenreise des Germanicus", *Chiron* 2, 349–365.

Herz P., 1980, "Der Aufbruch des Gaius Caesar in den Osten", *ZPE* 39, 285–290.

Herz P., 1993, "Die Adoptivsöhne des Augustus und der Festkalender: Gedanken zu einer Inschrift aus Messene", *Klio* 75, 272–288.

Herz P., 2001, "Das römische Heer und der Kaiserkult in Germanien", [in:] *Religion in den germanischen Provinzen Roms*, hrsg. von W. Spickermann, Tübingen, 91–116.

Hesberg H., Panciera S., 1994, *Das Mausoleum des Augustus. Der Bau und seine Inschriften*, München.

Hickson F. V., 1991, "Augustus Triumphator: Manipulation of the Triumphal Theme in the Political Program of Augustus", *Latomus* 50. 1, 124–138.

Hinz V., 1993, "Eine bekannte Tugend des Tiberius (*Tab. Siar.* Frg. I Z. 5)", *ZPE* 96, 59–63.

Hohl E., 1933, "Wann hat Tiberius das Prinzipat übernommen?", *Hermes* 68. 1, 106–115.

Hohl E., 1935, "Primum facinus novi Principatus", *Hermes* 70, 3, 350–355.

Hölscher T., 2011, *Sztuka rzymska: język obrazowy jako system semantyczny*, translated by L. Olszewski, Poznań [= *Römische Bildsprache als semantisches System*, Heidelberg 1987].

Holloway R. R., 1984, "Who's Who on the Ara Pacis?", [in:] *Alessandria e il mondo Ellenistico-Romano. Studi e Materiali Ist. Arch. Univ. Palermo* 6, 625–628.

Hurlet F., 1994, "Recherches sur la durée de l'imperium des « co-régents » sous les principats d'Auguste et de Tibère", *CCG* 5, 255–289.

Hurlet F., 1997, *Les Collègues du Prince sous Auguste et Tibère: De la Légalité Républicaine à la Légitimité Dynastique*, Roma.

Huttner U., 2004, *Recusatio Imperii. Ein politisches Ritual zwischen Ethik und Taktik*, Hildesheim.

Instinsky H. U., 1966, "Augustus und die Adoption des Tiberius", *Hermes* 94, 324–343.

Jacques F., Scheid J., 1992, *Rome et l'integration de l'Empire (44 av. J.-C. – 260 ap. J.-C.)*, I, *Les structures de l'Empire romain*, (second edition), Paris.

Jameson S., 1975, "Augustus and Agrippa Postumus", *Historia* 24, 287–314.

Janssen J., 1920, "Ad expeditionem Gaii principis in Germaniam", *Mnemosyne* 48, 205–206.

Jones A. H. M., 1956, "Numismatics and History", [in:] *Essays in the Roman Coinage presented to H. Mattingly*, eds. R. A. G. Carson, C. H. V. Sutherland, Oxford, 13–33.

Jung H., 1972, "Die Thronerhebung des Claudius", *Chiron* 2, 367–386.

Kantiréa M., 2007, *Les Dieux et les Dieux Augustes. Le culte impériale en Gréce sous les Julio-claudiens et les Flaviens. Etudes épigraphiques et archéologiques*, Athenes.

Keppie L., 1998, *The Making of the Roman Army. From Republic to Empire*, University of Oklahoma Press, Oklahoma.

Kienast D., 1982, *Augustus: Prinzeps und Monarch*, Darmstadt.

Kienast D., 1996, *Römische Kaisertabelle: Grundzüge einer römischen Kaiserchronologie*, Darmstadt.

Kleiner D. E. E., 2005, "Semblance and Storytelling in Augustan Rome", [in:] *The Cambridge Companion to the Age of Augustus*, ed. K. Galinsky, Cambridge, 197–233.

Kleiner D. E. E., Buxton B., 2008, "Pledges of Empire: The Ara Pacis and the Donations of Rome", *AJA* 112, 57–89.

Kleiner F. S., 1985a, "The Arch of Gaius Caesar at Pisa (CIL, XI, 1421)", *Latomus* 44, 156–164.

Kleiner F. S., 1985b, *The Arch of Nero in Rome. A Study of the Roman Honorary Arch before and under Nero*, Rome.

Kleiner F. S., 1997, "The Boscoreale Cups: Copies of a Lost Monument?", *JRA* 10, 377–380.

Koenen L., 1970, "Die laudatio funebris des Augustus für Agrippa auf einem neuen Papyrus (P. Colon. inv. nr. 4701; vgl. Taf. VIIIa)", *ZPE* 5, 217–283.

Koestermann E., 1953, "Der pannonisch-dalmatinische Krieg 6–9 n. Chr.", *Hermes* 81, 345–378.

Koestermann E., 1957, "Die Feldzüge des Germanicus 14–16 n. Chr.", *Historia* 6, 429–479.

Koestermann E., 1958, "Die Mission des Germanicus im Orient", *Historia* 7, 331–375.

Kokkinos N., 2002, *Antonia Augusta. Portrait of a Great Roman Lady*, London.

Kornemann E., 1930, *Doppelprinzipat und Reichsteilung im Imperium Romanum*, Leipzig.

Krüger J., 2012, *Nero. Der römische Kaiser und seine Zeit*, Köln–Weimar–Wien.

Kuhoff W., 1993a, *Felicior Augusto melior Traiano. Aspekte der Selbstdarstellung der römischen Kaiser während der Prinzipatszeit*, Frankfurt am Main.

Kuhoff W., 1993b, "Zur Titulatur der römischen Kaiserinnen während der Prinzipatszeit", *Klio* 75, 244–256.

Kunkel W., 1961, "Über das Wesen des augusteischen Prinzipats", *Gymnasium* 68, 353–370.

Kunst Ch., 2005, *Römische Adoption. Zur Strategie einer Familienorganisation*, Hennef.

Küntze C., 1985, *Zur Darstellung des Kaisers Tiberius und seiner Zeit bei Velleius Paterculus*, Frankfurt am Main–Bern–New York.

Künzl E., 1996, "Gladiusdekorationen der frühen römischen Kaiserzeit. Dynastische Legitimation, Victoria und Aurea Aetas", *JRGZ* 43, 383–474.

Kuttner A. L., 1995, *Dynasty and Empire in the Age of Augustus: The Case of the Boscoreale Cups*, Berkeley.

Lacey W. K., 1979, "*Summi fastigii vocabulum*: The Story of a Title", *JRS* 69, 28–34.

Lacey W. K., 1996, *Augustus and the Principate: The Evolution of the System*, Leeds.

Lebek W. D., 1987, "Die drei Ehrenbögen für Germanicus: Tab. Siar. Frg. I 9–34; CIL VI 31199a 2–17", *ZPE* 67, 129–148.

Lebek W. D., 1988a, "Die circensischen Ehrungen für Germanicus und das Referat des Tacitus im Lichte von Tab. Siar. Frg. II col. c 2–11", *ZPE* 73, 249–274.

Lebek W. D., 1988b, "Augustalspiele und Landestrauer (Tab. Siar. Frg. II col. a 11–14)", *ZPE* 75, 59–71.

Lebek W. D., 1989a, "Die Mainzer Ehrungen für Germanicus, den älteren Drusus und Domitian (Tab. Siar. Frg. I 26–34; Suet. Claud. 1, 3)", *ZPE* 78, 45–82.

Lebek W. D., 1989b, "Die Postumen Ehrenbögen und der Triumph des Drusus Caesar (CIL VI 31200 B col. I, 1–4; Tac. Ann. 4, 9, 2)", *ZPE* 78, 83–91.

Lebek W. D., 1990, "Welttrauer um Germanicus: Das neugefundene Orginaldokument und die Darstellung des Tacitus", *A&A* 36, 93–102.

Lebek W. D., 1991a, "Ehrenbogen und Prinzentod: 9 v. Chr. – 23 n. Chr.", *ZPE* 86, 47–78.

Lebek W. D., 1991b, "Der Proconsulat des Germanicus und die *auctoritas* des Senats: Tab. Siar. Frg. I 22–24", *ZPE* 87, 103–124.

Lebek W. D., 1992, "Die zwei Ehrenbeschlüsse für Germanicus und einer der "Seltsamsten Schnitzer" des Tacitus (Ann. 2, 83, 2)", *ZPE* 90, 65–86.

Lebek W. D., 1993, "Roms Ritter und Roms Pleps in den Senatsbeschlüssen für Germanicus Caesar und Drusus Caesar", *ZPE* 95, 81–120.

Lebek W. D., 1999, "Das senatus consultum de Cn. Pisone patre und Tacitus", *ZPE* 128, 183–211.

Lehmann G. A., 1991, "Das Ende der römischen Herrschaft über das "Westelbische" Germanien: Von der Varus-Katastrophe zur Abberufung des Germanicus Caesar 16/7 n. Chr.", *ZPE* 86, 79–96.

Lesuisse L., 1961a, "La nomination de l'empereur et le titre d'imperator", *AC* 30, 415–428.

Lesuisse L., 1961b, "Le titre de Caesar et son évolution au cours de l'histoire de l'empire", *LEC* 29, 271–287.

Lesuisse L., 1962, "L'aspect héréditaire de la succession impériale sous les Julio-Claudiens", *LEC* 30, 32–50.

Levick B., 1966, "Drusus Caesar and the Adoptions of A.D. 4", *Latomus* 25.2, 227–244.

Levick B., 1971, "The Beginning of Tiberius' Career", *CQ* 21, 478–486.

Levick B., 1972a, "Tiberius Retirement to Rhodes in 6 B.C.", *Latomus* 31, 779–813.

Levick B., 1972b, "Abdication and Agrippa Postumus", *Historia* 21, 674–697.

Levick B., 1975a, "Mercy and Moderation on the Coinage of Tiberius", [in:] *The Ancient Historian and his Materials. Essays in Honour of C. E. Stevens on his seventieth birthday*, ed. B. Levick, Farnborough, 123–137.

Levick B., 1975b, "Julians and Claudians", *Greece and Rome* 22, 29–38.

Levick B., 1990, *Claudius*, London.

Levick B., 1999, *Tiberius the Politician*, London–New York.

Levick B., 2010, *Augustus: Image and Substance*, Harlow.

Lewis J. D., 1970, "Primum facinus novi Principatus", [in:] *Auckland Classical Essays Presented to E. M. Blaiklock*, ed. B. F. Harris, Auckland, 165–184.

Liechtenhan E., 1947, "Das Ziel des Aufstandes der Rheinarmee", *MH* 4, 52–67.

Linderski J., 1990, "Mommsen and Syme: Law and Power in the Principate of Augustus", [in:] *Between Republic and Empire. Interpretations of Augustus and his Principate*, eds. K. Raaflaub, M. Toher, Berkeley–Los Angeles, 42–53.

Linderski J., 1995, "Julia in Regium", [in:] *Roman Questions*, Stuttgart, 375–394.

Lindsay H., 2009, *Adoption in the Roman World*, Cambridge.

Łuć I., 2004, *Oddziały pretorianów w starożytnym Rzymie: rekrutacja, struktura, organizacja* ("The Praetorian Units in Ancient Rome. Recruitment, Structure and Organization"), Lublin.

Łuć I., 2011, "The Military Coins of Caligula and Claudius: The Types Adlocut. Coh., Imper. Recept. and Praetor. Recept." [in:] *Studia Lesco Mrozewicz ab amicis et discipulis dedicata*, red. S. Ruciński, K. Balbuza, K. Królczyk, Poznań, 231–238.

Magie D., 1908, "The Mission of Agrippa to the Orient in 23 B.C.", *CPh* 3, 145–152.

Marsh F. B., 1931, *The Reign of Tiberius*, Oxford.

Maxfield V. A., 1981, *The Military Decorations of the Roman Army*, London.

Meise E., 1966, "Der Sesterz des Drusus mit den Zwillingen und die Nachfolgepläne des Tiberius", *JNG* 16, 7–21.

Meise E., 1969, *Untersuchungen zur Geschichte der Julisch-Claudischen Dynastie*, München.

Mellado Rivera J. A., 2003, *Princeps Iuventutis: la imagen monetaria del heredero en la época Julio-Claudia*, Alicante.

Meyer H., 2000, *Prunkkameen und Staatsdenkmäler römischer Kaiser. Neue Perspektiven zur Kunst der frühen Prinzipatszeit*, München.

Millar F., 1993, "Ovid and the *Domus Augusta*: Rome Seen from Tomoi", *JRS* 83, 1–17.

Miller S. G., 2006, *Starożytni Olimpijczycy. Sportowe życie antycznej Grecji*, translated by I. Żółtowska, Warszawa [= *Ancient Greek Athletics*, Yale University Press 2004].

Minto A., 1947, "M. Agrippa Postumus in Planasia (7–14 d. Cr)", *ASI* 105, 3–10.

Mlasowsky A., 1996, "Nomini ac fortunae Caesarum proximi. Die Sukzessionspropaganda der römischen Kaiser von Augustus bis Nero im Spiegel der Reichsprägung und der archäologischen Quellen", *JDAI* 111, 249–388.

Noreña C. F., 2001, "The Communication of the Emperor's Virtues", *JRS* 91, 146–168.

Ober J., 1982, "Tiberius and the Political Testament of Augustus", *Historia* 31.3, 306–328.

Olszewski L., 2003, [review:] A. A. Barret, *Livia: First Lady of Imperial Rome*, New Haven–London 2002, [in:] *Eos* 90, 2003, 366–370.

Olszewski L., 2011, "Haec mihi in animis vestris templa" (Tac. Ann. 4, 38, 2), czyli o naśladowaniu Oktawiana Augusta przez Tyberiusza ("'Haec mihi in animis vestris templa' (Tac. Ann. 4, 38, 2), or on Tiberius' Imitation of Octavian Augustus"), [in:] *Świat starożytny, jego polscy badacze i kult panującego*, red. L. Mrozewicz, K. Balbuza, Poznań, 335–352.

Osgood J., 2011, *Claudius Caesar: Image and Power in the Early Roman Empire*, Cambridge.

Paladini M. L., 1954, "La morte di Agrippa Postumo e la congiura di Clemente", *Acme* 7, 313–329.

Pani M., 1979, *Tendenze politiche della successione al principato di Augusto*, Bari.

Pani M., 1987, "La Missione di Germanico in Oriente. Politica estera e politica interna", [in:] *Germanico. La Persona, la Personalità, il Personaggio nel bimillenario della nascita*, Atti del Convegno (Macerata–Perugia 1986), a cura di G. Bonamente, M. P. Segoloni, Roma, 1–23.

Papano A. E., 1941, "Agrippa Postumus", *CPh* 36, 30–45.

Parker E.R., 1946, "The Education of Heirs in the Julio-Claudian Family", *AJPh* 67, 29–50.

Parsi B., 1963, *Désignation et Investiture de L'Empereur Romain (I et II siècles après J.-C.)*, Paris.

Pettinger A., 2012, *The Republic in Danger: Drusus Libo and the Succession of Tiberius*, Oxford.

Pigoń J., 1996, *W kręgu pojęć politycznych Tacyta: libertas – moderatio* ("Tacitus' Political Concepts of Libertas and Moderatio"), Wrocław.

Pistellato A., 2013, "Gaius Caesar, or the Ideal Non-Princeps: A Tiberian Issue", *Arctos* 47, 199–217.

Pollini J., 1986, "Ahenobarbi, Appuleii, and Some Others on the Ara Pacis", *AJA* 90, 453–460.

Pollini J., 1987, *The Portraiture of Gaius and Lucius Caesar*, New York.

Prévost M. H., 1949, *Les adoptions politiques à Rome sous la République et le Principat*, Paris.

Price S., 1987, "From Noble Funerals to Divine Cults. The Consecration of Roman Emperors", [in:] Rituals and Royalty. Power and Ceremonial in Traditional Societies, eds. D. Cannadine, S. Price, Oxford, 56–105.

Raaflaub K. A., 1987, "Die Militärreformen des Augustus und die politische Problematik des frühen Prinzipats", [in:] *Saeculum Augustum*, vol. 1, ed. G. Binder, Darmstadt, 246–307.

Raditsa L. F., 1980, "Augustus' Legislation Concerning Marriage, Procreation, Love Affairs, and Adultery", *ANRW* 2.13, 278–339.

Reinhold M., 1933, *Marcus Agrippa. A Biography*, Geneva–New York.

Requena M., 2001, *El emperador predestinado: los presagios de poder en época imperial romana*. Madrid (non vidi).

Rich J. W., 1980, "Agrippa and the Nobles: A Note on Dio 54, 29, 6", LCM 5, 217–221.

Ritter H. W., 1972, "Livias Erhebung zur Augusta", *Chiron* 2, 313–338.

Rivière Y., 2016, *Germanicus. Prince romain 15 av. J.-C. – 19 apr. J.-C.*, Paris.

Roddaz J. M., 1984, *Marcus Agrippa*, Rome.

Roehmer M., 1997, *Der Bogen als Staatsmonument. Zur politischen Bedeutung der römischen Ehrenbögen des 1. Jhs. n. Chr.*, München.

Rogers R. S., 1940, "Drusus Caesar's Tribunician Power", *AJPh* 61.4, 457–459.

Rogers R. S., 1943, *Studies in the Reign of Tiberius. Some Imperial Virtues of Tiberius and Drusus Iulius Caesar*, Baltimore.

Romer F. E., 1974, *G. and L. Caesar in the East*, Stanford University (Diss.).

Romer F. E., 1978, "A Numismatic Date for the Departure of C. Caesar", *TAPhA* 108, 187–202.

Romer F. E., 1979, "Gaius Caesar's Military Diplomacy in the East", *TAPhA* 109, 199–214.

Rose Ch. B., 1990, "Princes" and Barbarians on the Ara Pacis, *AJA* 94, 453–467.

Rose Ch. B., 1997, *Dynastic Commemoration and Imperial Portraiture in the Julio-Claudian Period*, Cambridge.

Rüpke J., Glock A., 2005, *Fasti Sacerdotum. Die Mitglieder der Priesterschaften und das sakrale Funktionspersonal römischer, griechischer, orientalischer und jüdisch-christlicher Kulte in der Stadt Rom von 300 v. Chr. bis 499 n. Chr.*, Band 2, Stuttgart.

Ryberg I. S., 1942, "Tacitus' Art of Innuendo", *TAPhA* 73, 383–404.

Sage M. S., 1982-83, "Tacitus and the Accession of Tiberius", *AncSoc* 13, 293–321.

Sajkowski R., 1994, "Antonia Młodsza a sukcesja Kaliguli" ("Antonia the Younger and Caligula's Accession"), [in:] *Wychowanie w rodzinie od starożytności po wiek XX*, Materiały z konferencji naukowej Katedry Wychowania (Bydgoszcz, June 1993), red. J. Jundziłł, Bydgoszcz, 49–61.

Sajkowski R., 2001, *Divus Augustus Pater. Kult boskiego Augusta za rządów dynastii julijsko-klaudyjskiej* ("Divus Augustus Pater. The Cult of Divine Augustus under the Rule of Julio-Claudian Dynasty"), Olsztyn.

Sajkowski R., 2006, "Kwestia sukcesji Tyberiusza w latach 4-14 n.e." ("The Problem of Tiberius' Succession from AD 4 to 14"), [in:] *Ad fontes: studia ofiarowane księdzu profesorowi A. Szorcowi w siedemdziesięciolecie urodzin*, red. Z. Jaroszewicz – Pieresławcew, I. Makarczyk, Olsztyn, 367–374.

Saller R. P., 1984, "*Familia, domus,* and the Roman Conception of the Family", *Phoenix* 38, 336–355.

Sattler P., 1960, *Augustus und der Senat. Untersuchungen zur römischen Innenpolitik zwischen 30 und 17 vor Christus*, Göttingen.

Sattler P., 1969, "Julia und Tiberius: Beiträge zur römischen Innenpolitik zwischen den Jahren 12 v. Chr. und den 2 n. Chr.", [in:] *Augustus*, hrsg. von W. Schmitthenner, Darmstadt, 486–530.

Sawiński P., 2004, "Agrippa's Mission in the East", *Eos* 91.2, 242–250.

Sawiński P., 2005, *Specjalni wysłannicy cesarscy w okresie od Augusta do Tyberiusza: Studium nad początkami pryncypatu* ("The Special Imperial Envoys in the Period of Augustus and Tiberius. The Study on the Beginnings of the Principate"), Xenia Posnaniensia – Monografie 4, red. L. Mrozewicz, M. Musielak, Poznań.

Sawiński P., 2007, "Some Comments on the Character of Germanicus' imperium during his Activity in Germany and in the East", [in:] *Haec mihi in animis vestris templa. Studia Classica in Memory of Professor Lesław Morawiecki*, eds. P. Berdowski, B. Blahaczek, Rzeszów, 221–226.

Sawiński P., 2008, "Oktawian jako mściciel Juliusza Cezara" ("Octavian as Julius Caesar's Avenger"), [in:] *Idy Marcowe 2050 lat później*, red. L. Mrozewicz, Poznań, 141–150.

Sawiński P., 2012, "Pogrzeby i formy pośmiertnego uhonorowania członków rodziny cesarskiej w okresie pryncypatu Augusta i Tyberiusza" ("Funerals and Forms of Posthumous Honouring of Imperial Family Members during the Principate of Augustus and Tiberius"), *Studia Europaea Gnesnensia* 5, 33–64.

Sawiński P., 2014, "Łuki triumfalne i honoryfikacyjne jako forma uczczenia członków rodziny cesarskiej w okresie pryncypatu Augusta i Tyberiusza" ("Triumphal and Honorific Arches as a Form of Honouring Members of the Imperial Family during Augustus' and Tiberius' Principate"), *Meander* 69, 109–139.

Schäfer T., 1989, *Imperii Insignia: Sella curulis und fasces: Zur Repräsentation römischer Magistrate*, Mainz.

Scheid J., 1992, "L'investiture impériale d'après les commentaires des arvales", *CCG* 3, 221–237.

Scheid J., Broise H., 1980, "Deux nouveaux fragments des actes des frères arvales de l'année 38 après J. – Chr.", *MEFRA* 92.1, 215–248.

Schillinger-Häfele U., 1988, "Die Laudatio Funebris des Tiberius für Germanicus (zu Tabula Siarensis Fragment II, col. B 13–19)", *ZPE* 75, 73–81.

Schmalz G. C. R., *Augustan and Julio-Claudian Athens. A New Epigraphy and Prosopography*, Leiden–Boston 2009.

Schmitt H. H., 1958, "Der pannonische Aufstand des Jahres 14 n. Chr. und der Regierungsantritt des Tiberius", *Historia* 7, 378–383.

Schmitzer U., 2000, *Velleius Paterculus und das Interesse an der Geschichte im Zeitalter des Tiberius*, Heidelberg.

Schrömbges P., 1986, *Tiberius und die Res Publica Romana. Untersuchungen zur Institutionalisierung des frühen römischen Principats*, Bonn.

Schrömbges P., 1992, "Zu den angeblichen Reichsteilungsplänen des Tiberius: (Dio 57, 2, 4 F)", *RhM* 135, 298–307.

Schumacher L., 1985, "Die imperatorischen Akklamationen der Tiumvirn und die auspicia des Augustus, *Historia* 34, 191–222.

Seager R., 1972, *Tiberius*, London.

Seager R., 2013, "Perceptions of the *Domus Augusta*, AD 4–24", [in:] *The Julio-Claudian Succession: Reality and Perception of the 'Augustan Model'*, ed. A. G. G. Gibson, Leiden-Boston, 41–57.

Segenni S., 2011, *I decreta pisana. Autonomia cittadina e ideologia Imperiale nella colonia Opsequens Iulia Pisana*, Bari.

Settis S., 1988, "Die Ara Pacis", [in:] *Kaiser Augustus und die verlorene Republik*, hrsg. von W. D. Heilmeyer, E. La Rocca, E. Künzl, Mainz, 400–426.

Severy B., 2000, "Family and State in the Early Imperial Monarchy: The Senatus Consultum de Pisone Patre, Tabula Siarensis, and Tabula Hebana", *CPh* 95, 318–337.

Severy B., 2003, *Augustus and the Family at the Birth of the Roman Empire*, New York–London.

Shaw M. L. G., 1990, *Drusus Caesar: The Son of Tiberius*, University of British Columbia (Diss.).

Shotter D. C. A., 1968, "Tacitus, Tiberius and Germanicus", *Historia* 17, 194–214.

Shotter D. C. A., 1971, "Julians, Claudians, and the Accession of Tiberius", *Latomus* 30, 1117–1123.

Shotter D. C. A., 1991, *Augustus Caesar*, London–New York.

Shotter D. C. A., 1992, *Tiberius Caesar*, London–New York.

Shotter D. C. A., 2005, *Nero*, London–New York (second edition).

Sickle C. E. van, 1928, *The Coregency and the Succession in the Early Roman Empire*, Chicago (non vidi).

Sidari D., 1978-1979, "Il ritiro di Tiberio a Rodi", *AIV* 137, 51–69.

Sidari D., 1979-1980, "Studi su Gaio e Lucio Cesare", *AIV* 138, 275–302.

Simon E., 1967, *Ara Pacis Augustae*, Tübingen.

Simpson Ch. J., 2005, "Rome's "Official Imperial Seal"? The Rings of Augustus and His First Century Successors", *Historia* 54. 2, 180–188.

Simpson Ch. J., 2008, "The Julian Succession and its Claudian Coda. A Different Perspective on the so-called Julio-Claudian Dynasty", *Latomus* 67, 353–365.

Smallwood E. M., 1967, *Documents Illustrating the Principates of Gaius, Claudius and Nero*, Cambridge.

Sordi M., 1979, "La morte di Agrippa Postumo e la rivolta di Germania del 14 d.C.", [in:] *Scritti in onore di Benedetto Riposati* 2, Rieti, 481–495.

Stevenson T., 2007, "Roman Coins and Refusals of the Title "Pater patriae"", *NC* 167, 119–141.

Stevenson T., 2013, "The Succession Planning of Augustus", *Antichthon* 47, 118–139.

Strack P. L., 1933, *Untersuchungen zur römischen Reichsprägung des zweiten Jahrhunderts*, vol. II, *Die Reichsprägung zur Zeit des Hadrian*, Stuttgart.

Sumner G. V., 1967, "Germanicus and Drusus Caesar", *Latomus* 26, 413–435.

Sutherland C. H. V., 1951, *Coinage in Roman Imperial Policy 31 B.C. – A.D. 68*, London.

Sutherland C. H. V., 1959, "The Intelligibility of Roman Imperial Coin Types", *JRS* 49, 46–55.

Syme R., 1958, *Tacitus*, I–II, Oxford.

Syme R., 1978, *History in Ovid*, Oxford.

Syme R., 1979, "Some Imperatorial Salutations", *Phoenix* 33, 308–329.

Syme R., 1984, "Neglected Children on the Ara Pacis", *AJA* 88, 583–589.

Syme R., 2002, *The Roman Revolution*, Oxford.

Syme R., 2009, "Imperator Caesar: A Study in Nomenclature", [in:] *Augustus*, ed. J. Edmondson, Edinburgh (reprinted from *Historia* 7, 1958, 172–188).

Talbert R. J. A., 1999, "Tacitus and the *Senatus consultum de Cn. Pisone patre*", *AJPh* 120.1, 89–97.

Temporini H., 1978, *Die Frauen am Hofe Trajans. Ein Beitrag zur Stellung des Augustae im Principat*, Berlin–New York.

Timpe D., 1962, *Untersuchungen zur Kontinuität des frühen Prinzipats*, Wiesbaden.

Timpe D., 1967, "Zur Geschichte und Überlieferung der Okupation Germaniens unter Augustus", *Saeculum* 18, 278–293.

Timpe D., 1968, *Der Triumph des Germanicus. Untersuchungen zu den Feldzügen der Jahre 14-16 n. Chr. in Germanien*, Bonn.

Toit L., 1980, "The Senatorial Debate on 17th September A.D. 14 and Drusus' Journey to Pannonia", *AClass* 23, 130–133.

Torelli M., 1982, *Typology and Structure of Roman Historical Reliefs*, Ann Arbor.

Treggiari S., 1991, *Roman Marriage. Iusti coniuges from the Time of Cicero to the Time of Ulpian*, Oxford.

Trillmich W., 1978, *Familienpropaganda der Kaiser Caligula und Claudius. Agrippina maior und Antonia Augusta auf Münzen*, Berlin.

Trillmich W., 1988a, "Münzpropaganda", [in:] *Kaiser Augustus und die verlorene Republik*, hrsg. von W.D. Heilmeyer, E. La Rocca, E. Künzl, Mainz, 474–528.

Trillmich W., 1988b, "Der Germanicus-Bogen in Rom und das Monument für Germanicus und Drusus in Leptis Magna", [in:] *Estudios sobre la Tabula Siarensis: Anejos de Archivo Español de Arqueología*, editado por J. Arce, J. González, Madrid, 51–60.

Uzzi J. D., 2005, *Children in the Visual Arts of Imperial Rome*, Cambridge.

Vassileiou A., 1984, "Caius ou Lucius proclamé princeps iuventutis par l'ordre équestre", [in:] *Hommages á L. Lerat*, éd. par H. Walter, Paris, 827–840.

Versnel H. S., 1980, "Destruction, Devotio and Despair in a Situation of Anomy: The Mourning for Germanicus in Triple Perspective", [in:] *Perennitas*. Studi in onore di Angelo Brelich, a cura di G. Piccaluga, Roma, 541–618.

Veyne P., 2008, *Imperium grecko-rzymskie*, tłum. P. Domański, Kęty [=. *L'Empire gréco-romain*, Paris 2008].

Von Premerstein A., 1937, *Vom Werden und Wesen des Prinzipats*, München.

Vout C., 2013, "Tiberius and the Invention of Succession", [in:] *The Julio-Claudian Succession: Reality and Perception of the 'Augustan Model'*, ed. A. G. G. Gibson, Leiden–Boston, 59–77.

Wallace-Hadrill A., 1982, "Civilis princeps": Between Citizen and King, *JRS* 72, 32–48.

Wallace-Hadrill A., 1986, "Image and Authority in the Coinage of Augustus", *JRS* 76, 66–87.

Wardle D., 2000, "Valerius Maximus on the "Domus Augusta", Augustus, and Tiberius", *CQ* 50, 479–493.

Watson G. R., 2014, Żołnierz rzymski, translated by P. Grysztar, Oświęcim [= *The Roman Soldier*, Cornell University Press 1985].

Webster G., 1998, *The Roman Imperial Army of the First and Second Centuries A.D.*, University of Oklahoma Press (Third Edition).

Weingärtner D. G., 1969, *Die Ägyptenreise des Germanicus*, Bonn.

Weinstock S., 1957, "The Image and the Chair of Germanicus", *JRS* 47, 144–154.

Weinstock S., 1966, "The Posthumous Honours of Germanicus", [in:] *Mélanges d'Archéologie et d'Histoire offerts à Andre Piganiol* 2, éd par R. Chevallier, Paris, 891–898.

Weinstock S., 1971, *Divus Julius*, Oxford.

Wellesley K., 1967, "The dies imperii of Tiberius", *JRS* 57, 23–30.

Wells C., 2005, *Cesarstwo rzymskie*, translated by T. Duliński, Warszawa [= *The Roman Empire*, Stanford University Press 1984].

Welwei K. W., 1986, "Römische Weltherrschaftsideologie und augusteische Germanienpolitik", *Gymnasium* 93, 118–137.

Welwei K. W., 2004, "Augustus als "vindex libertatis": Freiheitsideologie und Propaganda im frühen Prinzipat", [in:] *Res publica und imperium: Kleine Schriften zur römischen Geschichte*, hrsg. von M. Meier, M. Strothmann, Stuttgart, 217–229.

Wesch-Klein G., 1993, *Funus publicum: Eine Studie zur öffentlichen Beisetzung und Gewährung von Ehrengräbern in Rom und den Westprovinzen*, Stuttgart.

Wiedemann T. E. J., 2008, "Tiberius to Nero" [in:] *The Cambridge Ancient History* 10, *The Augustan Empire 43 B.C. – A.D. 69*, eds. A. Bowman, E. Champlin, A. Lintott, Cambridge (second edition), 198–255 (online edition).

Wilkes J. J., 1963, "A Note on the Mutiny of the Pannonian Legions in A. D. 14", *CQ* 13.2, 268–271.

Winterling A., 2011, *Caligula. A Biography*, Berkely, Los Angeles, London [= *Caligula. Eine Biographie*, München 2003].

Wolters R., 1989, "*Tam diu Germania vincitur*". *Römische Germanensiege und Germanensieg - Propaganda bis zum Ende des 1. Jahrhunderts n. Chr.*, Bochum.

Wolters R., 2002, "Gaius und Lucius Caesar als designirte Konsuln und principes iuventutis: Die lex Valeria Cornelia und RIC I.2 205ff", *Chiron* 32, 297–323.

Wood S. E., 2001, *Imperial Women: A Study in Public Images, 40 BC–AD 68*, Leiden–Boston (second edition).

Yavetz Z., 1999, *Tiberius. Der traurige Kaiser. Biographie*, München.

Zabłocka M., 1986, *Ius trium liberorum* w ustawodawstwie dynastii julijsko-klaudyjskiej ("Ius Trium Liberorum in the Legislation of the Julio-Claudian Dynasty"), Prawo Kanoniczne 29.1–2, 243–264.

Zanker P., 1999, *August i potęga obrazów*, translated by L. Olszewski, Poznań [= *Augustus und die Macht der Bilder*, München 1997].

Zanker P., 2005, *Apoteoza cesarzy rzymskich. Rytuał i przestrzeń miejska*, translated by L. Olszewski, Xenia Posnaniensia – Monografie 5, red. L. Mrozewicz, M. Musielak, Poznań [= *Die Apotheose der römischen Kaiser. Ritual und städtische Bühne*, München 2004].

Zetzel J. E. G., 1970, "New Light on Gaius Caesar's Eastern Campaign", *GRBS* 11, 259–266.

Ziółkowski A., 2004, *Historia Rzymu* ("A History of Rome"), Poznań.

Ziółkowski A., 2007, Prolegomena to Any Future Metaphysics on Agrippa's Pantheon', [in:] *Res bene gestae. Ricerche di storia urbana su Roma antica in onore di Eva Margareta Steinby*, a cura di A. Leone, D. Palombi, S. Walker, Roma, 465–476.

Index

The index only lists persons mentioned in the main body of the text, not counting the footnotes.